Jim Crow Capital

MARY-ELIZABETH B. MURPHY

Jim Crow Capital

Women and Black Freedom Struggles in
Washington, D.C., 1920–1945

The University of North Carolina Press *Chapel Hill*

This book was published with the assistance of the Greensboro Women's Fund of the University of North Carolina Press.

Founding Contributors: Linda Arnold Carlisle, Sally Schindel Cone, Anne Faircloth, Bonnie McElveen Hunter, Linda Bullard Jennings, Janice J. Kerley (in honor of Margaret Supplee Smith), Nancy Rouzer May, and Betty Hughes Nichols.

Set in Arno Pro by Westchester Publishing Services
Manufactured in the United States of America

The University of North Carolina Press has been a member of the
Green Press Initiative since 2003.

Library of Congress Cataloging-in-Publication Data
Names: Murphy, Mary-Elizabeth B., author.
Title: Jim Crow capital : women and black freedom struggles in Washington, D.C., 1920–1945 /
    Mary-Elizabeth B. Murphy.
Description: Chapel Hill : University of North Carolina Press, [2018] |
    Includes bibliographical references and index.
Identifiers: LCCN 2018012532| ISBN 9781469646718 (cloth : alk. paper) | ISBN 9781469646725
    (pbk : alk. paper) | ISBN 9781469646732 (ebook)
Subjects: LCSH: African American women political activists—Washington
    (D.C.)—History—20th century. | African Americans—Segregation—History—20th century. |
    African Americans—Civil Rights—History—20th century. | Washington (D.C.)—Race
    Relations—History—20th century.
Classification: LCC E185.86 .M9525 2018 | DDC 323.1196/07307530904—dc23
    LC record available at https://lccn.loc.gov/2018012532

Cover illustration: *Washington (Southwest Section), D.C., Negro Woman in Her Bedroom* (1942) by Gordon Parks (LC-USZ62-139542, Prints and Photographs Division, Library of Congress). The woman, seen here in reflection, would have been unable to vote but nonetheless registers her political views with a picture of Franklin D. Roosevelt hung above her mirror.

A previous version of chapter 4 was published as "'The Servant Campaigns': African American Women and the Politics of Economic Justice in Washington, D.C., in the 1930s." Special Issue: "African American Urban Electoral Politics in the Age of Jim Crow," edited by Lisa G. Materson and Joe William Trotter Jr., *Journal of Urban History* 44, no. 2 (March 2018): 187–202.

This book is dedicated to my parents,
John Murphy and Frances Lewis,
and to all of the women whose stories
for freedom and justice are
chronicled in these pages.

Contents

Illustrations, Graph, Map, and Tables

Jim Crow Capital

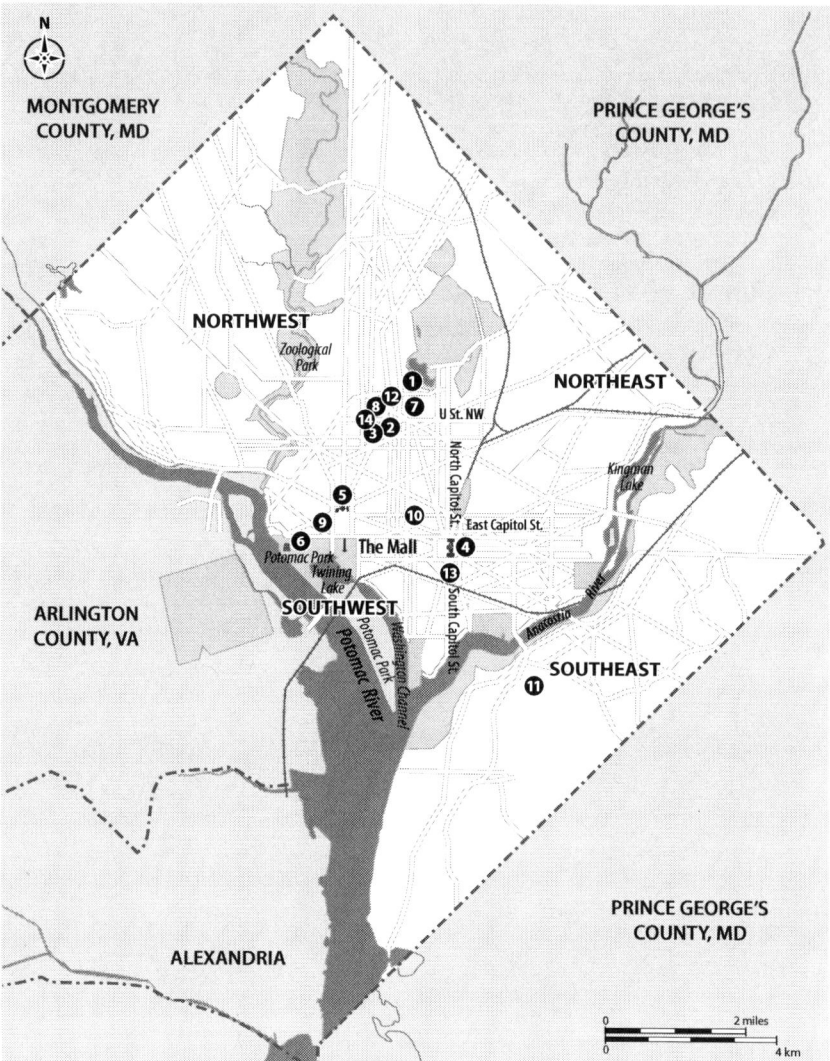

Washington, D.C., 1920–1945

❶ Howard University

❷ Phyllis Wheatley Young Women's Christian Association

❸ National Association of Wage Earners Headquarters

❹ U.S. Capitol

❺ White House

❻ Lincoln Memorial

❼ LeDroit Park Neighborhood

❽ U Street Business District

❾ Daughters of the American Revolution Memorial Continental Hall

❿ Police Court Building

⓫ Frederick Douglass House

⓬ Alpha Kappa Alpha Lobbying Headquarters

⓭ Colored Women's Legislative Headquarters

⓮ John Wesley AME Zion Church

Map prepared by Isabelle Lewis.

Introduction

Jim Crow Capital

On Tuesday, June 14, 1922 at one o'clock in the afternoon, 5,000 black Washingtonians gathered on Maryland Avenue in Washington, D.C., to march in a Silent Parade protesting the inhumanity of lynching. In January 1922, the U.S. House of Representatives had passed the Dyer Anti-Lynching Bill, and in just a few days after the parade, the Senate would begin its debates. This was an historic moment because it marked the first time both branches of Congress were holding hearings on a bill to make lynching a federal crime. Recognizing the importance of this occasion, African American women in Washington, D.C., planned a parade both to draw attention to the anti-lynching bill and to demonstrate the support of a broad spectrum of black Washingtonians for it. To organize the parade, women formed a Committee of One Hundred, which raised money, disseminated publicity, and recruited participants from churches, fraternal orders, civic associations, schools, and social clubs.

The Committee of One Hundred designed the Silent Parade to emphasize black Washingtonians' patriotism and organizational strength. It was determined that the parade would be held on Wednesday, June 14, which was Flag Day, a celebration in America's civic calendar. The Committee of One Hundred mapped the parade sequence—black fraternal orders first, followed by prominent women in the city, children of different ages, ministers, police officers, and veterans of foreign wars—to showcase a diverse cross section of black citizens and organizations who supported anti-lynching legislation. The parade began on Maryland Avenue and First Streets in Northeast Washington. African American men, women, and children waved flags and carried banners as they circled around the U.S. Capitol and passed the Senate and House Office Buildings. Parade participants then marched past the Treasury Building and ended on West Executive Avenue at the White House. Although Pennsylvania Avenue was not on the route, the parade was visible to employees in numerous government departments, including Pensions, Patents, the Land Office, the New Museum, the Post Office, and the federal courthouse; in fact, the Committee of One Hundred timed the procession so that marchers would reach government offices as workers were leaving for the day. The National

Association for the Advancement of Colored People (NAACP) issued a press release, drawing attention to the fact that participation in the parade involved African Americans from "every walk of life." This press release also emphasized that African American citizens living in Washington, D.C., were particularly well suited to represent black national interests since city residents had been born in every state throughout the nation, making this event a "national, as well as a local affair."[1]

For many marchers, this parade was personal because they had friends and family members who lived in states where they were vulnerable to racial violence. Newspaper articles about the parade appeared in both the local and national press, including the *Washington Post*, the *Washington Star*, the *New York Times*, the *Christian Science Monitor*, and the *Los Angeles Times*. Many of these articles mentioned that the Committee of One Hundred, composed entirely of African American women, had organized the Silent Parade.[2] In parading past important government buildings and offices, including the U.S. Capitol and the White House, African Americans pronounced themselves as citizens and claimed federal space in Washington, D.C., thereby broadcasting their support for the Dyer Anti-Lynching Bill to politicians, government workers, the nation, and the world.

Jim Crow Capital tells the story of how African American women in Washington, D.C., transformed civil rights politics in the United States between 1920 and 1945. Hundreds of black women living throughout the nation's capital waged political campaigns, such as the Silent Parade, to enact their visions of democracy and justice in the United States. Even though no resident of the nation's capital could cast a ballot, women nonetheless proclaimed their first-class citizenship rights by working to influence congressional legislation, lobby politicians, shape policy, and secure freedom and justice for all African Americans, both in Washington, D.C., and across the country. Black women in Washington, D.C., crafted a broad vision of citizenship rights, maintaining that full equality would never be achieved until everyone was equal in the eyes of the law; each person had the opportunity to earn a just wage and live decently; America's commemorative landscape celebrated the achievements of the nation's diverse citizenry; and all women, men, and children lived free of the terrors of violence. Women's political activism in Washington, D.C., influenced the postwar black freedom struggle and offers salient lessons for the current political moment.[3]

During the course of their political campaigns, African American women's relationship to federal and local politics underwent a fundamental transformation. During the 1920s, black women rode a wave of optimism about the possibilities of securing first-class citizenship. The nation had just fought a war based on a message of global democracy, and black soldiers had demonstrated bravery on the battlefield.[4] The ratification of the Nineteenth Amendment in 1920 granted woman suffrage, which enabled black women in northern and midwestern states to cast ballots in local and national elections.[5] And the return of the Republican Party—marked by the election of Warren G. Harding to the presidency and of a fresh roster of Republicans to the House of Representatives and Senate—engendered feelings of enthusiasm among black citizens that the GOP would return to its roots as the party of Abraham Lincoln and black citizenship rights. Encouraged by these circumstances, African American women living in the nation's capital pursued politics on a national scale by seizing on their location in Washington, D.C., to intervene in federal matters to improve conditions for their friends and family members who lived in the Jim Crow South and lacked a political voice.

During the 1920s, black women tapped their connections in churches, fraternal orders, labor networks, neighborhoods, and the women's club movement to organize and sustain their political campaigns. In particular, middle-class women used their networks in the National Association of Colored Women (NACW) and its local chapters throughout the nation as a building block to create new organizations and recruit constituents. Many women affiliated with the NACW were steeped in the politics of respectability and racial uplift, which shaped the character of their activism throughout the 1920s.[6] Women's attention to national politics did not mean, however, that they ignored local matters or that the nation's capital was a racially egalitarian city. Throughout Washington, activists fought for reduced streetcar fare for students; protested the expansion of racial segregation in the federal government, swimming pools, and neighborhoods; worked to improve conditions for workers; and lobbied to secure municipal services for black neighborhoods.[7] However, women's national campaigns often eclipsed their activism in local matters.

By the late 1920s, however, African American women turned their attention to focus more fully on local politics in Washington, D.C. Police violence surged as white officers assaulted black women and shot black men throughout the capital. Women tapped their organizing culture to address the growing crisis of interracial police violence. The Great Depression led to widespread unemployment and poverty for black residents across the city, prompting women to argue that all citizens of the United States deserved economic justice, which included decent employment, fair wages, family support, and government protections in cases of unemployment and old age.

During the 1930s, the club movement lost some of its influence, but seasoned leaders and a new generation of foot soldiers found important networks in sororities, leftist organizations, and interracial groups.[8] While most women focused on local affairs in Washington, some continued to use their location in the nation's capital to influence federal policy, especially as it pertained to New Deal programs and matters of citizenship and equality. Black women had always protested racial segregation and campaigned for the restoration of voting rights in Washington, D.C., but it was during the 1930s when activists achieved momentum in the struggle by writing a civil rights bill for the nation's capital and joining white residents to convince the city to hold a referendum election. Black women and men positioned the civil rights movement in Washington, D.C., as the opening wedge to black freedom movements across the country. When the United States entered World War II in 1941, black women drew on their two decades of activism to wage direct action campaigns for racial integration and resume their position as congressional lobbyists. By 1945, black women were guiding the nation's capital on a path toward legal equality and the restoration of home rule, while providing important strategies for the postwar black freedom struggle across the nation.

Jim Crow Capital joins a body of scholarship that illuminates early campaigns for black freedom in the United States, documenting the diverse ways that African Americans pressed for justice between the 1920s and 1940s.[9] It stands at the intersection of social and political history by connecting the leaders of political movements with their grassroots constituencies—not only exploring the gender and class compositions of activist campaigns but also illustrating the hard work of organizing.[10] Scholars have documented black Washington's rich cultural life, animated by literary societies, music, beauty salons, and fashion. *Jim Crow Capital* complements this historiography by illustrating black Washington's activism, organizing, and political culture.[11]

Civil rights protests and policies in Washington, D.C., often served as the experimental ground for political movements around the country. The historian Kate Masur shows that, during Reconstruction, elected officials used Washington, D.C., as a laboratory to test federal policy; she argues that when congressmen abolished local government and voting rights for residents of the nation's capital in Washington, D.C., they set the precedent for disfranchisement in the South.[12] *Jim Crow Capital* tells the second half of this story, revealing how black women's political campaigns in the nation's capital between 1920 and 1945 led to legal victories in Washington, D.C., and set the stage for the postwar black freedom struggle.

Early Activism in the Nation's Capital

When African American women waged their political campaigns in the twentieth century, they were following in the footsteps of their ancestors. In April 1862, President Abraham Lincoln signed the District of Columbia Emancipation Act, which abolished slavery in the nation's capital. Black Washingtonians banded together with their churches and mutual aid associations to assist the influx of migrants streaming into the city to claim their freedom. After the Civil War, African Americans in the city worked to make their vision of freedom a political reality by fighting for the right to vote in local and national elections and protesting all forms of segregation and discrimination. In 1867, Congress passed the District of Columbia Voting Rights Act that enfranchised all men, three years before the Fifteenth Amendment was enacted. Between 1867 and 1874, black men in Washington cast ballots, held patronage positions, and wielded influence in the local government. The Washington, D.C., City Council enacted ordinances that banned segregation in theaters, restaurants, and other establishments. Black women and men across Washington exercised their new rights of citizenship by attending congressional hearings, holding fundraisers on the executive lawn of the White House, and parading around federal buildings. While the city had two separate school systems, African Americans exercised control over their schools. In 1871, however, Congress created a territorial government for the District of Columbia with a governor appointed by the president of the United States and an elected House of Delegates. Three years later, all residents of Washington, D.C., lost the right to vote and most control over local governance. In 1878, Congress appointed a three-member Board of Commissioners to serve as the local government.[13] In 1900, Congress reorganized the school system by appointing a white superintendent to supervise the schools and selected black and white assistant superintendents to oversee the black and white school systems, respectively. With the end of home rule, the right to vote, and local control over the school system, African Americans lost significant political power.

Yet by the 1890s, Washington, D.C., developed a large and influential African American middle class. Since the main industry in the city was the government, some African Americans labored as clerks, messengers, and charwomen (office cleaners). A lucky few even received patronage appointments. Federal jobs paid higher wages than jobs in the private sector and offered the promise of stable employment. The city was home to Howard University, the premier university for African American education. Black students from all parts of the country traveled to the city to attend Howard for undergraduate studies or professional programs in law, medicine, pharmacy, zoology, and architecture; the university minted generations of black professionals. Even though public schools were segregated, the quality of education was high, and graduates of Dunbar High School attended prestigious colleges and universities.[14]

Through their churches, fraternal orders, and social and political clubs, black Washingtonians protested the declining status of African Americans across the country, marked by the spread of lynching, racial segregation, and disfranchisement.[15] At the local level, women worked to address poverty, employment, and child welfare among black Washingtonians. In 1892, African American women in the city formed the Colored Women's League, which united 113 different organizations, 85 of which were local.[16] The league was involved in the establishment of the Southwest Social Settlement in 1895, which offered women in that neighborhood the opportunity to improve their cooking and sewing skills and provided a kindergarten for black children.[17] The Colored Women's League merged with the National Association of Colored Women in 1896, which became the largest civil rights organization for African Americans until the 1920s.[18] African American women furthered their engagement in community service by forming the city's first Young Women's Christian Association (YWCA) in 1905 to address housing and employment for migrant women.

The political status of African Americans in Washington, D.C., declined significantly when Woodrow Wilson, a native of Virginia and a vocal opponent of African American civil rights, was elected president. In 1913, when Wilson took office, his administration installed racial segregation in government offices. The historian Eric Yellin demonstrates that African American civil servants not only faced humiliation imposed by separate offices, restrooms, and cafeterias but also that segregation thwarted black promotion and pay raises, which significantly hurt the black middle class in Washington.[19] The same year in which Wilson was inaugurated, women and men formed the city's chapter of the NAACP. While activists worked tirelessly with the NAACP to protest segregation, they were unable to integrate the federal government.

World War I created both opportunities and challenges for black Washingtonians. Under the leadership of political activist Nannie Helen Burroughs, black women held prayer meetings and circulated petitions that called on Congress to introduce a federal anti-lynching law. As the federal government expanded with the war effort, well-paying positions in government offices opened up, luring 15,000 migrants from South Carolina, North Carolina, Georgia, and Virginia to settle in the city.[20] This influx of migrants strained

TABLE 1 Population of Washington, D.C., by race and sex, 1920–40

Year	Black Women	Black Men	White Women	White Men	Total	Percentage Black
1920	59,111	50,855	174,292	152,031	436,289	25
1930	69,843	62,225	258,236	231,098	621,402	27
1940	98,594	88,672	246,305	228,021	661,592	28

Source: Fourteenth Census of the United States, vol. III: Population 1920 (Washington, D.C.: GPO, 1922); *Fifteenth Census of the United States*, vol. III: Population, parts I and II (Washington, D.C.: GPO, 1932); and *Sixteenth Census of the United States: 1940, Population*, vol. II (Washington, D.C.: GPO, 1943).

black women's resources, prompting members of the Phyllis Wheatley YWCA to petition the War Department's War Work Council for a new headquarters, and their request was granted.

Soon after World War I ended, the *Washington Post* began to print inflammatory articles claiming that African American men were attacking white women.[21] On the evening of Sunday, July 19, 1919, a group of white soldiers and sailors gathered near the White House and began to attack black residents of the city. White men pulled African Americans off streetcars and beat them. White soldiers threatened to storm into LeDroit Park, a middle-class black neighborhood in Northwest Washington. In response, black men from other parts of the city rushed into LeDroit Park to assist residents, and African American women formed a Home Defense Corps. Ultimately, white men killed six black Washingtonians and injured hundreds of African American residents.[22] The four-day riot only ended when 2,000 soldiers were sent to patrol the city. The race riot in 1919 was devastating and resulted in widespread concerns about black Washington's safety and citizenship rights in the nation's capital.

Black Women in the Nation's Capital in the 1920s and 1930s

By the 1920s, Washington, D.C., boasted a large and economically diverse black population. In 1920, African Americans were 25 percent of the city's residents; ten years later, that figure had climbed to 27 percent and by 1940 to 28 percent. By 1930, Washington, D.C., had the fifth largest black population in the nation and the third largest proportion of African American residents.

Between the 1920s and 1940s, African American women and men lived in each of the city's four geographic quadrants. Through their participation in the everyday activities of urban life—including work, streetcar travel, school,

TABLE 2 Population of Washington, D.C., by sex, race, and geographic quadrant, 1920–40

1920		*NW*	*NE*	*SE*	*SW*
	Black Women	37,955	5,775	8,511	6,870
	Black Men	31,210	5,287	8,161	6,197
	Total	69,165	11,062	16,672	13,067
1930		*NW*	*NE*	*SE*	*SW*
	Black Women	45,515	10,519	7,632	6,177
	Black Men	39,192	8,797	7,685	5,551
	Total	84,707	20,316	15,317	11,728
1940		*NW*	*NE*	*SE*	*SW*
	Black Women	63,834	9,949	16,034	8,777
	Black Men	55,810	9,105	15,710	8,047
	Total	119,644	19,054	31,744	16,824

Source: Fourteenth Census of the United States, vol. III: Population 1920 (Washington, D.C.: GPO, 1922); *Fifteenth Census of the United States*, vol. III: Population, parts I and II. (Washington, D.C.: GPO, 1932); and *Sixteenth Census of the United States: 1940, Population*, vol. II (Washington, D.C.: GPO, 1943).

shopping, and institutional and organizational life—black Washingtonians inhabited all corners of the city. As William Henry Jones, a sociologist of the city's black housing patterns noted in 1929, "It would not be an exaggeration to state that Negroes live in every residential block in Washington either as residents or as servants in somebody else's household."[23]

As this table illustrates, the majority of black Washingtonians lived in the Northwest quadrant of the city. Northwest also had a higher percentage of women, because single women who worked for the government or as domestic servants and boarded in houses tended to live in that section. Between the 1920s and the 1940s, the location of the black population shifted slightly, but not significantly. As black unemployment rose with the Great Depression, women and men moved into working-class neighborhoods in the Southeast and Southwest quadrants, where rent was less expensive. Northwest Washington was the largest quadrant in the city, and residents there had the best access to schools, police protection, and fire safety. African Americans who lived in Northeast, Southeast, and Southwest had more limited access to municipal services.[24]

Both federal and local authorities governed Washington during the 1920s and 1930s. A three-member Board of Commissioners formed the local government of the city. The president of the United States appointed two of the commissioners, while the Army Corps of Engineers selected the third. The Board of Commissioners oversaw the city's police officers, School Board members, public health officers, and public works funding. The president also appointed the judges to the District Superior Court. Congress's Committee on the District of Columbia convened special hearings on issues that arose in Washington. The U.S. Superintendent of Public Buildings and Grounds controlled the recreational spaces in the capital, including monuments, public parks, the zoo, and swimming pools. All residents of the city, regardless of race or sex, were disfranchised, having no vote in federal elections and no elected positions in local government. The only residents of the city who escaped these limitations were those who maintained residency in other states and voted by absentee ballot.[25]

Within this system of governance that blocked nearly all formal political participation, African American women and men nevertheless engaged actively in politics. In neighborhood associations and the umbrella organization, the Federation of Civic Associations, they submitted petitions to the Board of Commissioners, asking for municipal services ranging from street paving and expanded mail delivery to the employment of black police officers and firemen.[26] One African American resident served as the assistant superintendent of the school system, overseeing the city's black schools. It was customary for three black citizens to sit on the nine-member School Board, where they could address issues related to curriculum and the employment of teachers. Black Washingtonians also attended congressional hearings, lobbied elected officials, and used their connections as workers and servants in federal employment to secure meetings with congressmen, senators, and even the president.

Black Washingtonians worked to maintain more than 150 churches in neighborhoods across the city. The 1926 federal census of religious bodies revealed that 144,764 African Americans, or 60 percent of all black people in Washington, D.C., belonged to a church. The major denominations with which African Americans were affiliated were African Methodist Episcopal (AME), African Methodist Episcopal Zion (AMEZ), Baptist, Catholic, Christian Methodist Episcopal (CME), Congregationalist, Episcopalian, and Methodist Episcopal (ME). The actual number of church members was probably higher because this report tracked only members of official denominations, thereby excluding the women and men who attended services in holiness, spiritualist, alley, and storefront churches.[27] Black Washingtonians also operated more

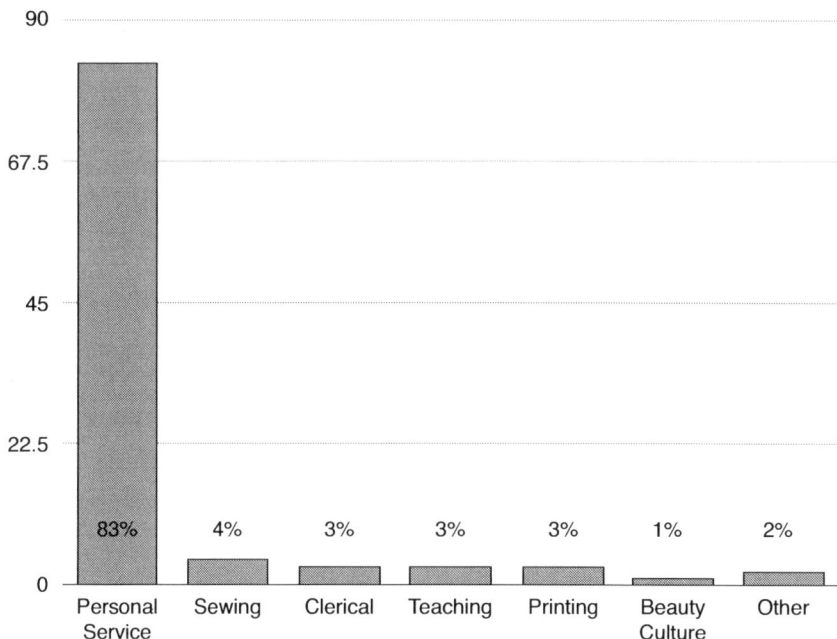

90

67.5

45

22.5

0

| 83% | 4% | 3% | 3% | 3% | 1% | 2% |

Personal Service | Sewing | Clerical | Teaching | Printing | Beauty Culture | Other

African American women's occupations in Washington, D.C., 1920.
Source: *Fourteenth Census of the United States: Population: Occupations. Males and Females in Selected Occupations* (Washington, D.C.: GPO, 1923), 897–900. The occupational census used the generic category of personal service to encompass diverse forms of personal service, such as cooks, live-in servants, maids, and domestic workers.

than 300 businesses, 162 mutual benefit and fraternal orders, dozens of political organizations, neighborhood associations, and the largest NAACP branch in the nation during the 1920s.[28]

For black women workers in Washington, D.C., few labor opportunities existed outside of personal service. In 1920, 83 percent of black women in Washington worked in personal service occupations: 45 percent worked as domestics, 25 percent worked as laundresses; 6 percent worked as charwomen (workers who cleaned offices), and 4 percent worked as waitresses. The remaining service workers labored in various jobs, such as stewardesses, untrained nurses, and cleaners.[29] Additionally, 1 percent worked as hairdressers, 4 percent worked as dressmakers and seamstresses, 3 percent worked as teachers, and 3 percent worked as printers and printers' assistants. While black women's high rates of service work in Washington closely paralleled labor patterns of other southern or mid-Atlantic cities, Washington, D.C., residents did enjoy prospects for federal employment, as clerks, stenographers, typists, and charwomen, making them highly desirable positions for black women workers.[30]

Black women did not constitute a monolithic political community. Washington, D.C., was a cosmopolitan city, filled with women who had been born in diverse states across the country, including South Carolina, Mississippi, Virginia, Colorado, Michigan, Illinois, Pennsylvania, and Massachusetts. Women's hometowns, residence in neighborhoods throughout the city, diverse labor experiences, and varied organizational and institutional connections shaped their political knowledge and flowed into their organizing and activism.

African American Women's Activism and Organizing in Washington, D.C.

In Washington, D.C., as elsewhere, African American women's networks formed the backbone of their politics. Whether in church on a Sunday, at a fraternal meeting, during a Friday evening game of bridge, in a meet-up on the streetcar, or an evening chat on the street, black women forged connections with one another. As women banded together to raise money for a church, canvass a neighborhood for potential members of a new organization, or circulate information about an event, they learned the craft of politics. Fraternal orders and churches were sites that taught black women political skills and cemented their bonds of attachment to each other.

Yet it was not a foregone conclusion that any black woman living in the nation's capital would participate in political campaigns. Political activism required time and deliberation. Many African American women in the nation's capital were focused on everyday survival for themselves and their families, securing adequate food, housing, employment, and childcare. That any black woman in Washington, D.C., was able to engage in political campaigns was exceptional, not inevitable. Women had to continually *perform* the hard work of politics and organizing, whether it was reaching into their networks to recruit new constituents, educating members about issues, or disseminating news about the importance of their activism.[31]

African American women living in the nation's capital practiced politics on many different levels. They pursued formal politics by creating partisan associations, lobbying politicians and elected officials, weighing in on legislation, attending meetings, testifying at hearings, and staging parades and protest marches to influence matters that affected the entire nation or specifically the residents of Washington, D.C. But African American women's politics also included workplace resistance, self-defense against violence, defiance toward racial segregation, and performances of racial egalitarianism, democracy, and citizenship in a city that often denied them all of these rights. *Jim Crow Capital* connects examples of black women's formal and informal politics to illustrate the complexity of their activism.[32]

While African American women's activism began as early as the seventeenth century, it was during the 1920s and 1930s that their political campaigns gained more visibility. Not only did black women form diverse partisan organizations and lobbying groups in those decades but they also employed calculated strategies to enact change. Black women seized on their conspicuous location in the nation's capital to stage parades and demonstrations in key sites across the city. When they held a Silent Protest Parade against lynching, they deliberately marched past the offices of the Senate and the House of Representatives and ended at the White House, which literally brought the struggle to lawmakers and the president. Black women had always been present in the U.S. Congress as cleaners, attendants, and observers, but they became more prominent in the 1920s and 1930s by testifying in Congress and government bureaus on a range of political matters. Speaking to audiences largely composed of white male senators, representatives, and staff, black women championed voting rights, freedom from violence, labor justice, and the construction of museums that commemorated black history. Some members of Congress who attended these hearings were southern Democrats, who were working to deny these rights to African Americans in their home states. In daring to confront these politicians through their testimony, black women upheld full citizenship rights for themselves and African Americans across the nation.

Black women's connections within Washington, D.C., and their access to the federal government shaped their political campaigns. It was challenging for black women in northern or midwestern cities and virtually impossible for southern black women to create such networks. Women in Washington, D.C., often viewed themselves as representatives of black women across the country, and, at various moments, acted on their behalf. Even though Washington, D.C., was a southern city, black women sued in court, met with local officials and national politicians, and served on juries. African American women in the nation's capital were litigious citizens, and when they felt their civil rights had been violated, they contested.

But black women's lives in the nation's capital should not be romanticized. Washington, D.C., was deeply segregated, interracial violence was rampant, and economic inequalities were stark. In the 1920s and 1930s, white southern men dominated the Democratic Party and held leadership positions on important committees in the U.S. House of Representatives and the Senate. The political scientist Ira Katznelson terms Congress in the 1930s the "Jim Crow Congress" based on white southern members' determination to enforce white supremacy and oppose civil rights.[33] Not only did white southerners wield power in Congress but they sometimes used racial matters in the nation's capital as a pawn in their white supremacist projects, which had major consequences for the rights of black Washingtonians.

Scholars have developed several approaches to the historiography of African American women's political history in the twentieth century. Historians have chronicled African American women's participation in electoral politics in Chicago, Memphis, and New York, examining how black women exercised the right to vote and championed legislation.[34] Others have documented women's wide-ranging contributions to the postwar black freedom struggle for legal equality, whether they served as leaders, rank-and-file participants, grassroots organizers, mothers, musicians, artists, or hairdressers.[35] Another cohort of historians has discussed black women's struggle for economic justice, analyzing the ways that women organized for fair wages and working conditions and pushed government institutions to provide decent housing, health care, schools, and welfare provision.[36] *Jim Crow Capital* integrates black women's activism in all of these contexts. It investigates how black women used their location in the nation's capital to lobby for legislation; illuminates women's broad participation in their early civil rights movement in the 1930s and 1940s; and demonstrates that black women's expansive visions of freedom included legal equality, economic justice, and safety from violence. *Jim Crow Capital* focuses on black women's experiences precisely because their level of formal organizing expanded during the 1920s and 1930s. As a study of women's history, *Jim Crow Capital* examines moments when black men joined women in their campaigns and analyzes gendered patterns of leadership and activism.

Outline of the Chapters

Jim Crow Capital chronicles three periods in African American women's politics in the nation's capital. Part I: Postwar Promises, 1920–1929, illuminates black women's optimism about the expansion of African American citizenship rights. In chapter 1, African American women harness the power of national organizations to influence federal policy. Chapter 2 examines women's campaigns to pass a federal anti-lynching bill. Part II: Political Crises, 1930–1940, documents the calamity of the Great Depression and rising racial tensions in Washington, D.C., which caused activists to turn toward local issues in the nation's capital. Chapter 3 documents women's crusades against interracial police brutality, chapter 4 assesses black women's struggles to secure economic justice during the 1930s, and chapter 5 surveys black Washingtonians' campaigns for racial integration, the restoration of voting rights, and the passage of a civil rights bill. In Part III: The Leverage of War, 1941–1945, black women express wartime militancy by fighting transportation segregation, staging sit-ins at lunch counters in the city, and lobbying for national causes, as described in chapter 6.

Black women's political activism in Washington underscores the importance of adopting a long view of the black freedom movement. Some of the political movements that African American women waged in Washington, D.C., eventually resulted in significant legislative change by the 1960s, including the end to legal segregation and the extension of voting rights to most citizens in the United States. But black women also confronted injustices that persist in the United States to the present day, including police brutality, racial and sexual violence, denial of voting rights, statehood for the District of Columbia, and the striking realities of economic inequalities, especially with regard to wealth accumulation. African American women's activism in Washington, D.C., not only demonstrates the importance of examining an earlier, more sweeping moment in political history but also reminds us that the quest for justice and citizenship is always an ongoing process that has not yet been fully realized.

Part I
Postwar Promises, 1920–1929

We are in politics to stay, and we shall be a stay in politics.

—National League of Republican Colored Women

There are enough Negroes in Washington to make Pennsylvania Avenue tremble.

—Nannie Helen Burroughs

CHAPTER ONE

The Women Will Be Factors in the Present Campaign

Women's National Politics in the 1920s

In the fall of 1920, a series of articles in the black-owned newspaper, the *Washington Bee*, applauded African American women's visibility in national politics. There were many reasons for black women's political prominence at that time. The Nineteenth Amendment, which granted suffrage to women, was ratified in August 1920, nearly doubling the number of eligible voters across the country. Its passage occurred just months before the presidential election, which pitted Democratic nominee James Cox against Republican nominee Warren Harding. Since black Washingtonians had witnessed their civil rights diminish under Democratic president Woodrow Wilson's administration, many residents of the nation's capital supported a Harding presidency. For years, African American women had been organizing in their churches, mutual benefit associations, and clubs. The ratification of the Nineteenth Amendment and the pending presidential election inspired women to connect their existing alliances with partisan causes, and the local press took note. "Though the women of the District of Columbia are suffering political slavery as well as the men," an article observed, "they are thoroughly organized and functioning to do their bit."[1] A columnist for the same paper remarked that he had "never seen so many would-be politicians in all of my life." He predicted that "the women will be factors in the present campaign. They are in many instances better vote-getters than the men." He concluded, "Our colored women exercise greater political sagacity than many of our men.[2] This recognition in the local press foreshadowed African American women's important contributions to national politics throughout the decade.

During the 1920s, African American women living in Washington, D.C., played a distinctive role in national politics. As residents of the nation's capital, they, like men and women of all races, were disenfranchised. The only Washingtonians who were eligible to cast ballots were those who maintained residency in other states and mailed in their absentee votes. The historian Alexander Keyssar notes that, by 1920, twenty states would supply an absentee ballot to any resident whose job prevented his or her presence at the polls.[3] Even though most black women in Washington could not vote, they established organizations to discuss political matters and champion legislation, traveled to neighboring states to encourage newly enfranchised women to vote, and reminded eligible citizens to mail in their absentee ballots. By discussing the significance of voting and electoral politics, black women in Washington presented themselves as citizens to their city and the nation.

Indeed, black women seized on their location in the nation's capital to advocate on behalf of African Americans living across the country. Pushing through heavy and intimidating doors, women testified in Congress, lobbied politicians and elected officials, and monitored the progress of legislation. Activists mobilized their newly formed political organizations to protest southern disfranchisement, champion the appointment of black women to administrative positions in the federal government, advocate for the rights of black women workers, support anti-lynching legislation and the Equal Rights Amendment, express opinions about Supreme Court judicial nominations, and weigh in on which monuments and memorials would grace the National Mall. In all of their different campaigns, black women in Washington claimed authority to represent the national interests of African American citizens.

Women founded national organizations, some of which were Republican; their membership ranged from neighborhood groups to national constituencies (see table 3). While the majority of these organizations worked to promote national causes, they each advocated for specific issues. The Colored Women's Republican League, which comprised absentee voters and disenfranchised residents of Washington, promoted the GOP; the Absentee Voter's League specifically encouraged absentee voting, the National Legislative Council of Colored Women tracked bills in Congress, and the National Association of Wage Earners championed labor justice for black women workers. Collectively, these organizations, with their respective aims, constituencies, and memberships, illuminate the complexity of black women's politics in Washington, D.C., animated by such concerns as absentee voting, congressional legislation, monuments and memorials, economic justice, and federal appointments.

Although hundreds of black women in Washington participated in national politics throughout the 1920s, three leaders—Mary Church Terrell, Marian Butler, and Nannie Helen Burroughs—spearheaded these campaigns. Terrell was born in Memphis in 1863 to former slaves. She attended Oberlin College and then settled in Washington, D.C., where she became a teacher, writer, and the first black woman to serve on the D.C School Board. She married Robert Terrell, who was appointed a judge in the Municipal Court of Washington in

TABLE 3 African American women's national organizations in 1920s Washington, D.C.

Name	Year	Constituency	Membership	Meeting Place
Colored Women's Republican League (CWRL)	1920	Ledroit Park: Northwest Washington	Republican absentee voters and Republican women	YWCA
Colored Women's Republican League Auxiliary	1920	Anacostia: Southeast Washington	Republican absentee voters and Republican women	Campbell ME Church
Women's Republican Forum of Deanwood	1921	Deanwood: Northeast Washington	Republican absentee voters and Republican women	Unknown
National Association of Wage Earners (NAWE)	1921	National	All black women	NAWE headquarters
Women's Political Study Club (WPSC)	1923	Washington, D.C.	Republican absentee voters	YWCA
National Legislative Council of Colored Women (NLCCW)	1923	National	All black women	Mazie Griffith's house
National League of Republican Women (NLRW)	1924	National	Republican women	NAWE headquarters
Absentee Voter's League	1924	Washington, D.C.	Absentee voters	Offices of the *Washington Bee*

Source: This information comes from a close reading of the *Washington Bee* and the *Washington Tribune* in the 1920s.

1910, and they had several children. Terrell served as the first president of the National Association of Colored Women (NACW), which was the largest black civil rights organization in the early twentieth century, and was a proponent of woman suffrage. As a middle-class woman, she was able to devote herself fully to social reform and politics. Terrell's affiliations with the NACW and the school system gave her access to many political networks, while attending her husband's confirmation appointments introduced her to the inner workings of the U.S. Congress.[4]

Marian D. Butler was born in Barnwell, South Carolina, in 1876.[5] She attended Benedict College and became a matron and fundraiser for the Jenkins Orphanage in Charleston, South Carolina, an institution that had a famous traveling band.[6] Her first husband was appointed the assistant postmaster of Blackwell, South Carolina, and after he died, she served in that position. As Marian Butler came of age in South Carolina, she witnessed the rise of Jim Crow, marked by racial violence, segregation, and disenfranchisement. In the 1910s, Butler returned to her post at the Jenkins Orphanage and, while on a fundraising tour in Washington, D.C., met and married her second husband, who worked as a government clerk. In 1920, she became a widow for the second time and supported herself in the nation's capital by editing the society page for the *Washington Tribune*, renting rooms in her home, and sewing dresses. But she struggled financially and, during the Great Depression, labored as a domestic servant. For Marian Butler, the disturbing memories of white supremacy in her home state of South Carolina inspired her political activism.[7]

Nannie Helen Burroughs was born in 1879 in Culpepper, Virginia. She moved to Washington, D.C., where she graduated from the prestigious M Street High School. She briefly moved to Louisville, Kentucky, where she worked as a bookkeeper and secretary for the Foreign Mission Board of the Baptist Convention. She was elected president of the Women's Convention of the National Baptist Convention, a large national organization of black women. In 1909 she returned to Washington, D.C., and opened the National Training School for Women and Girls in Lincoln Heights, a neighborhood in Northeast. The National Training School for Women and Girls provided instruction to black students in cooking, domestic service, sewing, and laundry. As the leader of a school for black women, she continually sought financial assistance from black and white Americans. Burroughs was involved in numerous causes throughout her life, but was most passionate about securing economic justice for black women.[8] As their biographies attest, Terrell, Butler, and Burroughs had significant political experiences before 1920, and they drew on these skills, networks, and knowledge to organize their campaigns in Washington.

Since black women and girls were excluded from many commercial and recreational spaces throughout Washington, D.C., the Phyllis Wheatley YWCA headquarters was an indispensable resource. The building contained a gymnasium, parlor rooms that could be divided to accommodate multiple meetings, a social hall with a fireplace, an elegant lobby, a cafeteria, and forty-four dormitory rooms. Census records reveal that women from a variety of economic backgrounds lived at the YWCA, including students, service workers, clerks, teachers, unemployed women, and out-of-town visitors. John P. Wymer Photograph Collection, Historical Society of Washington, D.C.

For activists in Washington, the Phyllis Wheatley Young Women's Christian Association (YWCA) was an essential resource. During World War I, YWCA leaders had petitioned the War Work Council for funds to construct a new headquarters, and they received $200,000 to build a "demonstration building for colored work." The new brick building was four stories tall, featuring dormitories, a gymnasium, a cafeteria, and many social spaces. The YWCA was located in LeDroit Park in Northwest, close to many churches, lodges, schools, Howard University, as well as the train station. The YWCA served local residents, as well as the hundreds of black women who journeyed to Washington for jobs, conferences, and inaugurations.[9]

A number of scholars have analyzed African American women's national activism in the 1920s. Rosalyn Terborg-Penn argues that, racism exhibited by

white women's suffrage groups in the aftermath of the Nineteenth Amendment, as well as growing economic inequalities, prompted black female activists to pursue reform strategies that aided all African Americans. Evelyn Brooks
Higginbotham acknowledges black women's reform work in the 1920s, but
maintains that they remained active in partisan politics, which laid the groundwork for the defection of African Americans to the Democratic Party. In her
analysis of middle-class black women's politics, Nikki Brown describes the
ways that black women worked to push the issue of racial justice onto the Republican Party platform throughout the 1920s. And in her study of black
women's politics in Illinois, Lisa G. Materson documents how southern
migrant women worked as "proxy voters" to represent the political interests
of their friends and family members.[10] These scholarly interpretations offer
important insights into black women's partisan activities, but aside from Materson, largely center around national leaders and organizations.

Jim Crow Capital builds on the historiography of black women's partisan
politics by connecting leaders and organizations with their local grassroots
constituencies and everyday activities. In their national political activities in
the 1920s, black women in Washington, D.C., cast absentee ballots and seized
on their federal location to give themselves the leverage of voters, using it on
behalf of themselves and African Americans living across the nation.

"Public Men, Women, and Things": Black Women's Political Organizing, 1920–1921

In September 1920, one month after the Nineteenth Amendment was ratified,
black women throughout Washington, D.C., founded Republican organizations to represent their new rights as citizens, even if most could not cast
ballots. Women in Northwest Washington formed the Colored Women's Republican League (CWRL) inside the parlors of the Phyllis Wheatley YWCA.
Rallying under the slogan, "Organize, Harmonize," members elected veteran
activist Mary Church Terrell to serve as the first president, while Nannie Helen
Burroughs chaired the Propaganda Committee. The CRWL's leadership board
largely comprised middle-class women who lived in LeDroit Park in Northwest Washington and were members of the local chapter of the NACW. Black
women in Anacostia, a working-class neighborhood in Southeast, banded
together as an auxiliary to the CWRL, meeting inside of the Campbell ME
Church, and elected Fannie Shipley, a teacher, to serve as president. The creation of an auxiliary enabled members to attend meetings at their local church,
rather than having to travel across the city to the YWCA in Northwest Wash-

ington.[11] Several months later, women in Deanwood, a working-class neighborhood in Northeast Washington, formed the Deanwood Women's Republican Forum.[12] The formation of Republican groups in three different neighborhoods throughout the city indicates that the passage of the Nineteenth Amendment resonated with many black women, even if they could not influence politics as voters.

Through their Republican organizations, black women worked to connect their networks in Washington, D.C., with electoral constituencies across the nation. Shortly after becoming president of the CWRL, Terrell traveled to New York City to recruit members for her new organization. While visiting the headquarters of the Harding-Coolidge campaign, she learned that she had been appointed the Republican Party's Eastern Representative for Colored Women, which required her to visit eastern cities for the remainder of the 1920s presidential campaign.[13]

In Terrell's absence, leaders in the CWRL sought to influence the 1920s election in the nation's capital. Their activities showed how disenfranchised black women in Washington presented themselves as citizens and articulated their political opinions. CWRL leaders contacted church ministers throughout the city, asking them to highlight absentee ballot submission in their Sunday sermons.[14] Washington, D.C., resident Julia J. Jeubius wrote a poem that was printed in the *Washington Bee*, endorsing Warren Harding for his positions on women's suffrage, a minimum wage for women workers, and global peace. Just days before the election, CWRL leader Fannie Clair organized a mass meeting at the Asbury ME Church, where her husband was the pastor. This event attracted a crowd of three hundred black Republican women, who heard addresses by Reverend and Fannie Clair, the white Republican leader Virginia White Speel, and lawyer Marie Madre-Marshall, as well as several "patriotic selections" from Asbury's choir. A newspaper article noted that all three hundred attendees made it "a truly Harding and Coolidge House" as they unanimously endorsed both candidates.[15] Teacher Eva Chase, an attendee, wrote a letter to Terrell that the "meeting at Asbury was the most successful we have had."[16] By encouraging absentee ballot voting, supporting candidates through the press, and endorsing Harding and Coolidge in a mass meeting, black women showcased their new citizenship rights conferred by the Nineteenth Amendment.

The black press in Washington, D.C., featured articles that described women's political organizing and praised their activities. The "Sage of the Potomac," whose weekly column in the *Washington Bee* was titled "Public Men and Things," chronicled political affairs across the city. After writing a series of articles on black women's political activities, the author broadened the title of his column to "Public Men, Women, and Things." In justifying the change, he remarked, "I have concluded to deal with women as well as men and things. Women have decided to place themselves on political and other equality with men hence they must receive what is to come." He announced that he "shall not be surprised to see the women ruling the world in a few years. They are more active and determined than the men."[17]

Black women's organizing for the Republican Party, both in Washington, D.C., and across the nation, paid off. In November 1920, Warren G. Harding was elected the nation's twenty-ninth president, and Republicans regained both houses of Congress. Members of the Republican National Committee recognized the important contributions of black women in Washington, D.C., even though they had not even cast ballots in the election. The Inaugural Executive Committee placed four women on the Information Committee in gratitude for their "splendid work in the last campaign." All four—Mary Church Terrell, Julia Mason Layton, Eva Chase, and Rachel Bell—were members of the CWRL.[18]

As the city prepared for a new presidential administration, activists turned to their next political priority: ensuring that all women could vote. During the recent election, most black women in the South had been subject to the same disfranchisement policies that had prevented black men from casting ballots since the 1890s.[19] In response, women in the nation's capital launched a two-pronged response to southern disfranchisement. In February 1921, prominent women gathered for a Republican reception at the storied Old Ebbitt House, which was one block from the White House. While white activists emphasized the need to bring women's suffrage to countries around the world, black speakers reminded reception attendees of the realities of disfranchisement in the United States. Julia Mason Layton, president of the Phyllis Wheatley YWCA and member of the CWRL, told reception attendees that "our duty now as colored women" was to "help all of our women" cast ballots as American citizens.[20]

Black women not only issued public statements about southern women's disfranchisement but also worked to lobby influential activists to take action. One week after the reception at the Old Ebbitt House, women from the CWRL banded together with NACW members representing twenty states and arranged a meeting in Washington with Alice Paul, a prominent suffrage advocate and the chair of the National Women's Party. This meeting would not be an easy one, considering Paul's weak record on race. In the 1913 suffrage parade in Washington, D.C., Paul had insisted that African American women march in a segregated section.[21] Aware of the impending difficulties, the women first gathered at the Nineteenth Street Baptist Church in Northwest Washington, where they strategized what they would say to Paul. This group of black women then walked from that church to the headquarters of the National Women's Party on Jackson Place in Northwest Washington. There, they greeted Paul and asked her to "lend her aid toward the enforcement of the Nineteenth Amendment to the Constitution" to enable "5,000,000 colored women" to vote. Paul was not receptive to this plea. While the activists were disappointed with Paul's response, an article in the *Washington Bee* noted that the "delegation left with a greater determination to go on and press the battle." After the meeting, the women went to the YWCA, where they enjoyed a luncheon and then held a strategy session.[22]

This interaction between the National Women's party and the NACW illustrates two important characteristics of African American women's partisan activities. First, black women received little assistance or moral support from white suffrage activists, who viewed black women's disfranchisement as an issue of race, not gender.[23] Second, Washington's landscape of racial segregation shaped African American women's participation in partisan politics. It was critical that black women had a space where they could convene for political purposes. The Phyllis Wheatley YWCA in Washington, D.C., offered not only a place for meetings but also a dormitory for out-of-town visitors and a cafeteria for activists to share a meal, a necessity in the city's segregated landscape. Activists saw it as their political duty to provide these resources to black women across the country. That partisan activists in Washington, D.C., were able to address these pragmatic considerations enabled them to focus more earnestly on supporting pressing issues for African American women, including voting rights and economic justice.

The National Association of Wage Earners and Economic Justice

A few weeks after the inauguration of President Warren G. Harding, Nannie Helen Burroughs built on this political victory by announcing the formation of the National Association of Wage Earners (NAWE), a labor organization for black women workers. Burroughs envisioned the NAWE as an advocacy group that would enable workers to fight for fair wages, address grievances against employers, and lobby for national legislation.[24] Between November 10 and 14, 1921, black women from across the country streamed into Washington, D.C., to attend the NAWE's founding meeting. Many of the same women who joined the NAWE had ties with the NACW and had been involved in Republican organizations in their home states.[25] At this meeting, members decided to open membership to all black women over the age of sixteen. The NAWE would be a "profit-sharing enterprise" whereby members could gain financial benefit from goods produced by the organization and especially, from their work as recruiters. Anyone recruiting another member earned 25 cents for each recruit. This national meeting affirmed members' commitment to organizing as many women as possible, with the aim of improving black women's economic situation across the nation.[26]

Between 1921 and 1926 1,800 women and men from thirty-seven states and the capital joined the NAWE; about one-third (679) had national memberships, and two-thirds (1,121) had local memberships in Washington, D.C.[27] The NAWE's chapter in Washington, D.C., was called the District Union. Members joined the District Union through formal recruitment, street connections, labor networks, churches, mutual benefit associations, and mass meetings. It became a cross-class organization through strategic recruitment processes and in order to fulfill its explicit purpose of assisting black working-class women. By the time the organization folded in 1926, 46 percent of the members in the District Union were service workers, including cooks, maids, laundresses, and charwomen.[28]

A close analysis of membership patterns in the District Union reveals the ways that recruiters helped to draw a cross-class coalition of women and men into the organization. The most successful recruiter was Sadie Tignor Henson. She joined at the founding meeting in November 1921, listing her occupation as a housekeeper. During the 1910s, Henson had worked as a truant officer in the public schools, traveling to different schools across the city to enforce attendance policies. In 1923, after returning to work as a truant officer, Henson canvassed diverse parts of the city and was able to enroll fifty members in the organization. Henson tapped both working-class and middle-class women and men, including maids and chauffeurs, butchers, printers, and government workers, as well as teachers, a social worker, a lawyer, a pharmacist, and a funeral home director. Available records do not designate those whom Burroughs accepted as official organizers, but given the pace and geographic scope of her recruiting, it is likely that in early 1923 Henson was acting in that capacity.[29]

Sadie Henson's neighborhood, institutional, labor, and organizational connections across the city help explain her diverse recruitment patterns. She had grown up in Southwest Washington. After she married James A. Henson, who worked as a clerk in the Bureau of Printing and Engraving, the couple moved across town to Northwest Washington. Both were active in mutual benefit associations. James held a leadership position in the Workers' Relief Association, while Sadie served as an officer in Chapter Number 3 of the Gethsemane Order of the Knights of Templar, which was a fraternal organization.[30] Five of Henson's recruits to the District Union—a live-in servant, two housekeepers, a housewife, and a government clerk—were officers in the Gethsemane Order. Henson's job as a truant officer required her to travel to different schools across the city, thus acquainting her with a variety of neighborhoods. In addition, she held leadership positions in the local chapter of the NACW and the Zion Baptist Sunday School. All of these different affiliations with neighborhoods, churches, mutual benefit associations, schools, and organizations flowed into Henson's work as a recruiter, enabling her to attract members who lived in different parts of the city and had a variety of jobs. For example, one year after Henson returned to work as a truant officer, three fellow attendance officers in the public schools, including the chief of the department, joined the District Union.[31]

Lucy E. Holland, a single waitress in her twenties, worked as another important recruiter for the District Union. She expressed an eagerness for the organization right away, filling out a membership card in November 1921 where she listed "herself" as her own recruiter. The following month, she recruited three members: a housewife, her husband who worked as a watchman, and their boarder, a janitor. Unlike Sadie Henson, Lucy Holland recruited close to her home, enlisting members from a discrete geographic area who were primarily engaged, like herself, in working-class jobs. Holland's recruits included four maids, three watchmen, three domestics, three housekeepers, two charwomen (office cleaners), two hairdressers, two laundresses, two who did not list their jobs, and a cafeteria director, a clerk, a cook, a dressmaker, a government laborer, and one housewife. None of her recruits were professionals, and most lived within thirteen blocks of Holland's home on L Street in Northwest.[32]

A comparison of the recruitment patterns of Sadie Henson and Lucy Holland illuminates how labor experiences, personal relationships, institutional connections, and everyday encounters in the city shaped African American women's knowledge networks. These processes also offer insights into the ways that black women canvassed members for other organizations and political causes. The District Union gathered a diverse set of members in Washington, D.C., precisely because of recruiters like Henson and Holland, as well as ordinary members who tapped neighbors, work friends, spouses, or fellow church members.

While Henson and Holland were recruiting potential members for the District Union on the local level, Nannie Helen Burroughs was advocating for black women workers in the federal government. On Thursday, January 7, 1923, the Women's Bureau in the Department of Labor convened a conference in which 300 delegates from states across the country met in Washington, D.C., to discuss issues affecting working women, including wages, safety, and homework (work such as sewing that was performed inside homes). President Warren G. Harding and the Secretary of Labor James J. Davis sent greetings of support to the Women's Industrial Conference, likely in recognition of women's new political power as voters.[33] Several black women spoke at the conference, but Burroughs delivered the most pointed address, where she used her location in the nation's capital to champion protection, dignity, and higher wages for black domestic workers living across the nation.

In her speech, Burroughs challenged delegates to consider the symbiotic relationship between black women's service labor and white women's industrial and professional work. "It is possible for large numbers of women in this country," Burroughs argued, to perform industrial labor and to volunteer because "there are women back in their homes now who are caring for their children, who are laundering their clothes, who are looking after their work, and who are doing those things faithfully; and they can be trusted." Burroughs argued that African American women were the "the backbone of the economic life, so far as the white women are concerned." Concretely, Burroughs championed three aspects of improved conditions for African American women: for them to receive both "finer and better service," and "better living conditions," as well as for "white women to feel and for colored women to feel that they have much in common, since the colored women are on your pay rolls." She noted that there was "a movement on foot on the part of the colored women to form a national association of wage earners" and that it was still in its infancy.[34] An article in the *Washington Tribune* noted that Burroughs received a "genuine ovation" following her remarks to the Women's Industrial Conference.[35]

While it was important that Burroughs described the work of the NAWE in a national conference sponsored by the Women's Bureau, on the ground in Washington, D.C., leaders in the organization worked to assist black women in their fight for economic justice. On July 15, 1924, the federal Personnel Reclassification Board issued new policies that adversely affected women who worked part-time as federal charwomen. Specifically, the policies reduced their hourly wages by 40 cents, limited their hours to three per day, required them to donate 2½ cents into a retirement fund, and eliminated additional pay on Sundays and holidays, which meant that workers earned less than $6 a week or only $288 a year.[36] Previously, part-time charwomen had earned between $320 and $480 annually and were eligible for a $120 salary bonus for overtime work. In response, 250 black and white charwomen from a variety of government bureaus met in the offices of Henry Lincoln Johnson, a black World War I veteran, lawyer, and prominent Republican activist. In this meeting, women criticized these salary reductions, which severely affected their livelihood, and pointed out that their cleaning tasks often exceeded the three-hour daily limit. Women then formed committees to protest these injustices. The three women who spearheaded these protests had working-class jobs and were raising families: Laura Langhorne (whose husband labored as a barber) had two daughters, one of whom was ten years old; Lena Ware (whose husband worked as a watchman) had a daughter who was fourteen; and Mary Porter had a large extended family.[37] Having their part-time wages cut and their hours limited placed increased strains on their families. A newspaper article noted, "In many instances, the meager salary received from the Government by these charwomen who toil after hours and in the early morning in the departments is their sole source of sustenance" and that reclassification of their wages had presented an "undue hardship."[38]

In September 1924, the District Union, the local chapter of the NAWE, decided to support these protests. An article noted that Nannie Helen Burroughs had "consented to swing the full force of her organization behind the government workers." It is likely that Burroughs selected this political cause because it would put her in touch with government workers. At this point, eighteen charwomen in the federal government were members of the District Union, along with forty-nine others who worked for the government in various capacities, such as clerks, messengers, elevator operators, and stenographers. They made up 9 percent of the District Union, thus making a significant proportion of the members vulnerable to government reclassification and explaining why the local union championed their cause. Charwomen, in cooperation with the District Union, organized a "monster mass meeting" in September at the Cleveland Elementary School to protest the low wages. An article on the meeting commented on the presence of the District Union, noting that "all women workers will join a cooperative movement with other government workers and make a nationwide appeal for relief."[39] Following the mass meeting, one charwoman and three government workers joined the District Union. In this instance, both the District Union and the grassroots protests benefited from working together on behalf of the government employees.

In November 1924, the NAWE opened a headquarters on Rhode Island Avenue in Northwest Washington, which enabled the District Union to expand its activities.[40] The headquarters' location in Northwest Washington—near the important black neighborhoods of Logan Circle and LeDroit Park; close to local institutions, such as Howard University, the Phyllis Wheatley YWCA, and the John Wesley AMEZ Church; and within walking distance of two street-car lines—made it a convenient and accessible site for many black Washingtonians. The headquarters featured "practice rooms" where domestic workers could sharpen their cleaning skills as well as bedrooms where workers could live. After the headquarters was opened, Burroughs told a reporter from the *Washington Tribune* that "the organization will show the world what Negro women can do in a labor movement."[41]

The NAWE's headquarters served many purposes. Between 1924 and 1926, local members of the District Union gathered at the headquarters on Thursday evenings for their monthly meetings. And each day, District Union members visited the headquarters to take classes to sharpen their skills as service workers, perfecting their crafts in the practice dining room, kitchen, and living rooms of the headquarters. These classes accommodated workers in a variety of service jobs, including cooking, waitressing, and maid service. The classes involved "drills in the ethics and fundamentals of their profession."[42] Once workers completed a class, they received a service card, which was sent to their employer. These classes were designed to increase black women's wages, as well as their value in the eyes of their employers.

The NAWE's headquarters was also an important site for black women's partisan activities. When Calvin Coolidge was inaugurated in March 1925, black women and men from all over the country traveled to Washington, D.C., to attend the ceremonies. The NAWE sought to assist some of these travelers by "having an open house during the entire Inauguration Week." A column in the *Washington Tribune* announced, "Visitors to the city may 'drop in' at any time between the hours of ten A.M. and ten P.M. for rest, refreshments, or conference."[43] Black women positioned their headquarters as both a space where visitors could come to learn about the work of the organization and a site where they could rest and enjoy a meal, a valuable benefit for out-of-town visitors who were barred from many hotels and restaurants. That same year, the NAWE wrote to the D.C. Board of Commissioners, protesting the Ku Klux Klan's intention to parade in Washington, D.C.[44]

While the NAWE was not able to address black women's economic concerns in very substantial ways on the national level, locally in Washington, D.C., more than one thousand people saw hope in the District Union. That the local chapter was able to recruit this membership demonstrates how black women's neighborhoods, churches, fraternal orders, and social networks

The National Association of Wage Earners headquarters was located at 1116 Rhode Island Avenue in Northwest Washington. When the NAWE headquarters opened its doors in 1924, it helped centralize the activities of the District Union. Members of the District Union gathered at the headquarters on Thursday evenings for their monthly meetings. And each day, members visited the headquarters to take classes to sharpen their skills as service workers, perfecting their crafts in its practice dining room, kitchen, and living rooms. These classes accommodated workers in a variety of service jobs. Library of Congress, LC-DIG-ds-10968.

offered important constituencies for political campaigns. Members of the District Union used the organization to rally on behalf of charwomen, visited the headquarters to sharpen their skills, and engaged with each other in conversations about economic justice. Even though the NAWE was focused specifically on labor issues, the organization's headquarters and membership networks assisted black women in other partisan activities throughout the 1920s.

"In Politics to Stay": Women's Partisan Activism in Washington, D.C., 1923–1930

Between 1923 and 1930, black women in Washington, D.C., expanded their presence in partisan politics. Building on the important groundwork laid by the Colored Women's Republican League, the National Association of Wage Earners, and neighborhood Republican clubs throughout the city, women founded ambitious organizations to advocate on behalf of African Americans. In 1923, lawyer Jeannette Carter formed the Women's Political Study Club, which was focused on voter education; that same year, women established the National Legislative Council of Colored Women; and in 1924, black women in the NACW organized the National League of Republican Colored Women. Each of these Washington organizations had a distinctive mission, and activists used them as instruments to lobby elected officials, track legislation, support black candidates and civil servants, and demonstrate the power and influence of black women's political networks, a duty uniquely suited to women living in the nation's capital.

Jeannette Carter, a lawyer in Washington and active member of the CWRL, created the Women's Political Study Club (WPSC) to enable absentee voters living in the city but maintaining residency in other states to make educated choices about candidates and issues. A native of Pennsylvania, Carter had moved to Washington, D.C., to attend Howard University Law School. While working with the Republican National Committee and canvassing for candidates, Carter had discovered how little most black women knew about the inner workings of politics. The WPSC's founding members were a relatively elite group of black women in Washington, D.C., who had been born in southern states, including dressmakers, housewives, and government clerks and stenographers.

At around the same time that Carter formed the WPSC, black women also created an independent political body, the National Legislative Council of Colored Women (NLCCW), which was responsible for monitoring legislation in Congress. Mazie Griffin, a prominent activist in the NACW, became the head of this association. In a letter to Nannie Helen Burroughs, Griffin wrote that she had "bought a house in <u>D.C.</u>—its not so large, but in a good location," which would serve as the headquarters for this new organization.[45] Griffin's house was located at 13 C Street in Southeast, only one block from the U.S. Capitol. Its proximity to the central site of American lawmaking enabled black women in the NLCCW to track the progress of various bills. Having a legislative headquarters so very close to the Capitol signaled the ways that black women were beginning to take up more visible space in American politics.

One year later in 1924, black women organized the National League of Republican Colored Women (NLRCW). At the conclusion of the NACW conference in Chicago that year, leaders Mamie Williams and Mary C. Booze gathered a group of women together to create the NLRCW, which adopted the slogan, "We Are in Politics to Stay and Shall Be a Stay in Politics."[46] Leaders decided that the organization would be national in scope and elected Nannie Helen Burroughs president, a strategic choice based on her location in the nation's capital and her vast networks with the National Training School and National Association of Wage Earners. As president of the NLRCW, Nannie Helen Burroughs drew on her experience with the National Association of Wage Earners to adopt similar organizing strategies and membership fees. For instance, Burroughs recommended that the NLRCW be divided into regional districts and "use lists of Districts made up for Wage Earners' Association."[47] Burroughs arranged for the NLRCW to have its headquarters in the NAWE building on Rhode Island Avenue. While the historian Lisa G. Materson claims that the NLRCW worked through mainstream churches, but missed opportunities to work directly with working-class women, it should be noted that domestic servants and cooks in Washington, D.C., used the NLRCW's headquarters for training classes, while some live-in servants slept in the building at night. The NLRCW might have neglected to organize working-class women nationally, but cooks, maids, lawyers, and clubwomen all used the headquarters in Washington, D.C.[48]

The formation of three new, distinctive political organizations created possibilities for conflict, whether characterized by competition, duplication, or even rendering existing partisan groups irrelevant. When the formation of the NLRCW was announced, women in Washington, D.C., discussed how this group would fit within the city's organizational landscape. Jeannette Carter, as president of the WPSC, argued that her organization was still important because "it was unique, it functioned between campaigns as well during campaigns," and was composed of a "group of business and professional women who reside in the District of Columbia, but who have voting status in other states."[49] In contrast, members of the Colored Women's Republican League voted that their organization be absorbed into the federated NL-RCW. But black women in Washington, D.C., wanted to ensure that a national organization would address the particular, local interests of black women in D.C., namely, absentee voting. On the same evening that the Colored Women's Republican League voted to join the NLRCW, a group of women representing twenty-six states met at the old offices of the *Washington Bee* in 1109 I Street NW, where they formed the Absentee Voters' League, electing Michigan resident and community activist Gabrielle Pelham as president.[50] With its formation, black women in Washington, D.C., had two organizations composed of citizens who voted in out-of-state elections, which reflected the unique structure of black politics in the nation's capital.

Between 1924 and 1930, activists steered the Women's Political Study Club, the National Legislative Council of Colored Women, and the National League of Republican Colored Women in different directions. True to its mission, the NLCCW tracked legislation on monuments and memorials, anti-lynching legislation, and marriage and divorce laws. As a neighbor of the U.S. Congress, Mazie Griffin could easily stay abreast on these political matters, and she held a conference on the campus of Howard University to educate women about these issues.[51] The National League of Republican Colored Women worked effectively on the local level in states where women voted, but in Washington, D.C., it mainly lobbied the Republican Party to adopt positions that would favor the interests of African American women and men. For instance, the NLRCW wrote letters to presidents, congressmen, and the heads of government agencies urging that African American women be appointed to various federal departments, such as Agriculture, Education, and Labor. Its members also met with elected officials, asking them to support enforcement of the Fifteenth and Nineteenth Amendments to the U.S. Constitution.[52]

The organization that had the most impact was the Women's Political Study Club because its activities focused on the important role that women in the nation's capital could play in federal politics. Members of the WPSC gathered weekly to learn from guest speakers, both black and white, who educated them on a range of political matters. During the 1920s, these speakers ranged from congressmen and civil servants to business leaders and professionals, who discussed diverse topics: racial prejudice, voter education, the U.S. Constitution, the movement to secure women's suffrage, and the Equal Rights Amendment.[53] The WPSC's vice president, Marian Butler, wrote the society page in the

Washington Tribune, where she documented information about the weekly activities of the organization. At a meeting in August 1924, for instance, the WPSC held a "very enthusiastic meeting." Teacher and NAACP activist Lafayette M. Hershaw addressed the organization on "How Presidents Are Made." The article noted that Hershaw was a "walking encyclopedia on this subject" and "the women expressed themselves as being greatly benefitted." Following the talk, Mary Fountain, a domestic servant, delivered an address to the group on why she supported the Republican Party.[54] This newspaper article indicates the ways that WPSC meetings encouraged members to make their own political declarations. In May 1928, an article reported that members of the WPSC discussed the Equal Rights Amendment, with a special guest from the National Women's Party, the organization led by Alice Paul.[55] The fact that members of the National Women's Party attended a WPSC meeting indicates that they saw black absentee voters as key players in the fight to pass the Equal Rights Amendment.

Members of the WPSC applied what they learned from these educational lectures to various political projects. Even though Woodrow Wilson was no longer president, government segregation persisted and continued to thwart promotion and employment opportunities for black civil servants.[56] In 1926, Emma Holcomb, a seamstress and executive secretary of the WPSC, offered a resolution "condemning removal of colored employees in disproportionate numbers from the office of the Register of the Treasury," and it was passed unanimously. The WPSC also arranged a meeting with Massachusetts senator William M. Butler, chairman of the Republican National Committee.[57] It is striking that black women in D.C. had enough leverage that Senator Butler would agree to meet with them about the matter of black civil servants. Two years later, when North Carolina representative William C. Hammer threatened to impeach the Recorder of Deeds, Arthur G. Froe, a black man, Legislative Chair Mary Lew offered a resolution for the retention of Froe, and WPSC members passed it unanimously.[58]

Women in the WPSC used their location in the capital to monitor the actions and opinions of Congress. In 1926, minister and political activist William Ferris delivered a talk in the home of WPSC member Jacqueline Cuney, in which he encouraged members to track the racial attitudes of members of Congress. Accepting this challenge, Cuney tapped her neighbor, Corelia B. Johnson, a hairdresser, to work with her. Together, they investigated the "attitudes and accomplishments of congressional aspirants and candidates for reelection regarding matters of concern to the colored race." Cuney's husband worked as an operator at the Bureau of Printing and Engraving, and it is possible that

Jacqueline benefited from his federal connections. It is unlikely that African American women living in other states would have been able to compile this survey since it required access to congressional documents and newspapers and possibly trips to the Library of Congress or congressional offices, which suggests the unique role that black women in Washington, D.C., played in partisan politics. In crafting this survey, black women in the WPSC performed a tremendous service for African Americans living across the nation since it enabled them to monitor the positions of elected officials in the states where they lived or wished to migrate.[59]

WPSC members also worked to influence electoral politics, traveling to neighboring states to encourage eligible women to vote. For instance, in August 1924, Jeanette Carter, Marian Butler, and Emma Holcomb "motored to Mechanicsville, Maryland to work for the Coolidge-Dawes campaign."[60] And in September 1924, the WPSC endorsed the candidacy of Calvin Coolidge for a full term in office. In their letter to President Coolidge, the WPSC pledged to the Republican Party "our undivided support and promise to do all in our power to lead back to the path of Republicanism those of our group that have blindly strayed therefrom, to the end that southern Democracy may be subverted and political equality and righteousness and the brotherhood of man may prevail throughout the United States." They explicitly opposed the Democratic Party because it was "the facile tool of Southern race prejudice and lawlessness." Similarly, they explained they were not supporting third-party candidate Robert LaFollette because his party "has maintained no interest whatever in in the conditions affecting our people in the South."[61] The WPSC's political endorsements suggest that its members registered strong support for the Republican Party throughout the 1920s, refusing to consider either the Democratic Party or a third-party candidate.

At the same time that women in the WPSC conducted political research and held meetings with elected officials, they performed activities that fell into traditionally female roles, such as hosting receptions, parties, and official visits. In June 1924, the WPSC held a reception in the private dining room of Harrison's Café, a popular restaurant in Northwest Washington, honoring George H. Woodson, chair of the Virgin Islands Commission.[62] When Thomas L. Jones was appointed the assistant district attorney in Washington, a committee comprising twelve members of the WPSC visited him on his first day in office in the Police Court Building and presented him with a bouquet of flowers to brighten his desk. Jones was the only African American man then holding this position, and black women wished to recognize that.[63] While this activity represented a "domestic" way that women could be in politics, it is possible that members of the WPSC hoped that black women might one day serve in these positions.

The WPSC members also brought their political activism into the halls of Congress. In 1926, Mary Church Terrell and Marian Butler both testified on behalf of black women's political organizations in support of a federal anti-lynching law, as described in the next chapter. And four years later, women in the WPSC worked to influence the composition of the Supreme Court. In March 1930, Supreme Court Justice Edward T. Sanford died in office, and President Hoover nominated John J. Parker, a North Carolina judge, to the Court. Parker, a Republican, had a well-documented history of racial intolerance toward African Americans. In a 1920 speech given when he was running for governor of North Carolina, Parker had stated that "the participation of the Negro in the political life in the South" was "harmful to him and to the community" and that African Americans had "no desire to participate in politics."[64] In another address, Parker characterized the relationship between African Americans and the Republican Party as "a source of evil" and a "danger to both races."[65] The prospect of a Supreme Court member who was so explicitly hostile to racial justice prompted African Americans across the country to oppose Parker's confirmation.

WPSC chair Marian Butler used her location in Washington, D.C., and her ties to the black club movement to fight and ultimately defeat Parker's nomination. Butler was the ideal person for this task. As a founding member of the WPSC, she had spent the past seven years studying politics and learning about the enormous power of the Supreme Court. And as a native of South Carolina, she understood firsthand the dangers of disfranchisement. She thus contacted local chapters of the NACW and black newspapers in every state where Republican senators favored Parker's confirmation. Tapping into her Washington, D.C., connections, she also wired telegrams to every Republican senator who supported Parker's confirmation, informing them of the NACW's strong opposition. "Through the colored press and the National Association of Colored Women's Clubs," Butler wrote to each politician, "I am asking the colored women to note your stand in the Parker case." Butler signed the telegram as the chairman of the National Political Study Club.[66] This telegram signaled the new strength of black women's voting and showcased the power of their political organizations and networks.[67]

On May 1, 1930, Ohio Republican senator Simon D. Fess read Butler's telegram on the floor of Congress, denigrating her efforts as "manufactured clamor."[68] In contrast, the black press, including the *Baltimore Afro-American* and the *Chicago Defender*, covered the Senate proceedings, highlighting her lobbying efforts. An article in the *Baltimore Afro-American* titled "Mrs. Butler's Anti-Parker Wire Peeved Senator Fess" featured the subtitle, "Washington Woman Reminded Ohio Senator that Women Helped Elect Him and Can Work Just as Hard for His Defeat."[69] In a letter to the *Baltimore Afro-American*, Marian Butler responded. "Senator Fess," she wrote, "referred to my wire as manufactured clamor." But he "seemed to have forgotten the manufactured clamor through Miss Hallie Q. Brown that he got when he wanted colored women's votes." She then weighed in on some of the southern demagogues who had spent the 1920s spreading hateful lies about black women on the Senate floor. She focused on the former governor in her home state, Ben Tillman of South Carolina, who had orchestrated a disfranchisement campaign and took no efforts to end lynching there. "Senator Ben Tillman said at least one true thing," Butler wrote. "'The colored woman is the more deadly of the species.'" She insisted, "We must not prove him false. We must hit back if we have to jump from party to party every four years." She foreshadowed the black migration from the Republican Party, predicting that "if the Democrats run Governor Roosevelt I hear thousands of colored men and women singing: 'I'm Republican bred and Republican born. But this is where the Republican is gone.'"[70] Butler then noted that there was a potential backlash among Republican women voters in Ohio and that she would work to ensure that black voters would not be taken for granted. Butler's advocacy was one part of a larger movement by the NAACP and numerous black citizens to block Parker's confirmation. These efforts were successful, and the Senate prevented Parker from ascending to the Supreme Court.

In the 1920s, black women in Washington, D.C., demonstrated that they were in politics to stay. Through their new organizations, such as the NLRCW, the National Legislative Council of Colored Women, and the WPSC, black women testified in Congress, sent telegrams and letters, met with elected officials, and tracked the opinions of all senators and representatives, circulating this information to black voters across the nation. Black women's political activities were visible in many spaces throughout the city and showcased their growing political acumen.

Black women's prominence in local politics was noted in 1928, when the U.S. House of Representatives convened a hearing that addressed voting rights in the nation's capital. Since the 1870s, black Washingtonians had been vocal proponents of restoring the suffrage, but faced formidable white opposition from both politicians and ordinary citizens. Some white Washingtonians feared that restoring voting rights would eliminate federal funding for the city, while others argued that black Washingtonians lacked the intelligence and wealth to make informed decisions.[71] At the hearing in 1928, white speakers articulated these opinions in their opposition to suffrage, but introduced one new factor: black women's participation in political activities, both in Washington, D.C., and across the nation. Grover W. Ayers, a white speaker, told the committee about black women's growing influence in politics. "There is now a negro woman who is a member of the State legislature in West Virginia," he stated, alluding to Minnie Buckingham, who had recently taken over her late husband's seat.[72] Ayers then referenced black women's prominence in politics in Washington, D.C, warning members of the committee that "since there are a greater number of negro women in the District of Columbia than there are negro men, it would only be right that there should be a negro woman elected to the United States Senate every once in a while." He cautioned that a black woman in the Senate would "mean that she could attend the White House receptions and things of that kind."[73] The fact that Ayers included a discussion of black women in his opposition to voting rights indicates their growing presence in partisan politics throughout the 1920s. This concern about the visibility of black women in spaces throughout Washington, D.C., such as the White House, connected to other debates about commemorative politics and black citizenship rights in the nation's capital.

"The Story Every American Should Know": The Politics of Commemoration

Black women in Washington, D.C., made public commemoration an important aspect of their political agenda. As residents of the nation's capital, African American women understood firsthand the power that monuments and memorials commanded in commemorating the history of a people and conveying notions of citizenship. Throughout the 1920s, many of the same women who joined partisan organizations in Washington, D.C., and lobbied for bills in Congress worked to create a civic landscape in the nation's capital that honestly depicted African American history and culture, in contrast to stereotypes from the 1915 film, *Birth of a Nation* and historical monographs that depicted slavery as benign and Reconstruction as an unfortunate moment in American political history.[74] In 1922, women in the NACW dedicated the Frederick Douglass House in Anacostia, celebrating the life of a man who fought for black freedom and citizenship. One year later, women vehemently protested the proposed "Mammy" memorial. And throughout the 1920s, women lobbied

Congress to dedicate a National Negro Memorial, which would be both a monument and a museum. African American women's work to influence Washington's memorial landscape formed an important component of their national political agenda and relied on their networks in the NACW, the Phyllis Wheatley YWCA, and political organizations.

Frederick Douglass, the famed abolitionist and civil rights activist, had lived with his wife at Cedar Hill, a stately house in Anacostia. After his death in 1895, Helen Pitts Douglass, his second wife who was white, willed the house and its mortgage to the male-run Frederick Douglass Memorial and Historical Association. This organization, however, was unable to raise sufficient funds to preserve the estate and pay off the mortgage. In 1918, African American women in the NACW then assumed control of the mortgage and established a Douglass Home Committee. For five years, the NACW conducted an ambitious fundraising campaign, securing donations from diverse sources, including black units serving in World War I, black women's clubs across the nation, and prominent businesswoman, such as the beauty culture magnate Madam C. J. Walker. In their organ, *National Notes*, women in the NACW tracked the financial progress of their fundraising efforts. Locally in Washington, D.C., Nannie Helen Burroughs and Mary Church Terrell made plans for the house. Finally, in 1922 African American women had raised $15,000, enough money to pay off the mortgage and restore the home. In August of that year, women in the NACW gathered in Washington to dedicate the Douglass house before a crowd of 250 people.[75] By showcasing the house of one of the most distinguished African Americans, women helped demonstrate ideas about African American dignity, respect, and citizenship to both black and white audiences in Washington, D.C. Activists used the house to celebrate African American women's history by displaying a sheaf of papers commemorating "our noted women" in the house and highlighting Douglass's activism on behalf of women's suffrage.[76]

In dedicating the Douglass house, activists showcased how women were taking up the challenge of history and preservation after men had been unable to raise the money to do so. As Burroughs argued in *National Notes*, the "women of this race have taken up the vigil and will guard, guide and direct, from the inspiring heights to which they are climbing the mental, moral, and spiritual destiny of their race."[77] In this article she linked the preservation of the Douglass house to the NACW's overall mission of uplift, most conspicuously through her use of the term "climbing." In a letter to Mary Church Terrell, president of the Colored Women's Republican League, Burroughs wrote, "The redeeming of the Home by our women, and now, the work of remodeling, is one of the biggest achievements to the credit of any race group. The women are planning to make Cedar Hill as beautiful as Mount Vernon."[78] Burroughs thus situated black women's commemorative practices within a code of American civic culture and memory. Just as white women had restored the house of the first president, black women were engaged in the preservation of the home of Frederick Douglass, arguably black America's most esteemed political figure.[79] Importantly, the first black museum in Washington, D.C., did not dilute the radicalism of Douglass's fight for justice in the nineteenth century. Three months earlier, a crowd of mostly white citizens had gathered at the Tidal Basin to dedicate the Lincoln Memorial. This racially segregated ceremony privileged Lincoln's legacy of reconciliation over his work for emancipation. In contrast, through the dedication of the Douglass House, black women honored the legacies of the Civil War and Reconstruction by emphasizing Douglass's advocacy on behalf of emancipation, civil rights, and women's suffrage.[80]

But the victory represented by the creation of the Douglass House was short-lived. As black women in the NACW were raising money to renovate the Douglass House, southern white women affiliated with the United Daughters of the Confederacy (UDC), a Confederate women's organization, lobbied members of Congress to erect a memorial to the faithful slave, "Mammy," in the nation's capital. Only months after black women dedicated the Douglass House, Mississippi senator John Sharpe Williams and South Carolina representative James Byrnes, introduced legislation to construct the Mammy Memorial in the nation's capital.[81]

The prospect of a Mammy Memorial spoke volumes about the intersections between race, gender, and politics. "Mammy" referred to a faithful and fictitious slave woman who labored in the plantation house and provided comfort and stability to southern white families. In the aftermath of the Civil War, white southerners waxed nostalgic about the institution of slavery, longing for the Mammy figure, who stood in stark contrast to the black women and men who demanded full civil rights and economic equality as freed people. Mammy was not just a figment of the imagination; she was a cherished character in literature and movies, and her image was emblazoned on syrup bottles, lunch boxes, cookie jars, and yeast packets, all evoking white southern sentimentalism for slavery.[82]

It was not coincidental that white women wanted to construct the Mammy Memorial in the 1920s. The passage of the Nineteenth Amendment had conferred equal citizenship rights on black and white women, and the Mammy Memorial would be a visual reminder of the legacy of slavery. The historian

Micki McElya argues that the local chapter of the UDC envisioned the Mammy Memorial as an instrument to shape current power relationships by freezing black women in a permanent servile mode as anti-citizens. Considering the fact that African American women had spent the past two years actively engaged in national causes—whether it was forming political and labor organizations, encouraging absentee voting, or lobbying politicians—the Mammy Memorial blatantly undermined black women's practices of citizenship.[83]

Black women across the nation, and especially in the nation's capital, mobilized their organizations and networks to prevent the construction of this statue. In the NACW's *National Notes,* the editor published a petition slip, inviting readers to sign it, circulate to others, and present to local officials expressing their disdain of this proposed memorial. Terrell, as president of the CWRL, wrote a scathing letter that appeared in local Washington, D.C., newspapers and even reached national newspapers, such as the *St. Louis Argus,* as well as the nationally circulated *Literary Digest.* Shattering the notion that black women received protection and care under slavery, Terrell outlined the painful realities of enslaved women's physical and sexual abuse. "The black mammy," Terrell wrote, "had no home life. In the very nature of the case she could have none. Legal marriage was impossible for her. If she went through a farce ceremony with a slave man, he could be sold from her at any time, or she might be sold from him, or she might be taken as a concubine by her master, his son, the overseer, or any other white man on the place who might desire her."[84] Terrell argued that women across the world should be angered by the prospect of the Mammy Memorial. "One cannot help but to marvel at the desire to perpetuate in bronze or marble," Terrell wrote, "a figure which represents so much that really is and should be abhorrent to the womanhood of the whole civilized world."[85]

Black women in the Phyllis Wheatley YWCA in Washington, D.C., worked on several fronts to defeat the Mammy Memorial. Board members issued a collective statement denouncing the proposal, in which they announced that they were speaking for "the colored women of the city of Washington." Black women perhaps issued this statement through the YWCA, and not one of their Republican organizations, as a way to make their critiques seem less partisan. "The colored women of the city of Washington," they wrote, "do not like to be vividly reminded of the unfortunate condition of some of our ancestors, as were the helots of Greece or the serfs of Russia. The old mammy as a slave, however well she may have performed her part as foster mother to many of the progeny of the South, represents the shadows of the past. Such irritants are not conducive to the harmony of citizenship."[86]

This statement, like Terrell's remarks, was reprinted in national publications, such as the *Literary Digest* as well as the very first issue of *Time Magazine*. YWCA women personally "carried the Resolution" to Vice President Calvin Coolidge and Speaker of the House Frederick H. Gillette. *Time Magazine*, in fact, credited women at the Phyllis Wheatley YWCA with striking down the proposal.[87] In their protests against the Mammy Memorial, women in Washington, D.C., utilized their organizing networks, raised awareness in the local and national press, and took advantage of their proximity to federal buildings to deliver their statements in person. Black women's protests in Washington were decisive in halting plans for the Mammy Memorial.

One year later, black Washingtonians staged their final monument campaign. In 1916, African Americans had formed the National Memorial Association (NMA), an organization dedicated to constructing a National Negro Memorial in Washington, D.C.[88] This classically styled building would serve three main functions. First, it would commemorate the black soldiers and sailors who had fought for the United States, their distinguished service stretching from the Revolutionary War to the Great War. Second, it would be a museum, documenting the contributions of Africans in the United States since the seventeenth century. The description noted that it would be a "great educational temple, where statues of Great Men and Women of our Race may be placed to give inspiration, hope, and pride to the youth in our land."[89] African Americans intended the National Negro Memorial to showcase African American citizenship in the United States. The National Memorial Association described the building as able to convey "the story every American should know."[90] In this statement, the NMA thus positioned the National Negro Memorial as part of American, rather than African American history. Finally, the building would be a meeting place that could accommodate up to five thousand people. This act of claiming a place in Washington, D.C., for the National Negro Memorial signaled ways that African American women and men proposed to use space in the city to champion their vision of racial democracy.

In 1924 and 1928, the U.S. House of Representatives convened hearings about the National Negro Memorial, at which African Americans who lived across the country and those who resided in the District of Columbia testified. In his remarks, Reverend Walter Brooks, pastor of the Nineteenth Street Baptist Church in Washington, D.C., argued that there were sharp distinctions between the Mammy Memorial and the National Negro Memorial. Brooks recounted how white women in the United Daughters of the Confederacy "proposed a statue here in the District of Columbia of black Mammy, but that was not what these colored people wanted." Brooks contended that the

National Negro Memorial, and not the Mammy Memorial, fulfilled African American visions of commemoration.[91]

In the House hearings in 1928, two black residents of Washington, D.C.— veteran activist Mary Church Terrell and Bureau of Printing and Engraving clerk Julia West Hamilton—testified. Both had worked to renovate and dedicate the Douglass House, protested the Mammy Memorial, and held institutional ties with the NACW, the National League of Republican Colored Women, and the Phyllis Wheatley YWCA. In her testimony, Hamilton emphasized African Americans' patriotism and nationalism, positioning the National Negro Memorial as an instrument to honor military veterans. She told the committee, "We appeal to you who have placed here in Washington, our Nation's Capital, numerous monuments to naval and military heroes of every nation, tribe, and section, to give or appropriate in some tangible way a monument to the valor of negro sailors and soldiers who love America so well, whose loyalty and patriotism are so unquestioned that they can be called on, as they were in the recent World War, first to defend the Nation's Capital and all the bridges and approaches leading thereto."[92] Terrell cast the memorial as an instrument of social change. Not only would it educate black and white children about the contributions of African Americans to U.S. history but it would also serve as a mechanism to promote social change and racial uplift. "Recognition of efforts by colored people to play their part effectively and nobly in the development of the United States," Terrell argued, "will spur the race as a whole to greater endeavor and will be an inspiration to our youth."[93]

In 1929, the U.S. House of Representatives debated the bill. Although the bill passed by a vote of 253 to 83, many white southern congressmen disparaged the prospect of a national memorial to commemorate the achievements of African Americans. White Mississippi representative John E. Rankin informed his fellow representatives that "I am not willing to expend the Government's money to build a memorial here to commemorate the achievements of the Negro race; nor am I in favor of spending money in this way on any race; not so long as the American congress refuses to erect a monument in the National Capital to the memory of Thomas Jefferson."[94] Rankin's thus openly expressed his opinion that white Americans mattered more than black Americans. After the Senate passed the bill, President Hoover signed it into law. However, the Great Depression drained the coffers for the memorial. After many decades of fundraising, lobbying, and construction, the National Negro Memorial finally opened on the national mall as the Museum of African American History and Culture in 2016.

Conclusion

In February 1925, Fannie Clair, a founding member of the Colored Women's Republican League, was dying; one of her final acts was addressing a monthly meeting of the Methodist Episcopal Ministers' Wives of Washington and Vicinity. In her address, Clair expressed happiness about "the visibility of the women of the race in Kingdom building and also in politics" and concluded with "the tender words of goodbye."[95] Her parting words captured the contributions of African American women over the decade: they were certainly visible in politics.

If a person visited Washington, D.C., in the 1920s, the political activities of African American women would be palpable. In the streets of their neighborhoods, African American women were recruiting members for the NAWE, the NLRCW, and the WPSC; discussing labor issues; and commenting on the viewpoints of elected officials and candidates. In churches on Sunday morning, pastors, at the urging of black women's organizations, stressed the importance of voting, whether it was to encourage eligible citizens to cast absentee ballots or to reflect on this act of citizenship. In the parlors of the YWCA, different organizations were meeting to plan campaigns, such as voting drives, a survey of the racial opinions of elected officials, and ways to support black civil servants. In the pages of the press, articles chronicled African American women's political meetings and events. And in various federal buildings—including the Department of Labor and the U.S. House of Representatives—black women were advocating for the rights of domestic servants, protesting the confirmation of Supreme Court nominee John Parker, sharply denouncing the Mammy Memorial, and passionately championing the construction of the National Negro Memorial.

Between 1920 and 1930, African American living in Washington, D.C., influenced federal politics. With the passage of women's suffrage in 1920, black women began to form partisan organizations that reflected their new citizenship status. As residents of the nation's capital, African American women listened carefully to the political conversations that were held in their city and transmitted this information to black citizens across the country. The next chapter investigates the ways that African American women in the nation's capital used their partisan networks to advocate for making lynching a federal crime.

CHAPTER TWO

The Eyes of the World Are upon Us
The Politics of Lynching

In May 1922, Theresa Lee Connelly, a teacher, member of the Colored Women's Republican League (CWRL), and chair of the women's Committee of One Hundred, invited churches, fraternal groups, and social and political organizations throughout the city to participate in an anti-lynching parade. "We are seeking ten or twenty thousand of our people," she wrote, "to march to muffled drums, to show Congress and the world that we demand the protection of ours and the passage of this law." She noted that this parade would coincide with the Senate's "consideration and discussion " of the Dyer Anti-Lynching Bill and ended her appeal with these words: "The eyes of the world are upon us. Let us make an outcry to the conscience of the world."[1] Here Connelly referenced black Washingtonians' visible location in the nation's capital, indicating that their activism against lynching would attract a global audience. In spearheading this Silent Parade, as it came to be known, black women in the Committee of One Hundred used their residency in the nation's capital to shape national politics.

In the 1920s and early 1930s, African American women living in Washington, D.C., worked hard to pass a federal anti-lynching law. Lynching was extralegal murder, and beginning in the 1890s, African Americans in the South were its victims. Between 1882 and 1918, 2,929 African Americans were lynched, and at least 130 of those who died were women.[2] Aware of their conspicuous location in the nation's capital, black women staged campaigns in different spaces across the city, including federal buildings, streets, public parks, and black churches, with the goal of generating national and international awareness about the inhumanity of lynching and the urgency of making it a federal crime. Over a period of fifteen years, women employed a range of protest tactics, including petitions, pickets, prayer meetings, congressional testimony, and a Silent Parade. Activists reached into their vast organizational networks, based in churches, fraternal orders, newly formed partisan clubs, the National Association of Colored Women (NACW), the National Association for the Advancement of Colored People (NAACP), and the Phyllis Wheatley Young Women's Christian Association (YWCA), to stage their different political protests. Black women's anti-lynching activism in Washington, D.C., was deeply connected to their political culture and long-standing strategies of opposition, which were deployed throughout the city.

Historians have written a great deal about the ways that African Americans worked to make lynching a crime and to end extralegal violence in the 1920s and 1930s. Robert Zangrando and Patricia Sullivan explore the role of black activists in the NAACP, who lobbied politicians to pass the Dyer Anti-Lynching Bill and press for other anti-lynching laws in those decades.[3] Additionally, Jacquelyn Dowd Hall, Mary Jane Brown, Angelica Mungarro, and Nikki J. Brown, examine the particular ways that African American women worked to pass anti-lynching legislation, especially through the formation of the Anti-Lynching Crusaders in 1922, which aimed to unite one million women against lynching.[4] However, scholars have not fully analyzed African American women's anti-lynching activities in the 1920s beyond this organization.

Connecting the local with the national reveals how black women living in the nation's capital used their community networks to press for the passage of anti-lynching legislation. For many activists in Washington, D.C., anti-lynching politics was deeply personal, based on their childhood experiences in the South or a relationship with friends and family members who continued to face the terrors of this violence. Black women reached into their personal memories and used their location in the nation's capital to press for national justice for their friends and family members throughout the 1920s and early 1930s.

Women on the Right Track

The horrors of lynching hovered in the consciousness of many black citizens in the nation's capital. While no resident of Washington, D.C., had died at the hands of a lynch mob, black citizens throughout the city were familiar with the lingering trauma of this racial violence. Many black Washingtonians maintained familial connections with the South or were southern migrants themselves, which made the quest for federal anti-lynching legislation both pressing and personal.

Black Washingtonians had placed anti-lynching activism on their agenda in the late nineteenth and early twentieth centuries. Citizens held mass meetings in churches throughout the city and issued resolutions about riots and racial violence occurring across the country.[5] The city's black newspaper, the *Washington Bee*, covered lynching incidents in the South and issued an annual report on the total number occurring each year.[6] Black women throughout Washington were members of the NAACP, the NACW, and the Woman's Convention of the Baptist Church (WC), all of which worked to end lynching.

When the United States entered World War I in April 1917, African American women in the capital expanded their activism against lynching, viewing this global conflict as an opportunity to pressure the federal government to promote democracy at home. Three months into the war, Nannie Helen Burroughs, in her capacity as superintendent of the NACW's Department for the Suppression of Lynching and Mob Violence, initiated a "vigorous campaign against lynching" by inviting black Washingtonians to meet every Wednesday morning at 6 A.M. in churches throughout the city to pray for the passage of an anti-lynching bill and to protest the recent violence in East St. Louis, in which more than one hundred women and men had been killed. An article in the *Washington Bee*, tellingly titled "Women on the Right Track," called these prayer meetings "something new under the sun" because women were wielding a "weapon of prayer." The article reported that Washington, D.C., was "under the spell" as "thousands flock to the 6 o'clock prayer meeting every Wednesday morning."[7] An article in the *Norfolk Journal and Guide* reported on a recent meeting where "5,000 Negro women" had gathered for a prayer service at the Metropolitan Baptist Church in Northwest Washington.[8] Burroughs expressed delight that the "City of Washington" was demonstrating "unabated interest in the campaign." She rejoiced that these meetings attracted a diverse community of women and men from "all walks of life," such as the "doctor and the ditch digger, the great and the small" who "meet at the mercy seat"—strategically acknowledging this broad participation in the WC's annual report.[9] That so many people attended these prayer meetings indicated not only widespread interest in anti-lynching politics but also the strength of black women's organizing culture in Washington, D.C., especially in the churches and the local NACW chapter.

Whenever black women engaged in activism, however, they risked angering their employers and losing their jobs. That is why these prayer meetings were held so early in the morning: servants, laundresses, cooks, teachers, and government employees were thus able to engage in political activity before they went to work. Moreover, congregating in a church did not invite suspicion that the cause might be political in nature. The use of churches for the meetings also enhanced Burroughs's ability to forge cross-class coalitions. Leaders in the Colored Women's Republican League and the Women's Political Study Club struggled to engage working-class members in other partisan activities throughout the 1920s. However, by meeting in churches across the city, African American women in the local NACW chapter used their everyday sites of worship to send a political message to black and white citizens about the need for anti-lynching legislation.

Only one month after these prayer meetings began, Burroughs moved black women's anti-lynching activism from neighborhood churches into the U.S. Congress. On August 3, 1917, she testified before the House of Representatives Rules Committee, which was convening a hearing on the riots in East St. Louis. Although Burroughs held many organizational affiliations, she identified herself in her testimony as the superintendent of the NACW's Department for the Suppression of Lynching and Mob Violence. Burroughs did not come empty-handed: she brought with her thousands of petitions from black and white citizens across the country, who were "extremely anxious that the Federal government do something in this matter." The petitions were "fixed in packages of fifty" and arranged geographically according to state. It would have been impossible for Burroughs to physically carry all of the petitions with her, but she informed the audience that there were "at least 100,000" petitions in total.[10]

In her testimony, Burroughs argued that federal enforcement of mob violence would make the United Sates a safer country for all citizens who wanted to live and work in peace. Employing a language of rights, she cast the need for an anti-lynching bill within the discourse of American citizenship while also tying it to labor rights for all. "The people who are seeking work," Burroughs argued, "the people who want to earn their bread, want to know whether the Federal Government is going to make America a safe place in which to live and not only to live but to labor, and we want to do both; but we are at the mercy of the Federal Government, and I come this morning to ask you, in behalf of my people, what are you going to do about this matter?"[11]

Two weeks after she testified before Congress, Burroughs published a letter in the local black newspaper, the *Washington Bee*, in which she recounted her recent activities. "Praise the Lord," she wrote. "I got a hearing for the National Association of Colored Women before House Rules Committee Friday." She also reported that, while she had been in the Capitol, she met with Congressman Leonidas Dyer, a white Republican representative from Missouri who was planning to introduce an anti-lynching bill; he had "urged her to stay with him in the fight" and informed her that his bill had received a favorable report from the Rules Committee. Burroughs announced that the "fight" was "on" and asked all readers to "flood Congressmen with petitions" as a way to demonstrate continuing enthusiasm among a broad spectrum of black Washingtonians.[12]

African American women in Washington, D.C., heeded this political advice. Two months later, the local chapter of the NACW invited veteran political activist and journalist Ida B. Wells, who had traveled across the country conducting investigations on lynching, to deliver a lecture to a "large audience" at the Asbury ME Church. An article in the *Washington Bee* reported that this meeting was "one of the largest ever held in in this section of the country."[13] Hearing Wells speak might have helped black women in Washington, D.C., keep their focus on the victims and their individual stories. Women affiliated with the ME Church also formed a Red Anti-Lynching Club and continued to hold prayer meetings.[14]

In 1920, glimmers of progress appeared when Missouri representative Leonidas Dyer introduced the first federal anti-lynching bill in the United States. It stated that "each person in the mob shall be guilty of murder" and that authorities who failed to stop a lynching could be subject to a fine of $5,000 or five years in prison.[15] However, an article in the *Chicago Defender* expressed disappointment that the first federal anti-lynching bill appeared to have been prompted by the recent lynching of Robert Paul Praeger, a German American man in Illinois. "This is the first attempt to make lynching a national offense," the article stated, "in spite of the three thousand members of our race who have been willfully murdered in the South."[16] Nannie Helen Burroughs expressed these precise concerns in a letter to Congressman Dyer shortly after he introduced his bill. Dyer responded by urging her to "correct the impression that seems to have gotten into some places, to the effect that I introduced this bill on account of the lynching in the name of Prager." Dyer emphasized his long-standing interest in a federal anti-lunching bill and urged Burroughs and other activists to "unite upon my Bill" and to keep him "fully posted as to your work in this matter."[17] By taking the time to respond to Burroughs's letter, Dyer not only expressed his dedication to the cause of anti-lynching legislation but also acknowledged his need for black women's political support.

With a bill before Congress, a diverse community of black women and men expressed continuing support and optimism for anti-lynching activities. Both the Red Anti-Lynching Club and the local chapter of the NACW continued to hold prayer meetings in churches throughout the city.[18] The local chapter of the NAACP also formed an anti-lynching committee to offer assistance.[19] In April 1919, students at Howard University decided to cancel their vesper service, choosing instead to attend the local NAACP's mass meeting at the Howard Theater to discuss the campaign against lynching. This meeting generated $300 in donations and $2,000 in subscriptions to the organization's magazine, *The Crisis*. An editorial in the *Howard University Record* stated, "We hope that many other meetings will take place not only in Washington, but also in the Southern cities where these foul crimes are perpetrated."[20]

Between 1917 and 1919, black women throughout Washington seized on the wartime climate to lobby for a federal anti-lynching bill and represent the interests of African Americans in national politics. Women attended prayer meetings, signed petitions, formed a new anti-lynching club, and made financial contributions to the cause. As the superintendent of the Department for the Suppression of Lynching and Mob Violence for the NACW, Burroughs testified in the House Representatives and personally lobbied Congressman Dyer to ensure that his bill would address extralegal violence against African Americans. These wartime activities demonstrated the strength of black women's organizing culture in Washington, which would be a vital resource as citizens worked to make the Dyer Anti-Lynching Bill a law.

"The Eyes of the World Are upon Us": The Dyer Anti-Lynching Bill

With the election of Warren Harding in 1920 and installation of a Republican Congress, many black women expressed cautious optimism that the new administration would enact policies of racial justice. Black women and men across the country, and especially in Washington, D.C., closely monitored the progress of the Dyer Anti-Lynching Bill. In May 1920, the bill finally moved out of committee onto the House floor. But it was not until January 1922 that Congress actually debated it. In anticipation of these congressional debates, black Washingtonians affiliated with the NAACP's local branch held a mass meeting with Congressmen Dyer at the Howard Theater during which he "outlined the provisions of the pending legislation."[21]

Black women in Washington, D.C., also forged a strategic relationship with Congressman Dyer. In November 1921, women affiliated with the Phyllis Wheatley YWCA invited him to deliver the keynote address for their fundraising drive, and he accepted their invitation. In Dunbar High School Auditorium, Dyer expressed his admiration for the Phyllis Wheatley YWCA, remarking that "every man, woman, and child should contribute to its support." He also offered to personally assist its fundraising campaigns.[22] Having Dyer as a supporter of their organization enabled YWCA women to connect their community outreach work with their fight for anti-lynching legislation.

In January 1922, the House of Representatives finally began the process of debating the Dyer Anti-Lynching Bill, and black Washingtonians eagerly followed these proceedings. Situated in the nation's capital, they had a unique vantage point. Black Washingtonians continued their tradition of occupying federal space to display and vocalize their support for congressional legislation.[23] An article in the *Baltimore Afro-American* noted the "big colored audience, numbering over seven-hundred" who climbed into the congressional galleries and "filled every available niche" to observe the hearings, expressing vocal protests when they disagreed with the statements of congressional opponents. Their voices were so loud that congressmen and the Speaker of the House ordered them to be quiet on several occasions.[24] Although the identities of the 700-plus black observers in 1922 are unknown, it is likely that a large number were residents of Washington, D.C., who might have had unique access to these buildings if they had a spouse, friend, or relative who worked as a charwoman, elevator operator, or messenger.[25]

The House of Representatives passed the Dyer Anti-Lynching Bill on January 26, 1922, by a vote of 231–119 and sent it off to the Senate, which scheduled its hearings for June.[26] African Americans in Washington, D.C., strategized about the best ways to advocate for the bill's passage. Toward this end, black women held a meeting in February with James Weldon Johnson, the executive secretary of the NAACP. He suggested that black citizens in Washington, D.C., stage a "silent parade" to show politicians that African Americans supported the passage of the bill. Johnson had organized a similar parade in New York City in 1917 in protest of police brutality experienced in the East St. Louis race riot.

In March 1922, Theresa Lee Connelly, a teacher and member of the newly formed Colored Women's Republican League (CWRL), organized the Citizen's Protest Parade Committee. She gathered a pantheon of elite black women called the Committee of One Hundred to help plan the parade and serve as the public face of the movement. Some of these activists were also members of the CWRL, including Mary Church Terrell and Julia West Hamilton. But other women joined as well, including housewife Leonora Scott, who was married to Howard University professor Emmett J. Scott; Phyllis Wheatley YWCA executive secretary Martha A. McAdoo; teachers Marie Madre, Emma F. G. Merritt, and Ella Lynch; and poet Carrie Williams Clifford. Many of these women were also affiliated with the NACW's Department for the Suppression of Lynching and Mob Violence.

Connelly, who taught at the prestigious Dunbar High School, drew on many different traditions of activism to organize the Silent Parade. She was in born in Boston, where her father, a native of Charleston, was active in city politics; he had served as a delegate for the Colored Equal Rights Association and protested the disfranchisement of African Americans in the South.[27] As a child, Theresa Lee formed a close friendship with Angelina Weld Grimké, the daughter of Archibald Grimké, a noted black politician; both girls' fathers had grown up together in Charleston. After Grimké returned from his diplomatic work in the Dominican Republic, he and Angelina lived with the Lee family in Boston for several years.[28] In 1915, Angelina Grimké wrote *Rachel*, the very first known play to protest lynching, which helped inspire several anti-lynching plays.[29] By organizing the Silent Parade, Theresa Lee Connelly not only emulated her father's political activism but also honored her good friend by working to make lynching a federal crime.

Connelly and members of the Committee of One Hundred spent May and June preparing for the parade. They held their meetings at the Phyllis Wheatley YWCA building, which offered ample space in which to plan the details of the parade. In that facility, women made hundreds of banners for black Washingtonians to carry. They also mapped the parade route, determined the marching sequence for black organizations and institutions, selected the dress code for all parade participants, and raised money.[30] Members of the Committee of One Hundred, working with lawyer Shelby J. Davidson and Minister Walter H. Brooks of the Nineteenth Street Baptist Church, also wrote to the director of parks and buildings to obtain permission to hold the parade.[31] They decided to march on June 14, which was Flag Day, thereby situating their struggle for justice within the American narrative of freedom. However, scheduling the march on a weekday limited participation to citizens who would be able to take the day off of work or who had flexible job schedules. Recognizing that participation might be difficult, Connelly sent a letter to the heads of institutions in black Washington—including churches, mutual benefit societies, fraternal groups, and social and political organizations—emphasizing the importance of the parade and urging them to encourage their members to march.

On June 14, 1922, five thousand black Washingtonians staged a Silent Parade against lynching. Through a deliberate choice of clothing, route and parade sequence, music, and signage, participants claimed a space in their city's monumental built environment. In her analysis of marches held in Washington, D.C., the historian Lucy G. Barber emphasizes the importance of location and parade formation to the effectiveness of each march's overall mission. Barber's insights help illuminate some of the strategic decisions that Connelly and other organizers made.[32] Black citizens marched around the U.S. Capitol, passed the Senate and House buildings, as well as numerous government bureaus, and ended on West Executive Avenue at the White House. Marching past these buildings, black Washingtonians raised the issue of lynching with elected officials and government workers. The sequence of the groups marching in the parade illustrated how black Washingtonians wished to define their community to their city, the nation, and the world. By beginning the parade with black police officers, they emphasized how African Americans played an important role in law enforcement in the city. The prominence of mutual benefit associations in the protest parade signaled their overall importance in black Washington. These institutions contained large memberships and often had chapters across the city. By choosing to represent black Washington through mutual benefit associations, members of the Committee of One Hundred underscored these organizations' political and economic strength. Having each of these organizations tap its own members to action also assured a mass base of participants for the parade. The presence of children of all ages showed not only that opposition to lynching was widespread but also that children, like adults, were at risk of this extra-legal violence. The parade sequence conveyed how African Americans imagined women, children, and men as all part of their community. Ending the parade with African American veterans offered an explicit reminder of the contributions of black military service members to the United States.

Marchers' banners and chants juxtaposed black patriotism against the barbarity of lynching. These messages were tailored to correspond to those holding the signs. For instance, one of the children's banners read, "We Are Fifteen Year Olds: One of Our Age Was Roasted Alive." Women's messages focused on their loss as mothers and on the lynching of women. Signs read, "What Would You Do if Your Sick Mother Were Hanged and Her Bones Burned?," "We Mourn as Mothers Whose Sons Might Be Lynched," and "We Protest the Burning of Babies and Women . . . American Cannibalism." The banners also situated African Americans as quintessentially patriotic Americans, demanding "Equal Protection under the Law" and "Make America Safe for American Citizens"; criticizing "mob trials instead of court trials"; arguing that "We Fought for Democracy: Give It to Us"; and concluding with the global message, "The World Looks on in Wonder at America, the Champion of Democracy." While black Washingtonians were not the only ones to hold an anti-lynching parade, theirs took on special significance in that parading through the nation's capital allowed them to speak more fully as American citizens representing the interests of African Americans across the country.

African American women played a visible and important role in this protest parade. Members of the Committee of One Hundred marched with ministers at the front of the parade, which showcased the leadership structure in the black community. By marching alongside ministers, black women demonstrated that they viewed these men as allies and partners in the campaign to legally outlaw lynching. Black women also dominated the membership ranks of mutual benefit associations, while the YWA's Girl Reserves and the Women in White were entirely female groups.[33] From the evidence available, it does not appear that black men in the city felt threatened that the Committee of One Hundred spearheaded this protest parade. Just as black men had voiced their support for women's political activism in the aftermath of the Nineteenth Amendment, they participated in this female-led campaign to support passage of the Dyer bill.

Following the protest parade, black Washingtonians vigilantly monitored the progress of the anti-lynching legislation. In late June, the Senate Judiciary Committee narrowly approved it by a vote of eight to six, sending it off to the Senate floor to be debated. The Citizen's Protest Parade Committee viewed this vote as a sign that the protest parade had registered a "wholesome effect . . . of the pending legislation and the Press at large." In a letter to Mary Church Terrell, Reverend Walter Brooks, an active member of the Citizens Protest Parade Committee, wrote, "We think that we do not claim too much when we state the vote of the Sub-Committee of Judiciary in the Senate of 8 to 6 in favor of the bill on June 30, was one of the far-reaching effects."[34]

During the summer of 1922, African Americans across the country continued to express their support for the Dyer Anti-Lynching Bill in the Senate. In July, students from several black colleges traveled to Washington, D.C., to present President Harding a booklet on mob violence.[35] Black women across the country formed a political organization called the Anti-Lynching Crusaders, which aimed to raise one million dollars by asking every woman across the country to donate one dollar to fund anti-lynching publicity and lobbying efforts. The organization's slogan was "One Million Women United for the Suppression of Lynching." At least 700 African American women volunteered as state workers for the Anti-Lynching Crusaders and staged prayer meetings across the country.[36] Before the Senate was about to begin debating the Dyer Anti-Lynching Bill, Nannie Helen Burroughs initiated another "day of prayer" in support for the bill in Washington, D.C., Black women unable to take off work to march in the Silent Parade might have participated in this day of prayer.[37]

But in September 1922, the prospects for passage of a federal anti-lynching law began to collapse. President Harding, who had previously voiced support for its passage, argued that the bill violated the Constitution. An article in the *Chicago Tribune* noted, "President Warren Harding at the last minute knocked all the wind out of the bag of hope that the entire country has held for the passage of the Dyer Anti-Lynching Bill."[38]

African Americans expressed keen disappointment in the loss of President Harding's support. Black Washingtonians reached out to sympathetic congressmen and leaders to sustain the momentum of the bill. Massachusetts senator Henry Cabot Lodge arranged for members of the Equal Rights League to have a private meeting with Harding, where they pleaded with him to support the bill.[39] Harding later reversed his claim that the bill was unconstitutional, but it was clear that opposition in the Senate remained fierce.[40] Later in September, a group of white southern Democrats in the Senate threatened to filibuster the bill. For three days, southern senators sharply denounced the prospect of anti-lynching legislation. Faced with the reality of defeat, liberal Republican Senators abandoned the bill in December 1922.[41] On August 3, 1923, President Harding unexpectedly died in office, and his vice president, Calvin Coolidge, assumed the presidency. This sudden shift offered African Americans a modicum of hope that the Dyer Anti-Lynching Bill might yet pass with the stronger backing of President Coolidge.

Thus, between 1919 and 1923, African American women in Washington, D.C., had made progress in their fight for a federal anti-lynching law. Black activists in the city, including Burroughs and leaders in the Phyllis Wheatley YWCA, personally reached out to Congressman Leonidas Dyer and expressed their enthusiasm and support for his anti-lynching bill. Once the Dyer Anti-Lynching Bill passed the House of Representatives, women mobilized 5,000 black Washingtonians to march in the Silent Parade, thereby demonstrating their support for this legislation. In all of these ways, African American women in Washington, D.C., used their local activities in the capital to influence federal politics. Women had helped secure a tremendous victory when the House of Representatives passed the Dyer Bill, but the Senate filibuster taught them that they needed support in both legislative bodies.

The People of This Country Are Looking to the Men on the Hill

With the election of Calvin Coolidge as president in 1924 for a full term and installation of a new Congress and Senate, politically active black women and men in Washington, D.C., began to strategize ways to continue to press for anti-lynching legislation. Before the election, President Coolidge had pledged his support for passage of the Dyer Anti-Lynching Bill[42]; after the election, he delivered a national address in which he declared that the "negro" was making progress and called on Congress to pass the bill.[43] Despite Coolidge's urging, progress in Congress stalled. In response, African American women in Washington, D.C., worked to keep the focus on the inhumanity of lynching. In January 1925, the Phyllis Wheatley YWCA invited NAACP assistant secretary Walter White to serve as the guest speaker for their Booklover's Hour and discuss his recently published book on lynching, *Fire in the Flint*.[44]

But it was not until the end of 1925 that the anti-lynching fight regained momentum. In December 1925, Congressman Leonidas Dyer reintroduced an anti-lynching bill in the House of Representatives, and Illinois senator William B. McKinley introduced it in the Senate. The legislation in 1925 differed slightly from the earlier bill because it would punish mobs regardless of whether the victim survived. Even with an ally in the Senate, Congressman Dyer knew that it was going to be a tough fight. In a letter to executive secretary of the NAACP James Weldon Johnson, Dyer noted that the bill would "be passed again easily by the House of Representatives," but "the only thing that stands in the way of it becoming law is the Senate of the United States," and he feared the looming threat of a filibuster. Dyer asked Johnson's assistance in convincing senators to support the legislation.[45]

In February 1926, a group of seven African Americans appeared before the Senate to testify at a hearing before the Judiciary Subcommittee on Senate Bill 121, "To Prevent and Punish the Crime of Lynching." The committee was made up of seventeen senators, several of whom were from southern states. In fact, Senator Lee S. Overman of North Carolina had been part of the effort to filibuster the Dyer Anti-Lynching Bill in 1922, arguing during his time on the floor that "the good negroes of the South do not want the legislation for they do not need it."[46] Four years later, seven African Americans—James Weldon Johnson; Reverend J. H. Branham, assistant pastor of the Mount Olivet Baptist Church in Chicago; James L. Neil, secretary of the National Equal Rights League, Thomas H. R. Clarke, a member of the National Equal Rights League; Edgar Brown of Chicago; Mary Church Terrell of the National League of Republican Colored Women in Washington; and Marian D. Butler, vice president of the Women's Political Study Club in Washington—testified in the Senate that Overman's claim was inaccurate.[47] The inclusion of two black women, representing two separate groups, reflected the growth of African American women's formal political organizing efforts in the 1920s.

Each witness described the urgency of the anti-lynching bill from a different perspective. In his testimony, James Weldon Johnson pointed to the statistical work conducted by the NAACP, which proved that African American men and women were the disproportionate victims of this crime. Reverend

Branham, in contrast, situated his message within the post–World War I context, arguing that "America is looked upon and regarded as the most outstanding nation in the world" and that the crime of lynching contradicted that perception.[48]

In her testimony, Mary Church Terrell boldly focused not on the victims of lynching, but on its perpetrators. Identifying herself as the first president of the NACW, Terrell announced that while she was testifying on behalf of African American women, her primary concern on that day was "to speak in the interest of the white women of the South." She told the committee that "when white women apply the torch to the Negroes burned at the stake they are brutalizing themselves and their children to come. . . . White women who apply the torch to burn colored men, as they have done more than once, when they become mothers of children, those children will undoubtedly by brutalized, and I think it is going to be more and more difficult to stop lynching, as had been suggested here, because the white mothers of the South are becoming more and more brutalized by these lynchings in which they themselves participate."[49] Terrell's fearless language starkly contradicted entrenched notions about southern white women, who were often depicted as innocent, pure, and the victims of rape at the hands of black men. By inverting this idea, she cast white women as perpetrators of lynching while also warning of the dangers to white children of being brought up in a society that allowed and even glorified such brutalization.

Marian Butler testified after Terrell, and she grounded her political argument within a personal narrative. To urge passage of an anti-lynching bill, Butler drew on the memories of her childhood in Barnwell, South Carolina, and the violence and terror she had witnessed. When she was thirteen years old, racial tensions in her town surged.[50] In October 1889, two black men, Mitchell Adams and Ripley Johnson, were in a saloon managed by Adams. When the white landlord, James Heffernan, was found dead, Johnson was accused of shooting him, and Adams was accused of assisting Johnson as an accomplice. The police arrested both men and put them in jail where they awaited trial. Shortly thereafter, six more black men were arrested and accused of killing the white son of a plantation owner, their employer. Just before sunrise on December 28, 1889, a mob of 100 white men wearing masks broke into the jail and seized all eight black prisoners and took them to the woods, where they hung them from trees and shot them dead. One witness noted that as many as "one hundred and fifty shots were fired."[51] When citizens in Barnwell woke up the next morning, they saw the disturbing sight of "eight bodies riddled with bullets by the roadside, just outside the town limits."[52] This horrific crime deeply affected the African American community in Barnwell, who raised the money to bury Adams and Johnson: their funeral attracted a crowd of 550 African Americans. Newspapers especially noted the grief among black women. One black woman shouted, "God should burn Barnwell to the ground."[53] African Americans in Barnwell urged the white community to pay for the burials of the six other men, which they did reluctantly. Only a few days after the Barnwell massacre, African American men across the state, mostly ministers, gathered at the Wesley ME Church in Columbia, South Carolina, to demand the "vindication of law and order."[54] Within a month of the lynching, black citizens in Barnwell staged mass meetings, where they discussed plans for migration out of the state.[55]

Thirty-seven years later, Marian Butler recounted the Barnwell massacre before a congressional audience. "I want to say something," she announced, "because as a child I lived through the terrors of lynching." She told them there were "eight men lynched in my town." In addition to her being an African American girl living in the town when these murders occurred, Butler had an even stronger personal connection to the crimes. Her younger sister, Rosa Ford, was married to Robert "Bob" Adams, the son of Mitchell Adams, who was lynched. Bob, like Marian Butler, was also thirteen years old when the lynch mob killed his father.[56] "My sister married the son of one of the men who was lynched—she married him afterwards, and so I know something about what a lynching means," Butler told the committee. After she married her husband and moved to Washington, D.C., Butler remained close to her sister through letters and visits.[57]

Butler then argued that lynching harmed not only the persons who were murdered but also inflicted trauma on the entire community: when a lynching occurred, a "whole town" could be "terrorized" with "women and children shrieking up and down the streets." She somberly remarked, "Never will I be able to get over it, never will I forget it. And so those kind of things are happening all over our country, every week the sad experience is being lived over by others."[58] Butler's testimony illustrated that the trauma, grief, and the memories of violence lingered for generations. The historian Kidada Williams argues that, for black victims of violence, offering testimony of their suffering was "a way of resisting and ending violence."[59] It was deeply important for Butler that she was able to articulate the collective suffering of her community in Barnwell, South Carolina, to a Senate audience.

During Butler's testimony, Senator William H. King of Utah, interrupted her and remarked that the number of lynchings were declining. Butler responded with an answer that honored grief and black suffering over numbers.

"Our papers," Butler told Senator King, "say that they are so often that it impresses one's heart as if it is almost every day, the sadness and horror of it is so great." In offering this reply, she educated Senator King—and other members of the Senate—about the experiences of being an African American in the United States, where citizens read report after report of lynching, disheartened with the knowledge that the perpetrators would not be punished. In this respect, Butler offered an interpretation of lynching that transcended numbers and instead reflected human emotion.

Butler concluded her testimony by eloquently arguing for the role of the federal government in stopping lynching:

> There is no hope of it being stopped by the states. . . . The people of the country are looking across to the men on this hill and if we lose the hope here, wither will our hope turn. We are looking to God and we are looking to the men who sit on Capitol Hill to pass some law, to do something that is going to make the lives of the negroes the United States safe, and that is going to make the lives of the negroes of this country sweeter and better, and thereby we make better citizens, and the white and the colored people will be happier and better. Thank you.[60]

Butler's emotional remarks embodied important linkages between episodes in her childhood and family life, the current political opportunity, and her ability to testify before a Senate hearing in Washington, D.C. Her experiences during her childhood and parts of her adulthood in South Carolina place into context her argument about the importance of federal action. In 1890, Ben Tillman became governor of South Carolina. Two years into his term, Governor Tillman announced his "lynching pledge" that when a black man was accused of raping a white woman, he would personally lead the mob. While Tillman's private actions contradicted his public rhetoric, this statement nonetheless symbolized African Americans' weakening political status in South Carolina.[61] Living in different cities and towns across the state, including Charleston, Barnwell, and Blackville, Butler would have witnessed firsthand the hardening of segregation practices. In moving to Washington, D.C., joining Republican organizations like the NLRCW and the WPSC, and recounting the racial terror of her childhood before a congressional audience, she was able to articulate the political interests of her sister and brother-in-law and her black community in South Carolina. The historian Lisa G. Materson writes about how black migrant women in Illinois served as "proxy voters" to politically represent the interests of their southern communities.[62] Similarly, black migrant women in the capital like Marian Butler could not cast ballots for their friends and relatives in the South. But they could seize on their geographic location in Washington, D.C., to press for racial justice, thereby serving as political surrogates.

It was also an incredibly courageous decision for Marian Butler to lend her voice to the anti-lynching struggle. As a resident of South Carolina, Butler would have been unable to cast ballots in any election or testify in the State House. Boldly standing before the committee, she represented a black women's political organization in the face of persistent disenfranchisement of African American women. The historian Hannah Rosen writes about the bravery of black women who testified in front of the House Select Committee about the Memphis Riot in 1866. Those black women who recounted their personal experiences with physical and sexual violence also had to contend with questions from white representatives that picked apart their testimony.[63] Within this context, both Mary Church Terrell and Marian Butler confronted white supremacy directly by declaring that black bodies, black mourning, and black suffering mattered in American public culture, both in the past and the present.

Despite these impassioned pleas, anti-lynching legislation in 1926 failed to be enacted. The following year in December 1927, President Calvin Coolidge delivered a pointed address to Congress, urging them again to pass an anti-lynching bill. Coolidge justified African Americans' citizenship and fitness based on their federal service, declaring that "fifty thousand negroes are on the payroll of the federal government" and that "their pay amounts to $50,000,000 a year." "No other race," Coolidge told Congress, "has accomplished as much in the same length of time." He believed that African Americans had "come up from slavery "to be prominent in education, the professions, art, science, agriculture, banking and commerce." Coolidge ended his address by urging Congress to "enact any legislation under the Constitution to provide for its elimination."[64] In addressing Congress about anti-lynching legislation, Coolidge's remarks about black federal employment implicitly referred to the black population in Washington, D.C., which formed the bulk of the black federal workforce. When Coolidge delivered this address, black Washingtonians would have been keenly aware that he was referring to them and perhaps would have been encouraged that their own efforts as a community of federal workers might influence the passage of federal legislation.

Two years later in May 1929, Leonidas Dyer tried one more time to pass the Anti-Lynching Bill in the House of Representatives.[65] In response, black Washingtonians staged an anti-lynching conference to sustain momentum and enthusiasm for anti-lynching legislation. In December 1930, a total of 135 delegates streamed into Washington, D.C., to lobby Congress.[66] But the power of southern Democrats was still too strong.

The Young People in Washington Have Set an Example for the Rest of the Country

During the early 1930s, as women continued to lobby for the passage of a federal anti-lynching bill, living conditions for black Washingtonians began to decline. The Great Depression in 1929 caused widespread unemployment across the city, and black Washingtonians slipped into poverty at higher rates than white Washingtonians. In the midst of these dire economic circumstances, white officers in Washington's Metropolitan Police became more violent, shooting, assaulting, and harassing black men and women at higher numbers. In response, black Washingtonians met with the Board of Commissioners, wrote articles in the press, and held neighborhood meetings. The disturbing context of black unemployment and interracial police brutality in the nation's capital shaped black women's ongoing advocacy for federal anti-lynching legislation, prompting them to identify connections between local and national patterns of violence.

Women and men in the Washington chapter of the NAACP spearheaded the fight for a federal anti-lynching bill in the early 1930s. Emma Merritt, a teacher, served as the local president in the early 1930s and after her death in 1934 was succeeded by Virginia "Jennie" Richardson McGuire, a truant officer.[67] Both Merritt and McGuire were seasoned organizers in the Phyllis Wheatley YWCA, and they, like their predecessors, utilized its building, programs, and political constituencies in their anti-lynching advocacy. In 1933, extralegal violence surged in the United States as twenty-eight citizens died from lynching. This violence hit close to home in October 1933, when George Armwood, a mentally challenged black man, was lynched in Princess Ann, Maryland, a town less than three hours away from the nation's capital.[68] One month after the Armwood lynching, activists in the NAACP held an anti-lynching conference under the direction of President Emma Merritt and board members Martha McAdoo and Mary Church Terrell. Guest speakers at this conference included lawyers Charles Hamilton Houston and Belford Lawson, along with George Murphy, editor of the *Baltimore Afro-American*.[69]

Black Washingtonians also banded together with white leftist and communist leaders in the city to form the Washington Provisional Committee against Lynching (WPCAL). This level of interracial activity and support from the white community had been rare in the 1920s, but was becoming more common in the 1930s, both in Washington and across the nation. In 1930, southern white women shocked the nation when they banded together to form the Association of Southern White Women against Mob Violence. This organization was radical precisely because white supremacy ideology and southern chivalry depicted white women as the innocent and helpless victims of black men's lascivious behavior and lynching was seen as the punishment to ensure white women's protection. Jessie Daniel Ames, the organization's founder, confronted the mythology of white supremacy directly when she argued that the "crown of chivalry was like a crown of thorns on our heads."[70]

In December 1933, members of the WPCAL held a mass meeting at the John Wesley AMEZ Church in Northwest Washington, where they offered a send-off for delegates who were to attend the Eastern Conference against Lynching in Baltimore the next morning. At the meeting, seasoned activists Mary Church Terrell and Charles Hamilton Houston delivered speeches.[71] In addition to Terrell, both social worker Laura B. Glenn and Lydia G. McIlwain, who at the time was working as a maid for a private family and would later be employed as a charwoman in the U.S. Capitol, attended.[72] The fact that this meeting attracted both a social worker and a servant suggests that important cross-class organizing occurred in this organization. It is noteworthy that McIlwain switched jobs from a maid working for a private family to a federal charwoman, possibly because she wanted to be closer to the center of American lawmaking.

While activists were working with the NAACP and the WPCAL, Nannie Helen Burroughs published a widely syndicated article titled "Americans Have Gone Lynch Mad," where for the first time a connection was made between the epidemic of lynching in the United States and the rise of police brutality. By December 1934, Washington, D.C., police officers had shot and killed several African American men for petty crimes, and they had attacked at least ten African American women. Burroughs's article first appeared in the local black paper, the *Washington Tribune*, but was reprinted in black newspapers across the country, including the *Baltimore Afro-American*, the *Chicago Defender*, and the *Pittsburgh Courier*. "We still have another factor contributing to the success of the lynching industry," Burroughs wrote, which now included "policemen, constables, guards, and officers of the law" who "club, shoot, beat into insensibility and murder." Burroughs acknowledged that the anti-lynching fight had gained momentum with the formation of the Association of Southern White Women against Mob Violence, which she praised. But Burroughs feared that a renewed emphasis on white victims would decrease attention to racial violence that continued to terrorize African Americans across the nation. She argued that "legislation will not cure lynching." Rather, she maintained that the only way to eradicate lynching was through enforcement of the Fifteenth Amendment, which would enable African Americans not only to elect police officers who would not tolerate lynching but would also change racial attitudes.[73] Burroughs's argument reflected a profound political change. As a political activist, she had been at the forefront of the movement to propose and support the Dyer Anti-Lynching Bill. Now she was certain that a bill might pass in the coming decade, but was skeptical that making lynching a crime would decrease these acts of violence. This shift perhaps reflected her awareness of changing circumstances in Washington, D.C., where African Americans were experiencing mounting hostility from the police, which was connected with the Great Depression, the climate of Prohibition, and militancy among black and white citizens.

As black women continued to lobby federal officials, they were heartened, briefly, in January 1934 when Democratic senators Robert J. Wagner and Edward P. Costigan introduced the Costigan-Wagner Anti-Lynching Bill in the Senate. One month later, black Washingtonians eagerly followed the hearings for the bill.[74] At the hearings, southern Democratic senators objected to the presence of black reporters, but they fought back and were seated in the press gallery.[75] However, it quickly became clear that some senators were deeply opposed to federal anti-lynching legislation and that the bill would likely meet the same fate as the Dyer Anti-Lynching Bill of 1922.

With discouraging news from Congress, activists turned to another branch of the federal government: the new administration in the White House. Although African Americans had not supported Roosevelt for president in 1932, some of his policies, and especially those of First Lady Eleanor Roosevelt, suggested that he might be sympathetic to civil rights causes. In March 1934, NAACP president Jennie Richardson McGuire learned about the brutal lynching of Claude Neal in Florida, in which a reported crowd of 20,000 had gathered to witness the burning of his body.[76] McGuire sent a pointed letter about the lynching to President Roosevelt, but received no response.[77] In May 1934, NAACP executive secretary Walter White met with the president for an hour-long meeting at the White House.[78]

A few months later, McGuire and other NAACP members learned that the upcoming National Crime Conference in Washington, D.C., had omitted lynching from its agenda. The National Crime Conference was an annual event attended by five hundred police commissioners, prison officials, lawyers, and judges, and this year it was to be held at Memorial Continental Hall at 1776 D

Street Northwest, a building owned by the Daughters of the American Revolution. Richardson and other NAACP activists contacted D.C. Commissioner Ernest Brown, asking his permission to picket the event, but he refused to grant them a permit.[79] Commissioner Brown's hostility reflected not only growing tensions between black citizens and the police but also the police's weariness with mass marches and militancy in Washington, D.C. Even though they did not receive a permit, activists decided to protest anyway.

On Monday, December 10, at 12:30 P.M., NAACP vice president Roy Wilkins, *Baltimore Afro-American* editor George B. Murphy, and lawyers Edward P. Lovett and Emmett Dorsey stood in front of Memorial Continental Hall carrying signs that called attention to the conference program's disregard for lynching. They timed this protest to coincide with the conference's lunch-break, which would enable them to alert all the attendees about the omission of lynching from the conference deliberations. But only five minutes into their demonstration, district police officers told them that they did not have a permit, informed them that they were violating the "sign law," and asked them to retreat from their positions. When the four men refused to budge, Washington police officers swiftly arrested them for protesting without a permit. In Police Court, Lovett, Dorsey, and Murphy all pled not guilty and were released on a bond of five dollars. Roy Wilkins had to return to New York City to pursue NAACP business, so he pled guilty. That evening, President Roosevelt addressed the Crime Conference and denounced lynching; he soberly stated, "Lynchings are no longer confined to one section of the country, unfortunately"—referencing the fact that the act of lynching had become more commonplace in states in the Midwest and West.[80]

While it was a victory that President Roosevelt condemned lynching, NAACP leaders were angry that the Washington Metropolitan Police Department had crushed their efforts to protest the National Crime Conference. President Jennie Richardson McGuire took the lead in crafting a response. She thought deliberately about ways to bypass police regulations, brainstormed about methods of protest going beyond carrying signs, considered potential participants in such protests, and crafted a backup plan in the event of more arrests. Only eleven months into her presidency of the Washington branch of the NAACP, McGuire had already handled several cases of police violence against black citizens.[81] These experiences likely pushed her to act with both precision and caution. She reached out to several faculty members at Howard University, who invited their students to join the protests. McGuire also tapped her networks at the Phyllis Wheatley YWCA, conceiving of this building as a central headquarters for her new protest plan. As mentioned, during the 1920s, several Republican organizations had met in this building, and it was a central location for black women's political activities.

On Thursday, December 13, a group of fifty-five men and women arrived at the Phyllis Wheatley YWCA. McGuire divided participants into groups of five, designating one person in each group as the movement leader who could be arrested in the event of police hostility. Richardson instructed each person to write an anti-lynching message on a small sign, so as to conform to police regulations. She also handed each person a piece of hemp rope about twelve inches in length to be slipped across the neck so as to evoke the victims of lynching. The fifty-five participants then departed the YWCA in cabs and traveled two miles across Northwest Washington to Memorial Continental Hall.[82]

Once they arrived, activists were instructed to stand on the sidewalk in front of the hall in their groups of five. No words were spoken, no verses were chanted, but through the ropes hanging from each person's neck and the small signs they clutched, the fifty-five activists registered their collective protests against lynching with unequivocal clarity to all who passed by. "Because these pickets were absolutely within the law," an article in the *New Negro Opinion* commented, "the police were helpless to stop the demonstration."[83] Through clever adjustments, McGuire had prevented the protests at the Crime Conference from being halted, modifying them to fit within police regulations. While historian Patricia Sullivan credits Charles Hamilton Houston with these new protest plans, all of my sources acknowledge his collaboration with McGuire. Given McGuire's connections with the YWCA, it makes the most sense that she would have centered her tactics on this building.[84]

Jennie McGuire tapped her deep networks in the YWCA, NAACP, labor groups, and churches to recruit members for the Rope Protests. Undergraduate students from freshmen to seniors at Howard University composed the largest group of protesters, numbering fourteen women and fifteen men. Additionally, there were three faculty members at Howard University, three ministers of local churches, two teachers, one newspaper editor, and one reporter. The two women who were not directly affiliated with Howard University were Bertha Lomack and Arnetta Randall. Bertha Lomack worked as a printer's assistant in the federal government, and her daughter Augusta Lomack was a student at Howard University and one of the participants.[85] Arnetta Randall was a teacher in the Washington public schools.[86] Lomack and Randall were both involved in the newly formed protest organization, the New Negro Alliance.[87]

Through their small signs, participants articulated their anti-lynching message. For instance, Owing Plummer, a student at Howard University and na-

This photograph depicts some of the fifty-five Howard University students who participated in the Rope Protests at the Crime Conference in December 1934. Owing Plummer is the woman on the far right who is clutching her schoolbooks. Her sign reads "4 Women, 45 Years," a reference to the four black women who had been lynched in her home state of North Carolina. Getty Images.

tive of North Carolina, clutched a small sign that read "4 Women, 45 Years." The message on Plummer's sign likely referenced the four black women who had been lynched in her home state of North Carolina between 1885 and 1930—a period of forty-five years. The women—Harriet Finch, Mrs. Joe Perry, Mrs. Bryant, and Laura Wood—had been lynched for a variety of reasons, including allegedly committing a murder and for the crime of being economically successful.[88] In her left hand, Plummer held a notebook and schoolbooks, perhaps to convey her status as a student. Plummer's protest spoke volumes. As a coed at Howard University in the nation's capital, Plummer was able to receive an education and pursue a career, while her counterparts in the Jim Crow South lived with the daily fear of lynching. Another activist held a small sign that read "5504 Lynchings in 80 Years." A photograph published in the *Baltimore Afro-American* featured three Howard students—Cassandra Maxwell, Jeanette Layden, and Carry Bell Hughes—who silently conveyed their protests against lynching. In the photograph, all three women were holding the bottom of the rope, perhaps alluding that their patience had come to an end. Both Layden and Hughes were undergraduate students at Howard, but Maxwell was a law student and in six years would be the first African American woman admitted to the bar in South Carolina.[89]

African American newspapers celebrated the innovative protest tactics that activists wielded in this anti-lynching demonstration. An article in the *Norfolk Journal and Guide* noted that the use of rope created a "grim and silent protest against the omission of the discussion of lynching by the conference."[90] Another piece described the ways that these tactics "caused wide-spread comment among the delegates and drew all newspaper photographers."[91] In assessing the significance of the protests, a piece in the *Christian Science Monitor* editorialized, "Actually, the Negroes are getting more attention by direct action than they could have by any single speech that might have been delivered— and lost in the welter of crime conference outpouring."[92] This article was particularly noteworthy by employing the language of "direct action," a method of nonviolent social protest that confronted the system of inequality, often through the body. Mahatma Gandhi employed direct action in his struggle against colonial rule in India. Black Washingtonians, such as Howard University president Mordecai Johnson, were intrigued by these ideas, and in turn he likely influenced the many members of the Howard community who participated in the Rope Protests. Beginning in the early 1940s, civil rights activists would use direct action to challenge segregation in transportation and private businesses.[93]

African American activists in Washington, D.C., celebrated the success of their protest experiment. By recruiting students, replacing signs with ropes, and bypassing police restrictions, the fifty-five protesters were able to powerfully articulate their anti-lynching pleas. The Washington branch of the NAACP issued a statement about the recent protests, noting that black activists in the city had successfully implemented a direct action campaign, which would be become a staple in the black freedom struggle. "No sacrifice is to great," the statement read, "to wipe out this barbarity. The young people in Washington have set an example for the rest of the country. We should use all our energies and all the money we can spare to fight lynching. No one of us should be too educated or too dignified to fight lynching. We defy anyone to read the report of the Claude Neal lynching and then to sit back contentedly on this 'respectability.'"[94]

An editorial in the *New York Amsterdam News* titled "Militancy" similarly celebrated the new strain of political activism palpable in the Rope Protests.

Not only did they succeed in "focusing the eyes of the nation on the country's greatest evil" but they also indicated that the "mass of American Negroes are willing now to fight for their rights."[95] An editorial in the *Baltimore Afro-American* titled "The Rope Pickets" concluded that the second day of protests were more successful because they were "smart and original."[96] In all of these instances, the national black press registered excitement with black Washingtonians' political militancy.

Locally, activists in Washington, D.C., also celebrated the power of black protest. One month after the Rope Protests, Nannie Helen Burroughs addressed a crowd of 1,000 black Washingtonians at the Vermont Avenue Baptist Church. "There are enough Negros in Washington," Burroughs declared, "to make Pennsylvania Avenue tremble"—referencing the ways that black Washingtonians used their position in the nation's capital to influence federal politics. Employing the dramatic verb "tremble" likely connected with the recent use of militant direct action, which had produced stunning results, both for this protest and for future campaigns in the black freedom struggle. Praising this militancy, Burroughs encouraged the audience to persist in this tradition of activism. "How will we demand our rights," she asked, "for who in the world will demand them for us?" She then called on the younger generation to participate in the campaign for freedom and justice.[97] After Burroughs's stirring address, Jennie Richardson McGuire delivered an address in her capacity as president of the local branch of the NAACP.[98]

In several ways, the Rope Protests in December 1934 marked a watershed moment in African American politics in Washington, D.C. First, they signaled the rise of college student activism in the city. Students had participated in politics before—whether by registering memberships in the NAACP Junior League or marching in an anti-lynching protest parade—but never before had college students been so visible in a political demonstration in Washington, D.C. Second, Jennie McGuire's brilliant strategy of bypassing police regulations gained national attention and helped educate other activists about the importance of direct action, college student participation, and detailed organization. Black citizens would draw on these tactics of direct action in their subsequent civil rights campaigns in the 1930s and 1940s. Third, the Rope Protests, like most anti-lynching activities in the 1920s, showcased black women's political skills and organizational networks. Most importantly, they caused activists to rethink their political priorities. It was not just that police officers had arrested black citizens because they lacked a permit and carried signs that exceeded a size limit. Since the late 1920s, white police officers had been harassing, attacking, abusing, and killing black men and women across the city. Not only did violence plague African Americans still living in the Jim Crow South but it was also an everyday part of life in black Washington.

When black women and men stood with ropes around their necks in 1934, it represented the last time that Washingtonians would collectively work to pass an anti-lynching bill. During the remainder of the decade, individual organizations, including the NAACP and the National Negro Congress, pressed for anti-lynching legislation, while the black press in Washington, D.C., continued to report on racial violence across the nation.[99] However, black citizens in the city stopped holding public demonstrations about lynching as many turned their attention more fully toward the matter of police brutality, which they would term "urban lynching."[100] One of the reasons why activists drew parallels between the two acts of violence was because police officers, like perpetrators of lynching, were rarely punished for their brutal behaviors toward black citizens. Many of the same women who had fought for the passage of an anti-lynching bill in Washington, including Nannie Helen Burroughs, Theresa Lee Connelly, Jennie Richardson McGuire, Arnetta Randall, and Mary Church Terrell, became activists against police violence. While the evidence is not available, it is possible that some of the rank-and-file citizens who observed anti-lynching hearings, signed petitions, attended prayer meetings, or marched in the Silent Parade in 1922 also became involved with collective demonstrations against police brutality. Black women's shift from an emphasis on national violence to local violence reflected the changing circumstances of politics in the city of Washington.

Conclusion

In a fifteen-year period, African American women could point to significant accomplishments in their campaigns against lynching. In the 1920s and early 1930s, African American women tapped their political networks to organize prayer meetings, petition drives, a Silent Parade with 5,000 participants, congressional lobbying, and direct action protests. Black women served as the leaders of most of these movements, many of which rallied both male and female constituents.

African American women's activism against anti-lynching also reflected the strength of their organizing culture. In their different campaigns, black women recruited a range of black Washingtonians to participate in anti-lynching activism, working within churches, fraternal orders, businesses, schools, and Howard University. The Phyllis Wheatley YWCA served as the anchor point for black women's anti-lynching activism, offering a place to design and store picket signs, a site for mass meetings and book talks, and a central gathering space.

African American women succeeded in generating national attention to the crisis of lynching. The two prominent protests—the Silent Parade of 1922 and the Rope Protests of 1934—bookend black women's political activism precisely because they illuminate the changes occurring over that time period in Washington, D.C. When activists staged the Silent Parade in 1922, it was legal for five thousand African Americans to carry protest signs of any size and march down Pennsylvania Avenue. But fourteen years later, it took fewer than five minutes for police officers to detain four men protesting at the Crime Conference. This moment decisively shaped the ways that black Washingtonians conceptualized politics, causing them to turn away from national campaigns and orient their efforts toward eradicating injustices closer to home. Although women did not serve in such prominent leadership positions as men, their campaigns attracted citizens from all walks of life, including working-class victims of police violence and veteran organizers from the anti-lynching fight who brought an arsenal of protest tactics to deploy in the hard and frustrating movement to end interracial violence against black Washingtonians.

Part II
Political Crises, 1930–1940

Washington is now Scottsboro.

—Chant of police brutality marchers

Washington, D.C., is seventy-five years behind the times.

—Nannie Helen Burroughs

CHAPTER THREE

Make Washington Safe for Negro Womanhood
The Politics of Police Brutality

In 1933, an editorial in the black-owned *Washington Tribune* titled "Women, Bravery, Freedom" recounted the remarks of former Alabama senator Thomas Heflin who, in a speech opposing interracial marriage in the Senate in 1930, referred to women as the "crowning glory of God's creation." Heflin's reference to "women" was racially coded to signify white women, and in this speech, he linked their protection and purity to bans on interracial marriage.[1] Assessing the contradictions in Heflin's argument, the editorial remarked, "We too look upon our women with high regard." It then described a recent episode of police brutality against two black women in Washington, D.C.: sixty-five-year-old Cornelia Diggs and her forty-eight-year-old daughter, Dedia Coates. The editorial wondered why in "this land of the brave, where women are the crowning glory of God's creation, two policemen—either drunk with liquor or authority—force their way into the privacy of a sober residence" and attack two women. While Diggs had witnessed "seventy years of racial oppression" she had never experienced the "forces of the law visited on her." The officers beat Diggs and then "dragged [her] by the hair out of the house" to arrest her. The editorial ironically concluded that the brutality inflicted on Diggs and Coates represented another example of the "crowning Glory of God's creation." Writers at the *Washington Tribune* thus reflected on the hypocrisy of figures like Senator Heflin, who vociferously defended the virtues of "women," but turned a blind eye toward the rising levels of white violence against black women in Washington, D.C.[2]

During the late 1920s, the number of reported cases of interracial police brutality against African American women in Washington, D.C., began to climb. This abuse fit into larger patterns of police violence, which terrorized all black residents of the city, but police brutality was a gendered process, which often affected black men and women differently. Between 1928 and 1938, white police officers shot and killed fifty citizens in the city, of whom forty were African American men. White police officers did not shoot and kill black women and girls, but over this time period subjected at least twenty-nine of them to a range of violent behaviors, including street harassment, racial epithets, physical assaults, and intrusions into their houses. In addition to these abusive encounters, white police officers and detectives in the Washington Metropolitan Police Department often employed a double standard by refusing to conduct thorough investigations when black women were abused, raped, or murdered; this was a form of negligence.

Interracial police violence created a culture of fear for all black Washingtonians. Known victims of police brutality lived in every quadrant of the city, ranged in age from fifteen to sixty-eight, and represented diverse class backgrounds. African American women living in the nation's capital held many connections to police brutality, whether they were victims, litigants, bystanders, family members of an injured party, or political activists.

Black Washingtonians politicized interracial police brutality precisely because policemen could be held accountable for these actions. As employees of the Metropolitan Police Department, officers were contracted to uphold the law and were subject to trial boards. Black Washingtonians could plead their case in Police Court and tap their political associations to pressure the Board of Commissioners to investigate officer abuse at a time when it was nearly impossible to prosecute civilian white men under the legal system in Washington. White police officers were not the only perpetrators of violence against black women in Washington, D.C., but they were the only ones who would be likely to face punishment for doing so. Women faced danger in every corner of the city, including in worksites, especially the homes where they labored as domestic servants; on streets and alleys; in streetcars, buses, and taxis; in places of public amusement; in schools and hospitals; and in their own houses.[3]

Historians have examined police brutality against black citizens in Washington, D.C., in the 1930s, but have not fully analyzed the broad spectrum of violence that affected African American women. In his study of the National Negro Congress, Erik Gellman does document black citizens' campaigns against police brutality in Washington, D.C., but he centers the majority of his study on the experiences of male shooting victims and the male activists who worked to reduce this violence. Gellman argues that black Washingtonians identified similarities between police brutality in Washington, D.C., and lynching in the U.S. South because racial violence in both settings had the effect of bolstering white supremacy.[4] However, his focus solely on victims of police shootings obscures the ways that gender shaped violence against black women.

Scholars in African American women's history have analyzed interracial police violence in other cities. In her study of Detroit during the 1920s and 1930s, Victoria Wolcott argues that black women's participation in underground economies—including bootlegging and prostitution—made them

TABLE 4 Female victims of police brutality in Washington, D.C.

First	Last	Age	Region	Year	Site of Attack	Source
Novella	Johnson	17	NW	1921	Street	Newspaper
Josephine	White	32	NE	1927	House	Newspaper
Anne	Burliegh	55	NW	1929	Street	Newspaper
M.	Body	Unknown	NW	1929	Street	Newspaper
Catherine	Brawner	46	NW	1929	Street	Newspaper
Constance	Spencer	24	NW	1929	Street	Newspaper
Ida	Turner	38	NW	1930	Street	Newspaper
Corinne	McCowe	Unknown	NW	1932	Street	Newspaper
Virgie	Togood	22	SE	1932	Street	Newspaper
Mattie	Ford	25	SE	1932	Street	Newspaper
Alberta	Young	54	SE	1933	House	Newspaper
Cornelia	Diggs	68	SE	1933	House	Newspaper
Dedia	Coates	48	SE	1933	House	Newspaper
Ida	Lindey	22	NW	1934	Beer Garden	Newspaper
Jeanette	Kidd	34	SW	1935	House	Newspaper
Jessie	Sterling	56	SW	1935	House	Newspaper
Mildred	deArellano	25	NE	1935	House	Newspaper
Jennie	Peters	45	NE	1935	House	Newspaper
Martha	Lloyd	17	NW	1936	Street	Newspaper
Ruth	Lloyd	15	NW	1936	Street	Newspaper
Georgia	Watkins	36	NW	1937	Street	Newspaper
Ruth	Clark	29	NW	1938	House	NNC report
Viola	Harris	Unknown	NW	1939	House	Newspaper
Lillie	Watson	Unknown	NW	1939	House	Newspaper
Ethel	McKinney	25	NW	1940	Street	Newspaper
Frances	James	Unknown	NW	1940	Street	Newspaper
Dorothy	Bowles	30	NE	1940	Street	NNC flier
Eva	Moxley	30s	Unknown	Unknown	Street	Newspaper
Dorothy	Wood	Unknown	Unknown	Unknown	Street	Interracial Committee report

Source: Washington Tribune, Washington Post, Baltimore Afro-American, Chicago Defender, the *National Negro Congress Report,* and the *Inter-Racial Committee Report.*

vulnerable to police brutality. She also links the absence of black police officers with escalating rates of violence. Cheryl Hicks's scholarship on black women in New York City argues that police officers instinctively linked African American women with crime to justify their violence. This historiography helps contextualize some of the violent encounters between white police officers and African American women in Washington, D.C. But, as Sarah Haley argues, scholars are only beginning this work, and she contends that police violence against black women and girls is part of "historical erasure."[5] This chapter chronicles police brutality through the eyes of black women like Cornelia Diggs and Dedia Coates and grapples with some of the reasons for this absence in the historical record.

Historians have applied different methodologies to their research into black women's violent encounters with the police. Since violence involves lingering trauma, a discussion of this experience is always fragmented, partial, and incomplete. As LaKisha Simmons argues, "Silence is absence; it is stories half-told, knowing glances, and narratives ignored."[6] The history of overt police violence and institutional negligence against black women brims with these very silences. This chapter draws on newspapers, organizational papers, records of the Washington Metropolitan Police Department, and census data.[7] While black newspapers offered the most comprehensive treatment of police brutality cases, it was rare for a particular case to be described in more than one article. Reporting on police violence required complex investigative journalism. Not only did this pose a financial burden to the cash-strapped black press but it also demanded that black reporters question white police officers, and these encounters could range from uncomfortable to violent.[8] This challenge posed by a paucity of sources is compounded by the reality that it was dangerous for black women to report violent encounters, especially those involving rape or sexual assault. Whenever a black woman in Washington, D.C., experienced violence, she faced a weighty decision about whether to disclose this assault because her morality would be questioned, her respectability scrutinized, and her future potentially compromised. As one unknown African American woman wrote in 1904, "A Colored woman, however respectable, is lower than the white prostitute."[9] It is significant that the historical record contains twenty-nine cases of brutality, but there were many, many more that were left unreported.

Relations between black Washingtonians and police officers had always been strained, but they worsened for a variety of reasons during the 1920s. In 1919, the Eighteenth Amendment banned alcohol in the United States, which prompted some Americans to engage in underground economies of smuggling and bootlegging. As historians have shown, police officers disproportionately punished African Americans for these activities.[10] Beginning in 1929, many black Washingtonians were plunged into poverty by the Great Depression, prompting more citizens to pursue petty theft or bootlegging for survival. As the Depression dragged on, black and white citizens staged militant marches in the nation's capital for economic relief, sometimes with the assistance of the Communist Party. All of these circumstances created more face-to-face interactions between white police officers and black citizens. The Washington Metropolitan Police Department and its Women's Bureau, which handled female offenders, were understaffed throughout the 1930s and did not hire enough black officers in proportion to the city's black population. Taken together, these conditions produced discernible patterns of interracial police violence against black Washingtonians, typified by arbitrary arrests, unnecessary force, home intrusions, verbal threats, and shootings.

As police violence increased in the late 1920s and early 1930s, black women and men responded to this crisis by filing lawsuits, engaging in investigations, and attending meetings, all while continuing their efforts to pass a federal anti-lynching law. A turning point occurred in December 1934, when Washington, D.C., police officers arrested anti-lynching activists for carrying large protest signs at the Crime Conference, as described in chapter 2. This event marked a crossroads for activists, showcasing the hostility of the police toward non-violent protest and illustrating their rough treatment of black citizens throughout the city. It convinced many veterans of the anti-lynching movement to reorient their activism toward local violence in the nation's capital.

Throughout the 1930s, a diverse group of black women protested police brutality. Women's campaigns to end police violence underscored the connections between their informal and formal politics, encompassing the individual citizens who resisted officers' aggressions and pled innocence in Police Court; the middle-class activists who lobbied government officials; and the dozens and sometimes hundreds of black women who read reports in the press, attended mass meetings, witnessed mock police trials, and marched in protest parades. While police brutality was not an exclusively women's movement, it utilized black women's networks in neighborhood associations, the Phyllis Wheatley YWCA, fraternal orders, and political organizations. African American women worked to make the city "Safe for Negro Womanhood," contending that the fight for justice and equality across the nation could never be achieved until it was realized in its capital.

Black Women and Police Violence in the Early 1920s

Both the federal and local government supervised law enforcement in Washington, D.C. The city's three Board of Commissioners appointed the police commissioner, who hired the officers, while the Congressional Committee of the District of Columbia approved the budget and oversaw the workings of the department. In 1920, 995 white men and 38 black men worked as police officers in the city.[11] After citizens were arrested, they could plead their case in Police Court, housed in a building located in Northwest Washington and presided over by four white male judges. During the 1920s and 1930s, the Police Court was busy. An article in the *Washington Post* reported that the "present congestion of the District Police Court interferes with adequate and sufficient consideration" of many cases. If black citizens were brave enough to plead their innocence in Police Court, then they faced long delays and crowded conditions.[12] When citizens believed that an officer had demonstrated abusive behavior and had not been reprimanded, they could appeal to the Police Trial Board and request a hearing; there a committee would recommend whether that officer should be suspended, pay a fine, receive a warning, or be dismissed from the force. Even though officers rarely faced significant punishments for violence against citizens, it was deeply important that black Washingtonians exercised their citizenship rights in the nation's capital by appearing in Police Court and appealing to the Trial Board for justice.

Throughout the city, police officers treated African American women and girls with suspicion. Records from 1917–20 show that black women in Washington were arrested at significantly higher rates than white women on various charges, including disorderly conduct, intoxication, and enticing prostitution.[13] Not only were African American women more likely to be arrested but also within the jails, *only* black women labored as laundresses, which reinforced their second-class status in these institutions. In a hearing before the U.S. House of Representatives, Assistant Superintendent of the Jails Thomas Rives argued that it was "necessary" to employ black women in these laundry facilities because it provided a "form of occupation for them" and "served a useful purpose for the jail." Rives cast black women as the natural population to work as laundresses in the city's jails and even expressed surprise that "disorderly" black women had not destroyed the laundry facilities, which indicated the poor image of black women in the eyes of law enforcement officials.[14]

In 1918, Mina Van Winkle, a white officer, worked to improve conditions for all women in Washington by forming a Women's Bureau in the Police Depart-

The Police Court Building was located on the corner of Fourth and E Streets. During the 1920s and 1930s, African American women appeared in this building to protest brutality among police officers. Black organizations also lobbied for the appointment of black judges in Police Court. Library of Congress, LC-USZ62-123897.

ment. As the bureau's director during the 1920s, Van Winkle ordered police-women to patrol the city and conduct "preventative and protective work."[15] She valued the importance of black policewomen. During World War I, she recruited prominent political activist Marian D. Butler to serve as a matron and attendant in the city's jailhouse. Butler likely accepted this position so that she could work to improve conditions for black women prisoners.[16] Van Winkle also hired twenty white women and two black women to serve as police offi-cers. While two female black officers was a small number for a city the size of Washington, D.C., consider that in 1923 there were only seven black police-women employed across the nation.[17]

Since African American policewomen were so rare, the black press ran sev-eral articles on the officers in Washington, D.C. The *Chicago Defender* labeled Washington a "pioneer" for having so many policewomen.[18] The *Southern Workman* profiled Washington's two policewomen, reporting that officers traded day and night shifts to ensure that at least one black woman officer was on call in the evenings. "Dance halls, cabarets, and theaters are visited and supervised, and the streets patrolled," the article noted, and if officers found "young girls in the streets or in questionable places of amusement" they would take them not to jail, but to their homes for questioning and rebuke. The officers acknowledged the high rate of arrests for black women and sought to lower it by working with reform and community organizations across the city. "The two colored policewomen," the article concluded, "have resolved to reduce this staggering number of arrests by prophylaxis," working with the YWCA, women's organizations, schools, and churches to keep women out of danger; the "results have been most gratifying."[19]

The evidence suggests that Van Winkle's leadership in the Women's Bureau and the individual advocacy of the city's two black policewomen were relatively effective: in the early 1920s, there was only one reported case of police brutality against a black woman. In 1921, Novella Johnson, a seventeen-year-old girl, was walking along Fairmount Avenue near Georgia Avenue in Northwest Washington at 5 P.M. Along the way, she noticed that two black boys were throwing stones at an iron post near a street lamp. A white woman saw this as well and began to chase after them. Presumably sensing that this situation could turn explosive, Johnson intervened, explaining to the white woman that the boys were throwing stones at the post, not the street lamp. E. C. Spaulding, a white police officer dressed in plain clothes, emerged on the scene and "slapped Miss Johnson down." Acting in self-defense and not realizing Spaulding was a police officer, Johnson grabbed a stone and struck Officer Spaulding in his left eye. Spaulding retaliated by choking her as he "pummeled her in the face," causing blood to pour from her nose and mouth. Spaulding continued to beat Johnson until a white bystander pulled him away.[20] Two black women witnessed this assault and swiftly called the police, informing them that a white man was attempting to kill a black girl. When the police officers arrived, they took Johnson to Garfield, a white hospital nearby, but then arrested her on charges of assaulting an officer.

Johnson's attorney, Royal Hughes, pressed the city of Washington, D.C., to convene a jury trial, but the case was deferred. Rather than punish Officer Spaulding, the Metropolitan Police Department transferred him to another precinct. An article about the incident noted, "The whole neighborhood was worked up on this inhuman attack on this young woman."[21] While disturbing and brutal, Johnson's assault in 1921, as mentioned, was the only recorded episode of police violence against black women.

While they did not face reported cases of brutality, black women continued to be arrested at high rates. During the 1920s, 11,623 African American women served time in prison, as compared to 1,810 white women: 88 percent of all women prisoners were black, although black women comprised only 26 percent of the female population in Washington, D.C.[22] This evidence indicates that police officers routinely arrested black women for their participation in underground economies, including bootlegging, drug peddling, and prostitution.[23] The fact that black women were the majority of police arrests among women and disproportionately dominated the population of female prisoners helped perpetuate stereotypes about all African American women in the city, linking them with crime and participation in underground economies. Black women in churches and social and political organizations, such as the Phyllis Wheatley YWCA, worked to shatter these myths by offering wholesome, recreational opportunities for women in the city and emphasizing the politics of respectability.

"D.C. Cops a Terror to Women": Brutality Surges

Beginning in the late 1920s and early 1930s, black newspapers began to report rising levels of police violence against black Washingtonians. There were many reasons for this increase. Despite the growing black population, the Metropolitan Police Department only employed forty black men and two black women as officers. In 1930, Henrietta Burwell, one of the city's two black policewomen, died suddenly, and she was not replaced for several years.[24] The Metropolitan Police Department also underwent administrative changes. In 1932, Ernest W. Brown, a white officer, was appointed police commissioner.[25] One year later in 1933, Mina Van Winkle retired as director of the Women's Bureau and was succeeded by Rhoda Milliken, another white officer. In interviews, black policewomen reported that they no longer patrolled the city, which created more opportunities for white officers to abuse African American women.[26]

In addition to these changes in the police department, the Great Depression transformed the culture of the city. If police officers had treated African Americans with suspicion before the stock market crash, the Great Depression rendered all black Washingtonians prime suspects for bootlegging, the illegal distribution of alcohol, and theft. As citizens streamed into the nation's capital and staged pubic demonstrations for economic relief, officers in the Metropolitan Police Department expressed frustration and concern. Its annual reports hint at struggles between officers and citizens. A report from 1931 noted that a "national hunger march" had brought "some 1,500 Communists and agitators" into Washington. Characterizing marchers as "agitators" signaled that police officers treated them with suspicion. One year later, 20,000 veterans from World War I camped in Washington, D.C., to demand payment of a bonus, which greatly strained the resources of the Metropolitan Police. A report in 1934 noted that there were "a number of smaller marches and gatherings" that "made problems for the police department"—thus equating public demonstrations with problems. These reports always made race central, highlighting the presence of African Americans and often linking them with communist activities.[27] Taken together, these personnel changes, a lack of black officers, Prohibition, the Great Depression, and political militancy led to violent encounters between white officers and black women in the late 1920s.

There were several different scenarios in which white officers would attack black women. Sometimes, policemen invaded their homes, especially when men were absent. In April 1927, Josephine White, a domestic servant, was sitting in her parlor with her fifteen-month-old son Wilbur, at their home at Linden Court in Northeast Washington, while her husband Charles, a laborer, was out.[28] Police Officer Clifton J. Gary barged into the home, inquired where Josephine White's husband was, and then "dragged her out into the alley and tried to force her into his automobile and beat her with a heavy stick."[29] White escaped from the officer and limped one block onto H Street, a business and residential street, where she collapsed and was taken to Casualty Hospital.[30] A few minutes later, three other policemen wearing plainclothes "began to terrorize the citizens living on the street." An article reported, "In their wild orgy they broke into people's doors, intimidated them, and in general created a disturbance." The riot finally ended when a sergeant from the Ninth Precinct arrested Gary, placing him in a cell and charging him with drunk and disorderly conduct. The case went to Police Court and five witnesses testified about the beating of Josephine White and police brutality on both Linden Court and H Street. However, Judge McDonald dismissed the case. An article in the *Baltimore Afro-American* titled "Justice Blind in Police Abuse Case" criticized Assistant District Attorney Bruce for "not vigorously cross-examin[ing] the witnesses" or "emphasiz[ing] the weight of the testimony against the white offender."[31] The fact that Officer Gary was inebriated suggests that he barged into Josephine White's home looking for alcohol.

Newspaper accounts in the black press emphasized Josephine White's respectability. An article in the *Washington Tribune* interviewed her neighbors, who described her as a woman of "small build" who had a "quiet, unassuming manner" and maintained an "excellent reputation for peace and good order." Other neighbors said that she was of "model character" and had lived at the address at Linden Court for "three years."[32] All of this language was precise, racially coded, and grounded in a language of sexual propriety. Her "small build" might contradict allegations of sexual promiscuity, while her "reputation" for peace and order would suggest the absence of loud visitors and disorder. Even though White resided at Linden Court, an alley often associated with disease, crime, and vice, this article noted that she had lived there for three years—thereby positioning her status as stable and permanent, rather than transient. The historian Cheryl Hicks argues that in times of violence, black working-class women clung to a discourse of respectability, and that was precisely the case with the depiction of Josephine White.[33]

In other situations, officers detained women on the street. In October 1930, Ida Wheeler Turner, a cook, was walking on Third and P Streets in Northwest Washington on her way home from church.[34] A white police officer, Arthur E. Fredette, suspected that she was intoxicated and tried to arrest her. When she protested, Officer Fredette struck her, badly bruising her face and temporarily blinding her. Officer Fredette arrested Turner, charging her with drunkenness, assaulting an officer, and resisting arrest. However, when Turner arrived at the police station, her husband informed the officers that she had previously been a patient at Gallinger Municipal Hospital in February, a public hospital in the city, where she had been treated for a nervous breakdown. That Turner had not yet fully recovered was indicated by her being confused when she was arrested and identifying herself by her maiden name, Wheeler, rather than by her married name, Turner. Her husband later confirmed that his wife often suffered from memory lapses and was known to wander around.[35] However, Judge Mattingly ignored her husband's testimony, found Turner guilty of disorderly conduct, and fined her $65.00.[36] The story of Ida Wheeler Turner illustrates that neither police officers nor Police Court judges expressed any kind of leniency when it came to mental illness, and it also signaled the levels of police cruelty toward black women in the city.

Archibald S. Pinkett from the local branch of the NAACP and Harry A. Dyson, Turner's lawyer, publicized her case and rallied on her behalf. According to an article in the *Washington Tribune*, Turner's mental state and her mistreatment by the police "attracted city-wide attention."[37] In October 1930 at a meeting of the Baptist Ministers' Conference at the Florida Avenue Baptist Church, attendees deplored the recent episode of brutality in the city. The Reverend J. P. Nichols denounced this violence, announcing that Turner's case "was simply the record of another brutal attack of the Police on defenseless Negroes," and he urged his fellow attendees to "rise up to protest this brutality."[38] Dyson was able to schedule a hearing for Officer Fredette before the Police Trial Board, but he was exonerated.[39]

Turner wrote a letter to the editor of the black newspaper in Washington, the *Washington Tribune*, where she publicly discussed the assault and narrated her experience with police violence. "I wish to thank the *Tribune*," Turner wrote, "for the kind interest shown during the trial I went through in reference to time I was assaulted by Officer Arthur Fredette." Turner noted that the *Tribune* had "rendered me valuable service" and "at all times presented my case to the public in the true light." She informed the public that her eye was healing, although the doctors warned her to be careful so as not to further jeopardize her vision.[40] The publication of Turner's letter underscored the important role of the black press, both in the nation's capital and across the country, in helping increase awareness of the white police violence that afflicted African American women and men. In contrast, in the 1920s and 1930s, the white newspapers in Washington, D.C. —the *Washington Post* and the *Washington Star*— failed to report episodes of police violence against African American residents of the nation's capital, instead restricting their coverage to incidents in which African Americans committed crimes.[41]

Ida Turner's encounter with street brutality was not uncommon. Given African American women's high representation in prisons for their work in the underground economy, it seems that police officers sometimes instinctively associated black women with crime. In September 1929, police officers knocked down Anne E. Burliegh in the streets. Burliegh was a fifty-five-year-old widow who worked for the federal government as a charwoman (office cleaner).[42] Three months later, a police officer detained Mrs. M. Body, who had been shopping; he checked her bag for liquor, which was currently illegal. In the process of searching her bag, he struck her. And in September 1930, Catherine Brawner, an operator in the Bureau of Printing and Engraving, and her daughter, Constance Spencer, a teacher, were walking down the street when an officer began to hurl racial epithets and abuse at Spencer. When Catherine Brawner protested, the white officer struck both of them in the face.[43]

The violence of white police officers toward black women in Washington was not very different from the treatment they received in the Jim Crow South. In June 1932, Police Officer Timothy J. McDonald located Corinne McCowe, who was currently living at the Phyllis Wheatley YWCA, and arrested her for stabbing her husband. It is telling that McCowe was staying at the YWCA, likely using this institution as a refuge for protection against her abusive spouse. When McCowe resisted arrest, pleading her innocence, McDonald dragged her bodily to the Second Precinct Police Station. McCowe was later released when it was revealed that she was not the wanted person, and she pleaded her innocence in Police Court, but she was found guilty of disorderly conduct.[44] McCowe, like many other victims, expressed a great deal of bravery in appearing in Police Court. Although she, like many others, did not win, her use of the legal system was a form of political activism.

Not only did police officers attack black women but they also assaulted citizens who tried to stop police brutality. On Thursday December 8, 1932, in the evening, two black women—Virgie Togood, who was pregnant, and her sister-in-law Mattie Ford—were walking toward Garfield Park in Southeast Washington when a police car pulled up and the officers began to shout disparaging remarks, yelling, "Hello babies, hello sweethearts." When Ford protested, the officers jumped from their car and slapped her. At that moment, George W. Beasley, an African American druggist and president of the Federation of Civic Associations, was closing his store with two companions when he noticed the altercation. Beasley appealed with the officers to stop assaulting Ford, reportedly pleading, "Don't do that." The officers responded by ordering Beasley and his two companions to line up against the fence. There an officer drew a pistol and rubbed it against their heads, threatening to "blow their brains out." While the officers were assaulting Beasley and his companions, Virgie Togood and Mattie Ford escaped. A newspaper article on this event noted that Garfield Park had been the site of many attacks on black women. As the owner of a drugstore in this neighborhood, Beasley exercised caution and always made sure that his customers "received protection on their way home" in the evenings.[45] This episode demonstrated that black bystanders were often powerless to stop white violence against black women. As the president of the Federation of Civic Associations, Beasley used his local influence to charge the officers in Police Court, but as in most such cases, the police officers were exonerated from all charges.[46] This attack prompted the *Baltimore Afro-American* to run a headline article titled "D.C. Cops Terror to Women," which underscored the escalating police violence toward black women in the city.[47]

In August 1933, a misunderstanding escalated into a case of brutality. Alberta Young, a fifty-four-year-old black woman who lived on Morris Road in Southeast Washington, testified in Police Court about an incident of police brutality following her attempt to secure welfare assistance for her brother, Roy Henderson. When a white welfare worker arrived at her house and mistook her for Henderson's wife, Alberta Young asked the woman to leave. The welfare worker reported the incident to the police, who came to the house and brutally assaulted both Alberta and her fifty-six-year-old husband, William Young, charging them with disorderly conduct. Alberta Young sued the officers in Police Court, appearing with a "blood bandage around her head and a wound that required six stitches to close." Despite the palpable evidence of Young's abuse, the judges in Police Court sided with the police officers rather than the victim.[48]

In October 1933, Ollie Rice, a maid at the Spanish Embassy in Washington, D.C., contacted the local branch of the NAACP, where she requested a meeting with President Jennie Richardson McGuire. In their meeting, Rice informed McGuire that an employee of the Spanish Embassy had tried to rape her. McGuire immediately reported the incident to the Spanish Embassy, discovering that the attempted rapist held diplomatic immunity through the Spanish Legation. She then reached out to the U.S. State Department to determine if there was any way to seek justice for Ollie Rice.[49] While this was not a case of police brutality, the unique circumstances of international law illustrated that black servants in Washington, D.C., were vulnerable to multiple forms of violence and that their perpetrators were rarely punished.

One of the worst episodes of brutality in the early 1930s occurred one month later with the beating of two black women— Cornelia Diggs, an elderly woman in her sixties, and her daughter Dedia Coates—in the middle of the night, described at the beginning of the chapter. Both women lived in Anacostia, a working-class neighborhood in Southeast Washington. At 2:00 A.M. on Tuesday, November 8, 1933, two white police officers, W. W. Humphreys and Henry Marzurski, fired shots into her home, striking a buffet in the kitchen and breaking glass near the stairs. The two police officers broke down two doors, and then bounded up the stairs, grabbed Diggs from her bedroom, and "dragged her by the hair from her bedroom to the first floor of the house and brutally beat her and her forty-eight year old daughter, Mrs. Dedia Coates." Diggs was still dressed in her nightclothes and later testified that she smelled alcohol on the breath of both policemen. The officers arrested both Diggs and Coates and took them to the Eleventh Police Precinct where they were charged with disorderly conduct. A reporter from the *Baltimore Afro-American* who visited Diggs in jail noted that she had "two blackened eyes, a badly battered face, and bruises about the shoulders and left leg."[50]

When black Washingtonians learned about these brutal beatings, they worked to ensure that Diggs and Coates could see some justice. Both Ivory Brown from the Hillsdale Civic Association in Anacostia and Jennie McGuire from the NAACP demanded a thorough police investigation into the beating.[51] Four months after their attack, Diggs and Coates appeared before the Police Court and were acquitted of their alleged crimes.[52] That same month, McGuire worked through the State Department to acquire a cash settlement for Ollie Rice, who, as mentioned earlier, was the victim of an attempted rape at the Spanish Embassy.[53] Diggs's, Coates's, and Rice's legal victories were rare. The only other known episode when police were held responsible for violence against black women occurred when Police Officer Middleton slapped Dorothy Wood. A fellow policeman, Officer Sanderson, observed this violence and felt it was uncalled for, forcing Officer Middleton to pay a fine.[54]

Black women were sometimes brutalized when they were arrested. In July 1934, the manager of the Atlantic Beer Gardens on Fourteenth Street in Northwest Washington had Ida Lindey, age twenty-two, arrested and charged with drunk and disorderly conduct. Lindey claimed that the white police officer "slapped her, threw her to the ground, and placed his knees on her breast." The officer reportedly stated that Lindey "really deserved it" and "should have been given a good beating."[55]

Middle-class black women used their social and political networks to protest gendered police violence. Corinne Martin, a teacher and assistant director of penmanship in the city's black public schools, served as a key activist in the campaign to end brutality. Martin's administrative position put her in contact with many different residents of the city, including students, parents, fellow teachers, and other administrators. In 1929, she was elected president of the East Central Civic Association, which represented the middle-class neighborhoods of Shaw and LeDroit Park in Northwest Washington.[56] In 1933, after the attacks against Virgie Togood and Mattie Ford, Corinne Martin led a delegation of black citizens to meet with Police Commissioner Ernest J. Brown of the police. At the meeting, Martin expressed concerns about the rising levels of brutality, especially the recent attacks against participants in the unemployment march. She told Commissioner Brown that the "brutal beating of half starved unarmed men and women by stalwart police" was "unnecessary" and urged him to pay closer attention to the actions of various police officers. Martin and members of the East Central Civic Association also presented Brown with a chart that starkly outlined the disproportionately few black police officers in the city: it showed that there was one white police officer or fire fighter for every 153 white people, in contrast to one black police officer or fire fighter for every 2,047 black residents. At this meeting, Brown was "visibly impressed with the facts presented by the committee" and "promised to look into the complaints" that were presented.[57] One month later in April 1933, Martin boldly declared that police brutality in Washington, D.C., posed a greater threat to American democracy than communism. She highlighted the recent example of Major Jones, who after leaving a barbershop was brutally attacked by two white police officers.[58] Martin's declaration positioned the threats of interracial police brutality as greater than those posed by communism and other forms of political radicalism, both in the United

States and around the world. This remark was especially provocative given the Red Scare in the United States, which had occurred not that long ago in 1919.

The Southwest Civic Group represented working-class residents of Southwest Washington, and women held several prominent leadership positions in the organization: Inez W. Clomax, a beauty operator, served as secretary, Mary Proctor was the vice president, and Lillian Dodson was the assistant vice president. In June 1933, its members held a meeting at Randall Junior High School with a special guest, Illinois representative Oscar DePriest, who was African American; his presence was noteworthy since he was the first black man to serve in Congress since 1901. At the meeting, residents discussed police violence in their section of the city. DePriest emphasized the "power to be wielded by an organization" and "advised block organization for real tangible service and contact."[59] The fact that members of the Southwest Civic Group reached out to a national politician to address their local concerns in Washington suggests that they felt a lack of responsiveness from the local commissioners.

A turning point in black women's activism toward violence occurred in December 1934 when, as described in chapter 2, police officers moved quickly to arrest NAACP members who were picketing the National Crime Conference. Police officers informed activists that they lacked a permit to protest and were holding signs that exceeded the legal size limit. Ten years earlier, these regulations had not existed. This moment signaled not only the hostility of Washington, D.C., police officers to political protests but also the surge in police violence in the nation's capital over the past several years, whether it was shots fired against unarmed black men or brutal force directed toward innocent black women. The arrests of the demonstrators echoed police violence toward black citizens in the city. They marked a watershed for anti-lynching activists, causing them to shift their attention toward combatting police brutality in Washington, D.C. Women and men applied the methods, institutional networks, and grassroots constituencies used in their fight for a federal anti-lynching bill to the local campaign of police violence.

Are Cops Brutal? Violence and Activism

By the mid-1930s, police brutality against women and men had increased across the city, but officers rarely faced professional consequences for their actions. Black citizens witnessed Officer George Struder beat a ninety-eight-pound black woman on the street, who was mentally ill. Struder's force was so intense that blood trickled from the location of the assault all the way to the call box.

When a local bystander, Eva Moxley, a widow in her thirties, observed this abuse, she asked Struder to stop beating the woman, and in response he promptly arrested her for disorderly conduct. While a judge in Police Court exonerated Moxley of the charges, Officer Struder kept his job.[60] In another instance, thirty-seven-year-old Georgia Watkins observed Officer N. T. Imlay killing a dog. When she protested, Officer Imlay attacked and arrested her for disorderly conduct; he was never punished.[61]

In April 1935, Jeanette Kidd, a single woman in her thirties who lived in a working-class neighborhood in Southwest Washington, charged that three white detectives broke into her house and grabbed her without consent, dragged her through the streets, and then struck her in the mouth. When she sued the officers in Police Court, the bruises on her body were still visible, but that made no difference to the legal outcome. Police officers charged that Kidd had, in fact, assaulted them, causing spectators in the court to laugh hysteri-cally.[62] The white judge sustained Kidd's charges of disorderly conduct while levying no punishment on the white officers.

The fact that police officers were rarely punished for police brutality often meant that they attacked multiple victims. In 1933, Detective Frank Ashley had used iron clamps as an instrument to force George Mahoney, a black man, to confess to a crime. Two years later, that same detective was hunting for a suspect who was Filipino. Without a warrant, he barged into the home of Mildred de Arellano, an African American woman who was married to the assistant secretary of the Philippine Trade Commission. Detective Ashley insulted both de Arellano and her mother, Jennie V. Peters, and even knocked Peters to the ground in his search for the suspect. He rifled through a desk in the house look-ing for incriminating evidence, but found none. Out of frustration, he report-edly shouted at the women that "niggers have no constitutional rights. The Constitution was made by and for white men."[63] Detective Ashley faced no professional consequences for his physical violence, unlawful entry, or verbal abuse against de Arellano and Peters.

In July 1935, black newspapers reported that Jessie Sterling, a fifty-nine-year-old woman, was another victim of police brutality. Sterling had smelled gas escaping from the pipes in her home at 807 Virginia Avenue in Southwest Washington. While Sterling had worked as a domestic servant during the 1920s, she had also supported herself in the underground economy through drug dis-tribution, earning the nickname "Sweets."[64] When she went out on her porch to call police for help, two white police officers, D. H. Mayo and George B. Reid, happened to be passing by in their patrol car. Officer Reid reportedly shouted at her, "Sweets, get back in the house." When Sterling protested,

Officer Reid forced her into the house and violently beat her. Reid's beating was so brutal that, when he was finished, Jessie Sterling had a black eye, scraped knees, a broken arm, and two missing teeth.[65] Officer Reid then arrested Sterling, charging her with disorderly conduct. Sterling claimed that Officer Reid also beat her in the Fourth Police Precinct.[66] In her study of black women in the underground economy in New York City, the historian LaShawn Harris argues that white police officers sometimes took advantage of black women who labored in the underground economy and framed them for crimes they did not commit.[67]

Sterling's assault prompted a response from black citizens and organizations across the city. The black press vigilantly monitored the case, and reporters interviewed Sterling in her house. A newspaper article in the *Baltimore Afro-American* titled "Are Cops Brutal?" featured a photograph of Sterling, providing a visual narrative of the violence inflicted on her body. A reporter noted that Sterling's left face and arms were "permanently disfigured" and her left eye sustained injuries that could not heal. This assault would remain visible for the rest of her life, most notably with the gaps in her mouth caused by the missing teeth. While reporters in the black press diligently circulated news of Sterling's assault, political organizations strategized about a legal response. Members of the Southwest Civic Association banded together to protest her beating, and its president, John T. Rhines, appointed a five-person committee to investigate mounting cases of brutality.[68] The local chapter of the NAACP also joined the fight. Jennie McGuire was no longer president of the local branch, but other women, including Nannie Helen Burroughs and YWCA executive secretary Martha A. McAdoo, were active in the organization's leadership. In a letter to the police, NAACP secretary Archibald S. Pinkett argued, "Nobody believes that a policeman is justified in blacking a woman's eye, bruising her body, and breaking her arms in attempt to maintain arrest."[69]

In August, Jessie Sterling appeared in Police Court where she pled not guilty. Only one month after the incident, Sterling's injuries were visible to all present. However, as a newspaper article noted, "A photograph and testimony of witnesses" were unable to persuade the judge of Sterling's innocence and Officer Reid's guilt.[70] Judge Robert E. Mattingly upheld Sterling's sentence and fined her for disorderly conduct. Five years earlier, Judge Mattingly had similarly upheld charges of disorderly conduct for Ida Wheeler Turner, who had been suffering from memory loss when Officer Fredette knocked her down, hitting her hard and damaging her eyesight. Black citizens were incensed that Officer Reid escaped punishment. James R. Cobb, a black municipal judge and civil rights activist in the city, arranged for Reid to be tried by a grand jury for his crimes, but it also found Officer Reid innocent.[71] Officer Reid already had a grim record on police brutality, having previously been involved in the death of another innocent black man, Daniel Woodland.[72]

This disturbing trend of officers attacking multiple victims continued in March 1936, when Martha and Ruth Lloyd, Dunbar High School sisters who were seventeen and fifteen years old, respectively, were traveling by bus from their school's cadet drill practice to their home. When their bus stopped at Tennessee Avenue and Fourteenth Street in Northeast, the sisters disembarked into the midst of a riot that was unfolding on the streets. While the sisters were running to escape the violence, a white man who was a police officer but was dressed in plain clothes grabbed Martha and pinned her to the ground. A uniformed police officer arrived at the scene and arrested both Martha and Ruth Lloyd, who had protested her sister's arrest. Officers grabbed the sisters and threw them into a police car where Officer John Sirola beat Martha on the head with a blackjack. In Police Court, Sirola defended his use of force, stating that Martha had "sassed him." Judge Isaac R. Hitt ruled that sixteen-year-old Martha Lloyd was guilty, upheld her charge of disorderly conduct, and fined her five dollars.[73] Historians have written that not all black girls enjoyed the rights and privileges of childhood, and Officer Sirola's treatment toward Martha and Ruth Lloyd reflected that sentiment.[74] Moreover, Officer Sirola had a history of violence. Five years earlier, Officers Sirola and Vivian Landrum had barged into the house of Henry Johnson, a veteran of World War I who worked as a Pullman porter. Both officers beat him with a blackjack and broke his skull. He sued them in Police Court for damages, and Sirola and Landrum were suspended from duty.[75] But in Criminal Court, Landrum was charged with simple assault and fined $100, while Sirola was acquitted.[76] That Sirola hit twenty-five-year-old Henry Johnson with a blackjack and received no punishment meant that five years later he was free to wield the same weapon on seventeen-year-old Martha Lloyd.

The attacks in the mid-1930s demonstrated that police brutality was an epidemic in Washington, D.C. In attacking black residents, white police officers in the city did not discriminate on the basis of age, sex, or mental fitness, which resulted in brutal treatment toward girls like Martha and Ruth Lloyd, elderly women like Cornelia Diggs and Jessie Sterling, and mentally ill women like Ida Wheeler Turner. Just as enslaved women were beaten and women in the Jim Crow era were lynched, black women were assaulted by the police in Washington, D.C., sometimes at the hands of the same officers who had attacked and shot black men. If police officers brutalized one victim and received little to no punishment, they were likely to repeat this behavior.

Between 1936 and 1938, black political organizations in the city united to address the epidemic of police brutality. The diversity of organizations that joined this movement reflected the complexity of black politics in Washington. Established organizations, such as the local branch of the NAACP, the Phyllis Wheatley YWCA, and the Federation of Civic Associations, were joined by newcomers founded in the 1930s: the Washington Interracial Committee (IRC), the National Negro Congress, and the New Negro Alliance. The IRC viewed interracial alliances as a fundamental resource to securing civil rights in the city, while the National Negro Congress and New Negro Alliance were left-leaning organizations that infused militancy into the struggle for justice in the nation's capital. Additionally, members of the local Morningstar Lodge of the Elks held a fundraising drive to secure legal funds for the fight against police brutality, and the Civil Liberties Bureau of the Elks brought their political expertise to bear on the issue.[77] While these organizations drew members from all corners of the black community in Washington, women emerged as crucial voices.

In particular, grassroots participants and veteran organizers from the anti-lynching movement joined the campaign to end police brutality. Arnetta Randall, a teacher who had taken part in the Rope Protests in 1934, was elected secretary of the New Negro Alliance; Natalie Moorman, a member of the Phyllis Wheatley YWCA, was a prominent member of the same group.[78] Five black women served on the board of the IRC: civic leader Mary Church Terrell, pharmacist Amanda Gray Hilyer, physicians Sarah Brown and Ionia Whipper, and teacher Mae Stewart Thompson. All of these women were also members of the Phyllis Wheatley YWCA. Terrell had marched in the Silent Parade and testified in Congress about the Dyer Bill. Jennie Richardson McGuire had organized the Rope Protests under the auspices of the NAACP; she then headed the local chapter of the National Negro Congress.[79] One woman who typified this political transformation from national to local politics was Theresa Lee Connelly Robinson. During the 1920s, as Theresa Lee Connelly, she had served as chair of the Committee of One Hundred, which mobilized churches, fraternal orders, schools, ministers, and social and political organizations to march in the Silent Parade against lynching in 1922. In the late 1920s, her husband died, and in the early 1930s, she remarried and became known as Theresa Lee Robinson. In the 1930s, Theresa Lee Robinson coordinated the police brutality effort as the assistant national chair of the Civil Liberties Bureau of the Elks.[80]

These examples not only illuminate the connections between lynching and police brutality but also underscore women's widespread participation as leaders, participants, and grassroots organizers. Black women shaped the police brutality movement in important ways. They brought their organizing skills to various political campaigns, helping spearhead mass meetings, protest parades, and petition drives. And within each organization, they described interracial political brutality as a gendered process that claimed both male and female victims.

Washington activists in the police brutality movement employed several strategies that they had tested in their anti-lynching campaigns. First, they used their location in the nation's capital to seek federal assistance. After meeting with several members in Congress, they found an ally in Byron N. Scott, a newly elected representative from California's 18th District, who agreed to introduce a resolution in the U.S. House of Representatives to launch a federal investigation into police brutality in Washington, D.C. The fact that black Washingtonians could turn to the House of Representatives for support in their local campaign against police brutality illustrated the unique political benefits of residency in the nation's capital. On January 19, 1937, Representative Byron Scott proposed House Resolution 77 calling for an "investigation of police brutality in the District of Columbia."[81]

At the same time that Representative Scott introduced his resolution in Congress, members of the IRC banded together with thirty organizations in the city to bring the issue of police violence to the Board of Commissioners. These local organizations then had federal leverage in their fight. IRC chair Charles Edward Russell, a white journalist, told the commissioners that it was unacceptable that fifty citizens had died at the hands of the police in less than ten years. Russell also emphasized that Washington's culture of violence included "cases of brutal beatings by police, invasion of homes of colored people without warrants, and the case of an officer who alleged criminally assaulted the wife of a colored man." He stated that, with one exception, all of the officers were still employed.[82] It is telling that Russell's assessment of police violence included male and female victims, which speaks to the influence of the five black women who served on the IRC board.

In addition to meeting with members of Congress and the Board of Commissioners, activists worked with different forms of media to ensure that police brutality did not disappear from black public consciousness, both in Washington and across the nation. They wrote press releases to maintain coverage of brutality in the black press. And on two occasions, activists addressed police brutality over the radio. In March 1937, National Negro Congress representative John P. Davis delivered an address on station WOL. Davis emphasized that while much media attention focused on male victims, "such assaults have not been confined to men or adults." He specifically mentioned the cases of Martha Lloyd, Jessie Sterling, and Eva Moxley.[83] By reciting the names of these women over the radio, Davis helped alert Washington's large black community about violence against women, perhaps reaching citizens whom the pages of the press did not. One month later, Representative Byron Scott appeared in a separate broadcast. He questioned why the Board of Commissioners "oppose such an unbiased search for truth on this question, in the light of the serious charges lodged with them." He also highlighted the lawlessness that existed in the nation's capital. "When the third degree is substituted for the judicial process and when punishment is meted out at the time of arrest by a policeman's night stick instead of by judges in a court of law," he stated, "then anarchy replaces the democratic process."[84] Representative Scott's politically charged words likely resonated with black citizens who had grown weary of acquittal after acquittal of brutal white police officers.

In addition to radio addresses, the IRC published a pamphlet that demonstrated that police violence in the nation's capital was not episodic, but an epidemic. Just as Ida B. Wells had tracked lynchings and analyzed them in publications to illuminate patterns, activists in the police brutality movement used searing language and selected disturbing examples to highlight the crisis of interracial brutality. Harlan Glazier, a white activist in the IRC, titled his pamphlet "Brutality Enthroned (with apologies to the Animals)," which provocatively argued that, for black citizens, the rule of law did not exist in Washington, D.C. "If any person should permit a mad dog to run at large," Glazier argued, "he would be denounced as a menace to the community; and yet, in this District of Chaos, our officials, over whom we have no control, allow the police of the city to commit crimes of the most dastardly sort against our citizenry."[85] The pamphlet summarized the scope of brutality cases in the 1930s, including examples of violence against both men and women. Glazier emphasized that half of the victims were shot in the back, which indicated that victims did not even know there was a potential for death.[86] He argued that the situation of police brutality in Washington, D.C., was "truly critical." The pamphlet concluded by encouraging readers to pressure Congress to end the crisis of brutality in Washington.[87]

Black citizens recognized that replacing existing judges in Police Court with fairer ones would help reduce the incidence of brutality throughout the city. In March 1937, black citizens gathered in a mass meeting at the Phyllis Wheatley YWCA. The term of one Police Court judge was set to expire, and meeting attendees vowed to lobby the Board of Commissioners to appoint a fair judge to succeed him.[88] Several days later, a delegation of black citizens sent a petition to the Board of Commissioners requesting that an African American serve as a judge on the city's Police Court. Prominent among those signatories was Nannie Helen Burroughs, who had personally carried anti-lynching petitions to Congress in 1917 to make lynching a federal crime, and YWCA President Julia West Hamilton, who had served on the planning committee for the Silent Parade in 1922.[89] The activism of Burroughs and Hamilton in local issues mirrored the shifting concerns among many African American women in Washington, D.C.

Despite mass meetings, petitions, pamphlets, radio addresses, and a congressional resolution, police violence persisted. Under these circumstances, activists elected to convene their own trial on police brutality at the storied John Wesley AMEZ Church. This event, which was open to the public, provided an opportunity for the black community in Washington to hear the facts of the different cases of brutality that were dismissed in Police Court and craft their own judgments. Importantly, the activists defined brutality as both murders and beatings, which allowed a discussion of male and female victims. This "trial" illustrated two important aspects of black political culture in the nation's capital. First, black Washingtonians, whether by virtue of their close proximity to Howard University Law School or the Supreme Court; or their eagerness to plead individual cases in Police Court, were litigious citizens, deeply familiar with the law and legal proceedings; this knowledge would prove helpful in their campaigns for economic justice and civil rights. Second, this community trial bespoke a fundamental aspect of black citizens' quest for justice in the United States. In their campaigns for black freedom, African Americans were merely asking for a fair trial in court, to be presided over by judges who took an oath to uphold the law of democracy and fairness. Judges in this trial included YMCA director Campbell Johnson, Howard University dean of women Lucy Slowe, Reverend Robert W. Brooks of the Lincoln Congregational Church, and Stephen Gill Spotswood, bishop of the African Methodist Episcopal Zion Church. A newspaper article noted that this public trial "provided a complete picture of the lawless police terrors which has reigned in Washington for the past ten years."[90] Through this act of political theater, some of the involved parties could symbolically witness justice being meted out to their perpetrators and receive the support of the black community.

Activists amplified their protest message in 1938. Natalie Moorman, a resident of Arlington, Virginia, who was affiliated with the New Negro Alliance, the Phyllis Wheatley YWCA, and the American Youth Congress, testified at a congressional hearing on the American Youth Act in March 1938.[91] In her testimony, Moorman urged the government to create programs for youth to promote their education, health, and, most importantly, safety. She began her testimony by saying that she could "talk perhaps 2 days about things that would be of interest here," but "decided to tell only one story." Before an audience of senators and representatives, Natalie Moorman described a recent case in which a seventeen-year-old boy in Arlington who burglarized a grocery store "was shot down by Arlington County deputies." She soberly noted, "There was no inquest and there was no investigation"; the lesson to be drawn was that "colored boys should not break into company stores" because they will become victims of police violence.[92] In her testimony, Moorman argued that economic injustice and a lack of a support system led to social disorder, as manifested as robberies. She pointed out that the boy's father was missing and his mother was in a state insane asylum. He was forced to support himself, which led to his crime, and ultimately, his death. Moorman's testimony powerfully illuminated the inhumanity of police violence and helped keep the focus on brutality in Washington, D.C.

In June 1938, representatives of a coalition of thirty organizations across the city—including churches, fraternal orders, and interracial organizations—met for two hours with a member of the Board of Commissioners, Melvin C. Hazen. In the meeting, Reverend Brooks, chair of the Committee of Churches, told Hazen that African Americans in Washington, D.C., "feared the police."[93] The fact that thirty organizations were organized against brutality not only reflected this issue's importance to the black community in Washington but also the strength of black political culture across Washington, D.C. Given the fact that black Washingtonians had exhausted other options, activists decided to stage a protest parade against police brutality in the nation's capital.

On the evening of Friday, July 9, 1938 in the evening, 400 white citizens and 1,600 black citizens staged a march against police brutality. The Washington branch of the Communist Party sponsored the parade, which lasted three hours and was endorsed by the National Negro Congress and the New Negro Alliance. Protesters started marching at the intersection of U and Fourth Streets in Northwest Washington and ended at Rhode Island Avenue and Ninth Streets. A crowd of ten thousand Washingtonians lined the route and witnessed its activist message. Mollie Davis McKnight, a laundress and widow of a recent victim of police violence, was a key figure in the parade. Mollie and her late husband, Wallace McKnight, had migrated to Washington, D.C., during the 1920s from South Carolina, along with Mollie's brother, View Davis.[94] Earlier that month, Wallace McKnight had been walking along Fifteenth and M Streets NW, carrying a large bag. Police officers stopped him to question him about the contents of the bag, and he began to run away; in response the police officers fired a shot that killed him instantly. The police officer was found guilty of manslaughter.[95] The National Negro Congress would later sue the city, but only won Mollie McKnight $85 in damages.[96]

The parade marchers had originally intended to carry black coffins to symbolize the victims of brutality, but police officers forbade them from doing so. Marchers instead carried signs that illustrated their protests against brutality; they read, "You May Be Next," "Prosecute Police Murders," and, perhaps most chillingly, "Washington Is Now Scottsboro."[97] By evoking the recent episode of racial injustice in Scottsboro, Alabama, in which nine African American teenage boys had been accused of raping two white women and were sentenced to death, protesters mounted an argument that police actions in the nation's capital resembled the worst practices of injustice in the Jim Crow South and that, before justice could be achieved nationally, it was necessary to intervene in local politics in the District of Columbia.

In the parade, protesters and police officers battled over boundaries of resistance and domination. In addition to barring coffins, police officers also forbade protesters from carrying signs and signatures that demanded the immediate dismissal of Major Ernest Brown. But protesters cleverly devised ways to convey their message without text. "Inspector Kelly took the signs," an article in the *Washington Afro-American* noted, "but the marchers did him one better by chanting 'Major Brown Must Go.'" This clever adjustment evoked the 1934 Rope Protests when activists replaced large signs with rope on their necks. In addition to repeating this activist message over and over, protesters also chanted "Police Brutality Must Stop," "Join the Big Parade," and "Stop Legal Lynching." By terming police brutality "legal lynching," marchers offered a powerful message that violence in their city mirrored the everyday terrors that black southerners confronted on a daily basis.

Important parallels, but also key differences, can be discerned between the anti-lynching parade in 1922 and the police brutality parade in 1938. Both parades rallied significant numbers of black citizens from all walks of life who carried protest signs to press for justice against violence. However, changes in black women's politics between these two parades illustrate the dramatic shift in African American activism. The five thousand black participants in the Silent Parade against lynching in 1922 were arranged in various formations according to organizational affiliation, and they circled around federal buildings to influence Congress, using silence as an instrument to draw awareness to their cause. Sixteen years later, the protest crowd was interracial, featuring black and white participants. In 1922 in the aftermath of the first Red Scare, it would have been politically toxic to ally with the Communist Party, but in the leftist climate of the 1930s, this alliance was more acceptable. In their protest against police brutality, participants marched through black and white neighborhoods, thereby illustrating that this parade was a local, and not a national affair, although activists did wish to attract press coverage. Perhaps most tellingly, in 1922, activists had received permission to stage their parade, and its legality had not been an issue. In fact, police officers supported the march and did not appear to question the marchers' paraphernalia, including the size of their signs. Sixteen years later, police and activists battled over the props that protesters carried and the messages emblazoned on their signs. The differences between these two protests illustrate first and foremost that the Washington Metropolitan Police Department had become much more hostile toward civil rights protests, especially when police actions were the subject of scrutiny.

The protest parade generated coverage in both local and national newspapers, and in its aftermath, activists continued to press for justice. In August 1938, the Washington Interdenominational Ministers' Alliance spearheaded a petition drive with the goal of sending fifty thousand signatures from black and white Washingtonians to President Roosevelt calling on him to personally intervene in cases of brutality.[98] Forging a coalition with ministers across the city, leaders advised them to educate congregants about brutality in their Sunday sermons and to urge them to sign these petitions.[99]

As citizens in Washington, D.C., channeled their energy into protesting and halting police brutality, they could point to a few small victories. Marshaling the support of thirty organizations across the city, activists found an ally in Congress, addressed the issue over the radio and in pamphlets, held a protest parade, and, most importantly, began to stage their own trials to seek justice when they could not find it in Police Court or the Trial Board.

"Make Washington Safe for Negro Womanhood": The Persistence of Violence

Despite citizens' coordinated campaigns against brutality, officers continued to attack black Washingtonians. On August 10, 1938, shortly after 5 A.M., three police officers banged on the door of Julia McKay's boarding house at 1340 Corcoran Street in Northwest Washington and demanded to be let in. McKay, a widow who worked as a seamstress and also ran the boarding house, was a prominent citizen of Washington who mingled in social reform circles, including the Tuesday Evening Club, which was an association of middle-class social workers. In 1940, eleven other women lived in her house.[100] The police officers were looking for a man named "Manassas" and asked to speak to Ruth

Clark, a black domestic worker who rented a room on the third floor. They entered her room, demanding to know if she was alone. Using a flashlight, they searched underneath her bed. One of the police officers also took his billy club and punched her in the stomach, uttering racial epithets at her and calling her a "god damn nigger." The woman in question, Ruth Clark, had moved to Washington, D.C., from Troy, Virginia, in 1930, and she worked as a maid for a physician. Clark's friend, Dorothy Brice, who worked as a beautician, submitted an affidavit in which she confirmed Clark's story.[101] Clark's experiences with police brutality underscore the collective nature of trauma and abuse. Because Clark lived as a boarder in a home filled with other women, all residents experienced that trauma.

This episode of brutality prompted black citizens in various organizations to speak out. Charles M. Thomas, civil liberties director of the Elks, told a reporter from the *Washington Post* that "support for anti-lynching legislation must be coupled with protests against police brutality" that would ensure "civil liberty for us all."[102] In this message, Thomas offered a rhetorical linkage between the dual imperatives of anti-lynching and anti-police violence legislation. This article was the first coverage given by the *Washington Post* of black protests against brutality. Additionally, activists in the National Negro Congress for the first time addressed the gendered nature of police brutality by issuing an open letter in August 1938 to the black women of Washington, D.C., titled "Make Washington Safe for Negro Womanhood." While the letter was unsigned, its deep familiarity with the intersections between gender, race, and safety in Washington suggests a female author, possibly Jennie Richard McGuire, who was the local chair. The letter began with this statement: "Dear Friends, if you are a colored woman enthroned in your house at five o'clock in the morning and a police sergeant weighing some three hundred pounds pushes his night stick onto your stomach and calls you a God Damn Nigger, there is NOTHING you can do about it." The letter writer stated that she had taken five witnesses to the district attorney's office and asked that a warrant be issued for Sergeant Sullivan, who had assaulted Ruth Clark. The district attorney, Mr. Underwood, declined to issue a warrant and insisted that no assault had taken place. The letter writer asked, "What would have happened if Miss Clark had been a white woman and Sergeant Sullivan had been a Negro Officer?"

The letter writer further argued that the Ruth Clark case fit into larger patterns of brutality against black citizens in Washington, D.C., where injustice stretched from the district attorney to rank-and-file police officers. "What happened to Miss Ruth Clark," the writer warned, "can and will happen to any other decent, self-respecting Negro woman of Washington and ACT NOW." She urged black citizens to sign their names to a petition to be forwarded to President Roosevelt, calling on "three thousand women of Washington representing the clubs and churches to not only sign their names to this petition, but to ask the petitions to be circulated to their friends for signature." She invited people to "collect 20,000 signatures to be sent to the President within the next ten days to demand that Washington be made a safe place for Negro womanhood."[103] This letter articulated the specific forms of injustice that afflicted black women, including verbal threats, physical intimidation, and vulnerability to sexual assault and rape.

One month after Ruth Clark's assault, the Washington Federation of Colored Women's Clubs of the District of Columbia held a meeting at the Phyllis Wheatley YWCA, where they endorsed the National Negro Congress and its campaign against police brutality. The women who signed onto this campaign included Marian Butler, Julia West Hamilton, and Nannie Helen Burroughs, all of whom were seasoned anti-lynching activists.[104] This endorsement demonstrated that African American women in the local chapter of the NACW were cognizant of the mounting violence—specifically the violence aimed at black women—and supported this organization in its fight against brutality.

Violence continued to afflict women and men across the city. In February 1939, police broke into the rented room of Viola Harris at 115 G Street NW, where they attacked her, Leroy Moses, and Lillie Watson. The National Negro Congress conducted an investigation of the incident.[105] Five months later in July 1939, Ethel McKinney was out walking with her mother, Frances James, on Fourteenth and Irving Streets in Northwest Washington. The two were peering into a store window when a white police officer, Charles S. Mills, "ran between them and knocked them aside." He reportedly shook James and knocked McKinney backward. As she extended her hands to protect herself, Officer Mills slammed into her body and threatened to knock her teeth out. The only protection McKinney had was her shoes, which she wielded as a weapon of self-defense. Officer Mills then threatened to "blow her head off" and hurled racial epithets at her. As James watched Officer Mills attack her daughter, she tried to wedge her body in between them. Two boys walking down the street witnessed the incident and scolded the cop, telling him "not draw a gun out on a girl like that."

In July, Ethel McKinney and Frances James filed suit in District Court for damages of $10,000 for verbal abuse, beating, and mental anguish. Officer Mills pled not guilty to the charges.[106] Newspaper articles about the McKinney and James case were quick to point out their class background and respectability.

Ethel McKinney was a secretary for the D.C. School Board and the wife of Roscoe L. McKinney, a professor of embryology and zoology at the Howard University Medical School. She also sued for damages in Police Court and received money for her troubles. It is possible that the elite status of Ethel McKinney might have been a factor in her acquittal and being awarded damages.[107]

The summer of 1940 proved dangerous for black citizens. On Sunday, June 9, the police entered the home of William and Susan Anderson at 2430 Snow's Court. The police officer assaulted and beat William; his wife Susan, who was pregnant at the time; and his sister, dragging all of them off to jail. The officer was never charged. One month later, in July 1940, Dorothy Bowles, a "hard working and law abiding Negro citizen," was involved in a conflict with a neighbor on K Street in Northeast Washington. A police officer who intervened in the dispute kicked and bruised her in the breast, and a judge in Police Court sentenced Bowles to a year of probation. A flier for a mass meeting distributed by the Citizens Committee against Police Brutality mentioned the Bowles incident and announced, "Do Your Part: Stop this Atrocious beating of innocent Negroes before you yourself are the next victim!!!!!"[108] That same month, one hundred men and women gathered in a mass meeting at the Zion Baptist Church to protest police brutality, especially those acts committed against residents in the Fourth Police Precinct.[109]

In September 1940, activists gathered at the Metropolitan Baptist Church to stage another mock trial. In the 1920s, that church had been one of the principal sites for black women's anti-lynching prayer protests, and in 1940 it was a place where black citizens staged a mock trial to seek justice when it was not being meted out at the local level. Belford V. Lawson, a lawyer who had represented many women in Police Court, including Frances James and Ethel McKinney, served as the defense lawyer. A number of women served as messengers, including Beatrice Morton, Thelma Dale, Marcella Moore, Charlotte Payne, Rachel Robinson, Marie Richardson, and Alice Wright. Women's participation at the trial signaled not only their interest in the epidemic of violence but also their desire to address racialized violence against women.[110]

While citizens continued to protest police brutality, other forms of violence against women emerged. Between 1939 and 1941, an unknown perpetrator began to attack black women in the nation's capital. Four black women—Josephine Robinson, Lucy Kidwell, Mattie Steward, and Ada Puller—were raped and murdered, while other black women, including Florence Dancy and Cora Doy, were robbed and attacked. The white press did not cover these deaths when they occurred, and police officers conducted minimal investigations to locate the culprit. While these murders did not occur at the hands of the police, the police department's apathetic response signaled an institutional culture of racialized negligence around black women's safety in the city, which was itself a form of brutality.[111]

This profound indifference toward black women was thrown into sharp relief in June 1941 when Jesse Elizabeth "Betty" Strieff, a twenty-two-year-old white clerk from Iowa, was raped and murdered. News of Strieff's murder made local and national headlines.[112] Representative Felix Edward Hèbert, a Democratic representative from Louisiana who served on the Committee on the District of Columbia, used Strieff's murder as an opportunity to conduct a federal investigation into the Washington Metropolitan Police Department. As Representative Hèbert argued, "There is no excuse for the failure of the department to check crime and solve a murder occasionally."[113] Only days before the official hearing, Mabel Everett, a black woman, was raped and murdered, presumably by the same killer.[114] It was noteworthy that Strieff's murder sparked a congressional investigation into the Police Department. Four years earlier, black Washingtonians had worked tirelessly to engage senators and representatives on the issue of police violence in the nation's capital. Although Representative Byron N. Scott had then agreed to issue a resolution on police brutality, no investigation materialized.

Over a period of two weeks in June and July 1941, the Committee on the District of Columbia convened hearings about the Washington Metropolitan Police Department. They were notable for what was said and what was omitted. Members of the House of Representatives and witnesses from the police department limited their discussion about gendered violence to Betty Strieff, ignoring the five black women who had also died and especially the most recent murder victim, Mabel Everett. Moreover, at several points during the hearings, Representative Hèbert justified the use of police brutality against black Washingtonians based on their alleged rates of crime by arguing, "Force begets force." He contended that black citizens were lawless and suggested that Washington police officers needed to locate "a way to handle those fellows"; otherwise officers were "going to have trouble." In this stunning statement, Representative Hèbert endorsed the use of police brutality in Washington, D.C., on the floor of the U.S. Congress.[115]

This congressional investigation undermined every aspect of the freedom struggle in black Washington waged for the past twelve years, in which activists had highlighted assaults against black women, protested the persistence of police violence, and sought a federal ally in the fight. Proceedings from the congressional investigation demonstrated that the federal government was not an ally, but a foe. The fact that Representative Hèbert, a Louisiana politician who embodied the mores of the Jim Crow South, could recommend the use of police force against African Americans in the nation's capital demonstrated that black Washingtonians lacked the political power to transform the culture of racialized and gendered violence in their city. In July 1941, an editorial in the *Washington Afro-American* appeared on the front page of the weekly newspaper titled "Don't Blame the Cops." This newspaper, which for the past decade, had been reporting case after case of police violence, provocatively remarked, "The police department is not wholly to blame." The article noted that police officers were men and women who "reflected the temper of the community which, in turn, is reflected by the Congressional chairmans who supervise the departments and have the right at will to probe into its operation." The editorial highlighted the critical importance of race in shaping reactions to Betty Strieff's murder versus those of the unnamed black women in Washington. Posing a powerful, rhetorical question, the editorial asked, "When colored citizens were shot down in cold blood, beaten, and maltreated by the Nazi-minded police officers, did Congress respond to the pleas of civic organizations to investigate?" Furthermore, the editorial described the numerous occasions when "colored girls and women were molested and raped by white perverts who crossed the color line to invade our neighborhoods after dark, was there any investigation of laxity? You may bet your life there wasn't." Discussing the fact that Betty Strieff and Mabel Evertt were murdered in the same month, the article grimly surmised that "Mabel wasn't very important." The editorial concluded by noting, "Is it any wonder that the police have so little regard for colored citizen when the Congressional bosses display such an attitude? At least that's one mystery which has been cleared up."[116]

Ironically, the congressional hearings convinced white Washingtonians that Commissioner Brown was ineffective in his job, an assessment black Washingtonians had been stating in petitions and chanting in protest parades for years. Within days of the congressional investigation, the *Washington Post* published an editorial that called for Ernest Brown to step down as head of the Washington Metropolitan Police.[117]

In August 1941, a black man named Jarvis Roosevelt Cato confessed to murdering six women in Washington, D.C., and one in New York City. Four of his victims were black and three were white.[118] African Americans supported his arrest and prosecution for his crimes, but worked to keep the focus on his black victims, and not on his crimes. An article in the *Baltimore Afro-American* highlighted the Washington Metropolitan Police Department's culture of negligence toward black women. "How through an investigation," the article asked, "did the police make when they found Mrs. Kidwell murdered? Mrs. Florence

Dancy ravished? Mrs. Ada Puller mutilated?" The article argued that the Cato murders "has exposed Washington's race prejudice and bigotry" and that the nation's capital was "blinded by prejudice."[119]

After Commissioner Brown stepped down in August 1941, black Washingtonians persisted in their visible and vocal opposition to police violence. Activists were determined to demonstrate that while certain members of Congress favored police brutality, black Washingtonians did not. Seven prominent citizens formed the Citizen's Committee against Police Brutality. The three women on the committee were government worker Ruby Hawkins, New Negro Alliance member Natalie Moorman, and veteran organizer Theresa Lee Robinson. That the organization's name was similar to the Citizen's Protest Parade Committee, which Theresa Lee Connelly had formed nineteen years earlier, reflected the ways that she applied her skills from the anti-lynching movement to her campaigns against police brutality. In September 1941, the Citizen's Committee against Police Brutality staged a mass march in Washington, D.C., in which an estimated two thousand women, men, and children marched through the streets. Participants carried placards with messages like "Old Jim Crow Has Got to Go," "Protect Our Civil Rights," and "Police Brutality Is a Disgrace to the Nation's Capital."[120] The protest parade route went through several sections of the city, including Northwest, Northeast, and Southeast, with the participants all converging at the corner of Tenth and U Streets in Northwest, which was at the center of the black community. The Citizen's Committee celebrated its collaboration with the Congress of Industrial Organizations in the parade.[121] The militancy of this protest parade demonstrated that black citizens were absolutely livid with the level of violence in their city. Terming Jim Crow "Old," they declared that they, a newer generation of activists, refused to accept that system of race relations. Calling police brutality a "disgrace" in the nation's capital indicated their awareness of international diplomacy and the reality that the United States was headed toward war. Staging a militant parade during this vulnerable time in the nation's political culture—when the country was on the brink of entering World War II—bespoke activists' calculation to abolish police brutality in the nation's capital.

Major Edward J. Kelly was named the new police commissioner in August 1941. Kelly was familiar with black activism. He had been present when African Americans staged the Rope Protests at the Crime Conference in 1934 and affirmed then that the participants' signs conformed to police regulations. He had also been an officer on duty during the 1938 protest against police brutality.[122] When Kelly was appointed, the NAACP and the National Negro Congress sent him a joint letter congratulating him on his new position, but tempered their enthusiasm by acknowledging ongoing police violence in the nation's capital. "Law abiding colored citizens must be made to know that policemen are the hired protectors of them," the letter read, "and not their law protected lynchers." This language was very direct and made clear that black citizens in Washington, D.C., would not tolerate any patterns of brutality and that they characterized police violence as "urban lynching."[123]

During his tenure as superintendent of the Washington Metropolitan Police, Commissioner Kelly listened and responded to the concerns of black civic organizations. In September 1941, Kelley held a meeting with 1,600 black citizens at the Metropolitan Baptist Church, which only one year earlier had been the site of a citizen's police trial. Kelly announced that he favored a change in the Trial Board to include both officers and civilians. He also signaled his disapproval of "holding persons for investigation without charges," which had been a common practice.[124] As police commissioner, Kelly worked to alleviate crowding in the Police Court by extending its hours so that citizens' cases could be heard in a more timely manner.[125] One year later in October 1942, the Police Court and the Municipal Court in Washington, D.C., merged, resulting in employee transfers. Armond W. Scott, a black judge in the Municipal Court, was assigned to the criminal bench. An article in the *Washington Tribune* noted that this was "the first time in history that a Negro judge has sat in this criminal branch" in Washington, D.C.[126] Judge Scott's appointment fulfilled the wish of many activists, who had lobbied for an African American to serve on the Police Court. Only one month after Judge Scott began his tenure, Mary Mason Jones, a social studies teacher at the Francis Junior High School and activist in the New Negro Alliance, brought her class to observe the court proceedings.[127] This opportunity for students whose communities had been ravaged by police brutality to witness an African American judge presiding over a court of law mattered tremendously and demonstrated the change that had occurred in the nation's capital.

The African American community in Washington, D.C., applauded the efforts of Major Kelly. In January 1943, the *Washington Afro-American* named Kelly to their annual Honor Roll, which was rare for white citizens. It stated that Kelly deserved this honor because he had been "made acting head at a time when he was under fire from all quarters, [and] he has since worked diligently to bring to it a high level of efficiency." It commended his administration for helping crime to decline by 35 percent as well as "a marked decrease in brutality."[128] Indeed, Kelly worked to address the demographic imbalance in the police force. By 1945, he had increased the number of black police officers from 42 to 138, of whom 6 were detectives, 4 were motorcycle patrolmen, and

4 were policewomen.[129] This shift in police personnel was a decisive factor in helping prevent further cases of brutality in the city of Washington, D.C.: comparatively fewer cases were reported after 1941. Kelly became a forceful advocate of racial justice by not only appointing more African American police office but also seeking to improve race relations in the city. In 1943, E. Franklin Frazier invited Kelly to speak at a roundtable on police violence at the University of Chicago, where he was lauded as an "example of a police chief who does his duty regardless of race."[130] In June 1945, Kelly held a meeting with the local chapter of the NAACP, where he told meeting attendees, "We will tolerate neither police brutality nor attacks upon police officers, regardless of race, creed, or color."[131]

Conclusion

Beginning in the late 1920s, African American women began to be the victims of a surge in police violence in Washington, D.C., whether they were walking down the street, protesting abuse, or even were fast asleep in their own homes. This rise in violence against women coincided with a wave of police brutality against men, making no black citizen safe in Washington, D.C., in this decade. Police officers attacked black women from all walks of life, including those who were model citizens and women who participated in the underground economy. But, regardless of their social standing, teachers, cooks, clerks, and maids all expressed their desire to be treated as citizens in the nation's capital by contesting brutality, whether by fighting back, suing in Police Court, or giving interviews to the local press.[132]

A cohort of middle-class activists joined the campaign against police violence by meeting with local officials, marching in the protest parades, circulating petitions, and attending mass meetings and citizens' police trials. Many of the same women who had been prominent in anti-lynching politics in the 1920s joined the campaign against police violence in the 1930s, including Nannie Helen Burroughs, Julia West Hamilton, Marian Butler, Arnetta Randall, Jennie Richardson McGuire, and Theresa Lee Robinson. Young newcomers, such as Thelma Dale and Natalie Moorman, banded together with these veteran organizers and assumed prominent positions in the National Negro Congress and the New Negro Alliance to address interracial police violence against women. Within this broad coalition, black women tapped their organizing culture in the Phyllis Wheatley YWCA and churches and fraternal orders to recruit large numbers of citizens to join the crusade. African American women's mobilization against police brutality showed the growth of their protest politics, which had begun to employ militant language, direct action resistance, and an unwavering quest for first-class citizenship in the United States. By the mid-1940s, activists successfully convinced Commissioner Edward J. Kelly to change the culture of the police department by hiring more black officers, adjusting the policies of the Police Court, and most importantly, demonstrating zero tolerance for brutality. Cumulatively, these changes lowered the patterns of police violence throughout the city streets.

The campaigns against police brutality also highlighted the importance of addressing other matters of racial justice in the nation's capital. If citizens of Washington, D.C., had been able to vote, it would have been easier to remove Commissioner Ernest Brown, appoint black judges to Police Court, and select trial boards composed of officers and civilians. The culture of segregation in the city nurtured police brutality precisely because it sanctioned a racial hierarchy, which constructed blackness as inherently deviant. Finally, many of the women who suffered from police violence in the 1930s worked low-wage jobs as maids and cooks and lived in poor neighborhoods with few public resources. Some were elderly and lacked family support. These conditions of poverty made women more vulnerable to police brutality. Activists recognized that police violence was only one dimension of a larger culture of oppression that afflicted African American women in Washington, D.C. The next two chapters investigate black women's campaigns to secure economic justice, racial integration, and voting rights in the nation's capital.

CHAPTER FOUR

Women Riot for Jobs
The Politics of Economic Justice

On Tuesday, October 11, 1938, by 8:00 P.M., black women carrying old news-papers, milk crates, and empty boxes began to line up outside the Fourth Po-lice Precinct in Southwest Washington. These women were not waiting in line for food, clothing, or handouts, but rather for job applications to work as fed-eral charwomen (office cleaners). By the next morning, newspapers estimated that between 10,000 to 20,000 black women—young, old, healthy, carrying young children, and leaning on crutches—had come to the precinct building. The sheer number of prospective applicants overwhelmed officials as traffic was blocked off, extra police were called in to contain the crowds, and eventu-ally the distribution of job applications was suspended. As the crowds grew restless and angry, police officers retaliated with violence, sending some women to the hospital with injuries. Essie Jackson, an unemployed widow who was thirty-eight years old, was one of the hundreds of black women who had waited all night, but did not receive a job application. "I waited a long time so I could be first in line, but I guess I lost my place in the rush," she told reporters of the *Baltimore Afro-American.* She lamented that she had "no job in view now" and worried about her future. One year later, Jackson was working as a maid for a private family.[1] Newspapers across the country covered the event, featuring dramatic photos of white police officers containing crowds of black women, whose bodies spilled into the streets; the coverage featured sensational head-lines such as "Twenty-Five Thousand Women Storm Jail to Apply for Char-women Job" and "Women Riot for Jobs."[2]

The images and words spoke for themselves. A substantial number of black women in Washington, D.C., were desperate for cleaning jobs in the federal government because they paid higher wages and offered holiday benefits. Although President D. Franklin Roosevelt's New Deal had created many programs to assist workers, the majority of African American women were excluded from them because they labored as domestic servants. By camping out at the Police Fourth Precinct and demonstrating their eagerness for jobs as charwomen, these thousands of black women in the nation's capital ex-pressed their collective visions for economic justice in the New Deal.

During the 1930s, many black women who had been engaged in national campaigns turned toward the economic crisis that was unfolding in the nation's capital. In the previous decade, women had seen the National Association of Wage Earners (NAWE) as a vehicle to improve wages, labor conditions, and dignity for workers, especially domestic servants. But the Great Depression inspired activists to amplify their demands for economic justice, to argue that black women deserved the opportunity to work in a job of their choice, earn a living wage, provide for their families, and enjoy full participation in government programs that regulated wages and hours or provided a safety net in old age.[3] Black women contended that they deserved the same rights in the United States as the "unemployed man," who was always coded as a white breadwinner.

A broad cross-section of black women—including housewives, domestic servants, laundresses, teachers, business owners, and even a maid in the White House—worked to enact their visions of economic justice in the nation's capital. Women followed different paths to achieve economic justice, engaging in both formal and informal political activity. Housewives participated in consumer boycotts designed to keep black earnings in the black community. Middle-class women lobbied to expand government programs, formed economic cooperatives, and worked with employment bureaus to alleviate unemployment for African Americans. The Great Depression thwarted the momentum of the NACW, but some women continued to use clubs as powerful advocacy organizations. Additionally, middle class women found activist networks in college sororities, economic cooperatives, and leftist organizations formed in the 1930s, as well as their reliable constituencies in the Phyllis Wheatley YWCA, churches, fraternal orders, schools, and neighborhoods. Working-class women joined economic cooperatives and sought training and employment opportunities, but they also practiced workplace resistance, appealed for government relief, and rioted for decent jobs.

Most African American women living across the city agreed that domestics represented the most exploited category of workers. In Washington, D.C., in the 1930s, 81 percent of all black women labored in domestic and personal service.[4] Even if black women did not themselves work as servants, many held deep connections to these workers as friends, relatives, neighbors, boarders, or business clients. Black women critiqued New Deal Programs for marginalizing domestics, whether through exclusion from the National Recovery Administration's (NRA) industrial codes, limited access to government relief programs, or most importantly, their ineligibility for benefits promised by the Social Security Act, arguably *the* landmark legislative achievement of the 1930s.

Black women's activism for economic justice in the 1930s is well studied. Deborah Gray White, Annelise Orleck, and Victoria Wolcott document housewives' boycotts that aimed to lower the price of food, rent, and public utilities, as well as alleviate black unemployment. Erik McDuffie and Keona Ervin illuminate attempts to organize domestic workers in the 1930s. Rhonda Williams, Lisa Levenstein, and Keona Ervin analyze black women's postwar campaigns to broaden government programs to extend decent housing, hospitals, schools, and welfare to African Americans.[5] However, there has been less attention to the ways that black women worked to secure economic justice outside of formal organizations. This chapter fills this gap and unites these historiographies by demonstrating the spectrum of black women who advocated for economic justice, whether they were household purchasers, labor organizers, lobbyists, business owners, job seekers, militant workers, or welfare applicants.

During the 1930s, black women and men worked to put the needs of domestic servants and other working-class women at the center of government programs and policies. Through their words and actions, black women contended that they were entitled to earn a just wage, live decently, and support themselves and their families as residents of the nation's capital and citizens of the United States. Women made economic justice central to their campaigns for black freedom in the nation's capital throughout the 1930s.

"Women out of Work": The Crisis of the Great Depression in the Nation's Capital

In July 1932 during the height of the Great Depression, Beatrice M. Murphy, a resident of Washington, D.C., and a columnist for the *Washington Tribune*, penned an article titled "Women out of Work: By One of Them." In her writing Murphy crystallized black women's visions of economic justice during the Great Depression. As a black woman who had struggled with unemployment, Murphy felt invisible.[6] "Today," she noted, "the stress is being laid on the unemployed men—heads of households." She recalled hearing "numerous speeches over the radio" that promised relief in various industries, including carpentry, painting, and gardening, but pointed out that all of these economic initiatives were limited to men. The visibility of the nation's unemployment crisis only magnified with the recent Bonus Army March when "thousands and thousands of men have trampled to Washington" to pressure Congress to offer financial relief. "The whole United States is sorry for them and is asking, what is to be done about the men out of work," Murphy reported. But she reminded readers that women were also heads of households and needed an income to support their families. She starkly noted, "We are women. We are supporting families. We did not fight in the trenches of France, but we are waging a desperate battle to make our children—the men and women of tomorrow—the kind of people that America wants and needs." Murphy argued that "ours" was a "double responsibility" because "nothing is being said about the unemployed woman." She called these women "hungry, ragged, and desperate," arguing that they did not have the luxury of marching on Washington because their responsibilities of caring for their families kept them closer to home. She detailed a long list of black women's economic concerns, which included being able to purchase clothing, coal, and food and pay the rent. Murphy then invited Congress, the president, and all those in Washington to "give a thought to the women of America and make jobs for them so that they may be able to meet the responsibilities which they are shouldering so bravely." She concluded by asking, "Are American women to say, 'We asked for bread and they gave us . . . a stone?'"[7]

In this article, Beatrice Murphy took the familiar narrative of an unemployed white man in the Great Depression and turned it upside down so that it centered on a working-class black woman in Washington, D.C. As she argued, the categories of white and male mattered a great deal in how the government and the American public addressed people's needs. For instance, while black women faced unemployment at high rates, city work relief projects were tailored toward male workers. Dissatisfied veterans of World War I could trek to Washington to demand payment of their bonus, while family obligations prevented black women from participating in marches and demonstrations. Finally, as mothers who were sometimes the breadwinners, black women were concerned with earning money to feed, clothe, and house their families. The conditions that Beatrice Murphy chronicled in her article reflected the economic predicaments of many black women throughout Washington in the 1930s.

In October 1929, the stock market crashed, pulling the United States into the most severe economic crisis in the nation's history. The Great Depression sparked widespread unemployment across the country, a drop in consumer spending, and a marked stagnation in wages. Some residents of Washington, D.C., did not experience the same immediate impact as the rest of the nation precisely because the federal government was the city's chief employer. In the black community, some middle-class women, including government workers and teachers, were shielded from the worst effects of the Depression. But, maids, cooks, laundresses, nannies, chauffeurs, and butlers were already living on the edges of poverty. As white families in Washington, D.C., struggled to cope with the straitened economic circumstances of the Great Depression, many either fired their hired help or significantly reduced their wages.[8]

Unemployed women could seek work at the Labor Department's U.S. Employment Service, which was located at 4 ½ Street in Northwest Washington. An article in the *Washington Post* termed this building a "servant mart," and it was always filled with prospective domestic workers. Because of the scarcity of work, the article noted that domestics, who previously earned between $40 and $50 a month, would now "work for $30 or $35 a month."[9] This article then illuminated the constricted landscape that characterized African American women's employment prospects during the economic crisis. Some black women were the sole wage earners for their families and had to support themselves and their children on less and less money. Furthermore, women competed against each other for employment at a center called a "servant mart" and worked longer hours for fewer wages. These descriptions painted a bleak portrait of black women's economic prospects during the Depression.

Those black women who were unable to work had few options for support. Alberta Goldman, a forty-two-year-old widow and mother of six children, lived in Southeast Washington. At some point around 1919, Goldman had migrated from South Carolina to Washington, D.C., with her husband and three children.[10] James Goldman soon found work as a laborer, and their family continued to grow. But in 1930 right after the stock market crash, James Goldman died, and Alberta was left to support six children at the outset of the Depression. She had appealed for assistance from the Board of Public Welfare, but this agency stated that all children over the age of sixteen had to earn twenty dollars a month. Goldman's oldest child, William, was unable to meet these income requirements, and he was forced to move out of the house. Her older daughter Beatrice was mentally ill, and Goldman made the difficult decision to commit her to an institution. The Board of Public Welfare punished Goldman for this decision by revoking her eligibility for relief payments, despite her unemployment status and four other dependent children: Pearl, Lillian, Henry, and Ivory. Working to achieve a modicum of economic justice for herself and her family, Goldman contacted Archibald S. Pinkett, the secretary at the local NAACP chapter, who wrote a letter on her behalf to the Board of Public Welfare. In his letter, Pinkett posed this question: "Where is she to get sustenance in these hungry days and lack of jobs?"[11]

In a desperate situation, Alberta Goldman resourcefully demanded government support for herself and her family, as well as her desire to be treated with respect, which reflected her visions of economic justice. Black women in Washington were aware that citizens like Alberta Goldman were neither treated fairly nor with dignity by white social workers and white charitable institutions. Racial segregation compounded these problems because educational institutions in the city that offered courses in social work barred black students. Esther Pope Shaw, a teacher in the city's public schools and the publicity secretary for the local chapter of the National Association of Colored Women (NACW), wrote a letter to the editor in the *Washington Tribune*, where she requested that Howard University offer courses in social services, so that they could train black professionals to assist women like Alberta Goldman.[12]

Sometimes conditions were so dire in Depression-era Washington, D.C., that they prompted some citizens to take their own lives. An article in August 1932 reported that, in the past six months, ten black Washingtonians had committed suicide and thirty-five had attempted it.[13] A glimpse into some of these stories illustrates these desperate circumstances. Flora Broadus, a sixty-two-year-old woman who was "despondent because of unemployment and financial worries," committed suicide at the residence of her daughter Essie Weaver. Broadus had recently moved to Washington, D.C., from Seattle and was seeking employment.[14] Her son-in-law was a laborer, while her daughter took in boarders. Their neighborhood on T Street in Northwest Washington was a mix of government workers and servants.[15] By moving to Washington, D.C., Broadus likely thought she would be able to find work for the government. Her decision to end her life signaled both her personal hopelessness and her desire not to be a burden to her family. Three years later in 1935, Jennie Thomas, a fifty-six-year-old widow who worked as a maid at the YWCA, fell from a third-story window. Police officers determined that her cause of death was suicide.[16] These stories reflect not only black citizens' extreme desperation but also their pessimism about the possibility of improving their personal situations.

Black Washingtonians' financial hardships in the Depression were so dire that 75 percent of the city's relief aid budget went to African Americans, which was the highest proportion in the nation. In August 1932, the municipal government created an Emergency Relief Bureau, and Congress appropriated $350,000 for relief in the city. When people arrived at the Emergency Relief Office, they were given up to three types of aid: cash, a voucher to obtain food, or a job at the municipal wood yard or sewing project.[17] "In no other city or state in the nation," reported the *Atlanta Daily News*, "is there such a wide variance between the white and colored persons on relief, according to the figures which show that the percentage of colored population of relief here is almost ten times the white population."[18]

Black women throughout Washington orchestrated campaigns to address hunger, homelessness, and unemployment. African American women and girls addressed the immediate crisis through donations of food and clothing. In November 1929, Anna S. Payne, a prominent activist in various social causes and a teacher at Shaw Junior High School in Northwest Washington, enlisted the aid of students and instructors to distribute food across the city.[19] Mabel Settle, who was thirteen years old and president of the Junior Needlework Guild at the Birney Community Center in Anacostia, a working-class neighborhood in Southeast Washington, joined her mother, Birdie Settle, a housewife, and Martha Ellis, a cleaner in a hotel, to donate twenty garments to the Home for Aged and Destitute Women and Children.[20]

As the Depression dragged on, women tapped the resources of their networks in churches, fraternal orders, schools, and sororities. These organizations and institutions had taught black women lessons about the importance of collectivism, and members employed these principles in their campaigns to address hunger and unemployment. In December 1930, the Health Unit of the Columbia Temple of the Elks held an annual Christmas dinner for poor children across the city at the Elks headquarters in Northwest Washington. Ruth Cumber, a real estate agent whose husband labored as a Pullman porter, chaired this event.[21] In February 1931, the Alpha Kappa Alpha (AKA) Sorority under the leadership of Eva Hilton Honesty held a "Night in Spain" at the Lincoln Colonnade to raise money for unemployed persons in the city.[22] In September 1932, a group of women at the Mount Carmel Baptist Church in Northwest Washington organized a daily luncheon of coffee and ham-and-tomato sandwiches for the unemployed men and women across the city. The chair was Mrs. D. E. Clark, the social worker in the church, and she was assisted by Hattie Holmes, servants Julia R. Davis and Charlotte Henderson, Emma Tolliver, Charlotte Henderson, Mrs. M. C. Wilson, Mrs. Willie P. Williams, Mrs. L. R. Adams, and Mrs. Marie Gray.[23] Additionally, women in the Independent Order of St. Luke (IOSL) delivered fifty food baskets to needy families across the city, along with twenty-three dresses.[24]

While most teachers were able to keep their jobs, they taught students who wore ragged clothes, were too hungry to learn, and, in the worst cases, did not show up to school. Since they had important insights into the challenges faced by struggling families, teachers throughout the city participated in relief efforts. In March 1932, a newspaper article described a social relief organization called the "It's Club." This group, made up of nine women who were mostly teachers in the city's public school system, had banded together for benevolent purposes. The club's purpose was to "to send provisions each week to some needy family until the fund is exhausted." In that particular week, the It's Club delivered "a tempting basket of groceries, sufficient for a week's supply" to a single mother and her eight children.[25] In December 1932, teachers at the Garnet-Patterson Junior High School recruited students to gather items for the poor. Students collected shoes, coats, caps, dresses, stockings, ties, sacks of coal, and a range of foodstuffs, including sugar, potatoes, apples, and canned goods. They deposited these items at the Mother-Child House in Southwest and at the Shiloh Baptist Church.[26]

As women and men continued to struggle during the Great Depression, the eyes of the nation turned to the 1932 presidential election. While many African American citizens considered President Herbert Hoover to be an ineffective leader in helping the nation cope with the circumstances of the Great Depression, most black voters were skeptical that New York governor Franklin D. Roosevelt, a Democrat, would craft programs to assist black citizens. In the 1932 presidential election, 77 percent of African Americans cast ballots for the incumbent, President Herbert Hoover, while only 23 percent voted for FDR.[27] However, most white citizens voted for change, and in November 1932, Franklin D. Roosevelt was elected as the nation's thirty-second president.

After the election, Nannie Helen Burroughs expressed her disappointment with the Democratic victory in a nationally syndicated article titled "Nannie Burroughs Pessimistic over Political Victory of the Democrats." For Burroughs, the Democratic Party was connected with the Jim Crow South, and she worried that conditions for African Americans would worsen under a Roosevelt administration. However, she did acknowledge that "no political party can cure our ills."[28] While not all voters were as vocal as Burroughs, most African Americans were skeptical that a white president associated with the party of Jim Crow and white supremacy would seriously alleviate the economic and political ills for African Americans.

"A White Man's Law": Early Years of the New Deal

In March 1933 on the eve of the presidential inauguration, an article in the *Pittsburgh Courier* featured interviews with prominent activists about their aspirations for Roosevelt's administration. Mary Church Terrell, the former president of the Colored Women's Republican League, hoped that FDR would not "reduce the salaries of Federal employees any more than they have already been cut." She passionately called on government programs to "deal more justly with women" and hoped that "they will receive greater recognition from it in every way than they did from the old." Terrell concluded by expressing a desire that Roosevelt's administration would "use its power and influence to give every citizen a square deal without regard to race, condition, sex, or creed."[29] In this article Terrell crystallized her vision for African American women to achieve economic justice in President Roosevelt's New Deal administration, whether it was through employment or full participation in government programs.

Within the first months of FDR's administration, economic conditions worsened for Washington's black residents. Only a few days after the inauguration, the Labor Department announced that the federal government would reduce government salaries by 15 percent, based on the fact that the cost of living in Washington, D.C., had declined by 21 percent in the past three years.[30] Landlords of white apartment buildings responded to these cuts by reducing rent or eliminating utility costs. However, racial segregation in the nation's capital meant that black residents had fewer options and were already paying disproportionally high rates for their living spaces; the pay cuts meant even less funds to pay the high rent. An article in the *Washington Tribune* noted that the effects of these salary reductions were "felt" among the black population, forcing government workers to move from rented apartments into rented rooms. The article concluded, "High rents have been the issue among colored tenants here for almost a decade."[31] The economic crisis thus brought issues of racial segregation into sharper relief.

In their coverage of the Roosevelt administration, articles in the black press noted that African Americans numbered more than half of the White House servants, which was a higher percentage than in previous administrations.[32] Two notable workers were Irvin and Elizabeth McDuffie of Atlanta. Irvin had served as FDR's valet during his gubernatorial term in New York, while Elizabeth had worked as a live-in servant for a prominent family in Atlanta. When FDR was elected president, both moved into the White House. The black press singled out Irvin and Elizabeth McDuffie, whom they viewed as cultivating important ties with the Roosevelts, thereby positioning their jobs as more than personal service work and as vehicles for their exercising meaningful political influence in the White House. A story in the *Washington Tribune* credited Elizabeth McDuffie with arranging for Etta Moten and Lillian Evanti to sing at the White House, the first black women to perform there.[33] When an organization dedicated to raising money for a polio foundation held a birthday ball for President Roosevelt in Washington, D.C., Elizabeth McDuffie attended as the official representative of the White House. The narratives coming out of the White House led the *New York Amsterdam News* to suggest that both Irvin and Elizabeth McDuffie possessed a "helpful influence in many directions where the welfare of the Negro is concerned."[34] These articles painted a portrait of the married couple not only as valuable members of the household staff but also as relatively prominent figures in the Roosevelt White House.[35]

While some black Washingtonians viewed Irvin and Elizabeth McDuffie as political allies, they did not pass judgment on the New Deal itself until they learned more about its economic initiatives. In June 1933, Congress passed legislation establishing the National Recovery Administration (NRA), which encouraged businesses to implement a set of codes that would establish fair working conditions, fix prices, and work to eliminate competition. The theory behind the NRA was that it would help stabilize existing industry and prevent further economic hardship. However, African Americans across the country demonstrated their concern that the NRA would not apply to black workers, especially domestic servants, by labeling it the "Negro Removal Act" or "Negroes Removed Again."[36]

Locally in Washington, D.C., women registered a variety of responses to the NRA. In September 1933, one thousand African Americans in the city organized a colored league of the NRA, with the intent of working to ensure that black workers could benefit from it. Workers rallied under the leadership of George Beasley, president of the Federation of Civic Associations. The colored league held a mass meeting at the Young Men's Christian Association (YMCA) for the purpose of placing the NRA symbol, the Blue Eagle, "in every home and every colored employer under a code." At the meeting, eighteen captains representing diverse occupations divided the city into different neighborhoods, where they canvassed homes and businesses and distributed more than 7,000 NRA pledge cards. The male captains whose occupations could be identified in the census included government workers, a fireman, a cement worker, a foreman, and a pharmacist.

Five of the eighteen captains were women: housewife Effie Pettis, beautician Inez Clomax, dressmaker and veteran activist Marian Butler, student Mildred Coleman, and federal clerk Elizabeth Bampfield.[37] Two held close ties with the NAWE: Marian Butler had served in a leadership position, while NRA captain Lloyd Cuney's wife, Jacqueline, had been a recruiter. The fact that Butler and Cuney had been active in the NAWE and were now affiliated with the NRA reveals how black women interested in economic justice wove their activism into the shifting organizational landscape of the city. It is also indicates that black women and men felt optimistic that the NRA programs would have a positive impact on African Americans.

Additionally, league members established an information bureau at the Phyllis Wheatley YWCA, where twelve volunteers answered questions about the NRA from nine in the morning until nine in the evening.[38] The fact that the NRA's information bureau was located at the Phyllis Wheatley YWCA signaled the institution's continued prominence in the city of Washington, D.C., especially for African American women's politics and activism.

Domestic servants in Washington, D.C., followed the establishment of the NRA closely and articulated their visions of economic justice by demanding that they be included in its programs. In September 1933, a black citizen in Washington wrote a letter to the *Washington Afro-American*, arguing that servants should not be excluded from the NRA. "Long hours similar to sweatshops are drummed out of these people," the writer announced. "A minimum of 30 cents an hour should be demanded and price of meals allowed out of that, eight hours a day." The writer concluded, "If this administration means fair business with us here, it is an opportunity for them to show it."[39] Another published letter appeared to be written by a group of domestic servants. The letter writers asked black citizens to support them in their quest for inclusion in the NRA. "Our group should not co-operate with the NRA," the letter writers stated, "unless equitable arrangements or code be provided for domestic help." The writers continued by pointing out that domestic work "is practically the only occupation this nation allows us" and recommended that activists "make it an industry." They concluded, "These people are just as human as other person and they are always the 'Forgotten Man.' They constitute the bulk of buying power in our group because of their numbers. If this administration means fair business with us here, it is opportunity for them to show it. It is up to you." The letter was simply signed "US."[40]

Thus these letter writers articulated their visions of economic justice by arguing that they deserved inclusion in government programs and respect as workers and consumers in the U.S. economy. Like Beatrice Murphy, they dismissed the idea that the "Forgotten Man" was the only group of people suffering in the Great Depression. Additionally, it is striking that domestic workers in Washington, D.C., followed federal legislation so closely, which indicates that some black women in the nation's capital continued to see themselves as representatives for black women across the nation. Although the second letter was anonymous, it is possible that a group of domestic servants banded together to publicly articulate their critiques of the NRA. In stating that domestic service was "the only occupation this nation allows us," they helped personalize this political issue and give a voice to the thousands of domestic servants who demanded that their occupations be classified as industries.

Even though black women who worked in the beauty culture industry were supposed to be included in the NRA, they faced a dilemma because domestic workers were their primary clients and so they needed to be open for longer hours than allowed by NRA regulations. The NRA regulation of the hours of beauty parlors revealed the racialized biases embedded in the program. Most black proprietors stayed open in the evenings to accommodate their primary clientele of domestic servants who were getting off of work, while white beauty parlors closed around 5 or 6 P.M. Ellen Bramlette, a salon proprietor in Washington and founder of the Hawaiian hair treatment, told a reporter from the *Washington Afro-American* that the National Recovery Administration was a "white man's program." She argued that it ignored both the needs and considerations of black women business owners and of black women workers. "It would be difficult for the colored operators to close their beauty shops at six," she argued, "when white employers work their help until eight or nine at night." Bramlette pointed out that black and white beauty operators served different sets of clientele. "Most of my trade is between 4 and 9 in the evening and if I close at six, I would have to go out of business and I am going to stand just as pat as the white housekeeper," she told a reporter. "They are not going to raise their maid's salary and are not going to lessen their working hours and are not going to be interrupted with any Industrial Recovery Code and neither am I."[41] Bramlette's reservations highlighted the ways that the interests of black middle-class business owners were bound together with the dignity and wages of domestic servants.[42]

Two months after Ellen Bramlette voiced criticisms of the NRA codes, a group of seventy-five beauty shop owners gathered at the Phyllis Wheatley YWCA, where they discussed the pending New Deal legislation. Collectively, these women rejected both the forty- and forty-eight-hour week "as well as the 7 P.M. closing time." A newspaper article on this meeting reported, "Local owners pointed out that the majority of patronage consisted of working people who find it impossible to visit beauty shops before 7 o'clock and fifty percent of colored patronage would be lost if time was set at a 7 P.M. closing."[43] In all of these ways, then, beauticians crafted a vision that they and their clients would all be treated equally under New Deal legislation.[44] During the first two years of the New Deal, black women worked to ensure that African Americans would be part of the NRA, and both hairdressers and servants denounced the exclusion of domestics from the codes. After it became clear that the NRA was not going to regulate the hours and wages of most black women's occupations, including domestic service, laundry, and beauticians, many black women turned their attention to the Social Security Act, then under debate in Congress.

"The Mudsill of the Social Order":
Debates over Social Security

In 1934, Congress began debating the Social Security Act, a broad piece of leg-islation that offered a government-provided economic safety net for U.S. citi-zens.[45] Two of its central programs were old age insurance and unemployment insurance, which were funded jointly by employers and employees and offered workers' compensation during periods of unemployment and a monthly pen-sion on retirement at age sixty-five or older. When the House of Representa-tives began fleshing out the specific details of the Social Security Act, the bill had provisions that excluded domestic servants and farmers from both forms of insurance. The rationale behind denying access to domestic servants was that their employment was short-term, making it difficult to track down em-ployers. However, with 1,600,298 African American women engaged in domes-tic and personal service and agriculture in the United States in 1930, the initial Social Security proposal threatened to exclude 87 percent of all black women workers and 55 percent of all black wage earners.[46]

The black press assiduously followed these political debates, educating read-ers about the potential consequences of this exclusionary legislation for most African Americans. At the hearings on Social Security held in January 1935, both George E. Haynes, former executive secretary of the National Urban League and representative of the Federal Council of Churches of Christ in America, and Charles Hamilton Houston, lawyer for the NAACP, testified about the importance of including black workers in this federal program. In his remarks, Houston pointed to the fragile status of black workers in the United States, arguing that they suffered higher rates of unemployment than white workers.[47] Their passionate remarks fell on deaf ears, and Congress passed the Social Security Act in August 1935 with the provision excluding farmers and domestic servants from coverage.[48] For African Americans, espe-cially black women, the Social Security Act created a dangerous precedent precisely because this federal legislation did not include a guarantee of eco-nomic justice for all Americans.

Leading black women activists—both in Washington, D.C., and across the country—attacked the exclusions in the Social Security Act. At the Nineteenth Biennial Convention of the National Association of Colored Women (NACW) in Cleveland, the issue of Social Security was on the agenda, and delegates passed a resolution vowing to "wipe from the statute books laws that discrim-inate against Negroes."[49] In August 1935, the Grand Order of the Elks held an educational conference in Washington, D.C., at which economist and lawyer

Sadie Tanner Mossell termed the Social Security Act a "sieve through which the majority of colored persons fall through."[50] African American women were cognizant of and outspoken about the exclusion of such a substantial portion of the black workforce from Social Security.

Nannie Helen Burroughs was one of the harshest critics of the Social Security Act. She joined fellow delegates in denouncing the Social Security Act as discriminatory at the Elks conference.[51] In an article in the *Baltimore Afro-American*, Burroughs broadened her critique, arguing that the federal government had made "domestic workers the mudsill of the new social order" and terming the Social Security Act "unjust, and undemocratic." By using the term "mudsill," Burroughs evoked nineteenth-century justifications for slavery, which presumed an inherent hierarchy in society. She thus powerfully connected the past exploitations of African Americans to contemporary circumstances. Even more, she pointed to the important role that domestics performed in enabling society to run smoothly, arguing that they were as responsible for the "the health, happiness, and social welfare of the nation as any other group." She ended her analysis by suggesting that "domestic workers and those who desire to build a new social order must address themselves to the task of training and organizing the grand army of workers who are engaged in personal service."[52] Burroughs's solution to exclusion from the Social Security Act was to set up training programs to improve wages and to organize domestic servants to collectively press for their rights. Although African American women issued stinging critiques of the Social Security Act, most were relatively powerless to alter this legislation.

Black women were not the only ones to denounce the limitations of the Social Security Act. In 1935, the Roosevelt administration wrote letters to churches across the country, seeking the opinions of ministers and their congregants about the New Deal. In Washington, D.C., black ministers registered their dissatisfaction. For instance, Arthur D. Gray, a political activist who was pastor at the Plymouth Congregational Church, noted that he was in "sympathy with and approve of the new Social Security Legislation" because it offered "old age pensions, aid for crippled children and unemployment insurance." But he ended his letter by "respectfully call[ing] your attention to the fact that Domestic Servants have not been provided for in this legislation."[53] Gray's letter conveyed not only his personal beliefs but also the political opinions of the women and men in his congregation, who either labored in domestic service or held connections to that category of workers and knew firsthand their disappointment in the Social Security Act.

One of the few African American women who was able to insert herself in debates around Social Security was Elizabeth McDuffie, the servant in the

White House. During the fall of 1936, she toured Midwestern states on the presidential campaign trail, urging African Americans to cast their ballots for FDR.[54] Nine days after FDR was reelected president in a landslide victory that claimed the majority of black voters, Elizabeth McDuffie was elected treasurer of the newly formed United Government Employees Union, Incorporated (UGE) in Washington, D.C., an advocacy organization created to improve working conditions for black government employees. Edgar Brown, a former tennis star, journalist, and employee in the Federal Emergency Relief Administration, served as president.[55] McDuffie used her position in the UGE to advocate for expansion of New Deal programs to benefit black women.[56] For instance, in February 1937, at a fundraiser for Indiana congresswoman Virginia E. Jenckes, McDuffie joined others on stage to advocate that all federal employees—including cleaners in government offices—should earn a living, minimum wage of $1,500.[57] Also in 1937, four black women contacted McDuffie, informing her that, as laundresses in Fort Myer, Virginia, they earned only $600 a year. McDuffie politicized their case, and Edgar Brown testified before a Subcommittee on Appropriations in the Senate, relaying the plight of these workers who earned menial wages while washing the clothes and linens for members of the armed services.[58] When the Senate voted to increase the laundresses' pay, the black press credited McDuffie and members of the UGE for their advocacy in seeking justice for service workers.[59] The fact that the laundresses in Virginia personally reached out to McDuffie suggests that black women workers viewed her as an approachable figure who could tap her political connections to fight for higher wages. However, most black women in Washington, D.C., lacked McDuffie's political connections, which prompted them to pursue projects of economic justice on the local level.

"The Rent Is Due and I Have Not Got It": Economic Justice at the Local Level

As Congress was grappling with ways to bring about an economic recovery, women in the nation's capital continued to address unemployment and poverty. In August 1933, a coalition of sixteen men and women formed the New Negro Alliance (NNA), an organization whose mission was to "protect the employment of Negroes in Washington under the NRA program."[60] Six of the founders were women: Howard University student Doris Risher; teachers Catherine Grey, Isadore Williams, Doris Shilmate, and Mae Thorne; and housewives Helen Nash and Peggy Williston Gray.[61] Male founders included Howard student Howard Fitzhugh, lawyers Belford Lawson and William Hastie, and teacher Clyde McDuffie. Since many members were affiliated with Howard University, they focused on issues in the university's neighborhood. One of the first incidents to be addressed occurred at a local restaurant. In August 1933, white managers at the Hamburger Grill on U Street in Northwest Washington, a hub of the black community, fired three black employees and replaced them with white workers.[62] In response, NNA members urged black Washingtonians to boycott this establishment to send a message about how black patronage was connected with black employment. The boycott was successful because the Hamburger Grill re-hired the fired workers. Most importantly, the boycott demonstrated the power of black consumers in the nation's capital.[63]

Soon after the protests at the Hamburger Grill, leaders in the NNA enlisted black women and girls to canvass black neighborhoods and gather signatures for petitions that called for the employment of black men and women.[64] It was vital to the effectiveness of the NNA that it have the support of a broad coalition of women in Washington, D.C., including both housewives and working-class women. Not only did women have deep networks across the city but they were also the chief purchasers for their families and, thus, the primary constituency for food boycotts. Since the beginning of the Great Depression, black working-class housewives in Detroit and other cities had been active in boycotts against vendors, landlords, and electrical companies.[65] Similarly, in Washington, D.C., forging alliances with housewives helped NNA members increase their economic pressure on businesses they were targeting. During the 1930s, members of the NNA picketed many of the chain stores in the city, including the Sanitary Grocery Company (which became Safeway) and the Atlantic & Pacific Tea Company (which became A&P). An article in the *Washington Tribune* in October 1933 commented on their recruitment progress. "A canvass of the community by the *Tribune*," the article reported, "discloses that housewives are in sympathy with the move of their youthful aggressors and that their continued co-operation would be assured members of the Alliance."[66] By 1938, the NNA had a membership of 10,000, and it likely that many of these members were housewives living throughout the city.

As an organization founded during the height of the Great Depression, the NNA's mission was to expand employment opportunities for African Americans, especially teenage girls and boys. In this respect it envisioned economic justice beyond traditional programs offered under the New Deal. In her analysis of economic boycott campaigns in Chicago, the historian Marcia Chatelin contends, "By casting the ideal worker as a teenage girl, the campaign built on decades of black girls' economic contributions to their families and communities."[67] The NNA trumpeted its success in having black clerks hired for the holiday season. The Capital Five and Ten Cents Store at 1248 Seventh Street Northwest had hired three Cardozo students: Ina Fox, Leah Glascoe, and Nellie Taylor. Edna Collins, a senior at Cardozo, worked at the Hollywood Shoe Store as a clerk, along with four young women who took orders for hosiery. A newspaper article celebrated that "the four young women within ten days sold 300 pairs of ladies hosiery."[68] Thus activism among NNA members resulted in holiday employment for African American girls in the city.

By the end of 1934, despite the great challenges, the NNA had fulfilled crucial aspects of its core mission. In that year alone, its members had succeeded in securing employment for fifty-two African Americans: thirteen clerks at the Atlantic and Pacific Tea Company, thirteen clerks at the Sanitary Grocery Company, four clerks at the Hamburger Grill, two clerks at High's Ice Cream, four clerks at the Capital Five and Ten Cents Store, one clerk at the Hollywood Shoe Store, one clerk at Brown's Corner, four clerks at Coney Island Barbecue, three clerks at Epstein's Meat Market, three clerks at the American Stores, and four clerks at Willis Cut-Rite Market.[69] That so many black clerks were hired while Washington, D.C., was still suffering from the Great Depression was significant.

NNA members used several strategies to achieve their mission, bringing throughout the 1930s a spirit of protest to campaigns for employment and supporting black-owned businesses.

They staged economic boycotts and picketed establishments that did not hire black workers. In 1938, police officers arrested some of those picketers, and the NNA appealed the verdict; the case ultimately went to the Supreme Court. In 1938, the Supreme Court handed down the decision of *New Negro Alliance v. Sanitary Grocery Company* 303 U.S. 552, which upheld the right of the picketers to protest.[70] But even a victory from the U.S. Supreme Court lacked teeth. One year after the ruling was handed down, in April 1939, Natalie Moorman was arrested for picketing a chain store at Fourteenth and U Streets in Northwest Washington.[71]

The members of the Phyllis Wheatley YWCA also worked to secure employment for girls in the city. In August 1934, YWCA president Julia West Hamilton created a camp to assist unemployed women who had worked in white-collar occupations; it later received $1,800 from the Federal Emergency Relief Administration (FERA) and accommodated a total of twenty-five girls. "So many unemployed young women," Hamilton argued, "need something of this kind to give them a new outlook on life." She also noted, "Much has been done for the domestic and laboring women, but little for the white collar women."[72] While the NNA and YWCA focused on employing girls as clerks and white-collar workers, other women in the city addressed unemployment for domestic servants.

In 1933, the Washington city government established the District Employment Center at 505 K Street NW. The center received funding from both the federal government and the local city government. In February 1933, Myra Colson Callis, a black social worker and long-standing advocate for women's economic opportunities, became the director of the domestic service division of the District Employment Center. Callis was an excellent choice for the position. A native of Virginia, she had worked for the YWCA in Ohio, Pennsylvania, and Chicago; had a master's degree in social work from the University of Chicago; and was committed to improving employment prospects for black women. In 1931, she and Lorenzo Greene published *The Employment of Negroes in the District of Columbia*, which included detailed sections on black women.[73] As a program director at the District Employment Center, Callis worked very hard to match black women applicants with positions as domestic servants and succeeded in connecting many women with jobs. A newspaper article reported that the center had found many positions for residents of Washington; in 1935 it was 15,132 jobs, 19,960 in 1936, 25,973 in 1937, and in the first nine months of 1938, that figure was 19,072.[74]

Myra Colson Callis shaped the culture of the District Employment Center to maximize the likelihood that black women would be matched for jobs. When they arrived, they filled out a detailed job application, met with an administrator, and sometimes had to take a test to assess their skills; if they passed, their file was placed in an "active file." The bureau was opened two hours earlier in the morning to accommodate "women who seek those jobs placed in temporary days' work." The Washington radio station WOL interviewed some of the job applicants on the air, and Callis arranged for Gertrude Butler, a maid, to be the first black woman interviewed.[75] Through instituting earlier hours and the radio interviews, Callis made the interests of black women workers central to the District Employment Center.

Correspondence between Callis and her clients illuminates how African American women envisioned economic justice in the New Deal era. All of these black women came to the District Employment Center with the explicit purpose of seeking employment. Those who reported satisfaction in their jobs specifically mentioned the hours, wages, and the temperament of their employers. Those workers who expressed frustration discussed the difficulty of their jobs, their poor relations with their employers, and the challenges of

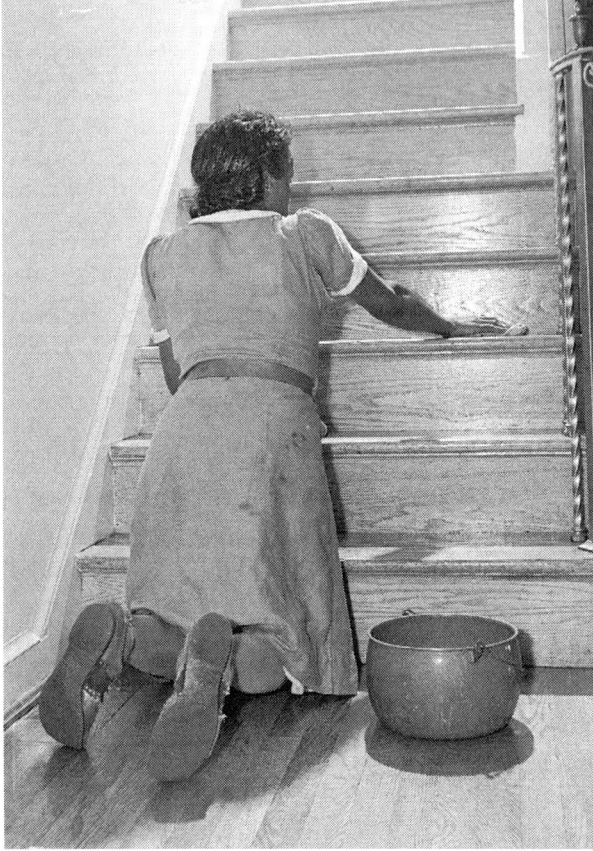

This photograph captures the grueling task of domestic labor in the nation's capital. During the 1930s, black women worked long hours, earned menial wages, faced physical and sexual abuse, and did not enjoy protections such as those provided by the Social Security Act. Having Myra Colson Callis at the District Employment Center as an advocate was deeply important for many prospective domestic servants in Washington, D.C. Library of Congress, LC-DIG-fsa-8c06134.

balancing employment with family commitments. These letters help give a human face to working-class black women during the New Deal.

Some letters are success stories, describing how prospective workers were matched with positions that fulfilled their visions of economic justice. For instance, in February 1933, Sara Ruth Barruss, a maid, wrote to Callis and thanked her profusely for helping her find a job. Barruss noted that her job was "easy" and she was grateful to have "a lovely upstairs room."[76] This letter is indeed telling because it indicates not only that Barruss needed a job but also that she was willing to "live-in" at her place of employment.[77] In May 1939, Lena Harper reported to Callis the following: "I hardly know what to say. I am so glad of my new job. I really like the people fine, they seem to be very nice people. My work isn't hard at all. I like the house. Now she told me Saturday he would go up on my wages if I continue the way I am doing. So right hear [*sic*] I want to give you thanks for giving me such a swell job."[78] And in November 1940,

Margaret Howard rejoiced, "I start at 5 a week and car fare at 6.50. When I get home at nights it's about 7 o'Clock."[79] These letters from Sara Barruss, Lena Harper, and Margaret Howard all indicate not only their thirst for work but also their gratitude to have obtained jobs with decent wages and hours and relatively kind employers.

These letters also demonstrate that Callis helped connect some black workers with positions that enabled them to support themselves and their families. Many clients expressed relief for having found a job and thanked Callis her for assisting them in the process. For instance, Elizabeth Simms personally thanked Callis for her "kind and prompt cooperation" in helping her to secure a position as a maid. She wrote to Callis to "thank you from the bottom of my heart" for her present job, but acknowledged that domestic service positions did not last forever and ended by saying, "Someday I may need your help again."[80] Simms's closing remarks reflected the reality that domestic workers frequently switched employers. The fact that Simms acknowledged this perhaps indicates her seasoned knowledge about the labor market for black working-class women. And in an undated letter to Callis, Janie Edwards wrote, "I appreciate your efforts in looking out for me." Edwards was currently sick, but when she recovered, she hoped to be able to start a job. At the end of the letter, she included "a little present I've wanted to give you"—a silk handkerchief embroidered with a flower.[81]

Other letters between Callis and the workers she assisted indicate that domestic service positions did not always allow black women to achieve their desire of economic justice. For instance, Marie Tibbs, who signed her name as (Maid) Marie Tibbs, commented on the difficulties of her job. She wanted to discuss her job with Myra Colson Callis, but "they are always sitting around and I don't have any day off by Sunday I am not able to see you then I can't afford to lose time because I have a sick child." The family Tibbs washed for grew after she was hired, and she was then required to clean "13 sheets, 20 towels, 12 pillow cases, 5 table cloths, 9 union suits, rugs, and handkerchiefs." After she listed all of the items she was required to clean, Tibbs lamented, "I can't stand it any longer." Tibbs's desperation came across in the text of her letter as she begged Callis multiple times to find her another position. She ended by asking Callis to call and ask for "Maid Marie (Tibbs). God Bless You."[82] The anguish in Tibbs's letter was palpable, and she seemed overwhelmed with balancing her demanding job while caring for her own sick child. Lillian McAdoo, another domestic worker, noted in October 1940 that her work was "hot and hard to do" and she did not know that her employer would be "so demanding."[83] In January 1941, Bernice Contree wrote to Callis that while she was somewhat comfortable with her existing job, she wanted "another job not staying nights." She noted that she liked her female employer and got along well with her, but "he's too much," indicating conflicts with her employer's husband, which could potentially escalate into physical abuse or sexual assault.[84]

Other letter writers had jobs, but were still struggling to survive economically in the midst of the Depression. Tellingly, all of these letters come from the late 1930s and early 1940s, which indicates that African American women were not the major beneficiaries of New Deal programs. For instance, in July 1940, Mary Berry, a maid, wrote Callis that "I really need the work *real* bad." She was caring not only for her daughter, who was enrolled in the Miner Teacher's College, but also for her sick mother. Berry wrote that she was trying to remain with her employer, but "I don't think I can put up with her any longer."[85] Christina Brown, a laundress, balanced working and caring for her own children, commenting that she was then substituting for other laundresses who were on vacation, but that, "as soon as school opens I can work on any time so I'll come in and see you then for a full time job."[86]

Many women revealed the desperation of their employment situations. For instance, Elizabeth Stanley told Callis that while she wanted to come see her, "I do not have the carfare." She had recently been fired from a hospital in Washington, D.C. Her only saving grace was that she had recently published a book. She wrote, "While traveling through the streets trying to advertise my book, I came in contact with quite a number of people who seemed anxious to have some one work for them, but because I could not direct them to where a reference could be given of my work, they could not believe my story." She further noted, "I have borrowed money and gone in debt with the green till my credit is just about exhausted."[87] In August 1939, Lillie Wilburn begged Colson to give her daughters work because "I ain't able to keep them all up and our rent is due and I have not got it."[88] In July 1940, Josephine Nalls asked Callis if she might assist her to "secure employment as I am certainly in dire need." She was so short on cash that she was unable to buy clothing, and her only purchases in a year were "two inexpensive hats." She listed her experience, noting that she had previously held positions "as an assistant general housekeeper, child's nurse," but that "days work cleaning" would be her "preference."[89]

Conversely, letters from employers indicates that some black women expressed opposition toward unfair conditions in the workplace. The historian Keona Ervin argues that through everyday practices of resistance, black women workers illuminated their role as "economic actors."[90] Ervin's insights help contextualize some of the activities of domestic servants. Virginia McCallig, a white employer, wrote to Callis, registering complaints about her servants and listing the qualities she would not tolerate. McCallig argued that one of her employees, Lucy Ann McNeil, had an "unpleasing voice," "talked too much," consumed alcohol, and smoked cigarettes on the job. McCallig also explicitly stated that she would reject any worker who displayed "Radical, Red, or any other socialist tendencies while on the job." McCallig's letter indicates that some of her employees may have brought revolutionary ideas into the workplace.[91]

If black women did not wish to work as domestic servants for white families, they could participate in relief cooperatives, either by working for wages or gathering lower-priced food to feed their families. In July 1934, Nannie Helen Burroughs announced that she would be working collaboratively with the Federal Emergency Relief Association to create the Northeast Self-Help Cooperative. It is telling that, in the 1920s, had founded the National Association of Wage Earners and, ten years later, established a neighborhood-based economic cooperative. Burroughs's transition from the national to the local mirrored this broader transformation in black women's politics. The Northeast Self-Help Cooperative was an important part of African American women's quest for economic justice in Washington, D.C. It assisted unemployed women or women who wished to escape domestic service by enabling them to sew garments, bake cakes, or construct chairs and, in return, earn credit for goods and food. Burroughs argued that this organization was trying to "solve the problem of unemployment."[92]

Little money was exchanged in the Northeast Self-Help Cooperative. To join the venture, participants were required to perform "nine hours of labor to purchase an entrance card." Once women and men joined, they could exchange goods. For instance, it took "six to eight towels to pay for a shampoo and two for a manicure." In addition to creating commodities, members could enter into exchanges with farmers in nearby Maryland for food. The cooperative sought to tap into women's many economic talents. For instance, it also featured a bakery, where people could exchange "cakes and pies" for "towels, shirts, shorts, and what-have-you," and "two hairdressers, connected with the cooperative, who give shampoos, manicures, and other beauty treatments in exchange for towels and uniforms."

Another venture of the Northeast Self-Help Cooperative was the construction of chairs from utilitarian barrels; they were then adorned with fabric, padding, and ribbons and sold. In June 1935, an article in the *Washington Afro-American* profiled this project. In an interview, Burroughs noted that women gathered all kinds of barrels, including "flour barrels, vegetable barrels—in fact, any kind of barrel except a liquor barrel." When asked how she came up with the idea, Burroughs stated that she was in the home of a very poor woman who used a "sawed-off barrel, with a piece of mattress on it for a cushion."[93]

Burroughs recruited a diverse coalition of women and men to join the Northeast Self-Help Cooperative. Organizational records list the names of 130 women living in Northeast Washington who joined between 1934 and 1935. When women filled out their membership applications, they listed their desired work preferences; it appears that some women saw the cooperative as an opportunity to do jobs other than domestic service. For instance, Mary Thomas labored as a domestic servant, but in her application, she expressed a desire to "cook or sew dresses."[94] Jeannette Reed, a widow who labored as a domestic, explicitly stated that she wanted to "Sew Dresses," as did another domestic worker, Sarah Harrington.[95] Other women affiliated with the Northeast Self-Help Cooperative were unemployed or working as domestics, maids, waitresses, laundresses, and seamstresses. Between 1933 and 1935, members of the organization manufactured 12,000 garments, 50 mattresses, and numerous towels, sheets, and other commodities.[96]

In August 1937, Nannie Helen Burroughs proudly announced the formation of the NE Cooperative Store at Fiftieth and Grant Streets in Northeast Washington. The store sold vegetables, eggs, and fresh pork, all grown or harvested on the cooperative's local farm—which had 125 hogs, 500 chickens, eggs, and fresh vegetables. An article noted, "The store is well stocked and the prices are a trifle lower than most chain stores." Both the store and the farm offered good jobs for members of the cooperative. Additionally, the farm formed a relationship with several clubs, restaurants, and private homes, selling them fresh and local products. Members who belonged to this organization received five dollars a year as well as "17 percent investment on their interest."[97]

The Northeast Self-Help Cooperative's effectiveness was enhanced by Burroughs's political connections. In October 1937, Mary McLeod Bethune, the Negro Adviser of the National Youth Administration, published a column in the *Washington Tribune* titled "From Day to Day." This column could have been adapted from First Lady Eleanor Roosevelt's popular newspaper column, "My Day." In her article, Bethune described her "visit to Nannie Burroughs's Cooperative Farm on Tuesday afternoon. . . . For a number of years, Nannie Burroughs has been talking and writing practical education and is now putting her talking and writing into concrete action." Bethune extolled the rich bounty of poultry, animal husbandry, and vegetables and concluded by noting, "We spent an evening together, enjoyed a wholesome delicious dinner, largely gathered from her garden, and talked over the things that are important to us at this time."[98] The fact that Bethune's column was printed in the pages of the *Pittsburgh Courier*, a nationally syndicated black newspaper, indicated its significance to a national audience; that she used the column to showcase Burroughs's work to address the crisis of unemployment and poverty in the nation's capital was also significant. In November 1937, a newspaper article in the *Washington Tribune* noted that members of the Pleasant Plains Civic Association wanted to form their own cooperative association, modeled on the NE Cooperative. Anita J. Anderson, a mother of three who took in boarders, spearheaded this venture for the Pleasant Plains Civic Association.[99] She invited members to come to her house on Irving Street in Northwest Washington, where they would "arrange to purchase food in different quantities and divide the articles."[100]

To black women, economic justice meant earning good wages, nourishing themselves, and being able to house their families in decent dwellings. Unfortunately, many black citizens in the nation's capital were living in squalid alley dwellings that lacked plumbing and running water. So during the early 1930s, when the Public Works Administration announced that it was constructing a housing project for black residents of Washington, D.C., hundreds filled out applications blanks and wrote letters requesting residency at Langston Terrace. Ultimately, 237 families moved into the modern housing project on Benning Road in Northeast Washington. Not only did black families receive modern living accommodations but black architects and workers also helped construct the project.[101]

All of these ventures illustrate how black women worked to enact economic justice. Housewives and activists in the NNA boycotted stores and worked to locate clerk positions for boys and girls. Nannie Helen Burroughs and Myra Colson Callis used the resources of the Employment Center and the NE Cooperative to elevate the lives of working-class women in Washington, D.C.

"Women Riot for Jobs": Grassroots Protest in the New Deal

Working-class black women in Washington, D.C., also articulated their visions of economic justice. Collectively, their actions—whether marching in demonstrations, camping out for jobs, or sitting in to receive benefits—evinced working-class black women's aspirations to improve material circumstances for themselves and their families.

In April 1938, Matilda Jones expressed her vision of economic justice by demanding government relief for herself and her family. Several months earlier, Jones had moved from South Carolina to Washington, D.C., with her husband

and two young children, presumably to seek work opportunities in the nation's capital. The family rented a one-room apartment on Nineteenth Street. But within a few weeks, her life began to fall apart. She gave birth to her third child in a hospital, her husband deserted the family, and she was evicted from her apartment. With three children in tow—ages three, fifteen months, and fifteen days—Matilda Jones visited the Emergency Relief Office on U Street to apply for financial assistance. But officials rejected her application because she was not a resident of the District of Columbia. They offered to pay for her to move back to her home state of South Carolina, but Jones "sternly refused." The fact that she did not want to move back to the South perhaps indicates her experience there with violence or a lack of economic opportunities. Even after administrators at the office reiterated that she could not receive any aid, Jones refused to leave: a photograph in the *Washington Afro-American* shows her cradling her children on the steps of the Emergency Relief Office. A newspaper article reported that she had remained in the office for a week, although she was currently missing. Tellingly, the article characterized her protest as a "sit-down strike."[102] By appealing to the Emergency Relief Office with her three children in tow and refusing to leave the office and move back to her home state, Matilda Jones articulated her vision of economic justice. She was in a truly desperate situation, yet Jones expressed her entitlement to services as a resident of Washington, D.C. Her sit-down strike was not about wages or hours, but her right to receive food, clothing, and shelter for herself and her family.

Matilda Jones was not the only black woman who struggled to receive financial assistance. One woman lost her job in June 1939 and stated that she was hard of hearing, had no food or fire, and "wonders where she will go in a few days when she gets orders to move."[103] One year later, members of the District Workers' Alliance visited the Welfare Board offices to "protest against alleged failure to provide relief for two colored women and their families." When officials argued that the two families were ineligible for welfare because each one had an "employable" member, "the delegation announced it would remain in Bondy's office until action of some sort was taken."[104] In November 1940, a newspaper article announced that "jobless, debt-laden" women were "facing eviction for nonpayment of rent, denied direct relief because they are certified as 'employable' by welfare agencies yet denied work." Under the auspices of the National Negro Congress, a citizens committee later met at the YMCA and crafted a list of objectives for "alleviating the suffering among Washington's poor as bitter winters draw near." Committee members called for an increase in benefits; the removal of the ceiling on direct relief, which was "causing great hardship, especially in large families"; a program for food stamps and milk distribution; and a more "inclusive program for abolishing unemployment."

The militancy expressed by women like Matilda Jones and citizens in the District Worker's Alliance in demanding government assistance indicates that employment was only one component of economic justice. All of these women demanded the right to food, shelter, and safety as residents of Washington, D.C. These cases illustrate the intersections of race, gender, and class in shaping black women's circumstances in the city. As single mothers of young children, these women needed flexible positions, but the job market limited black women's employment mostly to domestic service and laundry work.

In addition to appealing for government assistance, black women also applied for higher-paying jobs in the city. In 1938, the U.S. Civil Service announced that on Wednesday, October 12, it would accept applications for an estimated 2,000 charwoman jobs. Charwomen were the workers who cleaned the offices of the government and, despite their menial status, were on the federal payroll, received holiday benefits, and earned an annual salary of $1,080.[105] In contrast, wages for domestic servants in the District of Columbia ranged from $240 to $720 for long hours and had no holiday or retirement benefits.[106] While charwomen did not receive the retirement benefits promised by Social Security, the federal holiday benefits provided a measure of economic justice.

On Tuesday, October 11 by 8 P.M., prospective employees carrying milk crates, boxes, and newspapers began lining up outside the Fourth Police Precinct on E Street Southwest and prepared for a long night of waiting. The Fourth Precinct was located in a working-class majority (57%) black neighborhood located less than one mile from the U.S. Capitol.[107] As the hours went by," the *Washington Post* reported, "more and more women took their places." By the next morning, between 10,000 had 20,000 black women had arrived to receive applications. A newspaper article noted that "the avalanche of women forced officers of the Civil Service Commission to suspend distribution after 1,500 applications had been given out." When it was clear that applications were no longer being given, the crowds of women grew impatient and angry, causing police officers to silence them with their billy clubs and hoses. The large number of employees forced civil service officials to call on police reserves for backup assistance. The crowds were so great that they trampled over several prospective applicants.[108] Two women—T. E. Ryan (white) and Carrie Fields (black)—were injured and sent to the hospital, and an ambulance was dispatched to treat victims at the scene. The crowds also caused officers to redirect traffic on E Street Southwest between Fourth and Seventh Streets. Police officers arrested Edgar G. Brown, head of the United Government Employees union, charging him with "inciting the mob."[109] A columnist for the *Baltimore Afro-American* wrote, "That spectacle could hardly be duplicated in any other municipality because nowhere are jobs so attractive as in the Federal government, even for charwomen."[110]

Alice Miller had spent the night in line in front of the police station, curled up on a sheet of newspapers. She told reporters that "I could have gotten a chance at that blank and maybe went to work if that rush had not broken out."[111] Black women throughout the city viewed the charwomen position as a tremendous opportunity to improve their economic circumstances. By camping out at the Fourth Police Precinct, Alice Miller and thousands of other black women registered their visions for economic justice in the 1930s by expressing a strong preference for charwomen jobs in the federal government.

News of the eager job applicants circulated to black and white newspapers across the country, including the *New York Times*, the *Chicago Defender*, the *Los Angeles Times*, and the *Atlanta Daily Constitution*. Many of the articles also featured dramatic photo essays, revealing the stark juxtaposition between eager job applicants spilling into the street and police officers containing the crowds. Photographs showed black women of all ages at various times of day. In one photograph, three women dressed in dresses and coats stood on either side of an elderly woman seated on a barrel who was clutching a pair of crutches. The caption, "Some Came Crippled, Some Came Lame," depicted the varying physical conditions among the job applicants. The fact that women who struggled to walk sought applications for a physically taxing job as charwomen suggests their level of desperation.

Another photograph depicted three women seated on barrels, one cradling a child who appeared to be about five years old. Behind the seated women was a crowd of at least ten women, all whom looked eager for employment. A caption read "After All-Night Vigil," indicating that the women on barrels had spent the night at the Fourth Police Precinct.

In this episode, 10,000 to 20,000 black women in D.C. used their collective action to politically voice their discontent with the city's employment prospects. That thousands of women camped outside the police precinct hours before the distribution of job applications indicates their sheer desperation for employment that offered a decent salary and federal benefits. This movement was initially unplanned and spontaneous, and the evidence suggests that black women became increasingly politicized as police officers directed hoses and billy clubs at the crowd, shut down traffic, and arrested Edgar Brown. Police brutality against men and women was an issue of long-standing concern for

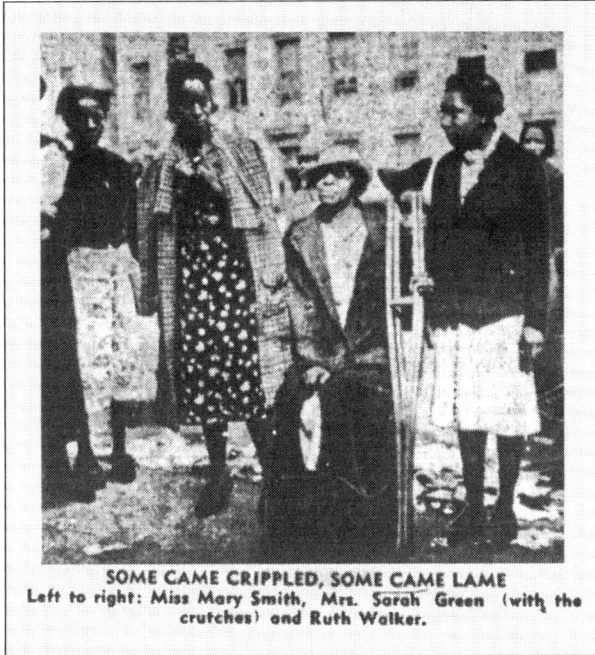

SOME CAME CRIPPLED, SOME CAME LAME
Left to right: Miss Mary Smith, Mrs. Sarah Green (with the crutches) and Ruth Walker.

Thousands of black women in Washington, D.C., were eager to apply to work as government charwomen. These jobs paid higher wages, offered more stable employment, and had an annual salary of more than $1,000. This photograph shows that even black women with physical disabilities camped outside the Fourth Police Precinct in October 1938 to receive applications to work as federal charwomen. *Baltimore Afro-American.*

African American residents in Washington, D.C., and this episode not only aggravated existing tensions in Southwest but also helped publicize this abuse to national audiences.[112] While the individual identities of most of the participants are unknown, it is very likely that many were either unemployed women or domestic workers who sought to improve their economic standing by obtaining steady wages and government benefits. In pressing for jobs as charwomen, African American women in Washington, D.C., used their bodies to help register their collective visions of economic justice for personal servants in the New Deal.

In the aftermath of the charwomen riot, the UGE held a meeting in which attendees sharply denounced the abuses that these women had faced. Edgar Brown, the president of the UGE who had been arrested in the riot, headed the meeting and was joined by a notable guest, Elizabeth McDuffie, a servant in the White House who had campaigned for President Roosevelt's reelection in 1936.[113] At the meeting, attendees cast votes on several resolutions that highlighted the abuse that the job applicants faced specifically, as well as their economic prospects more broadly. McDuffie asked meeting attendees to vote on a resolution that would allocate $10,000 to "make the Negro citizen's rights in the nation's capital and elsewhere something all men must recognize and respect, including police and civil service commissioners." McDuffie's resolution had overt, gendered language, casting black women as "citizens" who deserved "rights" and "respect," while police officers and civil service commissioners were the "men" who violated them. McDuffie then called for economic justice for black workers, arguing, "All those in high place who are responsible for the relief and employment opportunities throughout the country must heed the voice and feel the force the organization and demands for jobs and social security for one-tenths of the population of the 48 states who are colored Americans."[114] She and other meeting attendees passed a resolution calling for the removal of the superintendent of the police and condemned the "unnecessary roughness used by police in handling the women, who were standing in line to receive application blanks for jobs as federal charwomen."[115]

Two months after the charwomen riot, several domestic servants wrote letters that were published in the *Washington Post*. These letters indicate that workers' visions of democracy also reflected a quest for liberally guaranteed economic justice through inclusion in the Social Security Act. One woman, who signed her name, "A Self-Respecting Domestic Servant," called on Congress to expand the existing Social Security Act because servants "need protection when unemployed and when they become too old to work, just as industrial workers do." She concluded by noting that in the present circumstances, domestic servants rarely earned a "decent living" under "miserable working conditions."[116] Another woman who simply signed her name, "A Domestic," noted that she had been employed as a servant for the past twenty-eight years and claimed, "In many of the wealthy homes servants are working 15–20 hours daily underpaid with no pay for extra work or extra hours given off and are given less consideration than the family's pet dog."[117] Dissatisfied with their work and lack of government protections, these two women demanded economic justice rights through fair wages and better treatment.

Conclusion

In February 1936, Beatrice "Bessie" Mercer, who was the head of the District Beauticians League, discussed black women's economic circumstances with a reporter from the *Washington Afro-American*. "The real story of the Depression," she stated, "may never be written. We have heard of unemployment of white collar needs or of youth, but few stories of the heroism of our women." She went on to discuss how many African American women in Washington, D.C., were the sole wage earners and were supporting their families at low-paying jobs.[118] In this interview Bessie Mercer echoed the voices and sentiments of thousands of black women in the nation's capital during the Great Depression and New Deal eras.

During the 1930s, African American women were excited about the possibilities of the New Deal and worked hard to transform these government programs to benefit working-class women, whether by pressing for the inclusion of domestic workers in the NRA or critiquing domestic workers' exclusion from the Social Security Act. They also waged grassroots campaigns to secure economic justice. Activists in the New Negro Alliance recruited housewives to boycott stores that would not hire black workers and staged campaigns to secure employment for black girls and boys. As the director of the District Employment Center, Myra Colson Callis connected unemployed women with jobs in domestic service. Nannie Helen Burroughs formed the Northeast Cooperative to assist struggling citizens in that neighborhood. All of these ventures helped working-class women put food on their table. Working-class black women articulated their own desires to secure economic justice, whether it was writing letters to weigh in on economic policy, rioting for jobs as federal charwomen, or staging sit-ins to demand government assistance. African American women's activism and resistance evinced their desire to secure economic justice in the nation's capital.

Throughout their campaigns for economic justice, African American women increasingly recognized that their lack of civil rights in the nation's capital thwarted their broader goals. Black Washingtonians felt unsafe around police, faced a segmented labor market, had to contend with condescending policy officials, and could not elect their own representatives. The next chapter examines African American women's efforts to secure civil rights in the 1930s.

CHAPTER FIVE

Washington Needs the Vote

Women's Campaigns for Civil Rights in the 1930s

On Saturday, April 30, 1938, nearly 94,000 black and white citizens living in the nation's capital exercised one of the most sacred rights of American citizenship: they voted. The polls in Washington, D.C., had been closed for more than sixty years, since 1874 when Congress had taken control of the nation's capital. All residents of the city then lost the right to vote and were denied control over most local governance. Sixty-four years later, citizens participated in a referendum to determine if residents favored the franchise, which would enable them to vote in local and national elections and enjoy representation in Congress. Washington residents strongly supported voting rights, with 87,000 ballots cast for enfranchisement and only 6,832 in opposition. Voting rights found their strongest champions among black Washingtonians, who comprised 24 percent of the voting population: more than 99 percent of black Washingtonians endorsed local suffrage. "Colored residents without question," an article in the *Washington Afro-American* concluded, "took a very active part in balloting." Many of the citizens interviewed at the polls expressed enthusiasm about restoring voting rights in the nation's capital. When asked how she felt about voting, Sallie Carrington, a seventy-six-year-old woman, replied that she was "glad to have an opportunity" to do her "part," remarking, "I sure hope we get a vote here in the District."[1] The significance of this act of citizenship was not lost on this former resident of Virginia who was born in the 1860s as men and women were fighting to end slavery. During the 1930s, black women like Sallie Carrington evoked memories of the Reconstruction era as they worked to restore some of the freedoms that African Americans had lost when Congress had reorganized the government in the 1870s.

During the 1930s, black women and men worked to enact civil rights in the nation's capital. Inspired by the militancy of the Great Depression and influenced by ongoing campaigns for safety and economic justice, activists protested racial segregation, lobbied for the passage of a civil rights bill, and pressed for the restoration of voting rights to all eligible residents of Washington, D.C. The struggle for civil rights involved the restoration of full citizenship rights for African Americans in Washington, D.C., a matter of local concern that, at times, attracted a national and international audience. Throughout the

1930s, black Washingtonians, like their counterparts in other cities, worked to integrate the dressing rooms and restrooms in department stores so that black women would be permitted to use the facilities on the same basis as white women. This was about equal treatment, but it also concerned the visibility of black women's bodies in different spaces throughout the city. Late in the decade, this same issue resurfaced when the Daughters of the American Revolution forbade the famed opera singer Marian Anderson from performing in Constitution Hall. This matter circulated across the press wires and played out on a national stage, thereby alerting citizens across the country about where black women could and could not appear in the nation's capital. When Marian Anderson performed on the steps of the Lincoln Memorial on Easter Sunday in 1939, her concert helped raise national consciousness about racial segregation in the nation's capital.

Black Washingtonians waged their civil rights campaigns in the shadows of the Lincoln Memorial and the Frederick Douglass House, which nurtured discovery and revelation. During the 1930s, black women and men untangled the threads that connected the past, the present, and future. Nineteenth-century policies toward African Americans in Washington, D.C., were experiments that were implemented ahead of other states and helped shape national practice. For example, the city's slave trade ended in 1850, emancipation was decreed in 1862, and formerly enslaved men in the city were first in the nation to cast ballots. During Reconstruction in the nation's capital, black men received patronage appointments, and black women and men worked to influence local governance. But in 1874, Congress disfranchised all residents of the city, thereby ending the city's progress toward racial justice. In the 1890s, southern states began to follow suit. Black Washingtonians recognized that they had a unique role to play in securing freedom, first for themselves as citizens of the nation's capital and then for African Americans living across the nation. By the late 1930s, activists argued that residents of the nation's capital needed a second emancipation and Reconstruction to restore their full citizenship rights.

Black women joined new organizations and tapped connections in existing ones to conduct their civil rights campaigns. Many women who had been visible in national politics in the 1920s became civil rights organizers in the 1930s—recruiting citizens to support the restoration of voting rights, protesting segregation in department stores, or championing the passage of a civil rights bill. The city's organizational landscape broadened during this decade to include the National Negro Congress, the New Negro Alliance, the Washington Interracial Committee, the Citizen's Joint Conference on Welfare, the Alpha Kappa Alpha's Non-Partisan Lobby for Economic and Democratic

Rights, and several voting rights groups. Black women served in leadership positions in all of these organizations and mined their networks in social clubs, sororities, churches, and the Phyllis Wheatley YWCA to bolster each cause.

Dr. Ionia Rollin Whipper, a physician, served as a prominent leader in Washington's civil rights movement. Whipper's activism was rooted in her vocation as a doctor, her location in the nation's capital, and her family's political past. A native of Beaufort, South Carolina, she received her degree from Howard University Medical School in 1903. During the 1920s, she worked for the U.S. Children's Bureau, traveling to southern states to provide instruction for midwives under the auspices of the Shepard-Towner Act. In the 1930s, she oriented her activism toward local conditions in the nation's capital by working to end racial segregation and advocating for the restoration of voting rights. As a doctor, Whipper saw firsthand how segregation affected black health, and as a citizen of Washington, she understood that disfranchisement thwarted citizen's political power. Whipper's heritage also inspired her political activism. Her father, William James Whipper, was an abolitionist who fought in the Civil War and, during the 1870s, was a representative to South Carolina's constitutional convention and was elected to the legislature, where he championed voting rights for both African Americans and women. However, William Whipper also witnessed the transition from democracy to disfranchisement when a literacy clause was added to the South Carolina constitution in 1895. Whipper's mother, Frances Rollin Whipper, was a free woman of color from Charleston who had a distinguished career as a writer and political activist.[2] Ionia Whipper's family history epitomized the flourishing of black rights during Reconstruction, and she honored these memories in her political activism during the 1930s.

Comparing black politics in Washington, D.C., with struggles conducted across the nation reveals both parallels and differences. Scholars argue that, during the 1930s, African Americans across the country waged an "early" or "long" civil rights movement.[3] Thousands of African Americans united to improve working conditions, picketed white businesses to expand employment opportunities, challenged the legality of segregation, and mobilized voters to elect black politicians at the local and state levels.[4] Black women were especially visible in campaigns to organize domestic servants; establish economic cooperatives; and participate in New Deal programs, such as sewing rooms, theater productions, and oral history projects.[5] Black Washingtonians participated in these types of projects throughout the nation's capital, shaped by the local conditions in the city.

But the black freedom struggle in Washington, D.C., differed considerably from that waged in the rest of the nation. The transition from a focus on national politics to local affairs brought clarity to black Washingtonians about the precise needs for equality, freedom, and justice in the nation's capital. In their campaigns to end police violence, black citizens recognized that some members of the congressional Committee on the District of Columbia openly endorsed the police's methods of brutality and that the Board of Commissioners expressed apathy about their protest campaigns. Similarly, in their campaigns for economic justice, black Washingtonians expressed frustration that residential segregation forced black citizens to pay higher rents, were angry that black women had few labor opportunities beyond domestic service, and bristled at the stinginess of relief agencies toward poor black women who were supporting their families. All of these experiences underscored the need for racial integration, civil rights legislation, black voting rights, and local control over governance. Black Washingtonians were able to pursue these campaigns before their peers in southern states did precisely because of their charged location in the nation's capital, which was a crucial instrument in their protest politics. As memories of the Civil War and Reconstruction surfaced, activists applied the lessons from these decades directly to their political campaigns.

During the 1930s, black women and men worked to secure legal equality in Washington, D.C., although they were not naïve enough to believe that laws guaranteeing equal treatment would solve the injustices that plagued the nation's capital. Women's campaigns for integration and voting rights in Washington, D.C., intersected with their parallel struggles to secure physical safety and economic justice for black citizens. The civil rights movement for legal equality formed an important dimension of the crusade for democracy in the nation's capital. Cognizant of the unique place of Washington, D.C., in national politics, activists recognized that ending discrimination in the nation's capital was a critical first step in securing freedom and justice for black Americans living across the nation. Their campaigns soon became caught up in history, leading citizens to recognize that it was vital to enact racial integration, civil rights, and voting rights in the nation's capital and so serve as a model for the rest of the nation.

"Jim Crow Capital": The Fight against Segregation

For black and white Washingtonians, racial segregation was an everyday part of the urban landscape. In the 1930s, several different branches of government enforced these policies. The city's laws required schools, public hospitals, playgrounds, and swimming pools be segregated by race. The U.S. Park Police controlled 483 public parks in the city and restricted black Washingtonians' access to certain green spaces and picnic areas. Even though some agencies in the federal government had dismantled Wilsonian-era segregation practices by the 1930s, others still demanded that employees use separate bathrooms.[6] Through restrictive covenants, which the U.S. Supreme Court upheld in Washington, D.C., in 1924 in the landmark case, *Corrigan v. Buckley*, white citizens could prevent black citizens from purchasing homes in particular neighborhoods. Private establishments enforced a system of de facto segregation. Most white-owned theaters, restaurants, department stores, churches, and cemeteries either required black Washingtonians to occupy inferior spaces or banned them altogether.

The campaign against segregation in the nation's capital had been waged for decades, but the struggle intensified during the 1930s. As black women worked to abolish interracial police brutality and fight for economic justice, they recognized that racial segregation was a root cause of these issues. By the mid-1930s, black Washingtonians termed Washington, D.C., the "Jim Crow Capital," arguing that the discrimination in their city resembled the worst practices of the U.S. South. This charged language brought urgency to the struggle for integration. After they failed in their campaigns to abolish segregation, activists concluded that the only solution was to pass a civil rights bill for the District of Columbia.

Articles in the black press chronicled disputes over segregation throughout the city. In March 1932 during the Easter holiday, Olivia W. Baker was kneeling in a pew at the Church of the Immaculate Conception, located on Ninth Street in Northwest Washington. A white usher tapped her on the shoulder, demanded that she vacate the pew, and informed her that she could only pray in the segregated area of the church. Baker, incensed at the prospect of segregation in church, informed the parish that she would not be returning to worship there.[7] Four months later, citizens discovered that the U.S. Parks Department had issued new orders stipulating that African Americans could picnic only in certain areas of Rock Creek Park, which was a popular recreational destination for black Washingtonians, especially for women and girls affiliated with the Phyllis Wheatley YWCA.[8] A cohort of forty black ministers throughout the city protested this policy to Colonel Ulysses S. Grant, the U.S. Parks head and grandson of former Union general and Reconstruction-era president Ulysses S. Grant. After an unproductive meeting, ministers sent him a pointed letter that expressed their opposition to segregation. In response, Grant noted that he was "surprised" that "educated Negroes" were "objecting to equal accommodations in Rock Creek Park." Refusing to change the policy, he tried to ameliorate the situation by "consent[ing]" to allow African Americans into restricted sections "for this time." The Ministers Alliance sharply rejected this temporary policy. In a strongly worded letter, the Ministers Alliance told Grant that "Such discrimination under the shadow of the National Capitol not only belies the basic principle of American institutions—the equality of citizenship—but discredits your avowal of purpose to afford equal privilege and opportunity to all."[9] Thus black ministers acknowledged the contradictions of segregation in the nation's capital and articulated a vision of full citizenship.

Black women protested segregation by creating new organizations and working with existing ones. In 1932, a group of distinguished black and white Washingtonians affiliated with the local chapter of the NAACP formed the Washington Interracial Committee (IRC) to improve the status of African Americans in the city. Members focused on four areas of inequality: segregation, labor, culture, and education. Many women who had been involved in national politics during the 1920s joined the IRC, including Republican organizer Mary Church Terrell, physician Ionia Whipper, poet Carrie Williams Clifford, former YWCA President Frances Boyce, Dean of Women Students Lucy Diggs Slowe at Howard University, pharmacist Amanda Gray Hilyer, teacher Emma Merritt, and truant officer Coralie Cook.[10]

Members of the Washington Interracial Committee critiqued the ways that segregation created inequality in the city. Funding for black schools had decreased significantly in the 1932 municipal budget for Washington, D.C. IRC members staged a mass meeting in the auditorium of Garnet-Patterson High School to protest this paltry funding. Emma Merritt, a retired teacher, YWCA organizer, and president of the local branch of the NAACP, led the meeting, in which attendees noted the poor conditions of elementary schools, typified by overcrowded classrooms and part-time instruction.[11] The IRC also investigated segregation in chain stores across the city. Committee members Walter W. Brooks, YWCA membership coordinator Mae Stewart Thompson, and white activist Gertrude Stone visited various stores across the city. At one drug store, a manager informed them that drug stores in the city either served black customers on paper plates or refused them service altogether.[12] The IRC's campaigns highlighted that racial segregation in Washington, D.C., resulted in unequal funding for black schools and an inferior dining experience for black customers.

Racial segregation also affected black citizens' health and welfare. In 1934, black Washingtonians formed the Citizens' Joint Conference on Welfare at the

Phyllis Wheatley YWCA to advocate for improved health conditions. This group, which was part of the Federation of Civic Associations, focused on three areas: preventive health care, remedial health care, and public health administration. The committee comprised public health professionals and civic leaders, including physician Ionia Whipper, pharmacist Amanda Gray Hilyer, and YWCA president Julia West Hamilton. The fact that Whipper and Hilyer were in both the IRC and the Citizens' Joint Conference on Welfare during the 1930s indicates how seriously they took the issue of racial segregation. The Citizens' Joint Conference on Welfare submitted petitions to the D.C. Board of Commissioners, demanding better health care facilities and more funding for black Washingtonians.[13]

Members of the Citizens' Joint Conference connected black Washingtonians' poor public health to segregation and disfranchisement. In September 1934, an article in the *Philadelphia Tribune* ran with the dramatic headline, "Babies Die by the Hundreds in the Shadow of the U.S. Capitol." The article described how a lack of black hospitals and funding for public health initiatives increased black mortality. It noted, "Five hundred colored babies less than a year old died in Washington last year for lack of proper medical care, or better from lack of proper sanitary measure." Additionally, four hundred black adults died from tuberculosis. The Citizens' Joint Conference on Welfare issued this statement: "Washingtonians have not the right of franchise and they are appealing to colored people throughout the nation to prevail upon their Congressional representatives to force the Seventy-Fourth Congress to exert final authority over the District of Columbia, through the Congressional appropriation, for a program which will save the lives of colored citizens." The Joint Conference's statement marked an important reversal in black political strategies. During the 1920s, black Washingtonians had lobbied in Congress on behalf of African Americans around the country, and in the 1930s, they were asking black voters across the nation to influence Congress for their local interests.[14]

Finally, activists in the Alpha Kappa Alpha Sorority's local chapter, Xi Omega, formed a Non-Partisan Lobby for Economic and Democratic Rights in the nation's capital in 1938. AKA was a black women's sorority formed at Howard University in 1908, which had grown tremendously in the interwar years. In 1938 after a Founders May Meeting, members of Xi Omega decided that they needed a formal lobbying organization in Washington, D.C., to focus on housing, mortality, and economic inequalities. While the AKA lobbied on behalf of African Americans living across the United States, its local chapter was an important ally in the fight for democracy in Washington, D.C., through restoration of voting rights and the passage of a civil rights bill. The Xi Omega chapter selected Norma Boyd, a teacher and founding member, to serve as its first lobbyist. Other women on the lobbying committee included members of the local chapter of the AKA, such as Dorothy Boulding Ferebee and Marjorie Hollman.[15]

In addition to fighting segregation in education and health care, black women protested racial segregation in department stores. During the 1920s, department stores had been some of the few spaces in the city where black and white women were treated equally.[16] The largest department store in the city was the Hecht Company, which was known as the "Macys of Washington," and was located on F Street in Northwest Washington. In the mid-1930s, Hecht's reversed its policies and began barring black women from fitting rooms and forcing them to use restrooms in the rear of the store. Prominent women in the city, including Employment Center director Myra Colson Callis and Women's Political Study Club members Jacqueline Cuney and Jeannette Carter, were shocked and visited Hecht's to investigate these practices. Cuney, who also served as president of the Bloomingdale Citizen's Association, organized a mass meeting at the Tabor Presbyterian Church, where she and meeting attendees voted to send a letter of protest to the company.[17]

Since Hecht's Department Store did not respond to these protests, these activists invited more organizations to join the fight, including the Federation of Parent-Teacher Associations, the National Negro Congress, the NAACP, the Phyllis Wheatley YWCA, and the Baptist Minister's Union. Julia West Hamilton, then president of the YWCA, held a mass meeting at the center to which she invited a representative from Hecht's to speak to black Washingtonians. At the meeting Hamilton told the Hecht's representative that when the department store first opened, "you seemed very anxious for colored trade" and questioned whether it was "fair to begin now to discriminate against people who have helped make you who you are?" Attorney Belford Lawson from the New Negro Alliance argued that his organization represented "10,000 consumers and we want to know if you appreciate our business. We don't want to go to the press and say that the Hecht Company persists in this discrimination and ask patrons to stay away."[18] In June 1936, African Americans held another mass meeting at the Metropolitan Baptist Church in Northwest Washington, at which Howard University professor E. Franklin Frazier argued, "Colored businesses cannot match economic power with big business, but it can organize mass power." He urged black Washingtonians to emulate their strategy of maintaining ongoing boycotts of stores that did not hire black workers by canceling their accounts with Hecht's.[19] Despite these collective protests, black

Washingtonians were unable to convince Hecht's Department Store to disman-
tle its practices of segregation.

Black protests against segregation reached a turning point in 1935, when
white journalist Marguerite Young wrote a landmark article titled "Washington: Jim Crow Capital of the United States." This article was first published in
the *Washington Afro-American* and reprinted in black newspapers in the country, as well as the Marxist magazine, *New Masses*, which reported on African
American women's activism.[20] Young boldly underscored the contradictions
of black life in the nation's capital—a city filled with promise and opportunity
but marred by poverty, inequality, and violence, all within walking distance of
the U.S. Capitol. She claimed that Washington, D.C., had "echoes of the plantation" because many powerful members of Congress—who wielded control
over the nation's capital—were more "prominent in the scene than in years."[21]
Through this article, Marguerite Young not only connected Washington, D.C.,
with the worst symptoms of the Jim Crow South but she also linked this inequality with the lingering legacies of slavery.

Terming Washington, D.C., the "Jim Crow Capital" of the United States signaled activists' intentions to abolish racial segregation immediately. At the
same time that activists employed this rhetoric, men and women in the New
Negro Alliance began to discuss civil rights legislation for the nation's capital.
By the mid-1930s, sixteen states in the North and Midwest had passed civil
rights bills that forbade discrimination against African Americans. In 1935, the
state legislatures in neighboring Pennsylvania and New Jersey also passed civil
rights laws, presumably to protect the rights of southern African Americans
who had recently migrated to these states.[22] Black Washingtonians followed
this news with interest and curiosity. As an article in the *Washington Tribune*
explained, "The recent passage of similar bills in New Jersey and Pennsylvania has given impetus to the demand for such a bill in the capital of the nation."[23]

William Hastie and Charles Hamilton Houston, two Harvard-educated
lawyers in the leadership of the New Negro Alliance, wrote the text of a civil
rights bill for Washington, D.C.: it "penalize[d] by fine any person or corpora-
tion in the District of Columbia denying equal accommodations, advantages,
and privileges to any person because of race, creed, or color." Not only did
Hastie and Houston have legal training but they were also graduates of the
prestigious Dunbar High School in Washington, D.C. The historian Patricia
Sullivan notes that Dunbar's curriculum brimmed with African American history, with a particular emphasis on the Reconstruction era. It is likely, then,
that Hastie and Houston were inspired by their knowledge of Reconstruction
to write a civil rights bill for the nation's capital.[24] Hastie recognized the close

connection between the civil rights bill and other campaigns for justice across the city. He argued, "The fight for civil rights in work opportunities and political and social justice is so closely related to the fight for civil rights in general, until success and advancement in the cause of one brings success and advancement for the other."[25] He thus affirmed black Washingtonians' wide-ranging freedom struggles that prioritized economic justice, safety, and civil rights.

After they wrote the text of the bill, Houston and Hastie worked to locate a member of Congress to sponsor the legislation. They found an ally in Representative Herman P. Kopplemann, a Jewish Democrat from Connecticut whose family had emigrated from Russia to the United States to escape religious persecution. In June 1935, Kopplemann introduced a civil rights bill for Washington, D.C., in the U.S. House of Representatives and a variety of organizations in Washington supported its passage.[26] Kopplemann argued that twenty states in the United States had passed such legislation and that "the national capital should act as an example in this respect."[27] In June 1935, an article in the *Washington Tribune* reported that the New Negro Alliance (NNA) launched an "intensive drive" to "ensure speedy passage of the bill," tapping "civil, labor, fraternal, and religious organizations" to organize for civil rights.[28] One month later in July, the *Washington Afro-American* began running articles calling Washington, D.C., the "Jim Crow Capital" and focusing on different facets of injustice, including in housing, education, and public accommodations. Along with the black press, activists worked to educate the black community in Washington about the importance of civil rights legislation. In November 1935, they staged a mass meeting, and one month later, YWCA president Julia West Hamilton chaired a roundtable meeting of civic associations throughout the city about the civil rights bill.[29] However, progress was slow. As momentum stalled on the bill, activists redirected their energy toward restoring voting rights in the nation's capital.

"Washington Needs the Vote": The Push for Voting Rights

In July 1932, *Washington Tribune* columnist Beatrice Murphy endorsed the restoration of voting rights in the nation's capital. Murphy, a writer and social worker, argued that at the same time residents were facing discrimination at every corner, disfranchisement had rendered them powerless. "The D.C. citizen is denied a multitude of privileges that is the right of every American citizen," she noted, "which are enjoyed on the whole by men and women living under state banners." She called on the men and women of the nation's

capital to "fight not as individuals, but as a group for the privilege of voting—
for the certain inalienable rights which should be theirs as tax-paying American citizens."[30] In this column, Murphy identified voting as a right of
citizenship and foreshadowed black women's crusade for the restoration of
the suffrage.

During the 1930s, women channeled new energy and directed activist
networks toward the long struggle for voting rights in the nation's capital. In
the previous decade, many activists had focused on absentee voting, but in the
1930s, they argued that all residents of the nation's capital should be able to vote.
Activists tapped their networks in labor, politics, and social reform arenas to
rally citizens at the grassroots level. Working alongside male allies, they helped
encourage more than 23,000 black citizens to cast ballots in a referendum election in 1938, which unequivocally demonstrated that African Americans in
the nation's capital favored the franchise. In addition to possessing organizing
skills, black women also embodied respectable citizenship in the nation's capital. For some white Washingtonians, the history of voting rights in the nation's
capital evoked the era of Reconstruction, when black men had wielded power
and influence. Voting rights activists countered these false memories by strategically showcasing educated and elite black women as the model citizens who
should have the right to cast ballots in the nation's capital.

Black Washingtonians formed new organizations to press for local voting
rights. In April 1932, Beatrice Murphy organized the Young People's Study Club.
As a nonpartisan organization, the Young People's Study Club was designed
to "educate and interest the young Negroes in the principles of the political
parties and Governmental affairs" in order to uplift their "race and community." The organizing committee comprised four women and two men, and it
held weekly meetings at the headquarters of the National Association of Colored Women (NACW) on O Street in Northwest Washington.[31] While this
organization focused on educating young people in the city about politics,
Murphy, in her capacity as president, likely addressed the issue of local voting
rights. Activists in the Young People's Study Club were broad-minded about
politics. Not only did they invite Republican and Democratic officials to speak
to their club but they also hosted representatives from the Communist and Socialist Parties, which reflected the leftist climate of the 1930s. It is possible that
members quizzed all of these different politicians about their opinions on
voting rights in the nation's capital.[32]

Several months later, black men and women in Washington, D.C., organized
the Progressive Democratic Club. This organization's mission was explicitly
tied to local voting rights; its statement of purpose noted that it sought to in-

fluence the "management of our government to alleviate human suffering and to contend for the right of the franchise in the District of Columbia."[33] This organization was short-lived, but black citizens continued to fight for the cause throughout the decade. The Young People's Study Club and Progressive Democratic Club reflected black Washingtonians' long-standing engagement in partisan politics, but had an exclusive focus on local voting rights. The historian Elizabeth Gritter notes that, during the 1930s, African Americans throughout the South formed many voting organizations and leagues, and the activities of black Washingtonians mirrored these broader patterns.[34]

The black press in Washington, D.C., issued strong endorsements for voting rights through informative articles and compelling editorials. Each presidential election offered black Washingtonians another opportunity to reflect on their disfranchisement, which was ironic because black citizens resided in the city where each new administration worked. In June 1932, an editorial in the *Washington Tribune* titled "Washington Needs the Vote" outlined all of the benefits of voting in the nation's capital—having a voice in the local government, being able to elect the candidates of their choice for the Board of Commissioners or the School Board, or exercising governance over local transportation matters. "Can we truthfully say," the editorial asked, "that the District of Columbia is the land of the free?" The editorial concluded by succinctly stating, "Washington needs the vote badly."[35]

Another editorial in October 1936 contemplated the upcoming presidential election, which tested black voter's loyalty to the party of Lincoln against President Franklin D. Roosevelt's bold New Deal. Polls showed that 69 percent of African Americans across the country appeared to favor Presidential Roosevelt, which marked a major switch from the 1932 election. This editorial wondered whether black Washingtonians' political preferences matched national patterns. This was an important question, because, making up one-third of the city's population, black Washingtonians, if they voted in a bloc, would be a powerful force. "We want," the editorial insisted, "to make a fight for suffrage here."[36]

This editorial invited all readers to participate in a "voteless poll" by mailing their "ballots" into the newspaper office so it could track their voting preferences. Within one week, 5,707 black women and men, or approximately 4 percent of the black population in the city, complied. By performing the act of voting, black Washingtonians proclaimed their citizenship in spite of their disfranchisement. This "voteless poll" mirrored the tactic of staging citizen's police brutality trials, demonstrating black Washingtonians' desire to participate in the acts of citizenship. This informal poll soon gained the attention of

the white public. An article in the *Washington Post* released the findings, revealing that black Washingtonians favored Franklin D. Roosevelt, but only
slightly, with 2,976 votes for FDR and 2,731 votes for Governor Al Landon.[37]
The fact that black Washingtonians did not overwhelmingly favor FDR indicates that many citizens had not benefited greatly from New Deal programs.
However, the collective action of more than five thousand black Washingtonians to register their political opinions through stamps and envelopes showed
citizens' eagerness to cast ballots on a regular basis.

Not only were citizens enthusiastic about voting but they also understood
that the suffrage would grant them a stronger voice over the distribution of
funding throughout the city. In February 1934, the Senate's Committee on the
District of Columbia released its budget, which appropriated only 25 percent
of the education budget to black schools in Washington, D.C., despite the fact
that black students made up 34 percent of the student population.[38] In response, members of the Federation of Women of Washington and Vicinity
submitted a letter to the Senate committee, in which they highlighted black
citizens' disenfranchisement in the city with funding cuts for schools and public welfare. Black women told the committee that black citizens "would be
given less of a voteless voice as to how their taxes shall be spent." They further
argued that these funding cuts would delay important public works projects,
including street construction and electricity for public buildings and pointed
out that many unemployed citizens in the black community had been count-
ing on these jobs. In this pointed letter, members of the Federation of Women
of Washington and Vicinity argued that if black citizens could vote, they
could exercise more control over the distribute of funding in their city.[39]

This argument reflected a discernible shift in black women's political thinking as they now cast themselves as having a "voteless voice" and positioned
restoration of the suffrage as a top priority. Prominent political activists in the
Federation of Women of Washington and Vicinity included Nannie Helen
Burroughs, Julia West Hamilton, Marian Butler, and Emma Holcomb, all of
whom had been active in national partisan activities in the 1920s.[40] Emma
Holcomb had traveled to neighboring Maryland to encourage black women
to vote in that state, while Julia West Hamilton had lobbied for the construction of the National Negro Memorial. Marian Butler had visited Maryland to
encourage women to vote, but she had also testified in Congress on behalf of
anti-lynching legislation and had worked to prevent the confirmation of Supreme Court Justice nominee John J. Parker. Their efforts benefited black
women living across the country. Now, in the 1930s, these women argued
that casting ballots in their own city was essential for justice and democracy.

As residents of the nation's capital, most black women could not vote. However, women and men still registered their political opinions through meetings and organizations, participating in the *Washington Tribune*'s voterless poll, and supporting their candidates through posters, as shown in this photo of a woman in Southwest Washington with an image of FDR. Library of Congress, LC-USZ62-139542.

Ten months later, Nannie Helen Burroughs delivered a speech on racial violence where she pointed to the vote as the instrument of civil rights. While she did not specifically mention Washington, D.C., she was both a member of the Federation of Women of Washington and Vicinity and a resident of

Washington, D.C., so it was likely that local suffrage was not very far from her mind.[41]

As black citizens expressed renewed interest in local voting rights, they began to connect their struggle with memories of the Civil War and Reconstruction. Black women and men had always commemorated emancipation, sponsored pilgrimages to the Frederick Douglass House, and woven African American history into their political culture. But by the mid-1930s, these historical eras gained more salience as sources of inspiration. In 1935, renowned scholar and activist W. E. B. Du Bois published his magisterial *Black Reconstruction in America*, a revisionist history that celebrated the stunning achievements of interracial democracy in the 1860s and 1870s. In his book, Du Bois grappled with the unique history of Washington, D.C., in the era of Reconstruction. It is likely that at least a few black Washingtonians read this book or perused reviews of it in the black press. It is unclear if Du Bois ever delivered a Reconstruction lecture in the city during the 1930s, but he did speak to the local chapter of the NAACP on the subject of Italy and Ethiopia in 1936, when it is possible that the subject of Reconstruction arose.[42] That same year, Carter G. Woodson's Association for the Study of Negro Life and History, which was based in Washington, D.C., received federal funding to craft lessons for Works Progress Administration adult education classes on African American history; the unit on the Civil War and Reconstruction included a lesson plan written by Du Bois.[43] Two years later, the Association for the Study of Negro Life and History issued a set of themes for the upcoming Negro History Week. One theme posed the question: "How did the Negro help to win his own freedom during the Civil War?" while another asked, "Who were the corruptionists during the Reconstruction: Negroes or the whites to whom the Negroes sincerely trusted?" By urging citizens to investigate these matters during Negro History Week, Woodson encouraged African Americans to explore critical questions about the period of Reconstruction and untangle mythology from the truth in that unprecedented period of African American rights.

Civil rights organizations in Washington, D.C., also connected the era of Reconstruction with black rights in the nation's capital. Shortly before Juneteenth in 1936 commemorating the end of slavery in the United States, NNA president Howard N. Fitzhugh delivered an address focusing on the immediate postslavery era. Fitzhugh argued that in the "days immediately following the Civil War" there were "numerous barber shops and small hotels were operated by the Negroes for whites" in the nation's capital. But "the day . . . is gone when the Negro can operate a business."[44] Thus African Americans across the country and in the nation's capital were pondering the legacies of Reconstruction and working to disseminate this knowledge to the black community, whether through the pages of a scholarly book, a night school class, a community celebration, or a Negro History Week event.

As discussions about emancipation and Reconstruction spread across Washington, a cohort of black women and men increased their efforts to restore voting rights. At a mass meeting in August 1937 devoted to suffrage, NNA secretary Arnetta Randall read a resolution supporting voting rights in Washington, and fellow NNA members B. T. Montgomery and Wesley Hall endorsed her call.[45]

But while black Washingtonians were connecting the Civil War and Reconstruction with democracy, Mississippi senator Theodore G. Bilbo was working to reverse racial progress in the nation's capital. Bilbo, a former governor of Mississippi, embodied the mores of the Jim Crow South through his open endorsement of racial segregation and his affiliation with the Ku Klux Klan. A senator since 1935, Bilbo had emerged as one of the most stringent opponents to racial justice in Congress.[46] In 1938, he shocked most Americans when he endorsed black repatriation to Africa. Citing President Abraham Lincoln and the 1862 District of Columbia Emancipation Act, which allocated $100,000 for colonization, Bilbo argued that the United States was a nation for one, not two, races.[47] One month later, Bilbo introduced a bill in the Senate to ban interracial marriage in Washington, D.C. Black Washingtonians sharply denounced both of Bilbo's proposals. The fact that a senator from Mississippi could shape the laws for black citizens of the nation's capital only signaled the profound urgency of restoring voting rights.[48]

Prominent black activists, both women and men, banded together with the Citizen's Joint Conference on National Representation for the District of Columbia, a coalition of sixty white and black organizations that favored voting rights in Washington. The organization had been founded in 1917, but it was in the 1930s when it gained popularity.[49] NNA member and president of Local 27 of the Teachers Union, Mary Mason Jones was elected to the executive council of the Citizen's Conference. As the labor leader for one thousand black teachers in the city, Jones was in regular contact with parents, administrators, and students, making her an essential organizer for voting rights. Additionally, physician Ionia Whipper, an activist in the Tuesday Evening Club of Social Workers and member of the Citizen's Joint Conference for health equality, arranged for her organization to be part of this coalition.[50] Whipper was already a vocal critic of segregation in the city, and her family's history during Reconstruction likely inspired her activism for suffrage. Finally,

AKA's Xi Omega's Non-Partisan Lobby for Economic and Democratic Rights joined the Citizen's Conference.[51] Male leaders in the NNA, including government worker George Rycraw and civic activists Howard Woodson and Theophilus Houston, were also elected to the executive council of the Citizen's Conference.[52] Activists' networks in education, civil service, sororities, and political causes were thus critical for mobilizing a broad coalition of black Washingtonians to press for the restoration of voting rights.

In late March 1938, members of the Citizen's Joint Conference on National Representation for the District of Columbia convinced the D.C. Board of Commissioners to hold a referendum on suffrage on Saturday, April 30, from nine in the morning until nine in the evening. Any resident of the nation's capital who was over the age of twenty-one was eligible to cast a ballot on that day. The city's public schools would serve as the polling places, which meant that most black and white Washingtonians would vote separately.[53] Following the referendum, the U.S. House of Representatives would hold a hearing about the election results and would consider restoring voting rights in the nation's capital.

For black Washingtonians, this referendum was filled with promise, but fraught with danger. Over the past seventeen years, whenever the subject of local voting rights had arisen in the press or in congressional hearings, many white Washingtonians had expressed opposition, either by evoking the "tragic era" of Reconstruction or arguing that black Washingtonians should not be permitted to cast ballots because of their lack of education or wealth accumulation.[54] Under these circumstances, black Washingtonians' voting behaviors would be closely scrutinized and could potentially determine the fate of democracy in the city. The logistics of the referendum were also complicated. Activists had less than one month to raise awareness about the importance of voting, and for many black Washingtonians, this act of citizenship was unfamiliar. Black women and men thus reached out to churches, civic associations, schools, sororities, and social organizations to encourage African Americans across the city to cast ballots in the referendum. On the evening before the election, citizens across the city participated in a parade to celebrate the occasion.[55]

On Saturday, April 30, 1938, the eyes of the nation turned to the 23,172 black Washingtonians who cast ballots in eleven black schools across the city. The polls opened at nine in the morning, but at Garnet-Patterson School in Northwest Washington, 200 people were already waiting in line at 8:30 A.M. A newspaper article in the *Washington Afro-American* reported, "Young, old, rich, poor, the feeble, the halt, and even the blind were among those slipping ballots into the box" and that black voters' enthusiasm "bespoke an election spirit which may become a reality in the District."[56] It was quite significant that more than 20,000 black Washingtonians participated in this election after such a short period of preparation, demonstrating the effectiveness of activists in raising the political consciousness of citizens across the city. The vote was tallied by race but not by gender, so it is not known how many black women participated in the referendum; however, the evidence suggests that they were quite prominent. Many of the first people to cast ballots at various precincts were black women, such as beauty salon owner Marie Brent at Garnet-Patterson or Mrs. George Stanley at Browne Junior High in Northeast.[57]

Not only did black women cast ballots in the referendum but they also worked as election officials, registration clerks, and precinct judges, reflecting the strength of black women's networks throughout the city. For instance, Dr. Ionia Whipper, an advocate for voting, was active in the Tuesday Evening Club, and two women from this group volunteered at different precincts. Two women who were employed by the Bureau of Printing and Engraving worked the polls. Arnetta Randall, the secretary of the New Negro Alliance who had earlier issued a call for the restoration of the suffrage, served as a precinct judge. Gabrielle Pelham, a Michigan native who worked as a community center secretary, also volunteered as an election official. During the 1920s, Pelham had served as the president of the Absentee Voter's League in Washington, D.C., but now in the 1930s, she pressed for the right to vote in the nation's capital. The redirecting of Pelham's advocacy efforts between the 1920s and the 1930s typified the shift in black women's political activities throughout Washington. At least three teachers volunteered with the referendum, possibly at the urging of Mary Mason Jones, president of Teacher's Union, Local 27 and member of the executive council of the Citizen's Joint Conference on National Representation for the District of Columbia.

Teachers were not only prominent as volunteers but also as respectable voters. The *Washington Afro-American* interviewed many residents, including three teachers, at the polls to determine their thoughts about suffrage. While their responses represented a wide range of opinions, the consensus was that black Washingtonians strongly endorsed the right to vote. By featuring interviews with teachers, reporters at the *Washington Afro-American* cast voters as educated and enthusiastic. Helen Moore, a teacher at Francis Junior High School, said, "As long as residents are paying heavy taxes, I don't see why we can't vote." Another resident, Virginia Goode, a housewife, argued, "A governmental area without representation of vote is taking advantage of people." Myra Austin, a teacher at Shaw Junior High School, predicted that this event "should help residents of our city toward the point where they can have a say in government." Marie Perry, a teacher at Francis Junior High School, noted, "Every citizen should be greatly concerned in this important league." And Martha Hart, a charwoman, confessed she did not know the exact meaning of suffrage, but stated that "it has something to do with making things better for us, and that's what I want."[58] These interviews indicated that many black women understood the wide-ranging implications of their struggles for justice and democracy in the nation's capital.

By voting in this referendum in such large numbers, the black population in Washington sent a strong message about their thirst for democracy in the nation's capital. Of the black population, 12 percent cast ballots, and 99 percent of those who voted favored the franchise for elections and the restoration of local governance. Among white Washingtonians, 15 percent voted, and 90 percent of them favored local voting rights. It is striking that black Washingtonians favored local control more strongly than white voters. This data can likely be attributed to two factors. First, some black citizens had been residents of the South during the period of disfranchisement, and they understood that the right to vote was deeply connected with political power. Next, black support for voting rights was most heavily concentrated in Southwest, Southeast, and Northeast, working-class neighborhoods that historically received more limited municipal services—mail delivery, road paving, and police and fire protection. For instance, at Randall Junior High School in Southwest, the votes were 2,949 in favor of suffrage while only 2 people voted against it. Smothers, Burrville, Cardozo, Mott, Howard, and Garnet-Patterson were in other black districts that voted overwhelmingly for restoration of the suffrage.[59] Black residents in these neighborhoods likely viewed voting rights as an opportunity to improve their community.

Both black and white newspapers noted the impact of black voters on the election results. In the *Atlanta Daily World*, Florence Murray chronicled the struggles of black Washingtonians to visit local polling places. "Voting and a chance to vote in national and local representation polls throughout the city," Murray wrote, "were literally stormed April 30 when more than 95,000, black and white, rich and more, the lame and the blind, cast their votes in the informal referendum conducted by local citizens." Murray opined that African Americans in Washington had "long been the bone of contention in the argument for suffrage in the District." She surveyed the history of voting rights in the nation's capital, contending that the "privilege of voting in the nation's affairs was taken from District residents some 68 years ago because of irregularities at the polls, coupled with the fear of the rising power of Negroes as they

TABLE 5 Referendum election results in African American polling places, 1938

School Polling Place	Quadrant	Local Suffrage		National Representation	
		For	*Against*	*For*	*Against*
Mott School	NW	4,646	39	4,650	29
Garnet-Patterson Junior High	NW	4,471	8	4,437	18
Dunbar High	NW	2,971	58	3,002	34
Cardozo High	SW	1,907	10	1,899	11
Randall Junior High	SW	1,847	3	1,847	2
Burrville School	NE	1,700	3	1,696	4
Howard University	NW	1,628	14	1,626	12
Bell School	SW	1,171	18	1,173	16
Syphax School	SW	1,033	3	1,034	3
Smothers School	NE	1,008	10	1,003	8
Browne Junior High	NE	604	20	614	10
Total		22,986	186	22,981	147

Source: "How District Precincts Voted," *Washington Afro-American*, May 14, 1938, 18.

swarmed into Washington during the Civil War and Reconstruction period." She contended that the "real fight against suffrage here has been soft-pedaled by Southern elements dominating the District." She concluded by citing the efforts of NNA members George Rycraw, Howard Woodson, Theophilius Houston, and Mary Mason Jones, whose work on the executive council of the Citizen's Joint Conference on National Representation for the District of Columbia paved the way for the referendum.[60]

Shortly after black and white citizens went to the polls, the Judiciary Committee in the U.S. House of Representatives convened a hearing on voting rights in the nation's capital. For three days, black and white citizens weighed in on the question of suffrage, and racial issues loomed large. Many white speakers, explicitly or implicitly, perpetuated the mythology of black Reconstruction in Washington, D.C. The historian Jason Morgan Ward argues that many white Americans used memories of the Reconstruction era to bolster white supremacy during the 1930s.[61] Ward's insights nicely capture much of the white resistance toward the voting rights struggle in Washington, D.C. Admiral William L. Rodgers, who represented the DuPont Circle Citizens' Association, argued that the prospect of black voting demanded serious consideration. "While each of us know colored people whom we personally admire and whose character and intelligence we highly respect," he began, "in general they do not stand so high as the white race." Rodgers recalled that "the experience with suffrage in the District sixty-odd years ago" reinforced this point. He concluded that America was a "country of white people" and argued, "The National Capital should not be dominated by men of another race."[62] Admiral Rogers clearly believed the mythology of Reconstruction and repeated this false narrative in the U.S. House of Representatives. Alfred D. Calvert, the president of the Lincoln Park Citizens' Association, was equally concerned about the city's voting history. He told the committee that "when residents of the District formerly had the vote, colored people by the boatload were brought into Washington from Norfolk and intervening points and domiciled as repeaters about town." Calvert warned, "It could be as easily done as before, and under guidance customary in such cases could easily swamp the well-intentioned voters."[63] But, other white speakers endorsed suffrage for all citizens. Paul E. Lesh, vice chair of the Citizen's Joint Conference on National Representation for the District of Columbia told the committee, "No matter what the quality of our colored population is, there will remain those among our own white number in the District of Columbia who say that it is an undesirable voting constituency." Lesh stated unequivocally that that was "someone else's point of view" and he "did not adopt it."[64]

Five black Washingtonians also testified at the hearings, offering ringing endorsements for suffrage rights in the nation's capital. Three men—George H. Murray, a teacher at the Cardozo High School; Charles E. Hall, a former clerk in the Census Bureau; and Kelly Miller, a retired professor at Howard University—wrote a lengthy letter that was read aloud. It highlighted the accomplishments of the black community in Washington, D.C., including their diverse churches and organizations, their high rates of home ownership, and their success in employment and education. Furthermore, it pointed to African Americans' recent patterns of political independence in their opinions about national politics, contending that the "spread of education among the colored people has disintegrated past political traditions and allegiances." Furthermore, it attributed African Americans' broad support for President Roosevelt to his economic policies, citing it as evidence for the degree of thoughtfulness that African Americans brought to the political process. "Obviously then with this state of mind existing among the District's colored population," the men argued, "the fear of 'Negro domination' becomes wholly chimerical."[65] In his testimony, Dr. Arthur Gray, as a representative of the Washington Council of the National Negro Congress and pastor of Plymouth Congregational Church, stated that he represented thirty organizations across the city and that "we wish to go on the record as being in favor of local suffrage in the District of Columbia, and also of national representation." He concluded his remarks by arguing that the National Negro Congress and all other associations were "in favor of local representation and national participation in our Government."[66]

The only black woman who testified at the hearings was Cora L. Wilkinson, a fifty-nine- year-old activist who represented the Friday Evening Club. A native of Washington, D.C., she lived in Anacostia in Southeast Washington and was married to Robert Wilkinson, a mail carrier. Her brother-in-law, Garnet C. Wilkinson, was assistant superintendent of education and supervised black schools throughout the city. Cora Wilkinson was prominent in social reform efforts throughout the city through her affiliations with the Friday Evening Club, the Phyllis Wheatley YWCA, and the Red Cross. During World War I, she had volunteered extensively with soldiers and later held fundraisers for war veterans. As a black woman in Washington, D.C., Wilkinson thus embodied education, patriotism, and civic duty.[67] In her testimony, she argued that it would be "it is mighty nice to have a voice in the Government." Through her social engagements, she had worked with "a great many of women who represent the citizens of the District of Columbia" and that "we do want a voice in the government." In her testimony, Wilkinson thus spoke for the hundreds of black women in Washington, D.C., who were not able to speak at the committee hearing.[68]

While Wilkinson was the only black woman who testified, others publicly endorsed suffrage rights by affixing their signatures and organizational affiliation to the resolution from the Citizen's Joint Conference on National Representation for the District of Columbia, which was part of the public record of the hearings. Physician Ionia Whipper and teacher Mary D. Dodson signed their names as representatives from the Organization Committee of the District of Columbia, which appeared to be related to the Tuesday Evening Club, while Mary Mason Jones endorsed suffrage as president of the Washington Teacher's Union, Local 27. Whether they testified in Congress or signed their names to a public resolution, African American women represented diverse organizations in the city and helped express the opinions of the thousands black women who yearned to cast ballots and enjoy local representation.

Soon after the congressional hearing for voting rights was held, black citizens formed the D.C. Voter's League to continue to press for the restoration of local suffrage. Many of the women and men who were members of the Citizen's Conference or had volunteered as clerks and election officials during the referendum joined this organization, including Ionia Whipper,

Blanche Curry, Gabrielle Pelham, and Dorothy Boulding Ferebee.[69] The excitement for voting seeped into every inch of the culture in the nation's capital. James S. Chressey, a teacher in the WPA Adult Education Division, created a citizenship course for city residents to be given at the YMCA. An article in the *Washington Afro-American* publicized this course: "In an effort to prepare Washingtonians for citizenship in the event that suffrage is granted in the District, a course in government will be offered at the 12th Street YMCA on Mondays at 7 P.M." Moreover, the course would cover "the matter of precincts and wards and what effect voting will have on the District."[70] Additionally, at Cardozo High School's night school, students enrolled in the public speaking class were asked to deliver public presentations on the question, "Should the District of Columbia Be Granted the Right of Suffrage?"[71]

During the 1930s, black Washingtonians expressed their eagerness to restore voting rights, whether it was by forming organizations, testifying in Congress, or marching with their feet to cast ballots in the referendum. More than 99 percent of black men and women in Washington, D.C.—representing diverse ages, locations in the city, and economic situations—endorsed suffrage rights. Black Washingtonians took the zeal they had once brought to their campaigns for absentee ballots and infused it into the quest for local suffrage rights. The right to vote represented one of the freedoms that citizens had lost in 1874 when Congress reorganized the government. Voting rights captured both the idealism of emancipation and the promise of Reconstruction, but also the disillusionment of the Jim Crow era. Ironies about the Civil War and Reconstruction soon surfaced when it became impossible to secure a location for the famed opera singer, Marian Anderson, to perform in the city.

Washington, D.C., Is "Seventy-Five Years behind the Times"

In March 1939, Nannie Helen Burroughs publicly declared that the city of Washington, D.C., was "75 years behind the times." The Daughters of the American Revolution (DAR), a white organization with its headquarters in Washington, D.C., had forbidden Marian Anderson, the world-famous black opera singer, from performing in its large event space because she was black. In response, Burroughs argued, "The Revolutionary and Civil War conflicts have been moved from New England and Dixie to Washington—the capital of the greatest democracy on the globe." She claimed that Washington had an "antiquated" Board of Education whose policies reflected the sentiment of the popular novel and soon-to-be-released film, *Gone with the Wind*. Burroughs concluded, "In the field of race relations, Washington is exactly 75 years behind every large city in the world."[72] In this article Burroughs evoked the contested legacies of the Civil War and Reconstruction and directly connected them to the debacle of the Marian Anderson concert.

Marian Anderson frequently appeared in concerts abroad and was the recipient of numerous accolades. In the United States, her performances commanded record crowds. An article in the *Chicago Defender* described a typical concert where the "ten below zero which Chicago thermometers registers Sunday night did not deter the 4,000 music enthusiasts who packed the great Auditorium here to listen to the melting liquid notes from the voice of Marian Anderson."[73] Beginning in 1936, she participated in the Howard University School of Music's Lyceum Series. In 1936 and 1937, her Washington, D.C., concerts were held in the auditorium of Armstrong High School, which was a black school. But by 1937, it was clear that Anderson's popularity was growing and that her fan base included black and white citizens. In 1938, her concert was moved to the Rialto Theater, a black venue that could seat 2,000. But even that theater was not large enough, and concertgoers spilled into the aisles, prompting Howard officials to consider a larger space. Constitution Hall, owned by the DAR, could seat 4,000. In January 1938, Charles Cohen from the Howard University Music School contacted Fred Hand, the manager of Constitution Hall, inquiring about the possibility of Anderson performing a concert there on Easter Sunday. Hand replied that it was the policy of Constitution Hall to prohibit performances by African Americans; in fact, "every contract for the use of these halls contains a clause barring the appearance of any colored person."[74] Nationally, African American newspapers denounced the DAR's decision not to allow Marian Anderson to perform in Constitution Hall.

Five prominent Washington citizens—three black and two white Washingtonians—approached the D.C. School Board about the possibility of using another building in the city. This ad hoc group was led by Doxey Wilkerson, a veteran organizer in the New Negro Alliance; the other members were Charles Cohen, Gustave Auxene, Dorothy Klein, and Glen Dillard Gunn. It presented a six-page petition containing three-hundred signatures outlining why the School Board should provide a space for the Anderson concert. Initially, Elizabeth Peeples, the supervisor of the Community Center, contended that Washington had a dual system of education and that allowing the Marian Anderson concert to be held there would set a dangerous precedent. Frank W. Ballou, the superintendent of the Board of Education, affirmed Peeples' judgment.[75] In February, the issue came before a vote of the School Board. By custom, three African Americans served on the board, but on that particular day, two of the black members—John Wilson and former NAACP president

Jennie Richardson McGuire who had orchestrated the Rope Protests in 1934—were absent. The only black member present was Col. West A. Hamilton, who voted that Anderson should be allowed to perform. At the meeting, another board member, Charles Drayton, who was white, expressed the opinion that "board would be legally liable for any possible injury that may be sustained by any of the patrons and sustained that the board wasn't justified in granting a permit under these circumstances." Hamilton countered that the School Board routinely permitted both George Washington and Georgetown Universities to use school facilities for their athletic events and that there was never any problem. He also argued, "The whole question revolved into the query as to whether the board would be courageous enough to give use of the building for an American artist when other institutions in Washington denied her their facilities." In the end, the School Board voted no. An article in the *Baltimore Afro-American* was tellingly titled "School Board Apes DAR."[76]

The negative responses from both the DAR and the School Board illuminated black Washingtonians' second-class citizenship rights in the nation's capital. By now, articles about the concert debacle began to grace the pages of the *Christian Science Monitor*, the *New York Times*, and the *Jewish Exponent*. All expressed shock that these public and private institutions in the nation's capital had refused to allow Anderson to perform there. In February, a community of concerned black and white citizens banded together under the leadership of Charles Hamilton Houston to form the Marian Anderson Citizens' Protest Committee. Members canvassed neighborhoods, circulated petitions, and gathered signatures. By February 25, members had obtained 300 signatures on the petition, which stated, "We regard such action on the part of the board as contrary to the spirit of democracy and step toward developing racial goodwill in the District of Columbia."[77] Activists in the black community decided that they would look toward their own resources and stage the concert in a church, which could hold a maximum of 2,000 persons.[78]

A particularly pointed article appeared in the *Atlanta Daily World* titled "Marian Anderson Tests American Democracy." This article argued, "The fact that during the past years in the Nation's Capital the majority of her audiences have been white proves that the traditional Negro bugaboo has not yet swept the capital." It concluded by noting, "Since we must go on, remember that we are Negroes, citizens of this voteless District of Columbia." Many newspaper articles thus positioned the Anderson debacle as merely one symptom of black Washingtonians' utter lack of civil rights and second-class citizenship in the nation's capital.

The protests had escalated by March 1939 when First Lady Eleanor Roosevelt publicly resigned her membership from the DAR and two thousand black and white citizens staged a mass meeting to protest the Board of Education's action, under the leadership of Charles Edward Russell, the chair of the Washington Interracial Committee. By this time, seventy organizations were behind the protests.[79] Jennie Richardson McGuire wrote a letter to the *Washington Tribune* where she called for another vote of the Board of Education when all members could be present. "While it is true that we have a dual system of schools," McGuire wrote, "in the District we have one board of education, whose responsibility is to administer the educational program in the interest of the entire population." She added that this "emergency situation demands that the board of education see to it that no section of the population is deprived of cultural and educational advantages when it is within its power to regulate the facilities of the school service to accomplish."[80] The School Board did have another vote and, in a stunning reversal, permitted Marian Anderson to perform at the white Central High School. In this vote, six board members—three white and three black—voted to allow Anderson to perform.[81]

By late March, activists arranged for Marian Anderson to sing on the steps of the Lincoln Memorial in a concert on Easter Sunday. The fact that Anderson could inhabit a site controlled by the National Parks Service, but not the city of Washington, D.C., underscored the pervasiveness of racial segregation in the nation's capital. The historian Scott Sandage emphasizes that Anderson's concert marked the first time that the Lincoln Memorial was used as a site of black protest, which laid the foundation for the March on Washington in 1963.[82] The black and white press reacted differently to the outcome. For instance, an article in the *New York Amsterdam News* titled "Nazism in D.C." sharply denounced the events occurring over the past several months—"The real tragedy, is, however, that democracy and justice are flaunted so cruelly in the nation's capital"—and cited segregation in schools, theaters, and the city itself.[83] On the other hand, an editorial in the *Washington Post* called the concert at the Lincoln Memorial a "Happy Ending."[84]

In the aftermath of the Marian Anderson concert, Secretary of the Interior Harold Ickes initiated the process of racial integration in the nation's capital. He ordered the National Park Service to end segregation, thereby opening all parks in the city to African Americans. He also desegregated the offices of the Interior Department, and most government bureaus followed suit. It took a national embarrassment to force the federal government to pursue racial integration.[85]

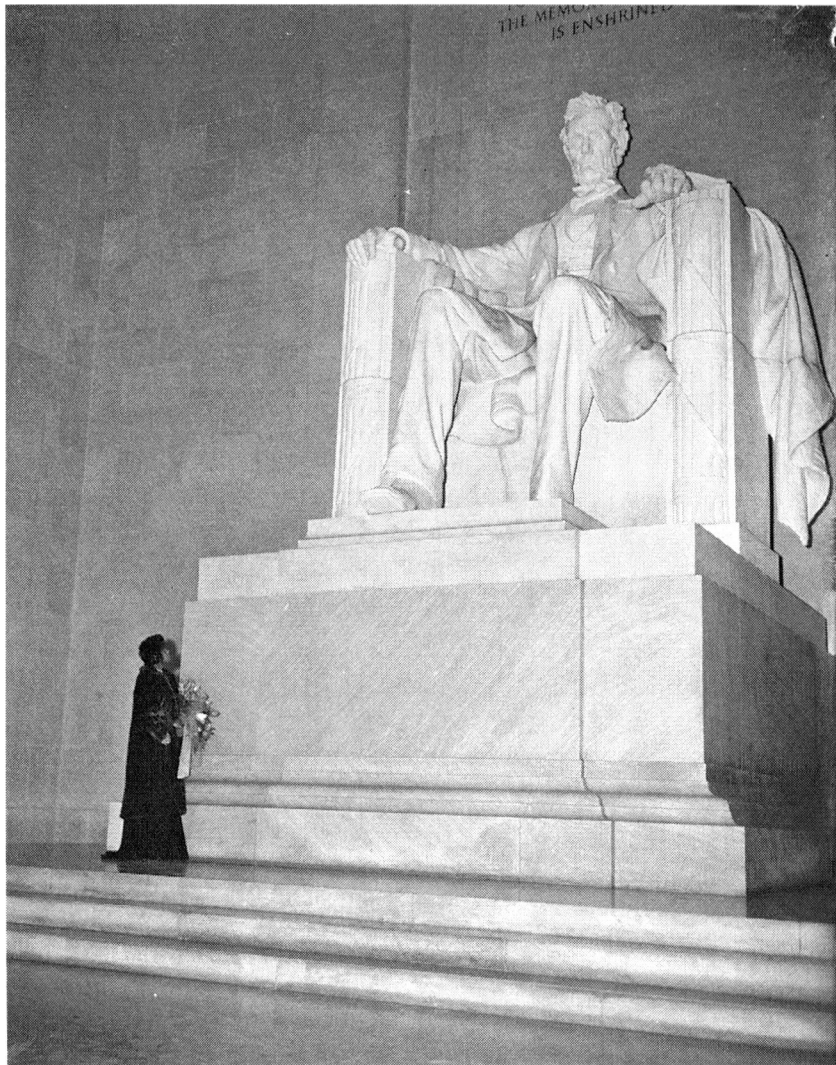

When Marian Anderson performed her concert in April 1939 on the steps of the Lincoln Memorial, her performance offered a poetic link between the Civil War in the 1860s and the civil rights movement in the nation's capital in the 1930s. Library of Congress, LC-DIG-hec-26448.

The Marian Anderson concert energized civil rights activists to press forward with their civil rights campaigns. The concert provided the visual link for citizens to connect the past and present in their campaigns for justice. Marian Anderson's performance on the steps of the Lincoln Memorial was poetry for the women and men who had been pondering the legacies of the Civil War and Reconstruction. Citizens in the city seized on the momentum of the event to lobby for the passage of a civil rights bill in the nation's capital.

"Let's Take Washington out of the Confederacy": Memory Politics at High Tide

After the Marian Anderson concert, an editorial in the *Washington Tribune* celebrating this bittersweet victory concluded, "We cannot rest as long as these hateful conditions continue."[86] For black Washingtonians, passing a civil rights bill would ensure that African American citizens could perform in any space in the city that they desired. In November 1939, the New Negro Congress submitted another civil rights bill for the consideration of Congress.[87] And one month later Mary McLeod Bethune, the Negro Advisor to the National Youth Administration, appeared at a meeting in Washington, D.C., where she stressed the importance of passing a civil rights bill for the District of Columbia.[88] Also that month, black citizens banded together to form a civil rights committee to spearhead passage of the bill. Arnetta Randall, the secretary of the New Negro Alliance and vocal supporter of voting rights, was part of this committee. A newspaper article reported, "At this meeting, more than 100 organizations are expected to have instructed delegates that the work of getting the bill introduced in the next week of Congress."[89]

In December 1939, an article in the *Atlanta Daily World* argued that Washington, D.C., was the "model" for segregation practices across the country. It detailed the various practices of segregation in Washington, focusing on hospitals as the root of inequality and injustice.[90] This landmark article situated the nation's capital as the prototype for segregation practices across the nation, thereby positioning civil rights activities in Washington, D.C., as having both local and national significance. While there is no record of commentary about this article, it is clear that many activists in the city agreed with this assessment and viewed the black freedom struggle in the nation's capital as an instrument to integrate the nation.

The connections between the Civil War and the city's black freedom struggle resurfaced when the premiere of the film *Abe Lincoln in Illinois* was held in the nation's capital. The film depicted Abraham Lincoln and his journey toward the White House from being a state senator in Illinois, to participating in debates with Stephen Douglas, to his arrival in Washington, D.C., as an opponent of slavery's expansion. The *Washington Daily News*, a white newspaper in the city, also sponsored a Lincoln look-alike contest, inviting all men who bore a resemblance to Abraham Lincoln, to enter. When it was discovered that

Thomas P. Bomar, an African American man who worked as a lawyer at the Post Office, in fact, most closely resembled Lincoln, the contest was canceled.[91]

The premiere of *Abe Lincoln in Illinois* was held at the Keith Theater, located on Fifteenth Street in Northwest Washington. The Keith Theater had a strict policy of racial segregation and barred all black patrons. In January 1940, hundreds of black men and women picketed the Keith Theater, highlighting the contradictions between showing a film about the Great Emancipator while barring from attendance the very people he was credited with emancipating. A newspaper article in the *Washington Tribune* compared the pickets with the Silent Parade against lynching, arguing that both protests had tremendous consequences for racial justice, both in Washington and across the country. It emphasized the contradictions of injustice in the nation's capital. "As many states have enacted laws providing stiff penalties and punitive damage for public places, which refuse to accommodate citizens on account of color or race," the article noted, it was despicable that "Washington, the seat of the Federal Government, has lagged behind and presents to the world a sad picture of hypocrisy and bigotry in the sheep's clothing of democracy."[92] Another article reported that activists carried protest signs emblazed with the words, "Colored Citizens May Not See Picture of Great Emancipator," "Negro Americans Are Deprived of Civil Rights," and "Where Freedom Is a Joke and Democracy Is a Sham."[93]

The *Abe Lincoln in Illinois* premiere presented a dilemma for First Lady Eleanor Roosevelt, who was an honored guest at the event. Roosevelt did cross the picket line to attend the film screening, but she later wrote a newspaper column recounting her complex feelings about the incident. "It seemed to me particularly ironic," Roosevelt wrote, "that in the nation's capital there should be a ruling, which would prevent this race from seeing this picture in the same theater with white people." However, she ended up justifying the policies, stating, "The organization had the right to sell tickets to whomever it wished."[94] One person who was particularly upset about Roosevelt's attendance was Pauli Murray, a political activist based in New York City, who often traveled to Washington, D.C., for political events. In January 1940, Murray wrote a letter to Eleanor Roosevelt, where she pressed her on her true feelings about racial segregation at the event. Murray told Roosevelt that she was "disappointed" that "you crossed a picket-line against your deeper feelings." Murray expressed confusion at Roosevelt's tacit acceptance of the right of the Newspaperwomen's Club to bar African American patrons from the event. She concluded by stating, "There can be no compromise on the principle of equality."[95] Murray's statement epitomized African American women's principled activism in fighting for justice and citizenship in the nation's capital. Pauli Murray would soon face these issues firsthand when she moved to Washington, D.C., to enroll in law school at Howard University.[96]

Though not allowed to attend the premiere, black citizens honored Lincoln and the Civil War by reflecting on the legacies of emancipation. The black press in Washington published a flurry of articles about the Civil War. An article in the *Washington Afro-American* chronicled "The Man, Frederick Douglass," and the paper also featured an editorial on the relationship between Douglass and President Abraham Lincoln; another reporter conducted investigative journalism to discover that much of downtown Washington had been built on the grounds of a former slave depot.[97] In February, black schoolchildren marched in a pilgrimage to the Lincoln Memorial, where they held their own services. The schools represented included Stevens, Morgan, Briggs-Montgomery, Phillips-Wormley, and Sumner-Magruder under the direction of L. S. Malone, who offered a blessing.[98] Black citizens in the New Negro Alliance staged an "Abraham Lincoln" mass meeting to discuss the importance of civil rights and suffrage in their city. At this meeting, a special guest was Thomas Bomar, the Abraham Lincoln look-alike. By labeling their meeting a "Lincoln Mass Meeting" and inviting Bomar to attend, NNA activists situated their fight for civil rights and voting rights in the spirit of Abraham Lincoln and the values for which he stood.[99]

While black citizens were celebrating the legacy of Lincoln throughout the city, some members of Congress continued to discuss a civil rights bill. By 1940, the cumulative impacts of the Marian Anderson concert, the *Abe Lincoln in Illinois* film premiere, and ongoing protests against segregation and disfranchisement caused citizens to equate the civil rights bill with emancipation. In March 1940, when Representative James Seccombe of Ohio introduced the civil rights bill, an article in the *Chicago Defender* argued, "The first step in the second emancipation the Race in Washington occurred here Tuesday."[100] The *Washington Afro-American* published an editorial titled "Let's Take Washington out of the Confederacy," which positioned the fight against racial segregation in Washington as having national significance. "Getting this bill introduced marks a step in the right direction," it observed, "and is the only legal means of correcting the evils of segregation and jim crow in the capital because it is the only efficient means of purifying the streams at the source." The editorial concluded by noting, "The job now is for Washingtonians from all straits of society to get solidly behind this measure and bring all possible pressure to bear to see that it is enacted."[101] By evoking the imagery of "purifying the streams at the source," this editorial, like the one in the *Atlanta*

Journal and Guide, positioned segregation in Washington, D.C., as the foundation for racial practices across the nation: both articles situated current events in the discourse of the Civil War and Reconstruction. Passing the bill would "emancipate" African Americans and take the nation's capital "out of the Confederacy." This historically charged language was not accidental and would fuel black citizens' determination to enact civil rights in the nation's capital.

Conclusion

During the 1930s, black women and men worked to secure civil rights for residents of the nation's capital. Women connected with existing organizations and formed new ones to attack racial segregation. They argued that segregation was not just about inconvenience. Instead, it shaped the course of a life, dictating the type of hospital where infants would be born, the type of health care they would receive, and the quality of education they would acquire. As black women organized for issues in their own city, they increasingly recognized that voting rights were an essential ingredient of full citizenship rights, prompting activists to rally residents across the city to march with their feet to the referendum vote. For an activist such as Ionia Whipper, these civil rights campaigns fulfilled her mission as a public health advocate and her heritage as the daughter of a Civil War veteran and Reconstruction-era politician.

Over the course of the decade, the struggle for civil rights in Washington became urgent and revolutionary. Activists labeled Washington the "Jim Crow Capital," and articles in the black press discussed how segregation in the nation's capital shaped national practices. Within this charged climate, memories of the Civil War and Reconstruction were the threads that wove these civil rights campaigns together by evoking feelings about black business ownership, citizens' right to cast ballots, legal equality through civil rights, and even the idea of Abraham Lincoln and the values that he stood for. As the United States inched closer to war in 1940, African Americans in Washington, D.C., and across the country contemplated a second emancipation to address many of the injustices that lingered three-quarters of a century after the Civil War.

Part III

The Leverage of War, 1941–1945

Lady lobbyist blazes trail in the nation's capital.

—*Chicago Defender*, 1945

The Civil War still rages along the jam-packed Potomac.

—Charlee Cherokee, *Pittsburgh Courier*

CHAPTER SIX

Jim Crow Must Go
Civil Rights Struggles during World War II

On Thursday January 7, 1943, shortly after midnight, Caroline K. Johnson and Mildred I. Turpin—black clerks in the Navy Department's Annex in Arlington, Virginia—boarded a bus bound for their homes in Washington, D.C. When the driver ordered the two women to move from the front to the rear, they refused, were arrested for violating Jim Crow laws, and spent the night in jail. At their hearing the next morning, they pled "not guilty," but were fined five dollars. Johnson and Turpin later met with officers in the local chapter of the NAACP, where they signed affidavits and appealed their case.[1] Three weeks later, Ruth Powell, Marianne Musgrave, and Juanita Morrow—all African American undergraduates at Howard University—visited the lunch counter at the United Cigar Store at 1201 Pennsylvania Avenue and ordered hot chocolate. When they were refused service, the students asked to speak with a manager, who was out. The students then discussed the matter with two police officers, who instructed a waitress to serve the women their order. When they received their bill, they discovered that they had been charged twenty-five cents for each cup, rather than the standard ten cents. In protest, the students paid thirty-five cents. After the women exited the store, police arrested them, loaded them into a patrol wagon, and transported them to the Women's Bureau at the Metropolitan Police Department, where they were detained for several hours.[2] The students' arrest became the catalyst for a sit-in movement at Howard University. These two cases in January 1943 were part of black women's campaign to secure civil rights in the nation's capital during World War II.

During World War II, African American women in Washington, D.C., worked to steer the city on a path toward racial integration. Black women's activism became more militant during the 1940s, influenced by the global fight against Nazism and fascism, the March on Washington for integration in the military and equality in wartime jobs, and ongoing campaigns for justice in the nation's capital. In the 1930s, hundreds of black women had worked to enact their visions of freedom. Black women had protested interracial police brutality; pressed for economic justice by writing in the press, demanding welfare relief, or rioting for jobs; and marched to the polls for the restoration of voting rights. During World War II, black women built on this tradition of resistance by refusing to move to the back of the bus and demanding to be served at lunch counters in the city. These expressions of direct action underscored the growth of black women's protest politics in the nation's capital, which included both formal and informal activism.

Seasoned activists banded together with newcomers in the city to wage political campaigns. A new cohort of students at Howard University honored the activist legacy of earlier classes by participating in civil rights activities. As male students departed campus to fight in the war, women crafted gendered arguments about civil rights, contending that it was their duty to fight for freedom at home. Other activists emerged from the rank-and-file community of workers who moved to Washington, D.C., to take government jobs. Finally, some women who had been active in politics for decades continued their campaigns for equality and justice.

While many activists worked to eradicate local inequalities in Washington, it was during the 1940s that some black women returned to national lobbying. In 1938, members of Xi Omega, the Washington chapter of Alpha Kappa Alpha Sorority, formed the National Non-Partisan Lobby for Economic and Democratic Rights. This group, which began on an experimental basis, operated initially on a budget of only $100 to advocate on behalf of African American women, especially around matters of economic justice and civil rights. Three years later, leaders in the AKA's national organization recognized the importance of this lobbying group, made it one of its central programs, and apportioned $7,500 from membership dues to support its advocacy efforts. Black women's participation in national lobbying, however, did not mean that the local struggle for democracy in Washington was over. In returning to lobbying, members of the AKA built on the tradition of advocacy set by the black women who had preceded them, including Mazie Griffin, Marian Butler, Julia West Hamilton, Mary Church Terrell, and Nannie Helen Burroughs.

Many accounts of the modern black freedom movement situate the Howard University students' sit-in movement in 1943 as a crucial point of origin.[3] In their discussions of these sit-ins, few scholars, however, acknowledge that these protests were one part of a larger movement that included federal lobbying campaigns, protests against transportation segregation, and ongoing engagement with the memories of the Civil War. Limiting the discussion of civil rights in Washington, D.C., to the sit-in movement paints the struggle as focused around only one issue while also depicting students at Howard University as the only activists in the city. The struggle against segregation at lunch counters was deeply connected with campaigns against segregation on interstate transportation: many of the same actors were involved with both movements, keenly shaped by the militancy of the wartime era and the local culture of black women' political protest in Washington, D.C.

Recognizing the multiplicity of actors who helped pave the way for momentous social change highlights the role of ordinary women and men in the black freedom movement while also illuminating new periodizations and geographies in the historiography of civil rights. Many historians trace the origins of the postwar black freedom struggle to events that occurred during World War II, pointing to the March on Washington Movement, migration to the North, black soldiers' military experiences, the growth of NAACP chapters, the collapse of colonial empires, and the landmark Supreme Court decision, *Smith v. Allwright*, that struck down whites-only primaries.[4] But, as this chapter demonstrates, by staging sit-ins at restaurants, resisting segregation on buses, and lobbying in Congress, African American women in the nation's capital laid a foundation for black activism in the postwar era.

During World War II, black women drew on two decades of activism and organizing in the city to wage grassroots campaigns against racial segregation and to lobby on behalf of African Americans across the nation. By the 1940s, some of the local and national aspects of black women's political campaigns in Washington, D.C., had fused. As residents of the nation's capital during one of the most dramatic moments in the nation's history, black women built on the visibility of their political campaigns and pushed the city on a path toward racial integration, making their politics and activism a model for the nation.

"Jim Crow Must Go": Militancy in Washington

Even before the United States entered World War II, African Americans understood the enormous implications of the conflict. The military was segregated, and during World War I, African Americans had been barred from most higher-paying wartime jobs. Some southern states even passed "Work or Fight" laws, which forced black women to work for white families in the South.[5] Not wanting that situation to be repeated, A. Philip Randolph, the president of the Brotherhood of the Sleeping Car Porters, announced that 10,000 African Americans would stage a March on Washington to achieve military integration and end discrimination in wartime jobs. "We colored, loyal Americans," Randolph argued in his call, which was published in the *Baltimore Afro-American* in January 1941 and reprinted in black newspapers across the nation, "demand the right to work and fight in our country." He contended that this march would "wake up and shock official Washington as it has never been shocked before."[6] Over the next few months, Randolph traveled across the country, forming March on Washington Movement (MOWM) chapters in Chicago, St. Louis, and New York. Many of these cities had attracted southern migrants in the 1920s and 1930s and in the 1940s boasted black electorates that were wielding political influence at the local and national levels. As Randolph gathered more supporters, he refined the details of his plan, broadening the scope of his call from 10,000 to 50,000 and even 100,000 participants and scheduling the march to occur on July 1, 1941.

Locally in Washington, D.C., expressions of black militancy appeared throughout the city, shaped by the MOWM, the coming of the war, and the ongoing culture of black protest. More than one hundred men and women in Washington joined the local MOWM chapter. Thurman L. Dodson, a veteran from the New Negro Alliance, was elected chair. Women leaders included Jeannette Welch, who was affiliated with the National Council of Negro Women; Velma Williams, the vice president of the Federation of Civic Associations; and Natalie Moorman, who had protested police brutality and participated in economic boycotts throughout the 1930s.[7] In February 1941, 6,000 members of the American Youth Congress, a leftist youth group, held a conference in the nation's capital and staged numerous demonstrations against Jim Crow by protesting segregation in eateries across the city, marching down Fourteenth Street to the Washington Monument, and picketing the War Department with signs proclaiming "Pass the Civil Rights Bill" and "Jim Crow Must Go." A newspaper article noted that traffic "became badly snared as motorists and pedestrians stopped to watch." The American Youth Congress protest helped make a national audience aware of racial segregation in the nation's capital.[8]

While black women registered members in the MOWM and participated in the American Youth Congress, they also utilized their own networks in sororities, neighborhoods, and the Phyllis Wheatley YWCA to ensure equal opportunities in wartime industries. In March 1941, the national chapter of the AKA and its lobbying arm, the National Non-Partisan Lobby for Economic and Democratic Rights, spearheaded a "National Legislative Weekend" of mass meetings and conferences. The Non-Partisan Council instructed AKA members to send letters, postcards, and telegrams to politicians and industry heads urging them to eliminate discrimination in wartime labor industries. Veteran activist and YWCA president Julia West Hamilton delivered a speech for the AKA's local D.C. Xi Omega chapter titled "The Woman and National Defense."[9] Several months later, the AKA and its lobbying group held a celebration for Citizenship Day. At this ceremony, speakers included Julia West Hamilton, Mary McLeod Bethune, Velma Williams, and Elsie Austin, who served as the president of Delta Sigma Theta, another black sorority.[10]

In this pre-wartime climate of activism in the capital, black women also protested racial segregation on buses that traveled between Washington, D.C., and neighboring Virginia. Within city limits, citizens could sit anywhere they wished, but when the bus wheeled into Virginia, black passengers were ordered to move toward the back. This policy of segregation underscored the arbitrary nature of racial practices because traveling only a half-mile outside of the city could bring into play a vastly different set of laws and codes for black citizens. Since the nineteenth century, hundreds of black women, both in Washington, D.C., and across the country, had been at the forefront of transportation segregation protests. In February 1868, Kate Dodson, an employee of the Senate, bought a ticket for passage in a Ladies Car while traveling by train from her home in Washington, D.C., to visit a sick relative in Alexandria, Virginia. On her return trip, Dodson refused to vacate the Ladies Car and was forcibly removed. Later, Dodson sued the railroad and ultimately secured damages.[11] Kate Dodson was only one of many black women who refused to move from their seats: during the 1920s and 1930s, several black women in Washington, D.C. protested segregated transportation on interstate buses and trains.[12]

Beginning in 1941, African American women began to resist transportation segregation in greater numbers. The coming of war and the slow unraveling of Jim Crow in the nation's capital helped inspire black women to openly defy the region's racial order. The historian Stephen Berrey argues that in Mississippi at the twilight of Jim Crow in the 1950s and 1960s, "every day presented opportunities to move or not to move, to act or not to act, as expected. Each opportunity affirmed or altered meanings of racial space." He argues that each "unexpected performance" that veered out of the ordinary helped strain the "normative racial roles of a Jim Crow world."[13] Berrey's insights illuminate some of black women's motivations for resisting Jim Crow segregation in the politically charged climate of the 1940s. One of the first women to undertake this campaign was Natalie Moorman.

On Wednesday, April 12, 1941, Moorman boarded a Washington/Fairfax Virginia bus at the Rosslyn, Virginia, station. On the bus, she refused to give up her seat to a white passenger and was arrested for violating Virginia's segregation laws. Charles Hamilton Houston, the noted civil rights attorney in Washington, D.C., represented Moorman in court. In the trial, the attorney representing the bus company contended that, as long as Moorman was offered a seat, it did not matter whether it was located in the front or the rear of the vehicle. But Houston argued "that the usual procedure of seating colored passengers from the rear was not dictated by Virginia law, but that it was the result of custom and usage." Furthermore, he contended that this practice "was in violation of the Fourteenth Amendment in view of the inequity of accommodations in the front and rear sections of the busses." Virginia Judge B. M. Hendrick refused to issue an opinion, levied a five-dollar fine against Natalie Moorman, and informed her that she was entitled to an appeal, which she pursued. An article summarizing the case noted, "The fight to end the South's jim-crow carrier laws broke out on a new front.[14]

Only one month after Natalie Moorman's trial, another woman was arrested for refusing to move to the back of the bus. On Tuesday evening, June 10, 1941, forty-one-year-old Daisy Willett had just finished a day of work and was headed home. She was employed as a domestic servant for John L. Lewis, the president of the United Mine Workers. Lewis and his family lived in Alexandria, Virginia, but Willett and her husband resided eight miles across the river in a working-class neighborhood in Southwest Washington, which meant that she had the daily experience of traveling in and out of cities with two different codes of law.[15] On that particular day, Willett boarded at the front of the bus on the A, B, & W bus line and found a seat near the front. When the bus driver, George Deihr, demanded that she move to the back, Daisy Willett said no. At the corner of Powhattan and Washington Streets in Alexandria, Deihr stopped the bus, and police officers arrested Willett for violating Jim Crow laws, while also charging her with disorderly conduct.[16] It is unclear whether Willett spent the night in jail, but she quickly contacted John Lewis, who rushed to her aid. At the hearing in Police Court, Judge J. M. Pancoast fined Willett $5.00 for Jim Crow violations along with $4.95 in costs, although the charges of disorderly conduct were dropped.[17]

Daisy Willett's case sparked attention in the black press because of the visibility of her employer. John L. Lewis had recently addressed an NAACP meeting in Philadelphia and was considered a civil rights ally.[18] It is likely that there were many more cases of domestic workers who, like Willett, used public transportation on a daily basis to travel to white homes. In her study of streetcar boycotts in the early twentieth century, the historian Blair L. M. Kelley argues that African American women served as "some of the most effective leaders and protesters in their fight for full citizenship and dignity."[19] It will perhaps never be known what sparked Daisy Willett's protest that Tuesday, but several theories can be offered. Natalie Moorman's recent arrest might have inspired Willett's defiance. It is also possible that segregation was not always enforced on the A, B, & W bus lines and that Willett's particular bus driver elected to enforce it that day. Daisy Willett's larger political world—shaped by the MOWM, black women's growing militancy in Washington, and her employer's struggles for economic justice—might have also factored into her decision. All of these circumstances may have been present when Daisy Willett refused to move to the back of the bus.

While Daisy Willett was dealing with her arrest, Natalie Moorman was working to appeal her case. A newspaper article in the *Washington Tribune* noted that Moorman was holding a "rights and anti-discrimination meeting" at her home in Alexandria, Virginia, with her lawyer, Charles Hamilton Houston.[20] Houston had also defended Moorman when she was arrested for picketing a drug store with the New Negro Alliance. The fact that Natalie Moorman held a meeting about her case indicates that she did not accept the legitimacy of her arrest and was determined to use the law as an instrument to integrate transportation across state lines. The militancy of Natalie Moorman and Daisy Willett demonstrates how black women began to defy Jim Crow more openly in Washington, D.C., as the nation inched closer to war.

The black press in Washington drew parallels between the current political moment and the Civil War era, thereby encouraging citizens to situate their current struggle within the narrative arc of the black freedom struggle. An article in the *Washington Afro-American* asked, "Will Roosevelt Profit by Lincoln's Mistake?" This article critiqued Lincoln for hesitating to enlist black soldiers and waiting until 1862 to issue the Emancipation Proclamation. Terming Lincoln "timid," the article argued, "Roosevelt will find out that we can't fight successfully for democracy abroad unless and until there is democracy at home." The article concluded by demanding that President Roosevelt integrate the military immediately or face the embarrassment of the impending March on Washington.[21]

One month before the March on Washington was scheduled to occur, First Lady Eleanor Roosevelt and New York City Mayor Fiorello LaGuardia held a secret meeting in Washington, D.C., where they tried to negotiate a solution that would simultaneously address racial inequality and avoid embarrassment for the United States. President Roosevelt feared that Randolph's March on Washington would weaken the nation's image before the world. In June 1941, FDR issued Executive Order 8802, which banned all discrimination in wartime employment and established the Fair Employment Practices Committee (FEPC) to intervene in matters of discrimination at worksites engaged in the war effort. This executive order marked a watershed moment in the federal government's intervention to eliminate discrimination; however, it did not address racial segregation in the armed services. Even so, Randolph announced the cancellation of the planned March on Washington,[22] and the black-owned *Washington Tribune* termed Executive Order 8802 the "Second Emancipation for Negroes." Locally, 2,000 African Americans held a celebratory rally at the

Watergate Outdoor Theater near the Potomac River, with guest speaker La Guardia. The site for this rally was chosen so that attendees could glimpse "the historic Lincoln Memorial, from which steps Marian Anderson thrilled 5,000 persons more than two years ago."[23] For black Washingtonians, there were many opportunities to encounter the memory of the Civil War, whether it was through the city's monumental landscape or the black press.

Not all citizens were pleased that the march had been canceled. An editorial in the *Washington Afro-American* captured these sentiments. "The general feeling," it noted, "is that it was a mistake call off the March on Washington, but a majority of people are willing to give the President a chance to work out a program for settling Jim Crow in industry without a demonstration." The editorial concluded, "Nothing will be satisfactory now except that which will quickly bear fruit."[24] This editorial reflected the spirit of activism that permeated Washington, D.C. Many black women and men knew firsthand that a gap existed between the language of nondiscrimination and its enforcement.

Four months later, Japanese planes bombed the U.S. military base at Pearl Harbor in Hawaii, and FDR asked Congress for a declaration of war. From December 1941 on, citizens across the United States were focused on the war effort. African Americans argued that they were fighting a "Double V for Victory"—victory from fascism and totalitarianism abroad and victory from discrimination at home—and black women and men in Washington, D.C., embraced that message. After Pearl Harbor, three hundred undergraduate students at Howard University signed a Student Council pledge to "give up their entire three-week Christmas vacation period in order to take special training courses in various phases of emergency civilian defense protection against air force raids," and many other students enlisted in the military.[25] Additionally, black citizens in the city gathered at the Phyllis Wheatley YWCA for a celebration of the 150th anniversary of adoption of the Bill of Rights. Nannie Helen Burroughs delivered a stirring address, while Robert Ming, a law professor at Howard, offered an interpretation of the Bill of Rights. This ceremony reflected black women's intentions to take their citizenship rights very seriously during the war.[26]

"The Civil War Still Rages along the Jam-Packed Potomac": Black Women's Protests against Transportation Segregation

World War II transformed Washington, D.C., as thousands of black and white citizens streamed into the nation's capital to fill wartime jobs—posing the most significant structural challenge to housing and traffic that the city had ever faced. Housing officials scrambled to build war housing and hotels to accommodate workers, but space was limited.[27] Population estimates for the area during World War II are unavailable, but in December 1942, the federal government encouraged all war workers to carpool to work to ease traffic and alleviate the parking shortage.[28] In April 1943, the federal government's War Housing Center requested that all "non-essential residents" leave their homes in the nation's capital so that war workers could take their place. "Families who are not bound to this community by reasons of employment," the War Housing Center argued, "would be making a contribution to the war effort if they sought living quarters elsewhere, thus relinquishing their present dwellings to war workers."[29]

Black women and men from both northern and southern cities relocated to Washington, D.C., for jobs. The city's landscape of racial segregation, however, made it difficult for them to find lodgings and places to eat. The only places where African American workers could eat meals were Union Station, government lunchrooms, and the cafeteria at the Phyllis Wheatley YWCA.[30] The federal government constructed multiple dormitories for white workers, but only two dormitories for black workers: Carver and Slowe Halls. This government housing for black workers was vastly insufficient, particularly given the reality that African Americans were excluded from residency in many apartment buildings in the city.[31] The Phyllis Wheatley YWCA, under the leadership of General Secretary Dorothy Height, opened an annex to provide extra dormitory space for African American women; its purpose was to t safely house black women, whether they were "travelers, students, working, or stranded girls."[32] Yet, the housing shortage remained acute throughout the war.

For black women in Washington, D.C., whether they were newcomers or long-time residents, World War II presented important labor opportunities. Many found positions that paid higher wages than domestic service. For the first time, black women were able to secure government jobs that had previously been off-limits to them; for example, the U.S. Botanical Gardens hired black women for the first time to tend the rose gardens. Women also filled the ranks of white-collar positions in the federal government as clerks, typists, and stenographers. By December 1942, 283,000 men and women were employed by the federal government, with large numbers working in the War and Navy Departments.[33] Office space in Washington, D.C., was so tight that the federal government constructed a Navy Annex in Arlington, Virginia, a city located across the Potomac River.[34]

The location of the Navy Annex in Virginia raised concerns about racial segregation for black workers. Members of the NAACP met with Senator Alva B.

During World War II, Washington, D.C., experienced a labor shortage, enabling black workers to obtain numerous positions in government bureaus. These African American women became the first black gardeners in the rose gardens of the U.S. Botanical Gardens. Library of Congress, LC-DIG-fsa-8d28925.

Adams, a Democrat from Colorado, about segregation in Virginia, but they were unable to secure a commitment of nondiscrimination.[35] In 1942, Dr. Leon A. Ransom, a representative of the NAACP's Legal Committee, met with R. T. Mitchell, the vice-president of the A, B, & W Transit Company, the bus line that had subjected Natalie Moorman and Daisy Willett to racial discrimination. Ransom and Mitchell reached an agreement that "there must be no attempt to segregate passengers using the line because of race." A newspaper article commented, "The ruling affects traffic to and from Washington and Arlington and follows the executive order banning discrimination of federal employees rather than the Virginia law which requires segregation."[36] While this agreement in May 1942 appeared to resolve the issue, it soon became evident that a large gap existed between theory and practice.

Transportation in the Washington metropolitan region became a racial battleground, and black women were often at the center of these conflicts. In June 1942, a columnist for the *Chicago Defender* discussed these difficulties in his weekly column, the "National Grapevine," under his pen name, Charlee Cherokee. "The Civil War," he told readers, "still rages along the jam-packed Potomac." He referred to a recent incident at the Navy Department Annex in Virginia that "brought Jim Crow laws into conflict." An African American employee of the Navy Department attempted to enter the cafeteria and was "beaten insensible by a guard."[37] This incident indicated that racial integration orders had not reached all corners of government offices in Virginia. By equating the contests over racial segregation in Virginia and Washington, D.C., D.C., with the "Civil War," Charlee Cherokee continued to evoke these memories for black citizens while also educating African Americans about these issues in the nation's capital.

For some black women in Washington, the global significance of the war shaped their political consciousness, fortifying them with the courage to protest situations of racial intolerance. In June 1942, an article in the *Baltimore Afro-American* recounted an incident that occurred on public transportation. An African American woman was riding a "crowded trolley" and finally found a seat next to a white sailor. According to the woman, the "man of the sea turned up his nose, raised the window, and spat to show his distaste for colored people in general and this woman in particular." The woman was cognizant of the situation, but elected to withhold her remarks until she was about to depart from the trolley, when she told the sailor, "You should be ashamed of yourself. Acting that way in that nice white uniform that Joe Louis bought for you." The article concluded by noting that "the word crowded is a masterpiece of understatement when used in connection with Washington."[38] It was abundantly clear, then, that the arrival of war workers and soldiers overburdened Washington's resources and contributed to the tense climate in the city. Importantly, this woman inverted the normative script by positioning the white soldier as indebted to Joe Louis, the famous black boxer who was serving in World War II and participating in charity matches to raise money for the war effort.[39] This encounter reflected the overall culture of protest that was brewing in the nation's capital.

In September 1942, Melvin B. Tolson, a columnist for the *Washington Tribune*, commented on the contradictions of segregation in the nation's capital during this dramatic moment in American history. Recognizing that the struggle against racial segregation in the nation's capital was a matter of national significance, he asked, "What is it that Negroes in the District of Columbia lack," answering, "Everything." He proclaimed, "The center of Negro propaganda in the United States should be in Washington, D.C.," precisely because it was the "hub of the world" and "place where the Four Freedoms will begin their march around the world." Tolson pointed to the visibility of the nation's capital in the broader freedom movement, noting the urgent need for a civil rights bill, an end to discrimination in the federal government, and the "destruction of Jim Crowism in the capital transit company."[40] The fact that Tolson situated the transportation segregation struggle alongside the other two goals indicated its utmost importance for the black freedom movement in wartime Washington, D.C.

In January 1943, two black clerks at the Navy Annex in Arlington protested the climate of segregation in the Washington metropolitan region. On Thursday, January 7, 1943, just after midnight, Mildred I. Turpin and Caroline K. Johnson boarded the Arlington and Fairfax Bus bound for Washington, D.C. Both women lived in Northwest Washington, Turpin on Girard Street and Johnson on Florida Avenue. Neither woman was a native of the nation's capital. As Turpin testified in her affidavit, she and Johnson "sat near the front." The driver requested that they move to the back, stating, "Colored move to the rear." Turpin remained silent, while Johnson replied, "No." Turpin then turned to the bus driver and informed him that she and Johnson would move to the back of the bus if the driver agreed to refund their fare. In response, the bus driver called the police. When the police arrived, they ordered Turpin and Johnson to move to the back of the bus. Turpin told the two police officers that "government employees can sit anywhere in the bus," to which he replied, "You are in Virginia and not in Washington." Neither Turpin nor Johnson would accede to these requests, causing the police officers to issue an ultimatum, threatening that "if you all don't move, you will be put in jail." Turpin and Johnson did not move. One police officer then grabbed Turpin's right arm, and she still refused to move. After she and Johnson did depart the bus, two officers shoved them into a police car, with one remarking, "It seems as if we will have a lot of trouble with" Mildred Turpin. At the Arlington County Jail, the women were charged with a "jim crow violation" and spent a cold night in the jail. At 9:55 A.M. on January 7, Turpin and Johnson were taken into court, where each woman pled "not guilty" and was fined five dollars. The judge later approached the women, informing them that they did not have to pay the fine and dismissed the case.[41]

During this incident, Mildred Turpin and Caroline Johnson displayed a great deal of courage. Turpin was the daughter of working-class immigrants from the West Indies who settled in New York City. Turpin's father died when she was still young, and her mother supported the family by working as a servant.[42] Caroline Johnson was also from a working-class family, who lived in Carlisle, Pennsylvania. Her father was a waiter in a hotel, while her mother worked as a servant for a family.[43] Both women moved to Washington, D.C., to serve as clerks in the Navy Department, relatively prestigious positions. Both had worked long days and were likely exhausted. It would have been more convenient to move to the back of the bus, but Johnson and Turpin chose protest over comfort. In his study of black resistance, the historian Robin D. G. Kelley argues that the circumstances of World War II—the contradictions of fighting for democracy abroad while suffering injustice at home, the migration of workers to cities, and the overflowing population—caused African Americans to amplify their protests against inequality in public transportation. In his study of Montgomery, Alabama, Kelley documents widespread patterns of black hostility toward segregation, which stretched from black passengers ringing the bells for the entire ride to refusing to move to the back of the bus.[44] Kelley's insights help illuminate some of the motivations that might have inspired Turpin and Johnson.

The black press quickly circulated the story of Turpin and Johnson's arrest, highlighting the contradictions of black women who were laboring for a patriotic cause, but were subject to inequality and humiliation. Stories appeared in the *Baltimore Afro-American*, the *Chicago Defender*, and the *New York Amsterdam News*, thus informing black citizens across the country about their ordeal.[45] An editorial in the *Baltimore Afro-American* stated, "It is bad enough under any circumstances when American citizens are subjected to such humiliations; but after innocent young women have slaved all day, doing their bit for democracy, it is even worse."[46] The verb "slaved" signaled the ongoing significance of the Civil War. Yet Turpin and Johnson were not the only ones to run into problems on buses traveling between Washington, D.C., and Virginia.

Several months later, the Civil Rights Bureau of the Benevolent Protective Order of the Elks (BPOE) held a meeting at the Metropolitan Baptist Church where they discussed civil rights in the city. Theresa Lee Robinson, a veteran organizer from the anti-lynching movement and police brutality campaigns, delivered "a very striking picture of what the Civil Liberties meant and what it hoped to do, not only in Washington but throughout America." Additionally, Senator Warren Barbour of New Jersey attended and discussed the possibility of passing a civil rights bill in Washington. A special guest named Carrie Mae Little described her experience with segregation. Little had been "recently badly handled by the Alexandria police" following an incident on a Greyhound Bus. The details are unclear, but it appears that Carrie Mae Little, like Mildred Turpin and Caroline Johnson, refused to move to the back of the bus and was arrested. After Little recounted her recent ordeal, J. Finley Wilson, the Grand Exalted Ruler of the Elks, "substantiated the words of Mrs. Robinson and the words of Miss Little to get this case before the proper persons."[47] The fact that Carrie Mae Little was arrested only one month after Turpin and Johnson indicates that black resistance to segregation on buses was ongoing in the city.

Shortly after Carrie Mae Little's arrest, another black woman in Washington, D.C., defied Jim Crow on the buses. On Sunday, May 23, 1943, Ilma Alice Jones, who lived on L Street in Northeast Washington, boarded a bus in Northwest Washington at 2:30 P.M. to travel to Alexandria, Virginia. She took a seat near the front. In her affidavit, Jones noted that the bus was crowded and many white people were standing in the aisles. When the bus stopped to fill up with gasoline on Monroe Avenue, the bus driver approached her, informing that she had to vacate her seat so that a white person could sit down. Jones replied that she had "paid my fare the same as they did" and was "a human just like they are." Jones did not budge from her seat. When the bus arrived at Union Station in Alexandria, Virginia, two police officers were on the scene. Initially, the bus driver told the police not to arrest Jones, and the officers began to leave the bus. However, while the officers were exiting the bus, white passengers began to snicker, jeer, and make audible comments. The reaction of the white passengers caused the officers to change their minds and arrest Jones for her defiance of Jim Crow laws. One police officer grabbed her by the wrist while the other officer snatched her purse and package. They loaded Jones into a car and drove to the police station in Alexandria, where she was charged with disorderly conduct and resisting arrest, while also being fined $100. The next morning, Jones pled not guilty to the charges in the Alexandria County Court; however, a judge found her guilty and fined her twenty-five dollars.[48]

What is telling about the Ilma Jones case is the reluctance on the part of the bus driver to enforce the law, compounded with the indecisiveness of the police officers about whether to press charges. The people who enforced the law on the bus on this day, ironically, were the white passengers. It was precisely *their* reactions to the prospect that Ilma Jones would not be punished that caused the officers to turn around and arrest her, charging her with both resisting arrest and disorderly conduct. The historian Stephen Berrey argues that, in segregated transportation systems, white passengers participated in racial surveillance to personally police Jim Crow. The evidence in this narrative suggests that black protests against Jim Crow had become routine. Both Ilma Jones and the bus driver picked their battles since they were positioned on opposite sides of a war over seating on the buses. Jones would not have been arrested had it not been for the white passengers who insisted the color line be preserved.[49] All of these stories suggest that the climate in the nation's capital was becoming even more militant. Black women throughout the city were at the forefront of resistance against segregation on buses.

"Why Can't We Eat Here?"
The Sit-In Movement in Washington, D.C.

Buses were not the only sites of black resistance. Students at Howard University also waged campaigns against racial segregation in restaurants and lunch counters throughout the city. When Pauli Murray arrived at Howard University in 1941 to begin her first year of law school, she could not locate housing. Murray was surprised that the city was so segregated, writing in her memoir that "segregation in the nation's capital was an especially galling indignity."[50] In a fortunate coincidence, she wound up living on the first floor of Sojourner Truth Hall, an undergraduate dorm for women, which helped nurture an important intergenerational bond between the students. "My room," Murray later reflected, "became an informal meeting place for undergraduate women interested in civil rights." She and many women students felt a call to duty. "We women reasoned that it was our job to help make the country for which our black brothers were fighting," she argued, "a freer place in which to live when they returned from wartime service."[51] As Murray and other women students discussed modes of activism, they talked about Gandhi's struggle against colonial rule in India and his use of nonviolent direct action to confront systems of oppression. She recalled, "Ideas about the use of nonviolent resistance to racial injustice, modeled on Gandhi's movement in India, were in the air."[52] The historian and sociologist Aldon Morris describes direct action as a nonviolent form of "mass protest" that "allowed the very bodies of blacks to become potential power instruments."[53] By discussing nonviolence and direct action, students at Howard University thought about the ways that they, as women, could directly engage in the struggle against racial segregation.

As described earlier, Howard University undergraduates Ruth Powell, Marianne Musgrave, and Juanita Morrow ordered hot chocolate at the United Cigar Store in Northwest and were refused service. After contesting their bill, the students were "arrested, placed in a patrol wagon, taken to the women's bureau and held for several hours."[54]

The arrest of these three young women helped spark the sit-in movement at Howard University. Immediately after the news had spread, undergraduate women gathered inside Sojourner Truth Hall to plan an action, with Pauli Murray as their legal advisor. Women formed a Temporary Committee on Campus Opinion, which educated students about the importance of passing civil rights legislation in the city while also polling their opinions on these issues. In addition, students formed a Direct Action Committee, chaired by Ruth Powell. This group decided to hold weekly sit-ins at local restaurants, where activists would politely request service and demand the same treatment as white customers. It decided to first work on integrating eating establishments that were located in black neighborhoods near Howard University and that practiced racial segregation, which meant that they would not serve black customers at the counter. These direct action protests built on the work of activists in the New Negro Alliance a decade earlier, in which both men and women staged pickets and boycotts of black stores and restaurants in neighborhoods that would not hire black workers. But in the 1940s, students steered the struggle from employment to patronage.

During the winter of 1943, Howard students engaged in an intense organizing drive on campus in preparation for their first sit-in. Working to educate the broader campus about the sit-ins, they first held fundraising campaigns. They procured hot-chocolate cups to symbolize the three students' earlier arrest and encouraged members of the student community to fill them up with donations to defray the costs of "postage, paper, and picket signs." They also held a campus pep rally and "drummed up support for our effort through noon-hour broadcasts from the tower of Founder's Library."

The students held a town hall to which they invited seasoned political leaders to educate the campus about nonviolent direct action. In their flier inviting students to participate, members asked, "Are you for Hitler's Way or the American Way?" Speakers at the meeting included Thomasina Walker Johnson, the lobbyist for the Alpha Kappa Alpha Sorority; Howard University law professor Robert W. Ming, who had previously spoken with Nannie Helen Burroughs at the YWCA about the importance of the Bill of Rights; and Albert B. Herman, the legislative aide for New Jersey senator Warren Barbour, who had introduced the civil rights bill. As a lobbyist for the AKA, Johnson was able to mine her vast networks and connections to introduce students to a legislative aid for Senator Barbour. This town hall underscored the unique connections that black women activists enjoyed in the nation's capital. At its conclusion, the Howard Players (who renamed themselves the Civil Rights Players) performed a skit titled "The Race's Problem Goes to Heaven."[55] As part of their educational campaign, the students also "conducted classes on the legal aspects of picketing and disorderly conduct in the District of Columbia, spent hours in small groups discussing public decorum, anticipating and preparing for the reactions of the black public, the white public, white customers and white management, respectively." As Pauli Murray remembered, "We stressed the importance of a dignified appearance, and the subcommittee directed that all participants dress well for the occasion."[56]

On Friday, April 16, nineteen Howard University students held their first planned sit-in at the Little Palace Café located on Fourteenth and U Streets Northwest, only blocks from the college campus. Initially, twelve students filed into the restaurant and demanded service at the counter; others were outside, on the ready with picket signs. Of the student participants, seven were men and thirteen were women, including veteran activist Natalie Moorman. The students were joined by AKA lobbyist, Thomasina Walker Johnson. It is striking that Thomasina Johnson waged two levels of politics by lobbying at the federal level to pass the civil rights bill and resisting at the local level to integrate Little Palace.

The white owner refused to serve them, but the students would not budge from their seats. Eventually, he ended the sit-in by closing his restaurant, eight hours earlier than the usual closing time. Once he locked the doors of the restaurant, the other students appeared bearing signs with phrases like "Why Can't We Eat Here? There's No Segregation Law in D.C. What's Your Story, Little Palace?" and "Our Boys, Our Bonds: Our Brothers Are Fighting for You." A reporter for the *Baltimore Afro-American* interviewed the owner, and he stubbornly stated, "I'd lose money, but I'd rather close up than practice democracy this way. The time is not yet ripe." However, it was clear that the Little Palace owner was on the losing side of these debates. The *Chicago Defender* reported, "The action was a planned part of their 'direct action' campaign to bring civil rights to the District of Columbia."[57]

Despite the lack of a clear victory after the first sit-in, activists pressed on and staged sit-ins during the next couple of months. When classes ended for summer vacation, some students remained in the area and continued to participate in the campaigns. In August 1943, an article in the *Washington Tribune* was headlined, "Interracial Experiments in D.C. Restaurants Prove Successful," highlighting the fact that the movement had broadened to include "interracial groups."

Groups of black and white citizens began to visit different restaurants across the city and demand to be seated together. They succeeded at Thompson's Restaurant at Pennsylvania and Eleventh Street and the People's Drug Store at Fourteen and U Street, both in Northwest Washington. NW. However, the sit-in at the People's Drug Store at Eleventh and G Streets in Northwest Washington was not successful. Its owner, a Mr. Snyder, was interviewed and asked why he did not serve black customers; he replied that it was "for business reasons."[58]

By initiating the sit-in movement in Washington, D.C., it is likely that activists saw it as a model they could introduce to cities across the country. The sit-in movement in Washington, D.C., became affiliated with the Fellowship of Reconciliation of the Congress of Racial Equality (CORE) under the direction of Bayard Rustin. CORE was an interracial and pacifist organization that had been formed in 1942. By uniting a local movement with a prominent, national civil rights organization, activists saw the black freedom struggle in Washington, D.C., as a model for the nation.

When classes at Howard University resumed in the fall of 1943 so did the student's sit-in movement. An article in September 1943 commented on the logistics of the sit-ins. For instance, an interracial group of students entered Murphy's Five & Ten Cent store at Fourteenth and Kenyon Streets in Northwest Washington and waited at the counter to be served. When the waitress only brought food to the white customers, those who were served cleverly "shifted the food and drinks over to the colored members—none of whom had been served." When the next interracial group arrived to take their place, the waitress would not serve any members of the group. The article noted, "An interesting sidelight of this experimentation is that the people visiting the store at this time assume that the store serves the colored seated at the counter." In addition to Murphy's, interracial groups successfully tested the enforcement of segregation at the Service Pharmacy, located at Fourteenth and L Streets, and at Stewart's Pharmacy at Sixteenth and U Streets, both in Northwest Washington.[59]

But the sit-in movement was unable to eliminate segregation at lunch counters across the city, and in October 1943, a newspaper article discussed the persistence of racial segregation in the city. The title of the article was "Eating in the Nation's Capital These Days Is Food for Thought about Jim Crow." It began by discussing a complete reversal in situations. "Getting a job these days in Washington is not much of a problem, but getting something to eat is something else—and it isn't a problem of ration points or black markets either." The article noted that "none of the downtown restaurants will serve Negroes, as a rule" and "the most democratic place is the Union Station lunch room and dining room." Additionally, the article mentioned the "cafeteria in the Lucy Slowe dormitories" and the "café in the Phyllis Wheatley YWCA, run by an enterprising Negro woman" as places where African Americans could be served. It was not at all surprising that these establishments were founded and run for and by African American women in the nation's capital.[60]

In September 1943, veteran civil rights leader Natalie Moorman departed the Washington, D.C., area to attend nursing school at the University of Minnesota. A newspaper column in the *Chicago Defender* commented on her departure, calling her "Washington's No. 1 colored woman fighter for race rights," warning, "Watch yourself Minnesota."[61] Sure enough in November 1944, Moorman's name resurfaced in connection to civil rights. When she attempted to make an appointment at the Campus Beauty Salon, she was refused service; in response Moorman cited Minnesota's civil rights law. Moorman knew that Minnesota had such a law since she had been part of the effort to pass a similar one in the nation's capital. Moorman's use of the legal system underscored her knowledge of her rights as a citizen in different states. As a result of her protests against segregation, Natalie Moorman became the first black woman to reside in the university's coeducational dormitories.[62]

"Lady Lobbyist Blazes Trail in Capital": Black Women's Local and National Lobbying

At the same time that black women practiced grassroots activism by resisting segregation on buses and demanding service at restaurants, they also worked to influence legislation at the local and national levels. Black Washingtonians had been lobbying to pass a civil rights bill since 1935, but their efforts gained momentum during World War II. By 1941, one hundred organizations throughout the city had united under the auspices of the Washington Civil Rights Committee to pass a civil rights bill.[63] During the 1940s, several members of Congress supported civil rights legislation, including New Jersey senator Warren K. Barbour, Illinois representative William D. Rowan, and Connecticut representative Herman Kopplemann. While it was a victory that activists had allies in both the House and the Senate, white Southern Democrats continued to register strong opposition. Two days after Kopplemann introduced the bill in the House, Representative John E. Rankin, a Democrat from Mississippi, denounced this legislation. In a pointed address titled "Stop Nagging the South," Rankin noted the climate of black militancy in the city, reflected in the March on Washington Movement, campaigns against transportation segregation, and rising student activism. "There is trouble brewing here in the District of Columbia," Rankin claimed, "where a few irresponsible Negroes, encouraged by a few radical whites, are stirring up trouble that is likely to blaze into a race riot at any time." He also menacingly stated, "The Negroes know their place and we know ours."[64] Rankin's speech depicted the civil rights bill as "radical" and part of a "fringe movement," rather than a crucial form of American democracy and citizenship. In response to this vocal opposition in the House of Representatives, African Americans living in Washington, D.C., worked to keep the focus on civil rights. Five hundred Baptist, AME, and AMEZ ministers in the city called for a united effort for civil rights legislation, and they asked that 40,000 ministers across the country join their crusade for equality.

Articles in the black press helped educate African Americans about the importance of civil rights legislation in Washington, D.C. In April 1942, Marjorie McKenzie, a writer for the *Pittsburgh Courier* whose well-known column was titled "Pursuit of Democracy," cast the civil rights bill as a matter of pressing concern not only for African Americans living in the nation's capital but also for those across the world: "There are nearly 200,000 Negroes in war-time Washington," and "the combined tragedies of their lives in the actual and psychological ghettos of Washington are now of cosmic import." McKenzie called out the real aim of the war effort: "America states that she is fighting for the great sweeping concepts of world freedom and justice and security." She contended that other nations who were "our allies in the struggle for democracy are China, and we hope, India." But she then starkly noted, "In the very capital of the Nation, the very heart of the arsenal of democracy, America practices race hate and segregation with calloused and unrelenting vigor." McKenzie passionately called on African Americans living across the country to lobby influential congressmen to pass the civil rights bill.[65] McKenzie, like other writers in the black press, thus positioned the civil rights struggle in Washington, D.C., as a matter of national significance. Another article in the *Washington Afro-American* in 1943 asked black voters across the nation to urge their senators and congressman to support the civil rights bill in D.C., pleading, "Let us have the fifth freedom in the nation's capital; freedom from prejudice."[66]

While activists lobbied Congress and students waged sit-ins, other black women in the city worked for civil rights by organizing campaigns and mass meetings. In February 1943, it was announced that the local NAACP chapter had reached 10,000 members. Ella Baker, field secretary for the national NAACP, had traveled from New York City to help organize the recruitment campaign, which was led by black women from churches across the city.[67] Black Washingtonians also staged a mass meeting at Garnet-Patterson High School, where they discussed the pending civil rights legislation and the arrest of the Howard students.[68] At this meeting, a community of black Washingtonians agreed to form a Civil Rights Committee, which operated under the assumption that "there is no Jim Crow in Washington and the practices as followed here are merely custom with no legal foundation." Members of the Civil Rights Committee argued that "it is possible to rid the capital of this insult and inconvenience by our action."[69] This activism indicated the two levels of politics that were practiced in the nation's capital: not only did activists work through traditional routes by lobbying representatives and senators to pass bills in Congress but they also staged their own grassroots campaigns.

Black citizens' optimism about the end of segregation in the nation's capital was affirmed in August 1943. That month, Bureau of Engraving clerk Tomlinson D. Todd had unearthed a law passed by the legislature of the District of Columbia in 1872 that banned discrimination.[70] It stated, "It shall not be lawful for any person or persons who shall have obtained a license from this District for the purpose of giving a lecture, concert, exhibition, circus performance, theatrical entertainment, for conducting a place of public amusement of any kind to make any distinction on account of race or color, as regards the admission of persons to any part of the hall or audience room where such lecture, concert, exhibition, or other entertainment is given."[71] The irony that black citizens were actively campaigning for the passage of a civil rights bill while one already existed was not lost on the black press. "While Washington organizations are clamoring for enactment of the civil rights bill for the nation's capital," an article in the *Baltimore Afro-American* noted, "it was revealed this week that such a law had already been passed, but conveniently forgotten."[72] With the discovery of this Reconstruction-era law, black Washingtonians had truly come full circle as they worked to restore many of the freedoms their ancestors had once enjoyed in the nation's capital. The question became "whether or not in the absence of a repeal the law is still effective, although it is not on the municipal government book."[73] Todd's discovery prompted activists to dig deeper. Pauli Murray consulted A. Mercer Daniel, the law librarian at Howard University, who performed further research. Importantly, Daniel "recalled talk among older Washingtonians of an earlier civil rights law in the District of Columbia."[74] The discovery of this civil rights bill was a fitting conclusion for black Washingtonians who had been contemplating the memories of the Civil War and Reconstruction through their voting rights campaigns, sit-ins, and push for a civil rights bill.

During the war, African American women engaged once again in national advocacy campaigns. In 1940, Thomasina Walker Johnson had been appointed the chief lobbyist for the AKA's National Non-Partisan Council. A native of South Carolina, Johnson had graduated from the University of Pennsylvania where she joined the local AKA chapter; she then worked as a hairdresser and teacher in Philadelphia. After her marriage, she moved to Boston with her husband, who was a musician; she was elected president of the Massachusetts Colored Women's Club and helped secure positions for black women as telephone operators. Her husband died at a young age, prompting Johnson to move to Washington, D.C., and accept the paid AKA position.[75] When she arrived, articles in the black press commented on the significance of her role in national politics. The *Pittsburgh Courier* called the AKA's lobbying project the product of the "far-seeing and constructive women" who recognized the importance of "having someone constantly on hand to observe congress and report findings to various chapters."[76] Johnson's networks of connections with the women's club movement, AKA members, and the beauty culture industry made her well suited for the position.

Between 1941 and 1946, Thomasina Johnson became a familiar witness in federal hearings as she championed economic justice, legal equality, and world peace. Johnson weighed in on a range of issues that affected African Americans across the country, including low-cost housing, the expansion of Social Security to all workers, the creation of a permanent Fair Employment Practices Commission, the equal distribution of funds for child care, government funding for hospitals, a federal school lunch program, and the creation of the United Nations, about which she spoke eloquently of the need for decolonization in Africa. One of Johnson's most significant lobbying efforts led to the enlistment of African American women as personnel and officers in the Navy in 1944.[77] Johnson's testimony was always detailed, relied on statistics and data, and advocated that African Americans be the beneficiaries of federal programs. Johnson was not always able to ensure that legislation would indeed benefit African Americans, but her legacy is apparent in volume after volume of federal hearings.

Thomasina Walker Johnson and the AKA's Non-Partisan Council garnered praise in the black press. Black women in AKA were proud that they had created this lobbying position in 1938, and until 1942, they were the only black lobbying group in the nation, representing men and women across the nation. An article in the *Chicago Defender* in 1945 summarizing Johnson's career was titled "Lady Lobbyist Blazes Path in Nation's Capital." Pointing to Johnson's testimony and legislative victories, the article concluded that she had "chalked up a record of accomplishments which today stands a monument to the foresight of Negro women." The article noted that when the NAACP established its own lobbying group in 1942, the AKA began to focus more specifically on legislation that affected black women and children. However, the article quoted Johnson as stating "with a twinkle in her eye," that "we do a supporting job on all legislation."[78]

Johnson's lobbying career during the 1940s reflected a discernible shift in black women's political activism in Washington, D.C. When Mary Church Terrell, Marian Butler, Nannie Helen Burroughs, Julia West Hamilton, and Cora

Wilkinson had testified in Congress for anti-lynching legislation, voting rights, and the construction of a National Negro Memorial, they had drawn on personal experiences, family memories, and Christian morality in their advocacy. All of these women were part of the black clubwomen's movement and were shaped by discourses of respectability. As congressional witnesses during the 1920s and 1930s, when woman suffrage was still relatively new, black women expressed humility about their political positions. Representing a range of political causes, these women were volunteers, and their organizations often operated on shoestring budgets. None of these groups had a paid staff, and most ran out of the Phyllis Wheatley YWCA. The Colored Women's Legislative Headquarters from 1925 was located inside of Mazie Griffin's house, conveniently one block from the U.S. Capitol. In contrast, Thomasina Walker Johnson was a paid lobbyist who had a staff and an office, making her more like a professional politician. Johnson represented a group of six thousand college-educated black women in the AKA who were affiliated with 165 local chapters in 46 states.[79] And as a resident of Philadelphia and Boston, Johnson had cast ballots in many state, local, and national elections. But her presence in the U.S. Capitol was facilitated by the pioneering women who had bravely testified in Congress and laid the groundwork for her political career.

Johnson also used her position as a lobbyist to advocate for African Americans in Washington, D.C. Because of her efforts, Alpha Kappa Alpha was one of the organizations that went on record in support of voting rights and local governance in Washington, D.C.[80] Johnson also organized several mass meetings to support the passage of civil rights legislation in Washington, D.C. In November 1943, the AKA Sorority held a meeting with Senator Warren Barbour, where members praised his position on civil rights. In turn, he told the AKA that he was "proud" of having introduced the civil rights bill for the District of Columbia. "Whether we have the franchise or not," Barbour argued, "I don't see why we can't give full privileges to everyone in public places."[81] African Americans also continued to lobby for the passage of a civil rights bill that would allow black citizens to patronize any establishment in the city on an equal basis.

The Foundations of All Jim Crow Laws Were Shaken a Little This Week

But at the same time that momentum was shifting toward civil rights in Washington, D.C., a white southern backlash in Congress solidified. In February 1944, Senator Theodore Bilbo, a Democrat from Mississippi, became the head of the Senate's Committee on the District of Columbia. In the preceding few years, Bilbo had already proposed legislation to ban interracial marriage in the nation's capital and openly supported black repatriation to Africa. Locally, African Americans in the nation's capital were devastated that an avowed segregationist had become the informal mayor of Washington, D.C. Arthur D. Gray, who was now president of the local branch of the NAACP, argued, "On the basis of Bilbo's record and statements, Negroes cannot expect any kind of fair treatment under his administration of District Affairs."[82] As committee chair, Bilbo announced his intentions to make Washington a "model city" for the entire country. Only one month after his appointment, he suggested that African Americans—as a race of people—were not suited for city life and recommended that black inhabitants of the District of Columbia migrate to the country. Bilbo was referring specifically to black inhabitants of the back alleys, but his message was clear that he intended Washington, D.C., to be a white city and that he was strongly opposed to voting rights in the nation's capital.[83]

Two months after Senator Bilbo became chair of the Senate's Committee on the District of Columbia, students at Howard University reenergized their sit-in movement. By working to integrate lunch counters and restaurants, students marched with their feet in opposition to segregation and Bilbo's political opinions. Veterans of the sit-in movement and newcomers banded together under the leadership of Pauli Murray to integrate the cafeterias at the John R. Thompson Company restaurant chain, which had three locations. Activists selected the location at Eleventh Street and Pennsylvania in Northwest Washington because this venue was open twenty-four hours a day and was within walking distance of several federal buildings; being able to eat there would be a blessing to weary black government workers. However, integrating this particular restaurant posed a challenge since it was not located in a black neighborhood. Activists thus doubled down on their preparation efforts, taking special care to train participants in proper decorum and etiquette.[84] They required all participants to sign a "pledge," which demonstrated each student's commitment to the black freedom movement. This pledge required them to take an oath, stating that one of the

> most precious of all human rights [is] the right of equal privileges in all places of public accommodation. . . . I conceive the effort to eliminate discrimination against any person because of race or color to be a patriotic duty and an act of faith in the American boys who are fighting for the Four Freedoms in foreign lands and to the young women who have

joined in serving the Armed Forces, and who have every right to expect a greater share of those freedoms when they return home. . . . I pledge myself to give full and vigorous support to the present campaign of the Civil Rights Committee and the NAACP Student Chapter in order to break down discrimination in restaurants, theaters, stores, and other places of public accommodation in Washington, D.C.[85]

On Saturday, April 22, 1944, black students began to enter Thompson's restaurant in pairs of two and three, ten minutes apart from one another. The wait staff at the restaurant refused to serve food to the students, prompting them to carry empty trays to vacant tables in the restaurant, thereby highlighting to other patrons the black students' lack of food. White students then entered the restaurant and questioned the white patrons about whether African Americans should be allowed to eat at Thompson's. Of the ten polled, only three favored racial restrictions. Outside of the restaurant, other black students formed a picket line, bearing signs with messages such as "Are You for Hitler's Way (Race Supremacy) or the AMERICAN Way (Equality)? Make Up Your Mind" and "We Die Together. How Come We Can't Eat Together?" The picket line soon attracted attention. Within a few minutes, six black soldiers witnessed the commotion and entered Thompson's, emulating the actions of the students. The soldiers asked to be served and were similarly refused. The staff at Thompson's panicked at the potential explosiveness of the situation and called their company's managers along with the Metropolitan Police. The white police officers asked the soldiers to leave, with a white lieutenant noting that this would be a "personal favor to the Army." Pauli Murray then challenged the officer, remarking that perhaps all members of the Army should leave the restaurant. The embarrassed soldiers complied. Within four hours, the crowed of patrons at Thompson's had thinned, and the black students were served a meal. For the next couple of weeks, activists continued to stage sit-ins at Thompson's, and a few African Americans were served. However, the president of Howard University, Mordecai Johnson, requested that students disband their sit-in movement. Howard received federal funding, and in this instance, President Johnson feared upsetting members of Congress.[86]

While the formal sit-in movement ended, women continued to resist segregation. On Sunday, May 14, 1944, at 6:30 P.M., eight female students at Howard University were returning by bus to campus after spending some time in Northern Virginia. These women included four freshmen—Ruby O'Hara, Doris King, Cynthia Kennedy, and Ruth Ann Robinson—as well as juniors Ruth Powell and Marianne Musgrave and seniors Angela Jones and Erma

McElmore. All of the women selected seats near the front of the bus. When the white bus driver, Mitchell B. Lee, told the students that they needed to move toward the back, according to an affidavit, they "sat silently, reading." He then told the women, "Well we'll just stay here until you move back," and then said that, if they did not move, he would alert the police. Again, the women remained in their seats. One of the passengers informed the bus driver that they could sit wherever they wished in compliance with the Interstate Commerce Clause. The driver responded by pointing to a sign at the front of the bus informing passengers about the Jim Crow law. The bus driver then departed the bus, and the eight women conferred among themselves. The upper-class students instructed the freshmen to move to the rear of the bus in order to avoid arrest, but refused to move themselves. After the freshman students returned to campus, they informed the director of the women's dormitories of the arrests of their fellow students and placed a telephone call to Charles Hamilton Houston, the dean of the law school and noted civil rights attorney.[87]

Thirty minutes after the women had first refused to move to the back of the bus, police officers arrested Musgrave, McLemore, Powell, and Jones. The women did not readily protest their arrest, although Jones questioned whether police officers had a warrant, and an officer replied that they would get that in prison. By 7:20 P.M. the women arrived at a jail in Fairfax, Virginia, where they were charged with violating Jim Crow law. When the women were allowed to make a telephone call, they phoned Pauli Murray who was staying at Professor Caroline Ware's farm in Virginia. The four women were released at 4:00 P.M. the next day under the recognizance of Caroline Ware, after she consulted with Charles Hamilton Houston.[88] It is clear that this activism had been planned. Both Powell and Musgrave were veterans of the sit-in movement and had spent the previous year working to integrate lunch counters across Washington, D.C. These women joined their case with that of Irene Morgan, which went to the Supreme Court and overturned segregation transportation segregation on interstate commerce.

In March 1945, an article in the *Chicago Defender* mentioned that all of these cases were traveling to the Supreme Court. "The foundation of Southern jim crow laws," the article stated, "were shaken a little this week" when the Virginia Supreme Court of Appeals decided to hear "five jim crow travel cases." It noted, "This question was raised by four Howard University students who were arrested in Fairfax county, Virginia last may for refusing to move to the rear of a bus traveling from Virginia to Washington, and Miss Irene Morgan, arrested last July 16 in Middlesex county for the same reason while enroute from

Virginia to Baltimore, Md." The article concluded by reporting that Leon A. Ransom and Charles Hamilton Houston were representing the Howard students.[89] Irene Morgan's case went through several appeals, and finally in June 1946, the U.S. Supreme Court ruled that racial segregation on interstate transportation violated the Commerce Clause of the Constitution.

That month, an article in the *Baltimore Afro-American* chronicled the long and tortuous struggle to end segregation on interstate transportation. "For over a quarter of a century," the article observed, "jim-crowing of colored passengers on busses, engaged in interstate transportation has made that mode of travel a dreaded experience among non-white people." The article noted the gender disparity in segregation transportation cases, observing that "among the legion of cases reported are those in which women, ministers, and persons in service to their country have been stranded, beaten, fined, and imprisoned." It concluded by noting that on Virginia buses "colored passengers are permitted to sit any place they desire."[90]

Black Washingtonians recognized that they had accomplished a great deal during the wartime period, and many women and men were determined to continue to whittle away at racial barriers in the city in the postwar era. In October 1944, students and faculty members in a public opinion class at George Washington University interviewed a cross-section of black and white Washingtonians to gauge their opinions about civil rights. Forty-six percent of respondents stated that they favored a civil rights bill for the District of Columbia, and 56 percent opposed school segregation; 61 percent denounced segregation on buses, while only 32 percent favored these policies and 7 percent registered no opinion on the question.[91] While there was still much work to do, this poll made it clear that some white Washingtonians favored civil rights and black equality in the nation's capital.

Conclusion

During World War II, black women's political campaigns developed urgency and momentum. Globally, nations battled epic battles between democracy and fascism. Nationally, African Americans witnessed firsthand the sharp disconnect between the language of democracy and antidiscrimination and the reality of intolerance and exclusion. In the charged location in the nation's capital, women seized on opportunities—whether it was on the seats of buses, the stools of lunch counters, the steps of federal buildings, or the stacks of libraries— to enact their visions of democracy, justice, and equality. These events did not occur in a vacuum, but rather helped inspire one another, and the black community in Washington, D.C., paid attention. When the students at Howard initiated their brave campaign against racial segregation at lunch counters, they acted in solidarity with black soldiers fighting on the battlefield; war workers battling segregation in Virginia; congressmen, senators, and AKA lobbyists pressing to pass civil rights legislation and other bills; and organizational allies, including the Civil Rights Committee, the NAACP, the Phyllis Wheatley YWCA, and the AKA.

At the conclusion of World War II, some of the hardest-fought elements of the struggle had already been realized. Activists achieved a victory in the landmark Supreme Court decision *Morgan v. Virginia*, discovered the 1872 civil rights law, and affirmed that nonviolent direct action was a successful protest weapon. In the postwar period, a group of women and men applied the twin forces of law and nonviolent protest to integrate the capital of the United States of America and, in turn, to inspire the postwar black freedom struggle.

Conclusion
Black Women and the Long Civil Rights Movement

In the aftermath of World War II, a community of black Washingtonians wielded their protest instruments to integrate the nation's capital. With the coming of the Cold War, the matter of legal segregation in the nation's capital had become an issue of national security. In November 1948, the National Committee on Segregation in the Nation's Capital released an eighty-nine-page report that outlined the scope of inequality in Washington, D.C. Its chapters documented the extent of segregation in housing, schools, and labor opportunities, calling Congress to action.[1] In January 1949, an article in the *Chicago Defender*'s "National Grapevine" was titled "It's a Strange World" and commented that "Washington has no civil rights law or equal rights law although the one recorded in 1872 has never been repealed."[2] Despite the release of this report, Congress remained inactive.

In April 1949, a team of lawyers in Washington, D.C., banded together with black women and men to devise a way to enforce the 1872 law. Two months later, activists held a meeting at the Phyllis Wheatley YWCA under the leadership of Mary Church Terrell to discuss how to implement these legal strategies. Neither the place nor the leader of this campaign could have been more fitting. The Phyllis Wheatley YWCA was a storied location in black women's politics since it was the meeting place for the Colored Women's Republican's League and the Women's Political Study Club, the planning site for the Silent Parade in 1922 and the Rope Protests in 1934, the headquarters for the NRA drive in 1933, and the meeting space for campaigns against police brutality throughout the 1930s. The eighty-five-year-old Terrell was a veteran organizer and seasoned activist in black women's politics in the nation's capital, personally witnessing its tilt from national to local affairs. Attendees at this meeting formed the Coordinating Committee for the Enforcement of D.C. Anti-Discrimination Laws (CCEAD) and elected Terrell as their leader.

In January 1950, members of the CCEAD—including Terrell, Geneva Brown, and the Reverend William H. Jernagin—attempted to eat at Thompson's Restaurant, located at 725 Fourteenth Street NW, an African American neighborhood. Six years earlier, students at Howard University had staged an iconic sit-in at Thompson's Pennsylvania Avenue location (see chapter 6). That sit-in had resulted in only short-lived integration. When the staff at Thompson's refused to serve Terrell, Brown, and Jernagin on account of their race, the activists politicized the case, claiming that their denial to eat violated the 1872 Civil Rights Law in the District of Columbia and sued Thompson's Restaurant.[3]

By 1950, the grassroots activism of black women and men had helped transform the climate of the city. In response to the lawsuit the three members of the Board of Commissioners, who were all white men, contended that the 1872 law was "in force" and used their powers to order all restaurants in the city to serve African American patrons.[4] Most restaurants in the city complied, but a few refused. In February 1951, *District of Columbia v. John R. Thompson Company, Inc., No. 1967* was argued before the Municipal Court of Appeals for the District of Columbia. Three months later, the court ruled that the 1872 and 1873 Civil Rights laws were valid.[5]

In January 1952, this decision was appealed, and the case traveled to the U.S. Supreme Court. The U.S. solicitor general and the special assistant to the attorney general each filed amicus curiae briefs in support of the lower court's ruling. In their briefs, the lawyers argued that "the problem of the Nation's Capital is for numerous reasons a matter of serious concern to the entire country." The lawyers defended their argument by noting that the federal government employed men and women who lived in all parts of the country and had a policy of nondiscrimination, and that numerous international embassies and consulates were located in the District of Columbia and were "likely to judge the country and its people by their experience and observation in Washington." Finally, the lawyers pointed out the existence of global diversity, making the case that the world was comprised of people of all races and creeds. Ringgold Hart, the attorney for Thompson's Restaurant, contended that Congress lacked the power to shape laws passed by the Legislative Assembly for the District of Columbia in the nineteenth century.[6] In June 1953, the Supreme Court upheld the legitimacy of the 1873 Civil Rights Act.[7] Segregation in places of public accommodation in the nation's capital was finally illegal. In October 1953, Mary Church Terrell celebrated this legal victory on her ninetieth birthday.[8]

While the end of racial segregation occurred earlier in the nation's capital than the rest of the country, the campaign for voting rights has lasted longer and is, in fact, ongoing. In 1961, states ratified the Twenty-Third Amendment to the Constitution, which enabled residents of the nation's capital to vote in presidential elections. In 1964, citizens of Washington, D.C., cast their first presidential ballots. Three years later in 1967, Congress passed a law that reorganized the local government. Walter Washington, an African American man, was appointed as the city's first mayor. Six years later, Congress granted home rule to the city, which allowed for residents to elect a mayor and thirteen members of the City Council. However, Washington, D.C., is not a state, which means that Congress—and not city residents—exercises control over matters of education, social services, and even civil rights. Currently, there is a vibrant movement afoot for statehood.[9]

The narrative arc of black women's politics, organizing, and activism in Washington, D.C., reveals both continuity and change. In 1920, black women celebrated the passage of the Nineteenth Amendment by creating political organizations, using them as instruments to lobby for national causes. Some of these organizations were affiliated with the National Association of Colored Women (NACW), but gathered members from churches, fraternal orders, social clubs, labor organizations, neighborhoods, and the Phyllis Wheatley YWCA. Since most black women in Washington could not vote, they either encouraged absentee ballot submission or traveled to neighboring states to urge women living there to cast their votes. Black women in Washington, D.C., also banded together with their networks and organizations to engage in a variety of national causes, including labor justice, federal anti-lynching legislation, Supreme Court appointments, and the memorial landscape in the nation's capital.

By the 1930s, the crises of interracial police violence and the Great Depression caused many of the same activists to turn toward local issues. In this decade, the NACW lost some of its power, and most of black women's local and national organizations declined in significance. Even though most organizations did not survive, black women's networks in churches, fraternal orders, neighborhoods, and the YWCA continued to be the organizing powerhouse in the black community and offered crucial constituencies in the campaigns for safety, economic justice, voting rights, and civil rights. The 1930s also witnessed the politicization of black sororities, such as Alpha Kappa Alpha and Delta Sigma Theta, as well as the emergence of leftist organizations, such as the New Negro Alliance and the National Negro Congress. During World War II, black women were able to build on two decades of lobbying, organizing, and resistance to wage their political campaigns for racial integration and civil rights. Women's organizations may have emerged and faded, but hundreds of black women were at the center of political campaigns in Washington, D.C., from 1920 until 1945.

Black activists in the nation's capital crafted a unique political culture that was rooted in the rituals of American citizenship and justice. In the moments when they were unable to exercise their rights or see justice materialize, activists organized their own ceremonies of citizenship. In the 1920s, hundreds of black citizens gathered in churches across the city to pray for the passage of a federal anti-lynching bill. Even though Congress never passed anti-lynching legislation, black women were able to use their prayers as a way to honor the victims of violence. During the 1930s, when, in case after case, white judges in the Police Court refused to punish white police officers for brutality against black citizens, African Americans in Washington, D.C., held their own police trials, where they stated the facts of each case and came to their own opinions. When black citizens were unable to vote in the presidential election in 1936, the black-owned *Washington Tribune* held its own election, asking citizens to mail in their ballots. By "voting by mail," black citizens participated in this act of citizenship.

Over the course of their campaigns for freedom and justice between 1920 and 1945, African American women transformed civil rights politics in the United States in several important ways. First, activists experimented with the method of direct action in their campaigns. Black women and men used this tactic in the Rope Protests in 1934 when they hung small pieces of rope from their necks to symbolize lynching victims, in 1938 when they carried empty coffins through the streets of Washington to evoke victims of police violence, and in the 1940s when students staged sit-ins at lunch counters demanding to be served. All three episodes were well publicized in the black press. While African American women were the not the first ones to pioneer direct action, they successfully applied this method to their different political campaigns, thereby offering peers in southern and northern cities practical strategies to implement in their own movements. The sit-in movement that erupted in 1960 in southern cities owed a major debt to their predecessors at Howard University in the 1940s. The black freedom struggle in Washington, D.C., also demonstrated the importance of students to political movements. Students had more time to participate in protests, did not always face employment consequences for political activism, and were eager to tackle injustice. At strategic moments in the 1930s and 1940s, the Washington, D.C., political campaigns thrived precisely because of black women's powerful political networks, the presence of students, and programs of mass action. When Ella Baker and other activists formed the Student Non-Violent Coordinating Committee in 1960, they continued the inclusive organizing vision that black women in the nation's capital had adopted.[10]

Familiar faces and names surfaced in the postwar black freedom struggle. Because activists in the nation's capital refused to compartmentalize or compromise their visions of justice, veterans from Washington, D.C., were active in postwar campaigns for legal equality, welfare rights, and feminism. After World War II, Thelma Dale moved to New York City and organized for progressive causes.[11] Both Pauli Murray and Natalie Moorman joined the Congress of Racial Equality (CORE) and helped plan its Journey of Reconciliation in 1947, which was an early freedom ride that sent black and white Americans on buses down South to test enforcement of *Morgan v. Virginia*. Murray and Moorman would have been on the buses, but male leaders decided to limit participation to men. As black women who had been arrested on buses, Moorman and Murray would have offered a wealth of experience to the Ride of Reconciliation, and it was their resistance that helped pave the way for the Supreme Court decision.[12] After she held a leadership position with the YWCA in Washington, D.C., Dorothy Height worked with Delta Sigma Theta and became president of the National Council of Negro Women. During the 1960s, she spearheaded Wednesdays in Mississippi, an interracial group that bridged divides between women across race and region.[13] After Pauli Murray graduated from law school, she traveled to the newly independent nation of Ghana and served on President John F. Kennedy's Commission on Women. As a lawyer and founding member of the National Organization of Women, Murray helped illuminate the intersections of race and gender in shaping black women's unequal citizenship, what she termed "Jane Crow."[14] Mary Church Terrell stayed in Washington, D.C., and became a crucial part of the integration struggle in the city. Beatrice Murphy, the noted columnist in Washington, D.C., who wrote about unemployment among black women and the urgent need for the vote, testified in Congress in the 1980s about the impact of President Ronald Reagan's budget cuts to Medicare on the elderly population; she was then in her seventies.[15] In addition to these direct connections, African American readers of the black press would have been familiar with the culture of black activism in Washington, D.C. Echoes of these different campaigns traveled to Birmingham, Selma, Newark, Oakland, and Ferguson: the connections between the black freedom movement in the nation's capital and the rest of the United States continue.

Yet, there were also differences between African American women's freedom movement in the nation's capital and the struggles waged in the rest of the United States. Some differences pertained to the different periodization of the black freedom movement in the nation's capital, but others were rooted in the exceptional circumstances of politics in Washington, D.C. In their civil rights campaigns, black women benefited from the ways that their political struggles captured both national and international attention. Whether they were staging a Silent Parade against lynching, waiting in line all night to receive applications as federal charwomen, protesting the rising tide of police brutality, or challenging businesses that would not hire black workers, African American women and men achieved a level of visibility from white journalists, photographers, and social critics that would rarely happen in the rest of the United States until the 1950s and 1960s. Black activists evoked America's heritage of liberty and democracy, pointing out the stark contradictions raised by inequality, tyranny, and injustice in the capital of the United States. Black women's arguments for freedom and justice clashed sharply with white politicians' concern that these causes would create embarrassment, diplomatic tensions, and political blowback, thereby accelerating the pace of racial integration in the nation's capital.

Black Washingtonians were cosmopolitan. Activists from the 1920s to 1940s hailed from diverse states, including Colorado, Michigan, Massachusetts, Illinois, Indiana, Pennsylvania, North Carolina, South Carolina, New York, Virginia, and Mississippi. Having connections with other states enabled women to cast absentee ballots, call on their state-based networks, and lobby their local elected officials. Those who moved to Washington, D.C, from states across the nation all had their own experiences as black women, and they infused that knowledge into the freedom struggle in the nation's capital.

The story of black women's freedom campaigns in Washington, D.C., offers salient lessons in this ever-challenging present moment, filled with mounting cases of voter restriction, police brutality, mass incarceration, the contested legacies of the Civil War and Reconstruction, and economic inequality. In the 1920s, women in the nation's capital, the majority of whom could not cast ballots, emphasized the importance of voting and citizenship rights. While they could not march with their feet to the polls, they walked in a Silent Parade, took their seats in congressional galleries, and testified in the U.S. House of Representatives and the Senate to champion a federal antilynching bill, lobby against Supreme Court nominees, and advocate for the construction of a National Negro Memorial. Some of these visions were realized. In 2016, the National Museum of African American History and Culture opened on the National Mall, although this building has been the site of vandalism and hatred.[16] In the 1930s, black women demonstrated that Black Lives Matter when they read the names of the female victims of police brutality on the radio and printed stories in the press as a way to shatter the silence. When the African American Policy Forum launched the hashtag campaign, "Say Her Name," in 2015 to honor female victims of police violence, they echoed black women's activism in Washington, D.C.[17] During World War II, black women decided that the city of Washington was on the wrong side of history and helped spearhead the racial integration of restaurants and buses. They also studied history, discovering that Reconstruction-era laws in 1872 and 1873 mandated equality before the "strange career" of Jim Crow was installed, enforced through law and violence, and passionately defended.[18] Black women's prescient visions for economic justice, safety from violence, and legal equality remain more relevant than ever before.

Acknowledgments

In my travels to becoming a professional historian, one of the sweetest rewards has been learning from the passionate scholars whose visions of social justice have been inspirational and revelatory. My intellectual journey began in my undergraduate education at Mount Holyoke College. There, Dan Czitrom, Michael Davis, Holly Hanson, Jeremy King, Lynda Morgan, Louis Prisock, Mary Renda, and Preston Smith provided a most rigorous education in history, politics, and visual culture, nurturing my curiosities around race and commitments to justice. Lynda Morgan taught me to write and research like a professional historian; Preston Smith modeled the life of a scholar and activist; and Dan Czitrom has continued to be a mentor and to offer sage advice in my career.

I was fortunate to attend graduate school at the University of Maryland, College Park, where distinguished scholars helped me take my passion for African American history and unite it with the richness of women's history. My dissertation advisor, Elsa Barkley Brown, set the highest standards for my research while posing the most difficult questions. Taking her classes and working as her research assistant transformed my understandings of activism illuminating black women's wide-ranging participation in politics from the seventeenth century to the present moment. Elsa Barkley Brown inspired this book. I was also privileged to study with Ira Berlin, Melinda Chateauvert, Sharon Harley, Alfred Moss, Leslie Rowland, Psyche Williams-Forson, and Francille Wilson, all of whom deepened my understandings of African American history in profound ways, and to learn from the cohort of grad students at Maryland and in the area working on race, including Millington Bergeson-Lockwood, Robert Bland, Tess Bundy, Naomi Coquillion, Dennis Doster, Thanayi Jackson, Jessica Johnson, Tina Ligon, and Eliza Mbughini. I would also like to warmly thank Richard Bell, David Freund, Gary Gerstle, Julie Greene, Clare Lyons, Robyn Muncy, and Michelle Rowley, who all offered words of encouragement and expressions of support.

Teaching at Drexel University, and now at Eastern Michigan University (EMU), has made me a better scholar. My department heads—Scott Barclay, Jim Egge, and Richard Nation—have all been generous and thoughtful mentors, and offered sage advice to me as a junior faculty member. My history colleagues at EMU have been deeply encouraging especially Kathy Chamberlain, Joseph Engwenyu, Mark Higbee, Jesse Kauffman, Linda Pritchard, Steven Ramold, Mary Strasma, and JoEllen Vineyard. Our department secretary, Rachelle Marshall, has been a beacon of support. I am deeply grateful for the collegial friendships of Kim Barrett, Ashley Johnson Bavery, Jim Egge, Ashley Falzetti, Melissa Jones, John Knight, John McCurdy, and Tomo Sasaki. I have learned so much from my students at Maryland, Drexel, and Eastern Michigan University, and teaching is one of the true delights of my job.

Eastern Michigan University generously supported this project through a Provost New Faculty Award, a Summer Research Award, and a Faculty Research Fellowship, which offered funding to conduct research and an entire semester's release from teaching. I also received release time through my participation in EMU's Culture of Research Excellence

Program, which provided a course release and a collegial environment for writing while teaching.

I would like to extend my tremendous gratitude to the hard-working staffs at the archives and libraries I visited. Over the past nine years, Jo-Ellen Bashir, Ida Jones, and the late Donna Wells have given me access to hundreds of boxes and several unprocessed collections at Moorland-Spingarn Research Center. Maida Goodwin at the Sophia Smith Collection generously introduced me to the labyrinth of YWCA records. The staff at the Manuscript Collection at the Library of Congress were incredibly generous, as were librarians and archivists at the FDR Library in Hyde Park, New York; the Robert Woodruff Library at Atlanta University; the Butler Theological Seminary at Columbia University; the Schomburg Center for Research in Black Culture at New York Public Library; the Smithsonian Anacostia Museum; and the Historical Society of Washington, D.C. I would also like to thank Julia Nims at Halle Library at EMU, who assisted with several interlibrary loan requests.

At conferences, I have been privileged to receive feedback from Shawn Alexander, Martha Biondi, Nikki Brown, Bettye Collier-Thomas, Sharon Harley, Samir Meghelli, Lisa G. Materson, Steven Reich, Joe William Trotter Jr., Deborah Gray White, Kidada Williams, and Nan Woodruff. I am grateful for all of their comments on my work. Happily, the field of Washington, D.C., scholars is growing, and I have personally learned a great deal from Chris Meyers Asch, Maurice Jackson, Kate Masur, Marya McQuirter, and Eric Yellin. I am grateful for all of these scholars for encouraging my own project and offering generous advice. This book would not have been possible without all of the scholars who have contributed to the richness of African American women's history since the 1980s.

Friends from childhood, college, and graduate school have sustained me and brought incredible joy to my life, although I am terrible at keeping in touch; these friends include Kris Alexanderson, Stephen Duncan, Caroline Eaton, Molly Gower, Melissa Kravetz, and Lindsay Theile. Moving to Michigan and writing about Washington posed the challenge of distance, but I am fortunate that my sister and Derek Groom, her most patient roommate, were so generous in letting me stay in their apartment every summer.

Working with the University of North Carolina Press has been a pleasure. My two anonymous readers offered incredible feedback and pushed me to write a better book. All errors and mistakes are mine. I am so grateful for Brandon Proia for believing in me and in this book, as well as Sherie Randolph, who first introduced us in Ann Arbor in 2014. Annette Calzone and her staff at Westchester Publishing Services did a tremendous job of copyediting this book.

My extended family has been unstinting in their support. I am deeply sad that my uncle, Michael Murphy, and cousin, Patrick Murphy, did not live to see this book's completion, but I am very grateful for the support of Virginia Kirk, Fred and Fayne Murphy, and Matt Murphy. My sister, Maggie Murphy, will rejoice that this book is completed so she doesn't have to hear about it anymore. She is my best friend, along with my mother, Frances Lewis, who has modeled an incredible life of kindness, hard work, and empathy. My father, John Murphy, marched on Washington in 1963 for Civil Rights, and fifty-four years later at the Women's March in 2017. Those bits of his biography speak for themselves and inspire me every day.

Notes

NNO	*New Negro Opinion*
NYAN	*New York Amsterdam News*
NYT	*New York Times*
PC	*Pittsburgh Courier*
PT	*Philadelphia Tribune*
RG	Record Group
RG-351	Record Group 351, Entry 9, National Archives
SW	*Southern Workman*
WAA	*Washington Afro American*
WB	*Washington Bee*
WC-Burke	Woman's Convention Papers, Burke Library, Union Theological Seminary
WP	*Washington Post*
WS	*Washington Star*
WT	*Washington Tribune*
YWCA	Young Women's Christian Association

Introduction

1. "Silent Protest Parade against Lynching Celebrates the Birth of Old Glory," 1922 in Box 34, Folder 16, National Association for the Advancement of Colored People (NAACP) Papers, Part I, Series G, Manuscript Division, Library of Congress, Washington, D.C. (hereafter cited as NAACP-LC).

2. "Negroes Stage Silent Parade," *LAT*, June 16, 1922, 12; "Silent Negroes March in Lynching Protest," *NYT*, June 15, 1922, 3; "5,000 Negroes Parade As Lynching Protest," *WP*, June 15, 1922, 2; "Foes of Lynching March in Silence," *CSM*, June 15, 1922, 2; "Citizens Parade in Washington for Dyer Bill," *CD*, June 24, 1922, 8; and "Colored Citizens Celebrate Flag Day in Silent Parade," Box 43, Folder 831, NAACP Washington, D.C., Branch Papers, Collection 78, Manuscript Division, Moorland-Spingarn Research Center, Founders Library, Howard University, Washington, D.C. (hereafter cited as NAACP-MSRC).

3. The historiography of black Washingtonian is rich, complex, and growing. Major works that have been useful for this project include Green, *Secret City*; Borchert, *Alley Life in Washington*; Harley, "Black Women in the District of Columbia"; Holloway, *Confronting the Veil*; Moore, *Leading the Race*; Masur, *Example for All the Land*; Yellin, *Racism in the Nation's Service*; Lindsey, *Colored No More*; and Asch and Musgrove, *Chocolate City*.

4. For information on African Americans during the World War I era, see Williams, *Torchbearers of Democracy*; Reich, "Soldiers of Democracy"; and N. Brown, *Private Politics and Public Voices*, 1–107.

5. For information on black women and electoral politics regarding the Nineteenth Amendment, see Terborg-Penn, *African American Women and the Struggle for the Vote*; Ma-

terson, *For the Freedom of Her Race*; Higginbotham, "In Politics to Stay"; and Gallagher, *Black Women and Politics in New York City*.

6. For treatments of black women's respectability politics, see Higginbotham, *Righteous Discontent*; Gilmore, *Gender and Jim Crow*; Wolcott, *Remaking Respectability*; Brown, *Private Politics and Public Voices*; Materson, *For the Freedom of Her Race*; and Lindsey, *Colored No More*.

7. Green, *Secret City*, 184–214; and Yellin, *Racism in the Nation's Service*, 175–206.

8. For information on the importance of black women's sororities to political activism, see Kiesel, *She Can Bring Us Home*; Chatelain, "The Problem Peculiar to Girls"; and Lindsey, *Colored No More*.

9. For works on the early black freedom struggle, see Lewis, *In Their Own Interests*; Kelley, *Race Rebels*; Hunter, *To 'Joy My Freedom*; Korstad, *Civil Rights Unionism*; Ortiz, *Emancipation Betrayed*; and Kelley, *Right to Ride*.

10. For scholarship that brilliantly connects African American social and political history, see Barkley Brown, "Negotiating and Transforming the Public Sphere"; Gilmore, *Gender and Jim Crow*; Dailey, *Before Jim Crow*; Kantrowitz, *Ben Tillman and the Reconstruction of White Supremacy*; Rosen, *Terror in the Heart of Freedom*; and Masur, *Example for All the Land*.

11. McQuirter, "Claiming the City"; Lewis-Mhoon, "Adorning Adversaries"; and Lindsey, *Colored No More*.

12. Masur, *Example for All the Land*.

13. Masur.

14. Moore, *Leading the Race*; and Taylor, *Original Black Elite*.

15. "The Congressional Lyceum," *WB*, December 18, 1897, 5; and "The District Conference of the African Methodist Episcopal Church," *WB*, September 12, 1903, 1.

16. Harley, "Black Women in the District of Columbia"; and Shaw, "Black Club Women and the Creation of the National Association of Colored Women."

17. Green, *Secret City*, 145.

18. Shaw, "Black Club Women and the Creation of the National Association of Colored Women," 19.

19. Yellin, *Racism in the Nation's Service*.

20. *Report of the Commissioners of the District of Columbia for the Year Ended June 30, 1917* (Washington, D.C.: GPO, 1917); and "Table 19: Native Negro Population of Each Division and Each State by Division and State of Birth: 1920," *Fourteenth Census of the United States*, Part II (Washington, D.C.: GPO, 1923), 636–40.

21. See, for instance, "Negroes Attack Girl," *WP*, July 19, 1919, 1.

22. Mellis, "'Monsters We Defy.'"

23. Jones, *Housing of Negroes in Washington, D.C.*, 57.

24. A full examination of black neighborhoods in Washington, D.C., is beyond the scope of this project. However, juxtaposing residential locations throughout the city reveals their differences. Neighborhoods in Northeast had a rural, small-town feel, as streets were mostly paved with granite and rubble or cobblestone. African Americans supported more than twenty-six churches and were served by four firehouses and two police stations in that neighborhood. Southwest, the city's smallest quadrant, was located at the confluence of the Anacostia and Potomac Rivers. The African American population living in

Southwest was primarily working class; many women toiled as domestics while men worked as laborers at the Navy Yard. The streets in Southwest were paved with asphalt or rubble, and citizens were served by three firehouses and one police station. Black Washingtonians worshipped at sixteen black churches in this section of the city. In Southeast, African Americans principally lived in three neighborhoods: Anacostia, Garfield, and Barry Farms. Black residents of Southeast were served by four firehouses and only one police station, and the streets were mostly paved with asphalt. African Americans supported and maintained sixteen churches in this area. In addition, there was a thriving black business and professional community, including physicians, dentists, undertakers, and druggists. All of this information comes from the *Report of the Commissioners of the District of Columbia for the Year Ended June 30, 1918* (Washington, D.C.: GPO, 1919), Record Group 351, Entry 9, National Archives, Washington, D.C. (hereafter cited as RG351-NA), as well as a close reading of black newspapers and *Sherman's Directory and Ready Reference of the Colored Population*.

25. For information on the federal and local government, see Green, *Secret City*, 111–17.

26. For these collections, see letters from citizens and civic groups to the Board of Commissioners, Vol. 231, Entry 11, RG351-NA.

27. Borchert, *Alley Life in Washington*, 201.

28. Borchert, "Washington, D.C.," 884; "Food Show Will Open for Colored People," *WS*, January 31, 1923, 33; and "These 'Colored' United States': The District of Columbia, a Paradox of Paradoxes," *Messenger* 5, no. 10 (October 1923): 839. The number of mutual benefit and fraternal associations was determined through a close reading of the *WB*, the *WT*, and the *WS*; Jones, *Recreation and Amusement among Negroes in Washington, D.C.*; and Boyd's *City Directory of the District of Columbia* in the 1930s.

29. *Fourteenth Census of the United States: Population: Occupations. Males and Females in Selected Occupations* (Washington, D.C.: GPO, 1923), 897–900. The occupational census used the generic category of personal service to encompass diverse personal service positions, such as cooks, live-in servants, maids, and domestic workers.

30. Haynes, "Negroes in Domestic Service in the United States," 421–26; and Greene and Callis, *Employment of Negroes in the District of Columbia*, 38–39 and 81.

31. Barkley Brown, "Womanist Consciousness"; Higginbotham, *Righteous Discontent*; and Ortiz, *Emancipation Betrayed*.

32. My thinking on this issue has been deeply influenced by Kelley, "'We Are Not What We Seem.'"

33. Katznelson, *Fear Itself*, 156–94.

34. Hendricks, *Gender, Race, and Politics in the Midwest*; Materson, *For the Freedom of Her Race*; Gritter, *River of Hope*; and Gallagher, *Black Women and Politics in New York City*.

35. Crawford, Rouse, and Woods, eds., *Women in the Civil Rights Movement*; Lee, *For Freedom's Sake*; Ransby, *Ella Baker and the Black Freedom Movement*; Greene, *Our Separate Ways*; Charron, *Freedom's Teacher*; McGuire, *At the Dark End of the Street*; Gill, *Beauty Shop Politics*; McDuffie, *Sojourning for Freedom*; Feldstein, *How it Feels to Be Free*; Theoharis, *Rebellious Life of Mrs. Rosa Parks*; Ford, *Liberated Threads*.

36. Williams, *Politics of Public Housing*; Orleck, *Storming Ceasars Palace*; Kornbluh, *Battle for Welfare Rights*; Levenstein, *Movement without Marches*; Sanders, *Chance for Change*; and Ervin, *Gateway to Equality*.

Chapter One

1. "Women's Republican League of D.C.," *WB*, September 25, 1920, 4.

2. "Public Men and Things," *WB*, October 9, 1920, 4.

3. Keyssar, *Right To Vote*, 151.

4. Mary Church Terrell's autobiography has important details of her life; see *Colored Woman in a White World*. For a scholarly treatment, see Quigley, *Just Another Southern Town*.

5. Census records offer several different years of birth for Marian Butler, ranging between the 1870s and 1880s. For her first mention in the census record which lists her birth year as 1876, see, "Marian Ford," *Tenth Census of the United States*, Enumeration District 24, sheet 3 (hereafter cited as ED).

6. The Jenkins Orphanage was founded in 1891 by Reverend Joseph Daniel Jenkins, a Baptist minister. The orphanage had a famous traveling band that performed in presidential inaugural parades and toured internationally. See Jack McCray, *Charleston Jazz*.

7. Historians have yet to write about Marian Butler as a political activist, although her name is mentioned in major accounts of the black women's club movement. Two principal reasons for her absence are that she is often listed as "M. D. Butler" and her name is spelled both "Marian" and "Marion." I gathered biographical information through a close reading of black newspapers; census records; one article, "Career Women of the Capital," *WAA*, April 13, 1940, 7; and a revealing letter from Marian D. Butler, Washington, D.C., to Nannie Helen Burroughs, Washington, D.C., June 5, 1927 in Box 3, Folder 4, Nannie Helen Burroughs Papers, Manuscript Division, Library of Congress, Washington, D.C. (hereafter cited as NHB-LC).

8. Higginbotham, *Righteous Discontent*; and Harley, "Black Goddess of Liberty."

9. "History of the Phyllis Wheatley Young Women's Christian Association," 7, YWCA Collection, Martin Luther King Junior Library, Washingtoniana Collection, YWCA Vertical File; and "Minutes of the Committee on Colored Work," New York City, March 9, 1918 in Box 710, Folder 10, Young Women's Christian Association Papers, Sophia Smith Collection, William Neilson Library, Smith College, Northampton, Massachusetts (hereafter cited as YWCA-SSC).

10. Rosalyn Terborg-Penn, "Discontented Black Feminists"; Higginbotham, "In Politics to Stay," 303–4; N. Brown, *Private Politics and Public Voices*, 132–33; and Materson, *For the Freedom of Her Race*, 140–43.

11. "Women's Republican League of the D.C.," *WB*, September 25, 1920, 7.

12. "Deanwood News," *WB*, February 8, 1921, 7.

13. Terrell, *Colored Woman in a White World*, 308–10; and Gustafson, *Women and the Republican Party*, 191–93.

14. Letter from Mary Church Terrell, New York, to "My Dear Friend," October 12, 1921, Reel 5, Frame 121, Mary Church Terrell Papers, Manuscript Division, Library of Congress, Washington, D.C. (hereafter cited as MCT-LC).

15. Julia J. Jeubius, "Nomination of Warren G. Harding," and "Women's Republican League at Asbury," *WB*, November 6, 1920, 2.

16. Letter from Eva Chase, Washington, D.C., to Mary Church Terrell, New York, October 27, 1920, Reel 5, Frame 158, MCT-LC.

17. "Public Men, Women, and Things," *WB*, December 11, 1920, 4. For a discussion of the black press's coverage of black women's political activities across the nation, see Higginbotham, "In Politics to Stay," 295–96.

18. "Colored Women on Inaugural Committee," *WB*, January 29, 1921, 3.

19. Gilmore, *Gender and Jim Crow*, 203–24.

20. "Republican Club Women," *WB*, February 5, 1921, 3.

21. Lindsey, *Colored No More*, 100–104.

22. "Colored Women Present Memorial," *WB*, February 19, 1921, 4; and Cott, *Grounding of Modern Feminism*.

23. Neverdon-Morton, *Afro-American Women of the South and the Advancement of the Race*, 205.

24. The NAWE receives brief mention in a number of historical works. For example, Evelyn Brooks Higginbotham describes how the NAWE embodied a "politics of respectability" that emphasized the dignity of black women's domestic labor. She situates the ideological program of the NAWE as extending from Burroughs's work in her Training School and her activism in the Women's Conference of the Baptist Church. Sharon Harley describes the NAWE as a "short-lived" organization that forged alliances between capital and labor. Deborah Thomas devotes an entire dissertation chapter to the NAWE, focusing principally on the process of organizing. She positions the NAWE as moving beyond the goals of the Training School through its work of political and labor organizing. She attributes the effectiveness of the NAWE to its ability to attract so many working-class women, citing the Great Depression as one of the chief causes for the organization's demise. See Barnett, "Nannie Burroughs and the Education of Black Women"; Higginbotham, *Righteous Discontent*; Harley, "Goddess of Liberty"; and Thomas, "Workers and Organizers."

25. Materson, *For the Freedom of Her Race*, 108–48.

26. Nannie Helen Burroughs, Washington, D.C., to J. W. Davis, Denver, 23 August 1922 in Box 308, Folder 8, NHB-LC.

27. The data on the NAWE membership come from membership cards, logbooks, and one letter, which are located in Box 308, Folders 1, 2, and 3, NHB Papers, LOC. The membership cards—containing members' names, street addresses, occupations, and the name of the person who recruited them—are found in Folders 1 and 2. The logbook lists the names and street addresses of the members and the dates when they joined the NAWE. A more extended discussion of the NAWE can be found in Mary-Elizabeth Murphy, "African American Women's Politics, Organizing, and Activism," chapter three.

28. Murphy, "African American Women's Politics, Organizing, and Activism."

29. For Sadie Henson, see *Fourteenth Census of the United States*, 1920, Washington, D.C., Enumeration District 204, Sheet 4A.

30. "Wage Earners," *WB*, April 17, 1917, 1; "Mrs. Lottie Tignor Dead," *WB*, June 8, 1918, 1; and "GPO Notes," *WT*, April 1, 1922, 2.

31. "Church and Sunday School," *WT*, April 27, 1928, 5; "School Heads back from Vacation," *WP*, September 5, 1923, 10; Davis, *Lifting as They Climb*, 409; "Zion Baptist Church Sunday School," *WB*, October 11, 1913, 1; "Celebrating Children's Day in Washington, D.C.," *BAA*, June 19, 1937, 19; and "Under the Capitol Dome," *CD*, January 19, 1924, 6.

32. For Lucy Holland, see *Boyd's City Directory of the District of Columbia* (1924), 779. For a list of her recruits, see Box 308, Folders 1, 2, and 3, NHB-LC.

33. "Seek Equality of Sexes in Industry," *Boston Daily Globe*, January 7, 1923, 2; and "President Will Greet 300 Woman Conferees," *WP*, January 8, 1923, 3.

34. Nannie Helen Burroughs, quoted in *Proceedings of the Women's Industrial Conference* January 11, 12, 13, Women's Bureau, Department of Labor, Washington, D.C. (Washington, D.C.: GPO, 1923), 100–102.

35. "Makes Plea for Women Who Work," *WT*, January 13, 1923, 1.

36. *Class Specifications for Positions in the Departmental Service: As Prescribed by the Personnel Classification Board in Accordance with Section 3 of the Classification Act of 1933* (Washington, D.C.: GPO, 1924), 11.

37. For Langhorne, see *Fourteenth Census of the United States*, ED 50, Sheet 2A; for Ware, see *Fourteenth Census of the United States*, ED 49, Sheet 10A; and for Porter, see *Fifteenth Census of the United States*, ED 212, Sheet 9A.

38. "Charwomen Protest Lower Wage Schedule," *BAA*, July 25, 1924, A2.

39. "Holds Monster Mass Meeting," *WT*, September 20, 1924, 1.

40. "Women Purchase Headquarters on R. I. Avenue," *WT*, March 1, 1924, 1; "The National Association of Wage Earners, Incorporated," *WT*, March 8, 1924, 1 and "Along the Banks of the Potomac," *PC*, March 8, 1924, 13.

41. "Women Purchase Headquarters on R.I. Avenue," *WT*, March 1, 1924, 1.

42. "List of Needs for Equipping the Practice House," in Box 308, Folder 8, NHB-LC.

43. "Wage Earners Will Keep Open House," *WT*, February 21, 1925, 2.

44. See letter from Daniel E. Carges, Washington, D.C., to National Association of Wage Earners, July 16, 1925, Vol. 231, Entry 11, RG351-NA.

45. Letter from M. Mossell Griffin, Washington, D.C., to Nannie Helen Burroughs (emphasis in original), Washington, D.C., undated, in Box 10, Folder 4, NHB-LC.

46. For a discussion of the NLRCW and its relation to clubwomen's politics, see Higginbotham, "In Politics to Stay."

47. "Plans: Executive Session, NLRCW," in Box 309, Folder 3, NHB-LC.

48. Materson, *For the Freedom of Her Race*, 141.

49. "Political Organizations among Colored Women," Box 1, Folder 7, Collection 12: Collection 12: Jeannette Carter Papers, Manuscript Division, Moorland-Spingarn Research Center, Founders Library, Howard University, Washington, D.C. (hereafter cited as JC-MSRC).

50. "Women Organize Political Clubs," *WT*, August 30, 1924, 1.

51. "Women's Organization Opens Legislative Headquarters Here," *WT*, March 24, 1923, 1.

52. Higginbotham, "In Politics to Stay."

53. "Talks on Race Prejudice," *WP*, May 4, 1925, 13; and "Speaker Interprets the U.S. Constitution," *WP*, March 8, 1926, 2.

54. "Locals and Society," *WT*, August 9, 1924, 2.

55. "To Discuss Equal Rights for Women," *WT*, May 25, 1928, 4.

56. Yellin, *Racism in the Nation's Service*, 175–204.

57. "Removal of Colored Workers Condemned," *WP*, June 14, 1926, 2.

58. "Froe Retention Urged at Study Club Session," *WP*, March 5, 1928, 16.

59. "Congress Inquiry Is Urged on Negroes," *WP*, January 25, 1926, 18; "Colored Women Plan Congressional Survey," *WP*, February 1, 1926, 18. For Corelia Johnson in the census see

Fourteenth Census of the United States, ED 211, Sheet 6B, and for Jacqueline Cuney see *Fourteenth Census of the United States*, ED 211, Sheet 7A.

60. "Locals and Society," *WT*, August 16, 1924, 3.

61. "Study Club Praises G.O.P. Stand," *CD*, September 20, 1924, A7.

62. "Women's Political Club Entertains at Banquet," *PT*, June 14, 1924, 14.

63. "Women Present Attorney Thomas L. Jones with Flowers," *WT*, June 1, 1925, 1; and "Thomas L. Jones Candidate for U.S. Attorney," *BAA*, May 23, 1925, A1.

64. John J. Parker in the *Charlotte Observer*, April 18, 1920, as quoted in Goings, *"The NAACP Comes of Age,"* 23.

65. Judge John J. Parker as quoted in the "Report of the Acting Secretary," April 1930, in Goings, *"NAACP Comes of Age,"* 24.

66. 71 Cong. Rec. S8115 (daily ed. May 1, 1930) (statement of Sen. Fess).

67. "Mrs. Butler's Anti-Parker Wire Peeved Senator Fess," *BAA*, May 10, 1930, A1.

68. "Mrs. Butler's Anti-Parker Wire Peeved Senator Fess."

69. "Senate Rejects Parker," *CD*, May 10, 1930, 1.

70. "Mrs. Butler's Anti-Parker Wire Peeved Senator Fess." For an analysis of Ben Tillman's political career, see Kantrowitz, *Ben Tillman and the Reconstruction of White Supremacy.*

71. An excellent analysis of these debates is found in Asch and Musgrove, *Chocolate City*, 173–78.

72. For information on Buckingham's career, see Bracks and Smith, eds., *Black Women of the Harlem Renaissance Era*, 32–33.

73. *National Representation for the Residents of the District of Columbia, Hearing before the Committee on the Judiciary in the House of Representatives*, 70th Congress, 1st session, 143–55 (1928) (statement of Grover W. Ayers).

74. For black protest against the film *Birth of a Nation*, see Franklin, "'Birth of a Nation'"; and Sullivan, *Lift Every Voice*. For a discussion of the ways that African American historians tried to disrupt stereotypes about slavery and Reconstruction in southern white historiography, see Hine, *State of Afro-American History*.

75. Brundage, *Southern Past*, 148.

76. For works that discuss the dedication of the Douglass home, see Johnson, "Ye Gave them a Stone this is in the bibliography"; Brundage, *Southern Past*; Morgan, *Women and Patriotism in Jim Crow America*; and Ruffins; "Lifting as We Climb."

77. Nannie H. Burroughs, "Cedar Hill—Beautiful for Situation: The Negroes Most Valuable Heritage, Women Have Taken up the Vigil," *NN*, 31, no. 5 (February 1929): 12.

78. Letter from Nannie Helen Burroughs, Washington, D.C., to Mary Church Terrell, Washington, D.C., February 8, 1922, in Reel 5, MCT-LC.

79. Johnson, "'Ye Gave Them a Stone,'" 67–68; and Brundage, *Southern Past*, 10–11.

80. Details about the dedication of the Lincoln Memorial are beyond the scope of this chapter. But on May 30 1922, Americans gathered to dedicate the Lincoln Memorial in a ceremony that privileged national reconciliation over emancipation. See letter from Shelby J. Davidson, Washington, D.C., to James Weldon Johnson, New York, May 31, 1922, Box G-34, Folder 15, NAACP-LC. For scholarly accounts, see Randall, "Democracy's Passion Play"; and Blight, *Race and Reunion*, 288-289.

81. 67 Cong. Rec. H1509 (daily ed. February 28, 1923) (statement of Rep. Byrnes).

82. For a discussion about the mythology of the Mammy figure in slavery, see White, *Aren't I a Woman*, 27–61.

83. McElya, *Clinging to Mammy*, 117–23. For other discussions of the Mammy Memorial controversy, see Johnson, "'Ye Gave Them A Stone,'" 62–86.

84. "For and against the 'Black Mammy's Monument,'" *LD*, 77 (April 28, 1923): 50.

85. "For and against the 'Black Mammy's Monument.'"

86. "Black Mammy of the South," *LD*, 77 (March 3, 1933): 56.

87. "Black Mammy of the South," 56; and "Black Mammy," *Time Magazine* 1, no. 1 (March 3, 1923): 6.

88. Wilson, *Negro Building*.

89. "Design of the Proposed National Negro Memorial," Reel 18, Frame 63, MCT-LC.

90. "Lest We Forget," Reel 18, Frame 84, MCT-LC.

91. *Monument or Memorial Building to the Memory of Negro Soldiers and Sailors: Hearings before the Comm. on the Library of Congress*, 68th Cong. 9 (1924) (statement of Dr. Walter H. Brooks).

92. *Public Buildings and Grounds No. 3: Hearings before the Comm. on Public Buildings and Grounds in the House of Representatives*, 70th Cong. (1928) (statement of Mrs. Julia West Hamilton, President Women's Relief Corps Auxiliary to Grand Army of the Republic and President of Washington and Vicinity of Federation of Women), in Reel 18, Frames 64–82, MCT-LC.

93. *Public Buildings and Grounds No. 3: Hearings before the Comm. on Public Buildings and Grounds in the House of Representatives*, 70th Cong. (1928) (statement of Mary Church Terrell, First President of National Association of Colored Women), in Reel 18, Frames 64–82, MCT-LC.

94. 70 Cong. Rec. H5081 (daily ed. March 2, 1929) (statement of Rep. Rankin).

95. Minutes of the M.E. Minister's Wives of Washington and Vicinity, February 23, 1925, Reel 5, p. 134, Records of the Asbury ME Church, Manuscript Division, Schomburg Center for Research in Black Culture, New York Public Library, New York City.

Chapter Two

1. Theresa Lee Connelly, Washington, D.C., to "Dear Friend," Washington, D.C., May 29, 1922, Box 43, Folder 827, NAACP-MSRC.

2. The number of African Americans lynched between 1882 and 1918 is found in Zangrando, *NAACP Campaign against Lynching*, 4–6. The number of women is found in Feimster, *Southern Horrors*, 235–39.

3. For the historiography of anti-lynching activism in the 1920s, see Zangrando, *NAACP Crusade against Lynching*; Brown, *Eradicating this Evil*; Waldrep, *African Americans Confront Lynching*; and Sullivan, *Lift Every Voice*.

4. Hall, *Revolt Against Chivalry*, 165–66; Brown, *Eradicating this Evil*, 144–50; Mungarro, "How Did Black Women in the NAACP Promote the Dyer Anti-Lynching Bill"; and N. Brown, *Private Politics and Public Voices*, 124–28.

5. "The District Conference of the African Methodist Episcopal Church," *WB*, September 12, 1903, 1; "Denounce Lynching," *WB*, September 29, 1906, 1; and "Meeting Asks Men to End Mob Violence," *WB*, July 13, 1910, 5.

6. See, for instance, "Lynching; Dispatches; Suspicion; Riddled," *WB*, December 25, 1886, 2.

7. "Women on the Right Track," *WB*, July 21, 1917, 3; and "Stop Lynchings through Prayer," *BAA*, July 28, 1917, 4.

8. "Washington, D.C.," *NJG*, July 21, 1917, 5.

9. "Working for a Real Democracy," *Annual Report of the Executive Board and Corresponding Secretary of the Women's Convention, Auxiliary of the National Baptist Church*, Volume 17, September 5, 1917, Muskogee, Oklahoma, Papers of the Women's Convention of the Baptist Church, Burke Library, Union Theological Seminary, Columbia University, New York City (herafter cited as WC-Burke).

10. "Working for a Real Democracy," WC-Burke.

11. *Riot at East St. Louis, Illinois: Hearings before the Committee on Rules in the House of Representatives*, H.J. Resolution 118, 65th Cong. 17–19 (1917) (statement of Nannie H. Burroughs, National Training School, Lincoln Heights).

12. "10,000 Petitions from 36 States," *WB*, August 18, 1917, 1.

13. "Self-Help, the Negro's First Duty," *WB*, October 13, 1917, 7.

14. It is possible that activists in the Asbury M.E. Church formed a "Red" Anti-Lynching Club to honor Ida B. Wells's 1895 anti-lynching publication, *A Red Record*. For evidence of this club, see Minutes of the NACW's Biennial Convention, Denver, Colorado, July 1918, Reel 1, Frame 542, Papers of the National Association of Colored Women's Clubs, Manuscript Division, Library of Congress, Washington, D.C. (hereafter cited as NACW-LC).

15. "H.R. 11279: A Bill to Protect Citizens of the United States against lynching in default protection of the United States," 65th Cong. (April 8, 1918), Box 242, Folder 1, Part 1, Series C, NAACP-LC.

16. "Anti-Lynching Bill Is Now before Congress," *CD*, April 13, 1918, 4.

17. I have been unable to locate the letter that Nannie Helen Burroughs wrote to Leonidas Dyer on April 17, but it is referred to in Leonidas Dyer, Washington, D.C., to Nannie Helen Burroughs, Washington, D.C., May 3, 1918, Box 242, Folder 1, Part 1, Series C, NAACP-LC.

18. Minutes of the NACW's Biennial Convention, Denver, Colorado, July 1918, 61, Reel 1, Frame 542, NACW-LC.

19. "Statement of Purpose," January 17, 1919, NAACP Papers, Part 1, Series G, Box 34, Folder 6, NAACP-LC.

20. Logan, *Howard University*, 219.

21. "Anti-Lynching Bill Topic," *WP*, April 18, 1921, 5.

22. "YWCA Notes," *WB*, November 19, 1921, 1.

23. Masur, *Example for All the Land*, 227–28.

24. See 67 Cong. Rec. H1721 (daily ed. January 25, 1922) (statements of Mr. Cooper, Mr. Fields, and Mr. Sumner); "Anti-Lynching Bill Precipitates Clash," *WP*, January 26, 1922, 3; "Anti-Lynching Debate Heard by Big Crowds on Yesterday," *BAA*, January 27, 1922, 1; telegram from James Weldon Johnson, Washington, D.C. to Walter F. White, New York City, January 25, 1922 in Part 1, Series, C: General Correspondence, Box C-243, Folder 5, NAACP-LC; and Sullivan, *Lift Every Voice*, 106.

25. Anti-Lynching Bill, 66th Cong., May 22, 1920.

26. Zangrando, *NAACP Crusade against Lynching*, 64.

27. For information on the Lee Family, see Gatewood, *Aristocrats of Color*, 112; and Schneider, *Boston Confronts Jim Crow*, 75. See also "For Equal Rights," *BG*, May 5, 1890, 4; and "To Congress: Petition from Boston Suffrage League," *BG*, March 31, 1904, 6. For a discussion of African American politics in Boston, see Bergeson-Lockwood, *Race over Party*.

28. *Twelfth Census of the United States*, Boston, Ward 12, ED 1322, Sheet 2; Bruce, *Archibald Grimké*, 79; and Shaw, *What a Woman Ought to Be and Do*, 39.

29. For information on Grimké and her play, see Hull, *Color, Sex, and Poetry*, 118–28; Young, "Female Pioneers in Afro-American Drama"; and Perkins and Stephens, eds., *Strange Fruit*.

30. "Silent Parade Report Made," *WT*, July 22, 1922, 5.

31. Letter from Col. C. O. Sherrill, Washington, D.C., to Shelby J. Davidson et al., Washington, D.C., June 13, 1922, Box 43, Folder 826, NAACP-MSRC.

32. Barber, *Marching on Washington*, 123–25.

33. For information on the YWCA's Girl Reserves, see "YWCA Notes," *WT*, January 17, 1925, 3. For examples of black women's numerical dominance in fraternal orders, see, for instance, "Locals and Society," *WT*, November 17, 1923, 3; "Catholic Women Elect Officers; Mrs. Locke, President," *WT*, January 28, 1927; and "Weekly Sunday School Lesson," *WT*, January 28, 1928, 5. For scholarly interpretations about black women's importance in fraternal orders, see Barkley Brown, "Womanist Consciousness," and Skocpol and Oser, "Organization Despite Adversity."

34. Letter from Reverend Walter Brooks, the Citizen's Anti-Lynching Protest Parade Committee, Washington, D.C., to Mary Church Terrell, Washington, D.C., July 16, 1922, Reel 5, Frame 371, MCT-LC.

35. "Harding Gets Facts on Mobs thru Booklet," *CD*, July 1, 1922, 3.

36. For an excellent analysis of the Anti-Lynching Crusaders, see Brown, *Eradicating this Evil*, 144–50; and Mungarro, "How did Black Women in the NAACP Promote the Dyer Anti-Lynching Bill, 1918–1923."

37. Brown, *Eradicating This Evil*, 144.

38. "Harding Tables Anti-Lynch Bill," *CD*, September 2, 1922, 1.

39. "President Hears Dyer Bill Plea," *CD*, November 11, 1922, 1.

40. "Harding Favors Dyer Bill," *NYT*, December 2, 1922, 2.

41. "South Flames into Filibuster on Lynching Bill," *CT*, November 29, 1922, 3.

42. "Dyer Declares Coolidge Is for Federal Anti-Lynch Legislation," *CD*, October 18, 1924, A9.

43. "Coolidge Asks Fair Play," *PC*, December 6, 1924, 1.

44. YWCA Notes," *WT*, January 17, 1925, 3.

45. Letter from Leonidas C. Dyer, Washington, D.C., to James Weldon Johnson, New York City, December 10, 1925, in Box C-247, Folder 5, NAACP-LC.

46. "Filibuster Kills Anti-Lynching Bill," *NYT*, December 3, 1922, 1.

47. Edgar Brown did not have an institutional affiliation when he testified at the hearings. He was active in politics in New York City and Chicago, and would be a founding member of the National Negro Congress in 1932. See "Negroes Seek to Elect Alderman in Fourth Ward," *Chicago Tribune*, November 21, 1930, 18.

48. Reverend Branham, as quoted in *To Prevent and Punish the Crime of Lynching: Hearing before a Subcomm. of the Comm. of the Judiciary of the United States Senate*, 69th Cong. (1926).

49. "Anti-Mob Bill Nears Senate Debate," *CD*, February 20, 1926, 1; *To Prevent and Punish the Crime of Lynching: Hearing before a Subcomm. of the Senate Comm. of the Judiciary of the United States Senate*, S.B. 121, 69th Cong. (1926) (statement of Mary Church Terrell).

50. Marian Butler did not explicitly refer to this lynching in Barnwell, South Carolina, in 1889, but I believe that she was discussing this lynching for the following reasons. She was born in Barnwell where eight men were lynched while she lived there; her congressional testimony matches the story of the Barnwell lynching; her sister Rosa married Robert Adams who was the son of a man who was lynched; and Rosa Adams visited Marian Butler on two occasions in Washington, D.C. in the 1910s. For census data on Marian Butler, see "Marion M. Ford," *Tenth Census of the United States*, 1880, Barnwell County, South Carolina, ED 24, Page 3. For Rosa Adams, see *Thirteenth Census of the United States*, 1910, Barnwell County, South Carolina, ED 39, Sheet 24B.

51. "Shot down in Cold Blood," *CNC*, December 29, 1889, 1.

52. "Shot to Death, Terrible Tragedy in Barnwell, South Carolina," *AJC*, December 29, 1889, 11; and "Eight Negroes Lynched," *NYT*, December 29, 1889. For more information on the lynching, see Finnegan, "Lynching and Political Power in Mississippi and South Carolina," 189–218; Kantrowitz, *Ben Tillman and the Reconstruction of White Supremacy*, 171–72; and Williams, *They Left Great Marks on Me*, 101–3.

53. "The Butchery in Barnwell," *CNC*, December 30, 1889, 1; and Finnegan, "Lynching and Political Power in Mississippi and South Carolina," 197.

54. "The Colored Conference," *CNC*, January 3, 1890, 1.

55. "The Negroes Are Going, Barnwell Will Soon Be without Its Colored Inhabitants," *AJC*, January 23, 1890, 1.

56. For information on Robert Adams, see *Tenth Census of the United States*, 1880, Barnwell, South Carolina, ED 24, Page 17; and *Fourteenth Census of the United States*, 1920, Barnwell, South Carolina, ED 49, Sheet 1A.

57. Rosa V. Adams visited Marian Butler in August 1915 and September 1916. See "The Week in Society," *WB*, August 28, 1915, 5; and "The Week in Society," *WB*, September 30, 1916, 5.

58. Testimony of Marian D. Butler, *To Prevent and Punish the Crime of Lynching: Hearing before a Senate Subcomm. of the Senate Comm. of the Judiciary*, S.B. 121, 69th Cong. (1926) (statement of Marian D. Butler).

59. Williams, *They Left Great Marks on Me*, 13.

60. Williams, 45.

61. Kantrowitz, *Ben Tillman and the Reconstruction of White Supremacy*, 156.

62. Materson, *For the Freedom of Her Race*, 77–80.

63. Rosen, *Terror in the Heart of Freedom*, 75-80.

64. "Wipe out Lynching," *PC*, December 10, 1927, 1.

65. "Dyer again Introduces Anti-Lynching Bill," *PC*, May 11, 1929, 3.

66. "Anti-Lynching Congress," *PC*, December 6, 1930, 10.

67. "Miss E. F. Merritt named Head of NAACP," *WT*, February 1, 1932, 1; and "Mrs. R. G. McGuire Named President of Local NAACP," *WT*, March 8, 1934, 1.

68. For information on the Armwood lynching and black activism in Maryland, see Cumberbatch, "What the 'Cause' Needs Is a 'Brainy and Energetic Woman'"; and Sartain, *Borders of Equality*, 27–29.

69. "Anti-Lynching Protest Meet at YWCA," *WAA*, November 4, 1933, 10.

70. For information on this organization, see Hall, *Revolt against Chivalry*, 167 and passim.

71. "Anti-Lynchers Plan Send-Off," *WAA*, November 18, 1933, no page given.

72. "Anti-Lynching Body Hears Secret Report," *BAA*, November 25, 1933, 3. For Lydia McIlwain, see *Boyd's City Directory of the District of Columbia* (1933), 1870, and (1934), 1877.

73. "Why Americans Have Gone Lynch Mad," *WT*, December 21, 1933, 1.

74. "Anti-Lynching Law Urged to Avert Anarchy," *WAA*, February 24, 1934, no page number.

75. "Attempts at Segregation Defeated by Negro Reporters at Anti-Lynching Hearing," *ADW*, February 21, 1934, 1.

76. For a discussion of the Claude Neale lynching, see James R. McGovern, *Anatomy of a Lynching*.

77. "White House Avoids Lynch Statement," *WAA*, November 10, 1934, n.p.

78. "Roosevelt and White Confer on Anti-Lynch Bill," *WT*, May 17, 1934, 11.

79. "Roosevelt Asks U.S. to Fight Crime on United Front," *WP*, December 11, 1934, 2.

80. "Roosevelt Calls for Unified Fight on Crime Problem," *LAT*, December 11, 1934, 1.

81. "Mrs. R. G. McGuire Named President of Local NAACP," *WT*, March 8, 1934, 1.

82. "Silent NAACP Pickets Let Crime Conferences Know the Horrors of Lynching," *NNO*, December 15, 1934, 1. All citations for the *NNO* come from the *New Negro Opinion* collection at the Smithsonian Institution's Anacostia Community Museum in Washington, D.C.

83. "Silent NAACP Pickets Let Crime Conferences Know the Horrors of Lynching."

84. For articles crediting McGuire, see "Silent NAACP Pickets Let Crime Conferences Know the Horrors of Lynching," *NNO*, December 15, 1934, 1; "Pickets against Lynching Arrested at Crime Conference," *CCP*, December 22, 1934, 1; and "President of NAACP Resigns," *WT*, April 27, 1934, 1. For Sullivan's description of the event, see Sullivan, *Lift Every Voice*, 197.

85. I was able to locate the identities of forty-one of the anti-lynching participants. See *The Bison* (Washington, D.C.: Horn Shafer Company, 1934); "40 Law Freshmen at Howard University," *BAA*, October 12, 1935, 5; "378 New Students at Howard; 275 in College Alone," *BAA*, September 29, 1934, 2; "World Horizon: Real Leadership," *PT*, December 20, 1934, 5; "Teachers Nip Jim Crow," *BAA*, September 4, 1937, 3; "Death Claims Dr. James. T. Williston," *NJG*, March 11, 1939, 3; "First Colored Woman Takes Bar in S.C.," *NJG*, November 12, 1938, 10; "Howard Women at 12th Dinner," *BAA*, November 4, 1933, 4; "Four Howard Faculty Members Will Sail," *BAA*, June 29, 1935, 2; "54 on Howard U Honor List," *BAA*, March 5, 1934, 23; "273 Howard Graduates Listed by States and Cities," *BAA*, June 15, 1935, 23; "76 Howard U Students Added to Honor Roll," *BAA*, December 1, 1934, 7; "Howard Players Seen in Richmond," *WP*, March 17, 1935, S10; "Howard Players Announce Season's Schedule of Plays," *NJG*, February 11, 1933, A16; "Howard's Grid Hopes Soar When Vets Arrive in Camp," *CD*, October 5, 1935, 13; "H.U. Junior Sails for Anti-War Meet," *BAA*, December 29, 1934, 16; "Howard University's Queen of May, Flanked by Court," *BAA*, May 26, 1934, 20; and "400 Gather for Women's Dinner in Howard Gymnasium," *NJG*, November 21, 1936, 5.

86. Arnetta Randall, *Fifteenth Census of the United States*, ED 114, Sheet 6A.

87. "As We Go to Press," *NNO*, February 5, 1934, 1.

88. Crystal Feimster constructed an excellent table listing all of the black and white women lynched between 1837 and 1965. Her research reveals that five African American women were lynched in North Carolina between 1885 and 1930: Harriet Finch (1885), Mrs. Joe Perry (1897), Mrs. Joe Perry (1915), Mrs. Bryant (1926), and Laura Wood (1930). See *Southern Horrors*, 235–39.

89. "Admit First Woman to State Bar," *CD*, December 20, 1941, 4.

90. "Military Precision Marks Crime Convo Demonstrations; Pro, Editor, Lawyer, Journalists," *NJG*, December 22, 1934, 1.

91. "Military Precision Marks Crime Convo Demonstrations."

92. "Negroes Picket Crime Meeting," *CSM*, December 13, 1934, 4.

93. For information on direct action, see Morris, *Origins of the Civil Rights Movement*, 124–74. For the relationship between African Americans and Gandhi, see Brown, "NAACP Sponsored Sit-ins," 274–77; and Chabot, *Transnational Roots of the Civil Rights Movement*, 74.

94. "55 Rope Picketers Picket Capital Crime Session," *BAA*, December 22, 1934, 1.

95. "Militancy," *NYAN*, December 22, 1934, 8.

96. "The Rope Pickets," *BAA*, December 22, 1934, 4.

97. "Let Pennsylvania Avenue Tremble, Says Nannie Burroughs in Speech," *WT*, December 29, 1934, 1.

98. "Washington Citizens Urged to Demand Their Rights," *WAA*, December 29, 1934, 13.

99. See, for instance, "Anti-Lynching Bill," *WT*, January 13, 1940, 4.

100. "Stop Police Brutality!! Washington's Record of Official Murder and Abuse, An Account of 'Urban Lynching,'" Washington Council of the National Negro Congress, July 1938, in Box 49, Folder 1060, NAACP-MSRC.

Chapter Three

1. J. Thomas Heflin, Washington, D.C., to H. Sam Reading, October 15, 1929, as reprinted in 71 Cong. Rec. H3173-3174 (daily ed. February 6, 1930) (statement of Rep. Heflin).

2. "Women, Bravery, Freedom," *WT*, November 16, 1933, 4.

3. African American women faced both intraracial and interracial violence in Washington, D.C. Legal records help illuminate some of the violent situations that black women faced. In nineteen court cases in Washington, D.C. during the 1920s, five (26%) of the plaintiffs who sued for divorce cited spousal abuse or cruelty in their petitions. See, for instance, "*Craney v. Craney*," March 29, 1927, Case Number 46786, Records of the District Court, Equity Case Files, Stack Area 16W3, RG 21, National Archives, Washington, D.C. For a discussion about interracial violence against black women, see "Brutes Flee after Girls Are Beaten," *CD*, August 19, 1922, 2.

4. Gellman, *Death Blow to Jim Crow*, 110.

5. Wolcott, *Remaking Respectability*, 111–14; Hicks, *Talk with You like a Woman*, 64–70; and Haley, *No Mercy Here*, 251.

6. Simmons, *Crescent City Girls*, 82.

7. The records of the Washington Metropolitan Police are thin between 1920 and 1945. I was able to locate the annual reports, prison statistics, and arrest records between 1910 and 1920. Records for the Police Court were not preserved.

8. In the early 1930s, the *Washington Afro-American* published a weekly paper and employed a staff of newspaper staff of six, along with agents and delivery workers. See "Afro Employs 396 in Washington," *WAA*, November 11, 1933, 2.

9. "Anonymous Black Woman, "A Colored Woman, However Respectable, Is Lower than the White Prostitute," 1904, in Lerner, ed., *Black Women in White America*, 167.

10. McGirr, *War on Alcohol.*

11. *Fourteenth Census of the United States*: Chapter VII: Males and Females in Selected Occupations, 898.

12. "Police Court Congestion," *WP*, September 10, 1923, 6; and "Police Court Congestion Blamed for Inadequate Administration," *WP*, January 15, 1935, 1.

13. "Reports of Arrests, 1917–1920," Entry Five, Records of the Metropolitan Police Department, RG 351, NARA. For newspaper accounts of black women and crime, see "Under the Capitol Dome," *CD*, July 22, 1922, 19; and "A Hundred Are Seized in a Hotch Raid," *CD*, February 17, 1923, 13. For government investigations, see *Repression of Prostitution in the District of Columbia: Hearings before the Committee On the District of Columbia of the United States Senate*, S. 1616, 67th Cong. (1921).

14. "Man Sues 2 Police on Beating Charge," *WP*, August 28, 1931, 2; and "Capital Jail Has Our Women Do All Laundry Work," *WAA*, April 13, 1935, 14.

15. *Repression of Prostitution in the District of Columbia.*

16. "Career Women of the Capital," *WAA*, April 13, 1940, 7.

17. "Did You Know?" *PC*, November 3, 1923, 11.

18. "Washington Policewomen Making Good," *CD*, April 1, 1922, 20.

19. "Colored Policewomen of Washington," *SW*, 135–36.

20. "Policeman Brutally Assaults Young Girl," *WT*, June 18, 1921, 1.

21. "Policeman Brutally Assaults Young Girl."

22. These statistics were calculated from the annual reports of the Washington, D.C., Board of Commissioners, 1920–30, using both population statistics and prison statistics. For these reports, see Records of the Temporary and Permanent Board of Commissioners, RG 351-NA.

23. See, for instance, "Booze Magnates Work Overtime in Washington," *CD*, September 10, 1921, 15; "A Hundred Are Seized in a Hotch Raid"; and "Liquor Splashes; Women Injured," *PC*, August 6, 1927, 9.

24. "Capital Policewoman Dies at Age 40," *NYAN*, April 30, 1930, 14; "Seven Whites Seek Vacancy," *WAA*, August 2, 1930, 2; and "Would Colored Police Reduce Crime?" *BAA*, May 21, 1932, 11.

25. "The Chief of Police," *WP*, October 22, 1932, 6.

26. "Days Work Curse of Women, Says District Policewoman," *WAA*, September 21, 1935, 11.

27. *Reports of the Board of Commissioners of Washington, D.C.*, 1931, 1934 (Washington, D.C.: GPO, 1932) in Box 67, Entry 9, RG 351.

28. For Charles and Josephine White, see *Boyd's City Directory of the District of Columbia* (1927), 1574.

29. "D.C. Woman Charges Cop with Attack," *CD*, April 16, 1927, 2.

30. "Woman and Baby Brutally Beaten by Policeman," *WT*, April 1, 1927, 1.

31. "Justice Blind in Police Abuse Case," *BAA*, April 16, 1927, 3.

32. "Woman and Baby Brutally Beaten by Policeman."

33. Hicks, *Talk with You like a Woman*, 53–90.

34. For Ida Turner in the census, see *Fifteenth Census of the United States*, ED 332, Sheet 21A.

35. "Policeman Brutally Beats Woman," *Washington Tribune*, October 11, 1930, 1.

36. "Officer Who Beat Woman Dismissed by Trial Board," *WT*, November 1, 1930, 1.

37. "Officer Who Beat Woman Dismissed by Trial Board."

38. "Brutal Beating of Woman Deplored by Baptist Clergy," *WT*, October 18, 1930, 1.

39. "Officer Who Beat Woman Dismissed by Trial Board."

40. "Our Mail Box," *WT*, November 29, 1930, 6.

41. See, for instance, "Three Women Held in Raid," *WP*, August 19, 1930, 3.

42. "Local News," *WT*, September 30, 1929, 1. For Burliegh in the census, see *Fifteenth Census of the United States*, ED 28, Sheet 7A.

43. "Brutal Police Stir City to Curb Menace," *WT*, December 27, 1929, 2. For Brawner and Spencer in the census, see *Fifteenth Census of the United States*, ED 208, Sheet 3A.

44. "Says Detective Dragged Her to Station House," *WT*, June 16, 1932, 1.

45. "White Capital Policemen Held for Assault on Woman," *BAA*, January 22, 1933, 1.

46. "White Policemen Held for the Grand Jury for Assault on Druggist," *WT*, January 20, 1933, 9. For information on Beasley's status, see "G. W. Beasley Remains Head of Civic Body," *WP*, November 26, 1933, R9.

47. "D.C. Cops Terror to Women," *BAA*, December 24, 1932, 11.

48. "Police Beat Her, Woman Charges," *WT*, August 24, 1933, 1. For the Youngs in the census, see *Fifteenth Census of the United States*, ED 337, Sheet 29A.

49. "Can't Arrest Her Assailant," *WAA*, October 7, 1933, 1.

50. "Dragged down Steps by Hair," *BAA*, November 25, 1933, 11.

51. "Brutality Arouses Ire of Citizens," *WT*, November 9, 1933, 1.

52. "Woman, 65, Acquitted of Assaulting Officers," *NJG*, March 10, 1934, 2.

53. "Mrs. R. G. McGuire Named President of Local NAACP," *WT*, March 8, 1934, 1.

54. Harlan Glazier, "Brutality Enthroned," Box 49, Folder 1060, NAACP-MSRC.

55. "Protest Arrest of Woman at Beer Garden," *WAA*, July 28, 1934, 8.

56. "East Central Civic Association Meets," *WT*, July 21, 1929, 6.

57. "Civic Association Protests Police Brutality," *WT*, March 24, 1933, 9.

58. "Police Brutality Greater Menace than Reds, Declares Civic Group," *WT*, April 21, 1933, 9.

59. "DePriest Speaks to Southwest Civic Group," *WT*, June 16, 1933, 9.

60. Glazier, "Brutality Enthroned." For Eva Moxley in the census, see *Fourteenth Census of the United States*, ED 4, Sheet 11A.

61. "Says Brutal Cops Broke into Home," *BAA*, April 24, 1937, 1; and Glazier, "Brutality Enthroned." For Watkins in the census, see *Fifteenth Census of the United States*, ED 1, Sheet 11A.

62. "Spectators Laugh as Cops Say Woman They Beat Assaulted Them," *WT*, April 13, 1935, 1.

63. Glazier, "Brutality Enthroned."

64. See, for instance, "On Bond, Arrested Again," *WP*, March 28, 1922, 5.

65. For details of Jessie Sterling's assault, see Glazier, "Brutality Enthroned"; and "Citizens to Protest Cop Brutality," *WT*, July 20, 1935, 11.

66. For Sterling in the 1940 census, see *Sixteenth Census of the United States*, ED 138, Sheet 3B.

67. Harris, *Sex Workers, Psychics, and Numbers Runners*, 132–33.

68. "Citizens to Protest Cop Brutality."

69. "NAACP Pledges to Help Fight Cop Brutality," *WT*, August 3, 1935, 7.

70. "NAACP Pledges to Help Fight Cop Brutality."

71. "Policeman Freed of Brutality," *WT*, August 17, 1935, 1.

72. Glazier, "Brutality Enthroned."

73. Glazier.

74. For Martha and Ruth Lloyd in the census, see *Fifteenth Census of the United States*, ED 264, Sheet 1B. For historians' treatment of black girlhood, see Simmons, *Crescent City Girls*; Chatelain, *South Side Girls*; and Cahn, *Sexual Reckonings*.

75. "Man Sues 2 Police on Beating Charge."

76. "Policeman Found Guilty of Beating Wielder of Stick," *WP*, December 12, 1931, 22; and "Cop Convicted of Assault, Fined $100," *BAA*, March 12, 1932, 4.

77. "Cop Brutality," *BAA*, March 6, 1937, 1.

78. "Join Meeting to Discuss Vote for District," *WT*, August 14, 1937, 1; "Forum Here to Hold Youth Act Symposium," *WP*, February 11, 1937, 15.

79. For Brown, see "YWCA News," *WT*, February 19, 1926, 5; for Hilyer, see "YWCA Notes," *WT*, February 17, 1923, 6; for McGuire, see "Local Unit of Congress Plans Mass Meeting," *WT*, January 24, 1936, 8; for Terrell, see Letter from Frances Boyce to Mary Church Terrell, March 8, 1928, Reel 6, Frame 296, MCT-LC; and for Thompson, see "YWCA News," *WT*, June 20, 1925, 2.

80. "The Elks' Real Job," *CG*, October 8, 1927, 1; and Letter from Theresa Lee Robinson, Washington, D.C., to Dr. Herbert Marshall, Washington, D.C., July 17, 1939, in Box C-38, Folder 19, NAACP-LC.

81. Byron J. Scott, "H.R. 77," *CR*, January 19, 1937, p. 313.

82. "Police Brutality Given Commissioners," *WT*, January 16, 1937, 1.

83. "Cop Exonerated in 53rd Killing," *BAA*, March 27, 1937, 1.

84. "Commissioners on Spot in Brutality," *BAA*, April 17, 1937, 1.

85. Glazier, "Brutality Enthroned."

86. "Half of Police Pistol Victims Shot in Back," *BAA*, April 10, 1937, 13.

87. Glazier, "Brutality Enthroned."

88. "Cop Brutality," *BAA*, March 6, 1937, 1.

89. "Delegation to Present Petition to Cummings for Negro Police Judge," *WT*, March 20, 1937, 1.

90. "Murders by Police in Nation's Capital Protested at Meet," *CD*, May 22, 1937, 3.

91. "Forum Here to Hold Youth Act Symposium"; and "YWCA Notes," *BAA*, February 13, 1937, 7.

92. *American Youth Act: Hearings before a Subcommittee on Education and Labor in the United States Senate*, 75th Cong. (1938) (statement of Natalie Moorman, Progressive Caucus of Arlington, Virginia).

93. "Citizens Protest Police Brutality," *WAA*, June 25, 1938, 3.

94. For Wallace McKnight, see *Fourteenth Census of the United Sates*, Maysville, South Carolina, 1930, ED 131, Sheet 2B; and for Mollie Davis, see *Fourteenth Census of the United States*, South Lynchburg, South Carolina, 1930, ED 18, Sheet 5B.

95. "Police Brutality Case in D.C. Called Plain Murder," *NJG*, July 16, 1938, 8.

96. "Warn Brutality May Cause Riots," *BAA*, August 13, 1938, 24.

97. "Coffins Barred as Reds March against Police," *WAA*, July 16, 1938, no page given.

98. "Warn Brutality May Cause Riots," *BAA*, August 13, 1938, 24.

99. "Washington Ministers Send Petition to Roosevelt," *ADW*, August 13, 1938, 2.

100. For Julia McKay in the Census, see *Sixteenth Census of the United States*, ED 163, Sheet 14A.

101. For information on this assault, see "Affidavit: Ruth Clark" and "Affidavit: Dorothy Brice" in Reel 12, Frames 85 and 86, respectively, National Negro Congress Papers, Manuscript Division, Library of Congress, Washington, D.C. (hereafter cited as NNC-LC).

102. "Civil Rights Important to All," *WP*, August 23, 1938, 7.

103. "Make Washington Safe for Negro Womanhood," August 30, 1938, Reel 18, Frames 71–72, NNC-LC. For a discussion of this episode, see Gellman, *Death Blow to Jim Crow*, 125.

104. "Washington, D.C., Federation Meets and Elects Officers," *CD*, October 8, 1938, 17.

105. "Brutality!" *WT*, February 11, 1939, 2.

106. "D.C. Matrons Sue Cop," *BAA*, July 29, 1939, 1; and "Police Brutality on the Increase in Washington," *CD*, October 14, 1939, 1.

107. For the McKinneys in the census, see *Sixteenth Census of the United States*, ED F31, Sheet 18A.

108. "Flash: Do Your Part," July 1940, Box 49, Folder 1060, NAACP-MSRC.

109. "100 Voices Protest Police in 4th Precinct," *PC*, July 27, 1940, 10.

110. It is likely that the women who worked as "messengers" performed clerical tasks in the mock trial. "Cop Brutality on Mock Trial September 26," *WT*, September 21, 1940, 1

111. "Solve 7 Sex Slayings in Washington, NY," *ADW*, August 30, 1941, 1.

112. See, for instance, "Government Girl Disappears on a Trip to Buy Butter," *WP*, January 16, 1941, 1.

113. "Legislators Seek Investigation of Police, FBI Intervention," *WP*, June 18, 1941, 3.

114. "Don't Blame the Cops," *WAA*, July 19, 1941, 1.

115. *Confidential Investigation of the Washington Metropolitan Police Department: Hearings before the Special Police Investigation Subcomm. of the House Comm. on the District of Columbia*, 77th Cong. (1941) (statement of Mr. Hèbert).

116. Don't Blame the Cops."

117. "Major Brown," *WP*, July 5, 1941, 6.

118. Solve 7 Sex Slayings in Washington, NY," *ADW*, August 30, 1941, 1. The Cato murders are very complicated and an in-depth analysis of the killer and his victims is beyond the scope of this chapter.

119. "Page Mister Ripley; Cato; Indicts Police!" *BAA*, September 20, 1941, 19.

120. "500 Negroes Protest 'Brutal' District Police," *WP*, September 15, 1941, 1.

121. "D.C. Citizens March to Protest Meet against Police Brutality," *BAA*, September 27, 1941, 24.

122. "55 Rope Picketers Picket Capital Crime Session," *BAA*, December 22, 1934, 1; and "Protest Parade Staged in Nation's Capital," *PC*, July 16, 1938, 4.

123. "New Police Chief Gets Protest," *WAA*, August 23, 1941, 1.

124. "Kelly Says He Won't Permit Police Brutality," *WP*, September 8, 1941, 24.

125. "Police Court Opens at 8 A.M.," *WP*, October 16, 1941, 36.

126. "Judge Scott, First Negro to Serve in Police Court," *WT*, October 3, 1942, 4.

127. "Students of Social Studies Visit D.C. Municipal Court," *WT*, November 21, 1942, 8.

128. "4 Women, 6 Men on D.C. Honor Roll," *WAA*, January 23, 1943, 3.

129. "Police Brutality Hit by D.C. Police Chief," *CD*, June 23, 1945, 4.

130. "Major Kelly Lauded by Chicago Roundtable," *WT*, July 10, 1943, 1.

131. "Police Brutality Hit by D.C. Police Chief," *CD*, June 23, 1945, 4.

132. For a call for scholars to write about black women's history beyond the duality of suffering and success, see Gross, *Colored Amazons*.

Chapter Four

1. "Coppers Pummel 10,000 Women Seeking 2,000 Jobs: Women Riot for Jobs," *BAA*, October 15, 1938, 1; and *Boyd's City Directory of the District of Columbia* (1939), 647.

2. "Twenty-Five Thousand Women Storm Jail to Apply for Charwomen Jobs," *LAT*, October 13, 1938, 20.

3. Keona Ervin's work most closely aligns with my definitions of economic justice. See *Gateway to Equality*, 3 and passim. For other works, see Kessler-Harris, *In Pursuit of Equity*, 12 and passim; Williams, *Politics of Public Housing*; Levenstein, *Movement without Marches*; and Moten, "More than a Job."

4. *Fifteenth Census of the United States: 1930: Occupation Statistics, United States Summary* (Washington, D.C.: GPO, 1932), 11–14; and *Sixteenth Census of the United States: 1940: Population*, vol. II (Washington, D.C.: GPO, 1943), 976.

5. Hine, "Housewives League of Detroit," 223–41; Wolcott, *Remaking Respectability*, 167–205; Orleck, "'We Are That Mythical Thing Called Public," 127–72; McDuffie, *Sojourning for Freedom*, 91-125; Ervin, *Gateway to Equality*; Williams, *Politics of Public Housing*; and Levenstein; *A Movement without Marches*.

6. Beatrice Murphy's column appeared in the *Washington Tribune* in 1932, but it is unclear how much money this paid. In a newspaper profile, Murphy lists her jobs throughout the 1930s as a secretary, a typist, and a published poet. See "Career Women of the Capital," *Washington Afro-American*, July 13, 1940, 7.

7. Murphy, "Women out of Work, by One of Them," *WT*, July 22, 1932, 8.

8. "How Washington Has Met Tenfold Increase in Demands upon Public Philanthropy in Hard Year," *WP*, October 15, 1933, SM8; and Green, *Secret City*, 219.

9. "Washington Has 25,000 Persons Employed in Domestic Service," *WP*, September 22, 1930, 4.

10. The *Fourteenth Census of the United States*, which was published in 1920, lists the Goldman family as having a child who was 11 ½ months and was born in Washington, D.C. All other children were born in South Carolina. See *Fourteenth Census of the United States*, ED 143, Sheet 14A.

11. "Mother and Two Small Children Face Starvation This Winter," *WT*, September 28, 1932, 1. For the Goldman family in the census in 1930, see *Fifteenth Census of the United States*, ED 124, Sheet 7A.

12. "NACW Requests Courses in Social Service at H.U.," *ET*, February 26, 1932, no page given.

13. "Suicide Record in D.C. Reaches New High," *BAA*, August 6, 1932, 10.

14. "Unemployed Woman Commits Suicide," *WT*, July 1, 1932, 1.

15. "Essie Weaver," *Fifteenth Census of the United States*, ED 1930, Sheet 4A.

16. "Y Employee Dies in Leap out Window," *ET*, February 23, 1935, 1.

17. "Plight of 3,000 Relief Transients Worries Capital," *WAA*, September 21, 1935, 11.

18. *Fifteenth Census of the United States*, vol. III: Population, Parts I and II; "Three-Fourths of Relief Given to D.C. Families," *WAA*, December 30, 1933, 8; and "Biggest Relief Percentage is in Washington," *ADW*, June 6, 1934, 1.

19. For Anna Payne's activism, see "Associated Charities Holds First Meeting," *WT*, October 18, 1923, 2; and "Dance for the Freedmen's Radio Fund," *WT*, June 6, 1925, 2. See also "Shaw Students Distribute Thanksgiving," *WT*, November 29, 1929, 5.

20. For Mabel and Birdie Settle, see *Fifteenth Census of the United States*, ED 339, Sheet 15B, and for Martha Ellis, see *Fifteenth Census of the United States*, ED 147, Sheet 10B. For their activities, see "Junior Needlework Guild Active," *WT*, December 6, 1929, 8.

21. "D.C. Society," *BAA*, December 27, 1930, 2. For Cumber in the census, see *Fifteenth Census of the United States*, ED 213, Sheet 7A.

22. "D.C. Society," *BAA*, February 7, 1931, 2.

23. "White and Colored Unemployed Given Free Lunch at Mt. Carmel," *WT*, September 30, 1923, 11.

24. "St. Luke's Gives 50 Baskets," *WAA*, January 7, 1933, 6.

25. "'Its' Sends Basket to Family of Eight," *WT*, March 18, 1932, 11. For the occupations of the members, see Evangeline P. Belle, *Fifteenth Census of the United States*, ED 269, Sheet 14B; Margaret E. and Ruth E. Harvey, *Fifteenth Census of the United States*, ED 225, Sheet 12A; Naomi Chatman, *Boyd's City Directory of the District of Columbia* (1932), 382; Dorothy Robinson, *Fifteenth Census of the United States*, ED 217, Sheet 5B; and Cordelia Jefferson, *Boyd's City Directory of the District of Columbia* (1932), 1059.

26. "Garnet-Patterson Students Rally to Aid Poor and Needy," *WT*, December 23, 1932, 1.

27. Grant, *Way It Was*, 340.

28. "Nannie Burroughs Pessimistic over Political Victory of the Democrats," *WAA*, December 3, 1932, 19.

29. "Nation's Leaders to Discuss What Roosevelt Regime Can Do to Improve Our Predicament," *PC*, March 4, 1933, A2.

30. "Federal Cuts Likely to Total 15 Per Cent," *WP*, March 28, 1933, 1.

31. "Salary Reductions Drive Families to Cheaper Quarters," *WT*, April 7, 1933, 9.

32. "Mrs. Roosevelt Picked Her Own Servants," *BAA*, September 16, 1933, 17.

33. "Plans President's Entertainments," *WT*, February 8, 1934, 8; "Clarksburg Plans Ball on Roosevelt Birthday," *WP*, January 3, 1934, 22; and "Plans President's Entertainments," *WT*, February 8, 1934, 8.

34. "Roosevelt Servitors Helpful in Contacts," *NYAN*, February 21, 1934, 9.

35. "New Dealers Girding Loins for Battle," *WAA*, June 30, 1934, 4.

36. As quoted in Weiss, *Farewell to the Party of Lincoln*, 56.

37. "1,000 Workers Launch N.R.A. Drive in Capital This Week," *WAA*, September 2, 1933, 1. For these occupations, see Marian Butler, *Boyd's City Directory of the District of Columbia* (1933), 2259; Mildred Coleman, *Fifteenth Census of the United States*, ED 20, Sheet 8A; Effie Pettis, *Fifteenth Census of the United States*, ED 197, Sheet 9B; Elizabeth Bampfield, *Fifteenth*

Census of the United States, ED 227, Sheet 12A; and Inez Clomax, *Fifteenth Census of the United States*, ED 104, Sheet 10B.

38. "NRA Drive Is Started by Workers Here," *WT*, August 31, 1933, 2.

39. "A Code for Domestic Needed," *WAA*, September 9, 1933, 14.

40. "A Code for Domestic Needed."

41. "The Spirit of T. G. Bramlette," *BAA*, July 23, 1927, A13; "Hawaiian Agents Extend from New York to Florida," *BAA*, October 27, 1928, 23; and "What Capital Employers Are Doing about the Codes," *WAA*, August 5, 1933, 6.

42. Gill, *Beauty Shop Politics*, 69–70.

43. "Mrs. Beatrice Woodland Elected Head of Local Beauticians League," *WT*, October 26, 1933, 9.

44. "Servants' Code Calls for $30 Week Wage," *WAA*, December 2, 1933, 1.

45. Poole, *Segregated Origins of Social Security*, 7–8.

46. *Fifteenth Census of the United States: 1930, Population, Vol. IV: Occupations by States* (Washington, D.C.: GPO, 1933), 25–34.

47. *Economic Security Act: Hearings before the Comm. of Ways and Means in the House of Representatives*, 74th Cong. 597–600 and 796–98 (1935) (statements of Mr. Haynes and Mr. Houston).

48. Poole, *Segregated Origins of Social Security*.

49. "Minutes of the Nineteenth Biennial Convention of the National Association of Colored Women, July 1935," Reel 2, Frame 72, NACW-LC.

50. "Women Fraters Lead Discussion on Economics," *PC*, August 31, 1935, A9.

51. "Women Fraters Lead Discussion on Economics."

52. "Educator Asks Social Security for Domestics," *BAA*, January 23, 1937, 9.

53. Letter from Arthur D. Gray, Washington, D.C., to Franklin D. Roosevelt, Washington, D.C., October 24, 1935, Collection 21A: Clergy Letters, Folder 2, Franklin Delano Roosevelt Presidential Library, Hyde Park, New York (hereafter cited as FDR-NY).

54. "White House Servants Even Campaign for F.D.," *BAA*, October 24, 1936, 16; and "Letter from Thomas J. Davis, Cleveland, Ohio, to Franklin Delano Roosevelt, Warm Springs, Georgia," November 17, 1938, in Box 1, Folder 43, Elizabeth and Irvin McDuffie Papers, Archives Research Center, Robert W. Woodruff Library, Atlanta University Center, Atlanta, Georgia (hereafter cited as EIM-Woodruff).

55. "New Deal Jobholders," *PT*, January 3, 1925, 5; and "U.S. Employees Form Alliance," *BAA*, November 28, 1936, 18.

56. "United Employees Hold Weekly Meet," *BAA*, December 5, 1936, 5.

57. "U.S. Workers to Hear Congressmen," *BAA*, February 13, 1937, 12. For the salary of government charwomen, see "Edgar Brown Fined as 20,000 Women Fight," *PC*, October 22, 1938, 12.

58. *Hearings before the Subcomm. of the Comm. on Appropriations, United States Senate, War Department Appropriation Bill for 1938*, H.R., 6692, 75th Cong., 166–72 (1937) (statement of Mr. Brown).

59. "Army's Laundry Workers Win $50,00 Pay Boost," *BAA*, May 8, 1937, 16; and "Wage Increase for Laundry Workers Urged: Recommendation Is Voted by Senate Sub-Committee," *NJG*, July 3, 1937, 5.

60. "New D.C. Group Plans to Wage Battle in Behalf of Workers," *WAA*, September 2, 1933, 3. An extended discussion of the New Negro Alliance is beyond the scope of this chapter. For more information, see Pacifico, "'Don't Buy Where You Can't Work," 66–88; Gellman, *Death Blow to Jim Crow*, 113–16; and Asch and Musgrove, *Chocolate City*, 260–64.

61. For Catherine Grey, see *Fifteenth Census of the United States*, ED 216, Sheet 10B; for Doris Risher, see *Boyd's City Directory of the District of Columbia* (1934), 1656; for Doris Shilmate, see "Appoint Summer Teachers," *PC*, July 9, 1932, A3; for Isadore Williams, see *Fifteenth Census of the United States*, ED 202, Sheet 11A; for Mae Thorne, see *Boyd's City Directory of the District of Columbia* (1935), 1941; and for Helen Nash, see "Activities of the Clubs," *WP*, January 13, 1924, EA3.

62. "Peaceful Boycott Breaking down Job Discriminations," *BAA*, September 16, 1933, 11.

63. Asch and Musgrove, *Chocolate City*, 260-263.

64. "Boycott Conducted by Negro Alliance," *WP*, September 3, 1933, 10.

65. For black women's campaigns, see Hine, "Housewives League of Detroit"; and Orleck, "'We Are That Mythical Thing Called the Public."

66. "New Negro Alliance Continues Picketing," *WT*, October 5, 1933, 1.

67. Chatelain, *South Side Girls*, 118–19.

68. "Girls Employed as Clerks in Five and Ten Cents Stores," *WT*, December 28, 1933, 2.

69. "NNA Activities of the Year," *NNO*, December 31, 1934.

70. *New Negro Alliance v. Sanitary Grocery Store*, 1938. For more information on the New Negro Alliance, see Asch and Musgrove, *Chocolate City*, 260-263.

71. "Demurrer Filed in Arrest of Picket," *BAA*, April 15, 1939, 24.

72. "Unemployed Women Get Highland Beach Camp," *WAA*, August 4, 1934, no page given.

73. Myra Colson Callis deserves more scholarly attention. For her scholarship, see Greene and Callis, *Employment of Negroes in the District of Columbia*. The most extended discussion of her career is discussed throughout Wilson, *Segregated Scholars*.

74. "Employment Center in D.C. Becomes of Age," *BAA*, October 22, 1938, 3.

75. "Employment Center in D.C. Comes of Age."

76. Sarah Ruth Barruss, Washington, D.C., to Myra Colson Callis, Washington, D.C., February 9, 1933, Box 42, Folder 7, Myra Colson Callis Papers, Collection 193, Box 42, Folder 8, Manuscript Division, Moorland-Spingarn Research Center, Founders Library, Howard University, Washington, D.C. (hereafter cited as MCC-MSCR).

77. For a discussion of living in, versus living out among black women workers in Washington, D.C., see Clark-Lewis, *Living In, Living Out*.

78. Lena Harper, Washington, D.C., to Myra Colson Callis, Washington, D.C., May 15, 1939, Box 42, Folder 7, MCC-MSRC.

79. Margaret Howard, Washington, D.C., to Myra Colson Callis, Washington, D.C., November 10, 1940, Box 42, Folder 7, MCC-MSRC.

80. Mrs. Elizabeth D. Simms, Washington, D.C., to Myra Colson Callis, Washington, D.C., April 15, 1940, Box 42, Folder 7, MCC-MSRC.

81. Janie Edwards, Washington, D.C., to Myra Colson Callis, Washington, D.C., Box 42, Folder 7, MCC-MSRC.

82. Marie Tibbs, Washington, D.C., to Myra Colson Callis, Washington, D.C., January 7, 1939, Box 42, Folder 8, MCC-MSRC.

83. Lillian McAdoo, Bethany Beach, Delaware, to Myra Colson Callis, Washington, D.C., October 7, 1940, Box 42, Folder 8, MCC-MSRC.

84. Bernice Contree, Washington, D.C., to Myra Colson Callis, Washington, D.C., January 16, 1941, Box 42, Folder 7, MCC-MSRC.

85. Mary Berry, Washington, D.C., to Myra Colson Callis, Washington, D.C., July 25, 1940, Box 42, Folder 7, MCC-MSRC.

86. Christina Brown, Washington, D.C., to Myra Colson Callis, Washington, D.C., August 22, 1940, Box 42, Folder 7, MCC-MSRC.

87. Elizabeth Stanley, Washington, D.C., to Myra Colson Callis, Washington, D.C., Undated, Box 42, Folder 8, MCC-MSRC.

88. Lille Wilburn, Washington, D.C., to Myra Colson Callis, Washington, D.C., August 25, 1939, Box 42, Folder 7, MCC-MSRC.

89. Josephine Nalls, Washington, D.C., to Myra Colson Callis, Washington, D.C., July 23, 1940, Box 42, Folder 8, MCC-MSRC.

90. Ervin, *Gateway to Equality*, 3–5.

91. Virginia McCallig, Washington, D.C., to Myra Colson Callis, Washington, D.C., January 2, 1940, Box 42, Folder 8, MCC-MSRC.

92. "Self-Help Projects," *WT*, July 19, 1934, 4.

93. "Barrel of Comfort in Nannie Helen Burroughs's Barrel Chairs," *WAA*, June 15, 1935, 1.

94. For Mary Thomas, see *Boyd's City Directory of the District of Columbia* (1934), 1552. For her membership application, see Box 49, Folder 2, NHB-LC.

95. For Jeannette Reed, see *Boyd's City Directory of the District of Columbia* (1934), 1304; and for Sarah Harrington, see *Boyd's City Directory of the District of Columbia* (1934), 731. Both of their membership applications are in Box 34, Folder 2, NHB-LC.

96. "Barrel of Comfort in Nannie Helen Burroughs's Barrel Chairs."

97. "Co-Op Store Opens Here Today," *WT*, August 21, 1937, 1.

98. "From Day to Day," *PC*, October 16, 1937 14.

99. For Anita J. Anderson, see *Sixteenth Census of the United States*, ED 409, Sheet 12A.

100. "Civic Group Starts Co-Op Movement," *WT*, November 20, 1937, 9.

101. For information on Langston Terrace, see Quinn, "Making Modern Homes"; and Asch and Musgrove, *Chocolate City*, 249–60.

102. "Ma, 15-Day Old Infant Stage Sit-In Strike," *WAA*, April 30, 1938, 4.

103. "Jobless Women Facing Eviction Receive Little Relief at District Agency," *WT*, November 14, 1940, 1.

104. "'Sit-Down' Threat Causes Eviction of Relief Group," *WP*, June 21, 1940, 5.

105. "Charwomen to Get Full Pay on Holidays," *WP*, July 26, 1935, 11.

106. These salary figures were taken from "Y Survey Shows D.C. Women's Wages Low," *BAA*, July 19, 1930, 3; "Letters to the Editor: Wages of Domestics," *WP*, November 30, 1938, 10; and "Servant Crises' Ironed Out at Job Center Conferences," *WP*, February 3, 1940, 3.

107. *Sixteenth Census of the United States: 1940: Population*, vol. II, 969.

108. "Coppers Pummel 10,000 Women Seeking 2,000 Jobs: Women Riot for Jobs," *BAA*, October 15, 1938, 1.

109. "20,000 Riot Seeking Jobs as Charwomen," *WP*, October 13, 1938, X16.

110. "Watching the Big Parade," *BAA*, October 29, 1938, 4.

111. "Coppers Pummel 10,000 Women Seeking 2,000 Jobs."

112. "Citizens Protest Police Brutality," *WAA*, June 25, 1938, 3; and "How Washington Protests Police Brutality," *WAA*, July 16, 1938, no page given.

113. More details about Elizabeth McDuffie's political activism are found in Murphy, "The Servant Campaigns."

114. "To Launch National Civil Rights Campaign, Wife of Valet to President Moves to Spend $10,000," *CD*, October 29, 1938, 6.

115. "Negro Congress Asks Ouster of Police Head," *BAA*, October 22, 1938, 3.

116. "Self-Respecting Domestic Worker," *WP*, December 16, 1938, 16. While the identities of the letter writers are unknown, it is extremely likely that they were African American since black women represented 88 percent of the population of domestic servants in Washington, D.C. in 1940. *Sixteenth Census of the United States: 1940: Population*, vol. II, 974–76.

117. "A Domestic," *WP*, December 16, 1938, 16.

118. "Beauty Culture Bill Has Okey of District League," *WAA*, February 1, 1936, 1.

Chapter Five

1. "District Hails Suffrage Vote," *WAA*, May 6, 1938, 15. For Sallie Carrington, see *Thirteenth Census of the United States*, ED 103, Sheet 6A.

2. For information on Whipper's career as a physician, see Moldow, *Women Doctors in Gilded-Age Washington*, 37–47; and Smith, *Sick and Tired of Being Sick and Tired*, 138. The Whipper and Rollin families are fascinating and deserve a book-length treatment. Information on their careers can be found in Holt, *Black over White*; and Gatewood, "The Remarkable Misses Rollin," 172–88.

3. Hall, "Long Civil Rights Movement and the Political Uses of the Past," 1233–63.

4. See, for example, Naison, *Communists in Harlem during the Great Depression*; McNeil, *Groundwork*; Korstad and Lichtenstein, "Opportunities Lost and Found," 786–811; Kelley, *Hammer and Hoe*; Bates, *Pullman Porters and the Rise of Protest Politics in Black America*; Korstad, *Civil Rights Unionism*; Skarloff, *Black Culture and the New Deal*; Gilmore, *Defying Dixie*; and Gellman, *Death Blow to Jim Crow*.

5. N. Brown, *Private Politics and Public Voices*; McDuffie, *Sojourning for Freedom*; and Blain, *Set the World on Fire*, 445–54.

6. Yellin, *Racism in the Nation's Service*, 175–203.

7. "Woman Ordered from Knees in Jim Crow Church," *WT*, March 25, 1932, 1.

8. For articles detailing excursions to Rock Creek Park, see "YWCA News," *WT*, December 5, 1925, 4; "YWCA News," *WT*, September 17, 1926, 3; and "Locals and Society," *WT*, August 2, 1924, 2.

9. "Ministers' Alliance Continues Its Fight to End Segregation in Parks," *WT*, September 30, 1932, 6.

10. "Interracial Group formed in District," *BAA*, February 13, 1932, 4.

11. "Protest against Unequal School Appropriations," *WT*, February 19, 1932, 1.

12. "Citizens Are Urged to Protest Chain Store's Jim Crow," *WAA*, February 16, 1935, 13.

13. "Plan Fight on Segregation in Halls, Theaters," *NJG*, February 20, 1932, 2.

14. "Babies Die by the Hundreds in the Shadow of U.S. Capitol as Congress Looks on Helpless," *PT*, September 27, 1934, 12.

15. "AKA Sorority Sets up Lobby to Further Social Legislation," *PT*, March 31, 1938, 1.

16. "Tribune Reporter Makes Survey of Department Stores," *WT*, November 24, 1929, 1.

17. "Segregated Rest Rooms in Style at Hecht Store," *WAA*, May 2, 1936, no page given.

18. "Hecht's to Keep J. C. Restrooms," *BAA*, May 23, 1936, 6.

19. "Both Races Unite in Fight against Hecht's Jim Crow," *BAA*, June 27, 1936, 15.

20. For information on *New Masses* reporting in other cities, see McDuffie, *Sojourning for Freedom*, 1.

21. "Washington, Jim Crow Capital of the United States," *WAA*, May 18, 1935, 12.

22. "Civil Rights Bill for New Jersey Assured," *WT*, June 15, 1935, 1. These states had civil rights laws by the mid-1930s: California, Colorado, Connecticut, Illinois, Indiana, Iowa, Kansas, Massachusetts, Michigan, Minnesota, Nebraska, New Jersey, New York, Ohio, Pennsylvania, Rhode Island, Washington, and Wisconsin.

23. "Civil Rights Bill for D.C. Pushed," *WT*, June 29, 1935, 1.

24. Sullivan, *Days of Hope*, 47.

25. "Anti-Lynch and Civil Rights Bills Held Most Vitally by Forum Speaker," *WT*, January 10, 1936, 1.

26. "Kopplemann Offers Civil Rights Bill," *HC*, June 7, 1935, 2.

27. "House Measure Provides Stiff Double Penalties for District Violators," *WT*, March 13, 1937, 10.

28. "Civil Rights Bill for D.C. Pushed," *WT*, June 29, 1935, 1.

29. "Civil Rights Mass Meeting Scheduled," *WT*, November 15, 1935, 11; and "Mrs. Julia Hamilton to Conduct Forum," *WAA*, December 14, 1935, 12.

30. "Voteless D.C.," *WT*, July 8, 1932, 8.

31. "Young Political Club Organized in Washington," *WT*, April 29, 1932, 2.

32. "Holds Open Forum," *BAA*, October 29, 1932, 19; and "Republicans Disappoint Negro Youth Group," *WT*, October 28, 1932, 10.

33. "Progressive Democratic Club Elects Officers," *WT*, July 22, 1932, 5.

34. Gritter, *River of Hope*, 114.

35. "Washington Needs The Vote," *WT*, June 24, 1932, 8.

36. "Voteless Washington," *WT*, October 13, 1936, 4.

37. "Roosevelt Vote Bid Called Aim of Howard Talk," *WP*, October 25, 1936, M1.

38. "Budget Slash Hits Schools in Washington, D.C." *NJG*, February 18, 1933, 14.

39. "Colored Women Protest Slash of D.C. Money," *WT*, April 14, 1933, 9.

40. See, for instance, "Federation of Women to Hear Lincoln Tribute," *WP*, February 15, 1926, 18; and "Washington, D.C., Federation Meets and Elects Officers," *CD*, October 8, 1938, 17. A full list of members is in Davis, *Lifting as They Climb*, 410–11.

41. "Why Americans Have Gone Lynch Mad," *WT*, December 21, 1933, 1.

42. "Dr. Du Bois in Speech before Capital NAACP," *CD*, February 22, 1936, 4.

43. "Group Plans U.S. Project on Race History," *CD*, July 13, 1935, 2.

44. "New Negro Alliance," *WT*, June 5, 1936, 13.

45. "Joint Meeting to Discuss Vote for District," *WT*, August 14, 1937, 1.

46. Katznelson, *Fear Itself*, 86–88.

47. For a discussion of the 1862 law, see Masur, *An Example for All the Land*, 25–27.

48. "What Bilbo Thinks of the Afro American," *BAA*, January 29, 1938, 7; and "Bilbo Aims Bill at Colored and White Marriages," *WAA*, February 26, 1938, 13.

49. For more information on this organization, see Asch and Musgrove, *Chocolate City*, 269.

50. "Delegates Report to Tuesday Evening Club," *BAA*, February 18, 1939, 12.

51. AKA is first mentioned as part of the Citizen's Conference in "Reorganization of the Government of the District of Columbia," U.S. Senate, 78th Cong. (Washington, D.C.: GPO, 1943), but many of the women affiliated with the sorority were part of the voting rights movement, which leads me to believe that the AKA joined the Citizen's Conference before it was first mentioned.

52. "Leaders Call Ballot April 30 on D.C. Vote," *WP*, April 9, 1938, X3.

53. Segregation was not enforced at the polls, but citizens did cast ballots at black and white schools throughout the city. See "Referendum on Suffrage Set on April 29," *WP*, March 30, 1938, X17; and "District Officials Voice Approval of Vote on Suffrage," *WP*, March 31, 1938, X2.

54. See, for instance, *Representation of the District of Columbia in Congress and the Electoral College: Hearings before the Comm. on the Judiciary in the House of Representatives*, H. J. Res. 11 and 32, 66th Cong., 157–60 (1921) (statement of Mr. Ayers).

55. "700 Draft Vote Plea," *WAA*, April 30, 1938, 1.

56. "Voteless D.C. Citizens Jubilant in Plebiscite," *WAA*, May 6, 1938, 15.

57. For Marie Brent in the census, see *Sixteenth Census of the United States*, ED 1-47, Sheet 63A.

58. "District Hails Suffrage Vote," *WAA*, May 6, 1938, 15. This newspaper article listed the occupations of these women, but not their home addresses. For Hart in the census, see *Sixteenth Census of the United States*, ED 147, Sheet 15A.

59. "D.C. Votes 7–1 for Self Rule, 13–1 for Seats in Congress," *WP*, May 2, 1938, X1.

60. "Negro Thought to be Bone of Contention in fight for Vote Power in D.C.," *ADW*, May 23, 1938, 1.

61. Ward, "Remembering and Refighting Reconstruction in the Roosevelt Era," 36–37.

62. *National Representation and Suffrage for Residents of the District of Columbia: Hearings before the House Comm. on the Judiciary*, H.J. Res. 232, 75th Cong., 3rd Sess. (1938) (statement of W. L. Rodgers).

63. *National Representation and Suffrage for Residents of the District of Columbia: Hearings before the House Comm. on the Judiciary*, H.J. Res. 232, 75th Cong., 3rd Sess. (1938) (statement of Alfred D. Calvert).

64. *National Representation and Suffrage for Residents of the District of Columbia: Hearings before the House Comm. on the Judiciary*, H.J. Res. 232, 75th Cong., 3rd Sess. (1938) (statement of the Honorable Paul E. Lesh).

65. *National Representation and Suffrage for Residents of the District of Columbia: Hearings before the House Comm. on the Judiciary*, H.J. Res. 232, 75th Cong., 3rd Sess. (1938) (statements of George Murray, Charles E. Hall, and Kelly Miller).

66. *National Representation and Suffrage for Residents of the District of Columbia: Hearings before the House Comm. on the Judiciary*, H.J. Res. 232, 75th Cong., 3rd Sess. (1938) (statement of Dr. Arthur Gray).

67. For Wilkinson in the census, see *Sixteenth Census of the United States*, ED 461, Sheet 2A. For articles on Wilkinson, see "At Red Cross Dedication," *BAA*, March 29, 1930, 2; and "Insurance Force Entertains Vets," *PC*, May 11, 1929, 9.

68. *National Representation and Suffrage for Residents of the District of Columbia: Hearings before the House Comm. on the Judiciary,* H.J. Res. 232, 75th Cong., 3rd Sess. (1938) (statement of Cora L. Wilkinson).

69. "Voters League Formed by Citizens' Committee," *WT,* May 21, 1938, 3.

70. "Plan Course in Citizenship for D.C. Voters," *WAA,* March 2, 1940, 3.

71. "Discussed D.C. Suffrage," *WAA,* March 29, 1941, 11.

72. "D.C. 75 Years behind Time—Miss Burroughs," *BAA,* March 4, 1939, 18.

73. "Chicago Acclaims Marian Anderson; 4,000 Brave Sub-Zero," *PC,* February 8, 1936, 9.

74. "DAR Blocks Appearance of Concert Singer," *PC,* January 28, 1939, 24; "DAR Insults Marian Anderson," *NYAN,* January 28, 1939, 1.

75. "School Board Apes DAR; Bars Marian," *BAA,* February 18, 1939, 1; and "Board of Education Denounced by Pickets," *PC,* February 25, 1939, 1.

76. "School Board Apes DAR; Bars Marian."

77. "Board of Education Denounced by Pickets."

78. "Bans Can't Still Marian's Songs," *BAA,* February 25, 1939, 1.

79. "Mrs. FDR Quits DAR," *BAA,* March 4, 1939, 3.

80. "Board Should Rescind Its Vote, Says Mrs. McGuire," *WT,* March 4, 1939, 2.

81. "School Board 'Backs Down' against Marian Anderson," *PC,* March 11, 1939, 1.

82. Sandage, "A Marble House Divided," 135–67.

83. "Nazism in D.C.," *NYAN,* April 8, 1939, 10.

84. "Happy Ending," *WP,* April 10, 1939, 8.

85. Green, *Secret City,* 262–63; and Quigley, *Just Another Southern Town,* 130–31.

86. "Let Freedom Ring!," *WT,* April 15, 1939, 1.

87. "Congress to Get Alliance Civil Rights Bill," *BAA,* November 25, 1939, 1.

88. "Mrs. Bethune," *WAA,* December 2, 1939, 2.

89. "Organizations Join to Back Campaign for Civil Rights," *WT,* December 16, 1939, 2.

90. "Washington Viewed as a Model of Segregation," *ADW,* December 22, 1939, 1.

91. For Bomar, see *Fifteenth Census of the United States,* ED 230, Sheet 7B. See also, "D.C. Suffrage Discussed at Mass Meeting," *BAA,* February 24, 1940, 23

92. "Action for Civil Rights," *WT,* January 27, 1940, 4.

93. "Citizens Picket Jim Crow Movie," *BAA,* January 27, 1940, 1; and "D.C. Picket Line Hits Abe Lincoln in Illinois," *CD,* February 3, 1940, 21.

94. Eleanor Roosevelt, "My Day," January 24, 1940, as quoted in Bell-Smith, *Firebrand and the First Lady,* 53–54.

95. Letter from Pauli Murray, New York City, to Eleanor Roosevelt, Washington, D.C., January 30, 1940, Box 1, Folder 1, Eleanor Roosevelt Letters: Pauli Murray File, FDR-NY.

96. "Mrs. F. D. Raps D.C. Jim Crow," *WAA,* January 27, 1940, 1.

97. "The Man, Frederick Douglass," *WAA,* February 10, 1940, 24; "Frederick Douglass, Abraham Lincoln," *WAA,* February 10, 1940, 4; and "Early Washington: Store and Offices Stand on Site of Slave Depot," *WAA,* March 1, 1941, 8.

98. "School Children Pay Homage to Lincoln," *WAA,* February 17, 1940, 24.

99. "D.C. Suffrage Discussed at Mass Meeting."

100. "D.C. Civil Rights Bill Reaches House Floor," *CD,* March 23, 1940, 7.

101. Let's Take Washington out of the Confederacy," *WAA,* March 16, 1940, 1.

Chapter Six

1. Affidavit of Mildred I. Turpin," January 8, 1943, Part 1, Series B, Box 191, Folder 2, NAACP-LC.

2. "Defy D.C. Jim Crow, H.U. Coeds Arrested," *BAA*, February 6, 1943, 16.

3. Lawson, *Running for Freedom*, 12–14; Wolcott, *Race, Riots and Rollercoasters*, 77–81; Catsam, "The Economic Civil Rights Movement in Washington, D.C."; and Bryant, "NAACP Sponsored Sit-Ins by Howard Students in Washington, D.C," 274–86.

4. For a discussion about the impact of World War II, see Plummer, *A Rising Wind*; Tyson, *Radio Free Dixie*; Bates, *Pullman Porters and the Rise of Protest Politics in Black America*; Ransby, *Ella Baker and the Black Freedom Movement*; Gilmore, *Defying Dixie*; Sullivan, *Lift Every Voice*; and Jones, *March on Washington*.

5. Hunter, *To 'Joy My Freedom*, 222–35.

6. "10,000 Should March on D.C., Says Randolph," *BAA*, January 25, 1941, 3.

7. "Randolph Protest March Launched in Washington," *WT*, May 10, 1941, 5.

8. "D.C. Schools to Mark Negro History Week," *WAA*, February 8, 1941, 5; "Democracy at Work in Nation's Capital," *WT*, February 15, 1941, 1; and "Youth Demonstrate against D.C. Jim Crow," *WAA*, February 15, 1941, 10.

9. "AKA Plans Series of Mass Meetings," *WAA*, March 29, 1941, 11.

10. "AKA Group Plans Citizenship Day," *WAA*, May 17, 1941, 11.

11. The details of this story are vividly told in Masur, "Patronage and Protest in Kate Brown's Washington," 1047–71.

12. See, for example, "W.B.A. Loses in Jim-Crow Case," *BAA*, October 11, 1918, 5; for cases described in that article, see "Cases of Jim Crow Show Barbarity of Policy," *BAA*, June 15, 1946, 11.

13. Berrey, *Jim Crow Routine*, 59.

14. "Va. Bus Jim Crow Still Holds despite Ruling," *BAA*, May 17, 1941, 11.

15. For Daisy Willett in the census in 1930, see *Fifteenth Census of the United States*, ED 292, Sheet 1B; and in 1940; for Willet in the 1940 census, see *Sixteenth Census of the United States*, ED 161, Sheet 62B.

16. "Maid Balks at Va. Bus Jim Crow; Nabbed," *WT*, June 14, 1941, 1.

17. "John L. Lewis's Maid Fined in Jim-Crow Case," *PT*, June 26, 1941, 12.

18. "NAACP in Philly for Annual Meet," *PC*, June 22, 1940, 1.

19. Kelley, *Right to Ride*, 11. For another discussion of black women's refusals to adhere to Jim Crow during World War II, see Greene, *Our Separate Ways*, 52.

20. "Rights Meet to be Held in Arlington," *WT*, June 14, 1941, 1.

21. "Will Roosevelt Profit by Lincoln's Mistake?," *WAA*, April 10, 1941, 4.

22. "Postponed," *PC*, July 5, 1941, 6.

23. "La Guardia to Speak Here," *WT*, June 30, 1941, 25.

24. "The President's Anti-Jim Crow Committee," *WAA*, August 1, 1941, 4.

25. "Howard U Students Give up Christmas to Enter Defense Class," *CCP*, December 27, 1941, 1B.

26. "Rally to Mark Anniversary of Signing of Bill of Rights," *WAA*, December 13, 1941, no page given.

27. "606 Southeast Negroes Ordered by Court to Move by May 15; Destitute," *WT*, April 18, 1942, 28; Green, *Secret City*, 261.

28. "War Workers Are Asked to Share Cars," *WT*, December 5, 1942, 4.

29. "Non-Essential Residents Urged to Leave District," *WT*, April 24, 1943, 3.

30. Murray, *Song in a Weary Throat*, 200.

31. Green, *Secret City*, 261.

32. "Phyllis Wheatley YWCA Opens Annex," *WT*, January 6, 1940, 3.

33. "Federal Government Jobs Rise to 100,000 in Each of Six States," *CT*, December 27, 1942, A7.

34. "U.S. to Build Navy Offices in Arlington," *WP*, September 21, 1940, 1.

35. "Jim Crow Feared in Virginia Offices," *PT*, September 6, 1941, 17. See also, "NAACP Warns against Jim-Crow if Government Offices Move to Va.," *CCP*, August 23, 1941, 1B.

36. "D.C. Bus Line Orders, 'No Discrimination,'" *PT*, May 30, 1942, 10. See also, "No Jim Crow on District-Va. Bus Line," *BAA*, May 30, 1942, 3; and "D.C. Bus Line Orders No Segregation," *PC*, May 30, 1942, 3.

37. "National Grapevine by Charley Cherokee," *CD*, June 6, 1942, 15.

38. "Crowded Washington, War Capital, Where Identification Badges Are Needed," *BAA*, June 13, 1942, 1.

39. For information on Joe Louis and his image during World War II, see Philips, *War!*, 31–35.

40. "Caviar and Cabbage: Is Race Prejudice Increasing?," *WT*, September 19, 1942, 6.

41. "Affidavit of Mildred I. Turpin," January 8, 1943, Part 1, Series B, Box 191, Folder 2, NAACP-LC.

42. For Mildred I. Turpin in the census, see *Fifteenth Census of the United States*, ED1051, Sheet 3A.

43. For Caroline K. Johnson in the census, see *Sixteenth Census of the United States*, Carlisle, Pennsylvania, 1940, ED 2114, Sheet 6B.

44. Kelley, "Congested Terrain," 55–75.

45. "2 Girls Jailed for Flouting Jim-Crow Bus Rule," *NAYN*, January 23, 1943, 24; and "2 Jailed for Violating VA. Bus Jim Crow," *CD*, January 16, 1943, 8.

46. "Kick the Rascals Out—An Editorial," *BAA*, January 23, 1943, 6.

47. "Civil Rights Bill for D.C. Aim of Group," *WT*, May 22, 1943, 5.

48. Affidavit of Ilma Alice Jones, May 1943, Part I, Series B, Box 191, Folder 4, NAACP-LC.

49. Berrey, *Jim Crow Routine*, 104.

50. Murray, *Song in a Weary Throat*, 200.

51. Murray, 205.

52. Murray, 201.

53. Morris, *Origins of the Civil Rights Movement*, 42–43.

54. "Defy D.C. Jim Crow, H.U. Coeds Arrested," *BAA*, February 6, 1943, 16. This narrative is also recounted in Murray, *Song in a Weary Throat*, 201.

55. "Leaflet, The Civil Rights Committee of Howard University," undated, in Box 1, Folder 5, Pauli Murray Papers, Collection 75, Moorland-Spingarn Research Center, Founders Library, Howard University, Washington, D.C. (hereafter cited as PM-MSRC).

56. Murray, *Song in a Weary Throat*, 207.

57. "Howard Students Picket Jim Crow Restaurant," *CD*, April 24, 1943, 5; and "HU Students Pickets Force Restaurant to Drop Jim Crow," *WAA*, April 24, 1943, 14.

58. "Interracial Experiments in D.C. Restaurants Proves Successful," *WT*, August 7, 1943, 9.

59. "Interracial Group Continues Experiments in Restaurants," *WT*, September 11, 1943, 21.

60. "Eating in Nation's Capital These Days Is Food for Thought about Jim Crow," *CD*, October 2, 1943, 1.

61. "National Grapevine," *CD*, September 25, 1943, 15.

62. "Blames Negroes for Minnesota Segregation," *CD*, February 26, 1944, 6.

63. "New Drive for Civil Rights Bill Gets Underway," *WT*, March 1, 1941, 1.

64. Representative John E. Rankin, "Stop Nagging the South," *CR*, April 1942, Appendix, A1199.

65. "Pursuit of Democracy," *PC*, April 4, 1942, 7.

66. "Washington Scene," *BAA*, May 22, 1943, 7.

67. "NAACP Membership Nears 2,000 Mark," *WAA*, February 28, 1943, 5.

68. "Meeting Here Friday to Urge Civil Rights Law," *WT*, February 13, 1943, 2.

69. "The Civil Rights Committee," undated, Box 1, Folder 6, PM-MSRC.

70. Tomlinson Todd had also worked for the federal government as an elevator operator. For his records, see *Boyd's City Directory of the District of Columbia* (1928), 1626; and *Sixteenth Census of the United States*, ED 415, Sheet 8B.

71. "Statutes in Force in the District of Columbia," 219.

72. "D.C. Civil Rights Bill Conveniently 'Forgotten,'" *BAA*, August 14, 1943, 12. For the bill, see "Statutes in Force in the District of Columbia," U.S. House of Representatives, 42nd Cong. (Washington, D.C.: GPO, 1872).

73. "D.C. Civil Rights Bill Conveniently 'Forgotten.'"

74. Murray, *Song in a Weary Throat*, 229.

75. For Thomasina Johnson in the census, see *Fourteenth Census of the United States*, 1920, South Carolina, ED 125, Sheet 19A. For biographical information, see "Thomasina W. Johnson to Lobby for AKA Sorority," *PC*, September 12, 1942, 10.

76. "Thomasina W. Johnson to Lobby for AKA Sorority." For a scholarly account of Johnson's work, see Franklin and Collier-Thomas, "For the Race in General and Black Women in Particular."

77. See, for example, "Adopt Hospital Bill with Race Amendments," *ADW*, June 6, 1940, 1; "20,000 Child-Care Bill Opposed," *NJG*, June 26, 1943, 4; "Officials of AKA Support School Lunch Program," *ADW*, April 18, 1944, 6; "Urge Negro Women to Enlist in Waves, Spars," *CD*, November 4, 1944, 8; *The Charter of the United Nations: Hearings before the Committee on Foreign Relations of the United States Senate*, 79th Cong. (1945) (statement of Thomasina W. Johnson, National Non-Partisan Council on Affairs of the Alpha Kappa Alpha Sorority); and *Amendments to Social Security: Hearings Before the Committee on Ways and Means* 79th Cong. (1946) (statement of Thomasina W. Johnson, National Non-Partisan Council on Affairs of the Alpha Kappa Alpha Sorority).

78. "'Lady Lobbyist' Blazes Path in Nation's Capital," *CD*, June 16, 1945, 6.

79. Johnson offered this information in *The Charter of the United Nations: Hearings before the Committee on Foreign Relations of the United States Senate*, 79th Cong. (1945) (statement of Thomasina W. Johnson, National Non-Partisan Council on Affairs of the Alpha Kappa Alpha Sorority).

80. *Reorganization of the Government of the District of Columbia: Hearings before a Subcomm. of the Comm. of the District of Columbia of the U.S. Senate*, S. 1420, S. 1527, and S. J. 87, 78th Cong. (1943)(Alpha Kappa Alpha Sorority).

81. "Barbour's Fair Policy in Senate Praised by AKA's," *PC*, November 6, 1943, 7.

82. "Bilbo Becomes Mayor of D.C.," *CD*, February 12, 1944, 2.

83. "Says D.C. Is Negro's Home, but They Will Be Happier in the Country," *WT*, March 18, 1944, 6.

84. Murray, *Song in a Weary Throat*, 221–23.

85. "Pledge: 1944," Box 1, Folder 9, PM-MSRC.

86. This incident is recounted in Murray, *Song in a Weary Throat*, 222–24.

87. "Statement of Facts: Virginia Bus Incident, May 14, 1944," Box 1, Folder 11, PM-MSRC.

88. "Statement of Facts: Virginia Bus Incident, May 14, 1944"; "Jim Crow Law May be Tested in Supreme Court," *WP*, December 9, 1944, 3; and "Co-Ed's Bus Jim-Crow Case Heads for High Court," *BAA*, December 16, 1944, 1.

89. "Travel Case to Va. High Court," *CD*, March 17, 1945, 5.

90. "Cases of Jim Crow Show Barbarity of Policy," *BAA*, June 15, 1946, 11.

91. "Poll on Discrimination Shows: Both Whites, Negroes in D.C. Oppose Jim Crow on Buses," *WP*, October 15, 1944, B.

Conclusion

1. Landis, *Segregation in Washington.*

2. "National Grapevine: It's a Strange World," *CD*, January 1, 1949, 6.

3. "Three Refused Service to Test 1872 Bias Law," *WP*, March 1, 1950, B2.

4. "D.C. to Test Discrimination Law of 1873," *WP*, February 22, 1950, 1; and "14 D. C. Eateries Rule out Discrimination; Maryland U Yields," *PC*, April 22, 1950, 17; "14 Washington Restaurants Have Dropped Color Bar," *ADW*, April 21, 1950, 1.

5. "District Civil Rights," *WP*, July 16, 1951, 6. For the case, see *District of Columbia v. John R. Thompson Company, Inc., No 967*, Municipal Court of Appeals for the District of Columbia; argued February 28, 1951, and decided May 24, 1951, 81 A.2d249 (1951). For more information, see Asch and Musgrove, *Chocolate City*, 300-304.

6. "Café Segregation Case Argued before U.S. Court," *NJG*, January 19, 1952, A3.

7. For the Supreme Court case, see 346 U.S. 100 (1953); and "Brownell Hails Decision on Washington Café Segregation," *ADW*, June 11, 1953, 6.

8. "A Well Deserved Tribute for a Champion of Battle," *NJG*, October 24, 1953, 14.

9. Kate Masur, "Capital Injustice," *NYT*, March 28, 2011.

10. Ransby, *Ella Baker and the Black Freedom Movement.*

11. Biondi, *To Stand and Fight*, 221.

12. Arsenault, *Freedom Riders*, 30.

13. For more information on Wednesdays in Mississippi, see Tuuri, "'This Was the Most Meaningful Thing I've Ever Done.'"

14. Rosenberg, *Jane Crow.*

15. *Impact of Reagan Administration Proposed Medicare Cuts, Select Committee of Aging in the U.S. House of Representatives*, 98th Cong., 1st sess. (1983) (statement of Beatrice Murphy Campbell).

16. Matthew Haag, "Noose Found inside African American History Museum in Washington," *NYT*, May 31, 2017, 3A.

17. The African American Policy Forum, through its hashtag campaign #Say Her Name#, has helped publicize the plight of black women and girls who have suffered from interracial police violence and brutality; see www.aapf.org/sayhername.

18. The historian C. Vann Woodward's body of work demonstrated the circuitous process by which southern states crafted segregation laws and enacted policies of white supremacy. He argues that segregation in the 1890s was an entirely new system that was enforced through law, attitudes, and violence, but was enacted to counter the threats of biracial coalitions of black and white southerners facilitated by populism and other third-party movements. The story of black rights in Washington, D.C. demonstrates how the system of Jim Crow created a mythology, which conveniently ignored all of the legislation that mandated equality. It was fitting for activists to discover a never-overturned Reconstruction law. See Woodward, *Strange Career of Jim Crow*.

Bibliography

Primary Sources

MANUSCRIPT COLLECTIONS

Georgia
 Robert Woodruff Library, Atlanta University Center
  Irvin and Elizabeth McDuffie Papers
Massachusetts
 Sophia Smith Collection, William Allan Neilson Library, Smith College, Northampton
  Young Women's Christian Association Central Files
New York
 Hyde Park, New York
  Franklin Delano Roosevelt Presidential Library
   Eleanor Roosevelt Papers
   Franklin Delano Roosevelt Papers
 New York City, New York
  Butler Theological Library, Union Theological Seminary, Columbia University
   Records of the Woman's Convention, Auxiliary to the National Baptist Church, USA
  Schomburg Center for Research in Black Culture, New York Public Library
   Asbury United Methodist Church Records
   Ebenezer United Methodist Church Records
   Shiloh Baptist Church Records
Washington, D.C.
 Columbia Historical Society of Washington, D.C.
  Photographs Collections
   Remembering U Street Photograph Collection
 Library of Congress
  Manuscript Division
   Nannie Helen Burroughs Papers
   William Depre Houston Papers
   Mary Church Terrell Papers
   Carter G. Woodson Papers
   National Association for the Advancement of Colored People Papers, National Office, Washington, D.C., Branch
   National Association of Colored Women's Clubs Papers
   National Negro Congress Papers
 Martin Luther King Jr. Library, Washingtoniana Division
  Washington Star Photography Collection

Vertical file on the National Zoo
Vertical file on the Phyllis Wheatley YWCA
Moorland-Spingarn, Founders Library, Howard University
　The Bison, 1920–45
　Howard University Alumni Directory, 1867–2005
　Manuscript Division
　　Myra Colson Callis Papers
　　Jeannette Carter Papers
　　Angelina Weld Grimké Papers
　　Archibald Grimké Papers
　　Charles Hamilton Houston Papers
　　Kelly Miller Papers
　　Pauli Murray Papers
　　Lucy Diggs Slowe Papers
　　Myra L. Spaulding Papers
　　Mary Church Terrell Papers
　　Carter G. Woodson Papers
　　National Association for the Advancement of Colored People, Washington, D.C.,
　　　Branch Papers
National Archives
　Government of the District of Columbia, Record Group 351
　　Correspondence of the Board of Commissioners, 1920–45
　　Records of Arrests, 1920–25
　　Records of the Metropolitan Police, 1920–45
Smithsonian Anacostia Community Museum
　New Negro Opinion Newspaper Collection

MAPS

Sanborn Fire Insurance Maps, 1867–1970
　Washington, D.C., 1927–28

NEWSPAPERS

Atlanta Journal and Guide
Baltimore Afro-American
Chicago Defender
Cleveland Gazette
New Negro Opinion
Norfolk Journal and Guide
Pittsburgh Courier
Washington Afro American
Washington Bee
Washington Post
Washington Star
Washington Tribune

OTHER PERIODICALS
Crisis
National Notes
Negro Yearbook
Opportunity

PUBLISHED GOVERNMENT DOCUMENTS
Census
Tenth Census of the United States. Washington, D.C.: Government Printing Office, 1880.
Eleventh Census of the United States. Washington, D.C.: Government Printing Office, 1890.
Twelfth Census of the United States. Washington, D.C.: Government Printing Office, 1900.
Thirteenth Census of the United States. Washington, D.C.: Government Printing Office, 1910.
Fourteenth Census of the United States. Washington, D.C.: Government Printing Office, 1920.
Fifteenth Census of the United States. Washington, D.C.: Government Printing Office, 1930.
Sixteenth Census of the United States. Washington, D.C.: Government Printing Office, 1940.

Congressional Documents
Congressional Record, 1920–45
Riot at East St. Louis, Illinois: Hearings before the Comm. on Rules, H.J.R. 118, 65th Cong. (1917).
High Cost of Living in the District of Columbia: Hearings before a Subcomm. on the District of Columbia on S.R. 150, 65th Cong. S (1919).
Public School System of the District of Columbia: Hearings before the Select Comm. of the United States Senate, 66th Cong. 2nd sess., pursuant to S.R. 310: Raising a Select Committee of Five Senators to Investigate the Public School System of the District of Columbia, 66th Cong. (1920).
Representation of the District of Columbia in Congress and the Electoral College: Hearings before the Comm. on the Judiciary in the House of Representatives, 66th Cong. (1921).
Repression of Prostitution in the District of Columbia, 67th Congress (1921).
Monument or Memorial Building to the Memory of Negro Soldiers and Sailors: Hearings before the Comm. on the Library Congress of the United States, 68th Cong. (1924).
To Prevent and Punish the Crime of Lynching: Hearing before a Subcomm. of the Comm. of the Judiciary of the United States Senate on S.B. 121, 69th Cong. (1926).
National Representation and Suffrage for Residents of the District of Columbia: Hearings before the Comm. on the Judiciary of the House of Representatives, 70th Cong. (1928).
Public Buildings and Grounds No. 3: Hearings before the Comm. on Public Buildings and Grounds House of Representatives, 70th Cong. (1928).
Reduced Car Fares for School Children: Hearings before the Comm. of the District of Columbia. United States Senate, 71st Cong., pursuant to H.R. 12571: A Bill to Provide for the Transportation of School Children in the District of Columbia at a Reduced Rate of Fare (1930).

Economic Security Act: Hearings Before the Committee of Ways and Means, House of
Representatives, 74th Cong. (1935).

*American Youth Act: Hearings before a Subcommittee on Education and Labor in the United
States Senate*, 75th Cong. (1938).

*National Representation and Suffrage for Residents of the District of Columbia: Hearings
before the Comm. on the Judiciary of the House of Representatives*, 75th Cong. (1938).

*Confidential Investigation of the Metropolitan Police Department: Hearings before the Special
Investigation Subcomm. of the Committee of the District of Columbia, House of
Representatives*, 77th Cong. (1941).

Other Government Documents

*Proceedings of the Women's Industrial Conference Called by the Women's Bureau of the United
States Department of Labor, Washington, D.C., January 11, 12, and 13, 1923*. Washington,
D.C.: GPO, 1923.

Religious Bodies: 1926. Vols. 1 and 2. Washington, D.C.: GPO, 1926.

Report of the Commissioners of the District of Columbia. Years 1920–45. Washington, D.C.:
GPO.

ARTICLES, BOOKS, NEWSPAPERS, SPEECHES, AND PERIODICALS

Callis, Myra Colson and Lorenzo J. Greene. *The Employment of Negroes in the District of
Columbia*. Washington, D.C.: Association for the Study of Negro Life and History, Inc.,
1931.

Cooper, Anna Julia. *A Voice from the South*. Xenia, Ohio: Aldine Printing House, 1892.

"Covenant Prohibiting Sale of Property to Negro is Constitutional." *Virginia Law Review* 11
(November 1924): 68–69.

Davis, J. Arthur. *"The Missing Link" and the Howard Theatre*. Washington, D.C.: Murray
Brothers Press, 1911.

Du Bois, W. E. B. *Efforts for Social Betterment among Negro Americans*. Atlanta University
Publications, no. 14. Atlanta, Ga.: Atlanta University Press, 1909.

Ellington, Duke. *Music Is My Mistress*. Garden City, N.Y.: Doubleday, 1973.

Grimké, Angelina Weld. *Rachel: A Play in Three Acts*. Boston, Mass.: Cornhill Company,
1920.

Grimké, Archibald H. "The Sex Question and Race Segregation." *Occasional Papers nos. 18
and 19*. Washington, D.C.: American Negro Academy, 1916.

Greene, Lorenzo J. *Working with Carter G. Woodson, the Father of Black History: A Diary,
1928–1930*, edited by Arvarh E. Strickland. Baton Rouge: Louisiana State University
Press, 1989.

Haynes, Elizabeth Ross. "Negroes in Domestic Service in the United States: Introduction."
Journal of Negro History 8, no. 4 (1923): 424–25.

———. "Two Million Negro Women at Work." *Southern Workman* 15 (February 1922):
64–66.

Haynes, George Edmond. *Negro Newcomers in Detroit: The Negro in Washington*. Reprint
ed. New York: Arno Press, 1969.

History of the Helping Hand Club of the Nineteenth Street Baptist Church. Washington, D.C.:
Associated Publishers, 1948.

Hull, Gloria T., ed. *Give Us Each Day: The Diary of Alice Dunbar-Nelson*. New York: W. W. Norton, 1984.

Johnson, James Weldon. *Along this Way: The Autobiography of James Weldon Johnson*. New York: Viking Press, 1933.

Jones, William H. *The Housing of Negroes in Washington, D.C.: A Study in Human Ecology*. Washington, D.C.: Howard University Press, 1929.

———. *Recreation and Amusement among Negroes in Washington, D.C.: A Sociological Analysis of the Negro in an Urban Environment*. Washington, D.C.: Howard University Press, 1927.

Kuhn, Clifford M., E. West, and Harlon Joye, eds. *Living Atlanta: An Oral History of the City, 1914–1948*. Athens: University of Georgia Press, 1990.

Landis, Kenesaw. *Segregation in Washington: A Report of the National Committee on Segregation in the Nation's Capital*. Chicago, Ill.: National Committee on Segregation in the Nation's Capital, 1948.

Lerner, Gerda, ed. *Black Women in White America: A Documentary History*. New York: Random House, 1972.

Logan, Rayford W. "Growing up in Washington: A Lucky Generation." *Records of the Columbia Historical Society of Washington, D.C.* 50 (1980): 500–507.

Lutz, Tom, and Susanna Ashton, eds. *These "Colored United States": African American Essays from the 1920s*. New Brunswick, N.J.: Rutgers University Press, 1996.

Miller, Kelly. "Separate Communities for Negroes: The Causes of Segregation." *Current History* 25, no. 6 (March 1927): 827–31.

Murray, Pauli. *Song in a Weary Throat: An American Pilgrimage*. New York: Harper and Row, 1987.

Pickens, William. *Nannie Burroughs and the School of the Three Bs*. New York: William Pickens, 1921.

Perkins, Kathy A., and Judith Louise Stephens, eds. *Strange Fruit: Plays on Lynching by American Women*. Bloomington: Indiana University Press, 1998.

Report of the Conference on the Betterment of Race Relations in the District of Columbia. Washington, D.C.: Washington Federation of Churches, 1935.

Robinson, Joanne Gibson. *The Montgomery Bus Boycott and the Women Who Started It: The Memoir of JoAnne Gibson Robinson*. Knoxville: University of Tennessee Press, 1987.

Scott, Emmett J. *Negro Migration during the War*. New York: Oxford University Press, 1920.

Seder, L. "Property Covenants in Deed and Contracts Not to Sell to Negroes." *Boston University Law Review* 5 (June 1925): 213–15.

Sellow, Gladys. *A Deviant Social Situation: A Court*. Washington, D.C.: Catholic University of America Press, 1938.

Severson, William H. *History of Felix Lodge, No. 3 F.A.A.M. or Freemasonry in the District of Columbia from 1825 to 1908*. Washington, D.C.: H. L. Pendleton, 1908.

Shannon, A. H. *The Negro in Washington: A Study in Race Amalgamation*. New York: Walter Neale, 1930.

Terrell, Mary Church. *A Colored Woman in a White World*. Washington, D.C.: National Association of Colored Women's Clubs, 1968.

Weller, Charles F. *Neglected Neighbors: Stories of Life in the Alleys, Tenements, and Shanties of the National Capital*. Philadelphia, Pa.: J. C. Winston, 1909.

CATALOGS, GUIDES, AND DIRECTORIES

N. W. Ayer and Son's American Newspaper Annual and Directory. Philadelphia, Pa.: N. W.
Ayer and Sons, 1919–29.

Boyd's City Directory of Washington, D.C. Washington, D.C.: R. L. Polk, 1920–45.

Directory of the Public Schools in the District of Columbia. Washington: D. C.: L. G. Kelly
Printing Company, 1916.

Directory of Recreational Facilities for Negroes in the District of Columbia. Washington, D.C.:
Community Center and Playgrounds Department, n.d.

Hillyer, Andrew F. *The Twentieth Century Union League Directory: A Compilation of the
Efforts of the Colored People of Washington for Social Betterment.* Washington,
D.C.,:N.p. 1901.

*Progressive Negro Washington: A Souvenir Album of Some of the Beautiful Negro Churches,
Halls, and Public School Buildings.* Washington, D.C.: R. L. Pendleton, 1909.

*Sherman's Directory and Ready Reference of the Colored Population in the District of Columbia
1913.* Washington, D.C.: Sherman Directory Company, 1913.

Simms, James N. *Simm's Blue Book and National Negro Business and Professional Directory.*
Chicago, Ill.: James N. Simms Publisher, 1922.

Secondary Sources

Abbott, Carl. *Political Terrain: Washington, D.C. from Tidewater Town to Global Metropolis.*
Chapel Hill: University of North Carolina Press, 1999.

Abernathy, Lloyd M. "The Washington Race War of July, 1919." *Maryland Historical
Magazine* 58, no. 4 (1963): 309–24.

Anderson, Carol. *Eyes off the Prize: The United Nations and the African American Struggle
for Human Rights, 1944–1955.* New York: Cambridge University Press, 2003.

Anderson, Karen. "Brickbats and Roses: Lucy Diggs Slowe, 1883–1937." In *Lone Voyagers:
Academic Women in Coeducational Institutions, 1870–1937,* edited by G. Clifford, 283–307.
New York: Feminist Press, 1989.

Aptheker, Bettina. *Woman's Legacy: Essays on Race, Sex, and Class.* Amherst: University of
Massachusetts Press, 1982.

Aron, Cindy Sondik. *Ladies and Gentlemen of the Civil Service: Middle Class Workers in
Victorian America.* New York: Oxford University Press, 1987.

Arsenault, Raymond. *Freedom Riders: 1961 and the Struggle for Racial Justice.* New York:
Oxford University Press, 2007.

———. *The Sound of Freedom: Marian Anderson, the Lincoln Memorial, and the Concert
that Awakened America.* New York: Bloomsbury Press, 2009.

Asch, Chris Meyers, and George Derek Musgrove. *Chocolate City: A History of Race and
Democracy in the Nation's Capital.* Chapel Hill: University of North Carolina Press,
2017.

Ayala, Adriana. "Negotiating Race Relations through Women's Activism: Women
Activists and Women's Organizations in San Antonio, Texas during the 1920s." PhD
diss., University of Texas at Austin, 2005.

Baldwin, Davarian L. *Chicago's New Negroes: Modernity, the Great Migration, and Black
Urban Life.* Chapel Hill: University of North Carolina Press, 2007.

Barber, Lucy Grace. *Marching on Washington: The Forging of an American Political Tradition*. Berkeley: University of California Press, 2002.

Barkley Brown, Elsa. "Negotiating and Transforming the Public Sphere: African American Political Life in the Transition from Slavery to Freedom." *Public Culture* 7, no. 1 (1994): 107–46.

———. "What Has Happened Here: The Politics of Difference in Women's History and Feminist Politics." *Feminist Studies* 18, no. 2 (1992): 295–312.

———. "Womanist Consciousness: Maggie Lena Walker and the Independent Order of Saint Luke." *Signs* 14, no. 3 (1989): 610–33.

Barkley Brown, Elsa, and Gregg D. Kimball. "Mapping the Terrain of Black Richmond." *Journal of Urban History* 21 (March 1995): 296–346.

Barnett, Evelyn Brooks. "Nannie Burroughs and the Education of Black Women." In *The Afro-American Woman: Struggles and Images*, edited by Sharon Harley and Rosalyn Terborg-Penn, 100–102. Port Washington, N.Y.: Kennikat Press, 1978.

Bates, Beth Tompkins. *Pullman Porters and the Rise of Black Protest Politics in Black America, 1925–1945*. Chapel Hill: University of North Carolina Press, 2001.

Bell-Scott, Patricia. "To Keep My Self-Respect: Dean Lucy Diggs Slowe's 1927 Memorandum on the Sexual Harassment of Black Women." *NWSA Journal* 9, no. 2 (1997): 70–76.

Bell-Smith, Patricia. *The Firebrand and the First Lady: Portrait of a Friendship; Pauli Murray, Eleanor Roosevelt, and the Struggle for Social Justice*. New York: Vintage Books, 2017.

Bender, Thomas. "Wholes and Parts: The Need for Synthesis in American History." *Journal of American History* 73, no. 1 (June 1986): 120–36.

Bergeson-Lockwood, Millington. *Race Over Party: Black Politics and Partisanship in Late Nineteenth-Century Boston*. Chapel Hill: University of North Carolina Press, 2018.

Berrey, Stephen A. *The Jim Crow Routine: Everyday Performances of Race, Civil Rights, and Segregation in Mississippi*. Chapel Hill: University of North Carolina Press, 2015.

Biondi, Martha. *To Stand and Fight: The Struggle for Civil Rights in Postwar New York City*. Cambridge, Mass.: Harvard University Press, 2003.

Blain, Keisha. *Set the World on Fire: Black Nationalist Women and the Global Struggle for Freedom*. Philadelphia: University of Pennsylvania Press, 2018.

Blair, Barbara. "True Women, Real Men: Gender, Ideology, and Social Roles in the Garvey Movement." In *Gendered Domains: Rethinking Public and Private in Women's History*, edited by Dorothy O. Helly and Susan Reverby, 154–66. Ithaca, N.Y.: Cornell University Women's Press, 1992.

Blair, John L. "A Time for Parting: The Negro during the Coolidge Years." *Journal of American Studies* 3, no. 2 (1969): 177–99.

Blee, Kathleen M. *Women of the Klan: Racism and Gender in the 1920s*. Berkeley: University of California Press, 1991.

Blight, David W. *American Oracle: The Civil War in the Civil Rights Era*. Cambridge, Mass.: Harvard University Press, 2011.

———. *Race and Reunion: The Civil War in American Memory*. Cambridge, Mass.: Harvard University Press, 2001.

Blumenthal, Henry. "Woodrow Wilson and the Race Question." *Journal of Negro History* 48 (1963): 1–21.

Borchert, James. *Alley Life in Washington: Family, Community, Religion, and Folklore in the City, 1850–1970*. Urbana: University of Illinois Press, 1980.

———. "Urban Neighborhood and Community: Informal Group Life, 1850–1970." *Journal of Interdisciplinary History* 11, no. 4 (1981): 607–31.

———. "Washington, D.C." In *Encyclopedia of the Great Black Migration*, edited by Steven A. Reich, 880–95. Westport, Conn.: Greenwood Press, 2006.

Borchert, James, and Susan Danziger Borchert. "Migrant Responses to the City: The Neighborhood, Case Studies in Black and White, 1870–1940." *Slovakia* 31 (1984): 8–45.

Bowling, Kimberly Crandall, and Kriste Lindenmeyer. "How Did a Multiracial Movement Develop in the Baltimore YWCA, 1883–1926?" 2003, in Kathryn Kish Sklar and Thomas Dublin, eds. *Women and Social Movements in the United States 1600–2000*. Accessed through the Library of Congress, http://womhist.alexanderstreet.com/bywca/intro.htm.

Boyle, Kevin. *Arc of Justice: A Saga of Race, Civil Rights, and Murder in the Jazz Age*. New York: Henry Holt, 2004.

Bracks, Lean'tin L. and Jessie Carney Smith, eds. *Black Women of the Harlem Renaissance*. Lanham Md.:, Rowman & Littlefield, 2014.

Bradbury, William C., Jr. "Racial Discrimination in the Federal Service: A Study in the Sociology of Administration." PhD diss., Columbia University, 1952.

Breen, William J. "Black Women and the Great War: Mobilization and Reform in the South." *Journal of Southern History* 44 (1978): 421–40.

Brown, Bernard B. "Civil Rights in the District of Columbia." MS thesis, Howard University, 1940.

Brown, Flora Bryant. "NAACP Sponsored Sit-Ins by Howard University Students in Washington, D.C., 1943–1944." *Journal of Negro History* 85, no. 4 (Autumn 2000): 274–86.

Brown, Letitia Woods, and Elsie M. Lewis. *Washington in the New Era: 1870–1970*. Washington, D.C.: National Portrait Gallery, 1972.

Brown, Mary Jane. *Eradicating this Evil: Women in the American Anti-Lynching Movement, 1892–1940*. New York: Routledge, 2000.

Brown, Nikki. *Private Politics and Public Voices: Black Women's Activism from World War I to the New Deal*. Bloomington: Indiana University Press, 2007.

Brown, Tamara Lizette. "Lingering Lights from America's Black Broadway: Negro Renaissance to the Black Arts Movement, African American Concert-Theatrical Dance in Washington, D.C." PhD diss., Howard University, 2004.

Brown, Tullia Kay. "The National Association of Colored Women, 1896–1920." PhD diss., Emory University, 1978.

Browne, Dorothy M. *Setting a Course: American Women in the 1920s*. Boston, Mass.: Twayne Publishers, 1987.

Bruce, Dickson D., Jr. *Archibald Grimké: Portrait of a Black Independent*. Baton Rouge: Louisiana State University Press, 1993.

Brundage, W. Fitzhugh, ed. *The Southern Past: A Clash of Race and Memory*. Cambridge, Mass.: Harvard University Press, 2005.

———. *Where these Memories Grow: History, Memory, and Southern Identity*. Chapel Hill: University of North Carolina Press, 2000.

Bryand, Karl John. "Changing Race, Changing Place: Racial, Occupational, and Residential Patterns in Shaw, Washington, D.C., 1880–1920." PhD diss., University of Maryland, 1999.

Bryant, Flora J. "NAACP Sponsored Sit-Ins by Howard Students in Washington, D.C., 1943–1944." *Journal of Negro History* 85, no. 4 (Autumn 2000): 274–86.

Burkhalter, Nancy. "Women's Magazines and the Suffrage Movement: Did They Help or Hinder the Cause?" *Journal of American Popular Culture* 19, no. 2 (Summer 1996): 13–24.

Cahn, Susan K. *Sexual Reckonings: Southern Girls in a Troubling Age*. Cambridge, Mass.: Harvard University Press, 2012.

Camp, Stephanie M. H. *Closer to Freedom: Enslaved Women and Everyday Resistance in the Plantation South*. Chapel Hill: University of North Carolina Press, 2004.

Carby, Hazel V. "Policing the Black Woman's Body in an Urban Context." *Critical Inquiry* 19, no. 4 (1992): 738–55.

———. *Reconstructing Womanhood: The Emergence of the Afro-American Woman Novelist*. New York: Oxford University Press, 1987.

Carter, Patricia. "Becoming the 'New Women:' The Equal Rights Campaign of New York City Schoolteachers, 1900–1920." In *The Teacher's Voice: A Social History of Teaching in Twentieth-Century America*, edited by Richard J. Altenbaugh, 40–58. Washington, D.C.: Falmer Press, 1992.

Cary, Francine C., ed. *Washington Odyssey: A Multicultural History of the Nation's Capital*. Washington, D.C.: Smithsonian Books, 1996.

Catsam, Derek Charles. "Early Economic Civil Rights in Washington, D.C.: The New Negro Alliance, Howard University, and the Interracial Workshop." In *The Economic Civil Rights Movement: African Americans and the Struggle for Economic Power*, edited by Michael Ezra, 46–56. New York: Routledge, 2009.

Chabot, Sean. *Transnational Roots of the Civil Rights Movement: African American Explorations of the Gandhian Repertoire*. Lanham, Md.: Lexington Books, 2012.

Charron, Katherine Mellen. *Freedom's Teacher: The Life of Septima Clark*. Chapel Hill: University of North Carolina Press, 2012.

Chatauevert, M. Melinda. *Marching Together: Women of the Brotherhood of Sleeping Car Porters*. Urbana: University of Illinois Press, 1998.

———. "The Third Step: Anna Julia Cooper and Black Education in the District of Columbia, 1910–1960." *Sage* (1988): 7–13.

Chatelain, Marcia. "'The Problem Peculiar to Girls': Black Sorority Women, Vocational Guidance, and Professional Identity in Chicago, 1927–1940." *Journal of Illinois History* 14, no. 3 (Autumn 2011): 185–206.

———. *South Side Girls: Growing Up in the Great Migration*. Durham, N.C.: Duke University Press, 2015.

Cherkasky, Mara. "'For Sale to Colored': Racial Change on S Street, NW." *Washington History* 8, no. 2 (1996–97): 40–57.

———. "Slices of the Pie: Black and White Dupont Circle from the 1920s to the 1950s." MA thesis, George Washington University, 1985.

Clark, Nina Honemond. *History of the Nineteenth Century Black Churches in Maryland and Washington, D.C.* New York: Vantage Press, 1983.

Clark-Lewis, Elizabeth. *Living in, Living Out: African American Domestics in Washington, D.C., 1910–1940.* Washington, D.C.: Smithsonian Institution Press, 1994.

Clark-Lewis, Elizabeth, and Stanley Nelson. *Freedom Bags.* New York: Filmmakers Library, 1990.

Cohen, Robert. *When the Old Left Was Young: Student Radicals and America's First Mass Student Movement, 1929–1941.* New York: Oxford University Press, 1993.

Collier-Thomas, Bettye. *Jesus, Jobs, and Justice: African American Women and Religion.* New York: Alfred A. Knopf Press, 2010.

Corrigan, Mary Elizabeth. "A Social Union of Heart and Effort" The African-American Family in the District of Columbia on the Eve of Emancipation." PhD diss., University of Maryland, 1996.

Cott, Nancy F. "Feminist Politics in the 1920s: The National Woman's Party." *Journal of American History* 71, no. 1 (1984): 43–68.

———. *The Grounding of Modern Feminism.* New Haven, Conn.: Yale University Press, 1987.

Countryman, Matthew. *Up South: Civil Rights and Black Power in Philadelphia.* Philadelphia: University of Pennsylvania Press, 2006.

Crawford, Vicki L, Jacqueline Anne Woods, and Barbara Woods, eds. *Women in the Civil Rights Movement: Trailblazers and Torchbearers, 1941–1965.* Bloomington: Indiana University Press, 1993.

Cumberbatch, Prudence. "What 'the Cause' Needs is a 'Brainy and Energetic Woman': A Study of Female Charismatic Leadership in Baltimore." In *Want to Start a Revolution?: Radical Women in the Black Freedom Struggle,* edited by Dayo F. Gore, Jeanne Theoharris, and Komozi Woodard, 47–71. New York: New York University Press, 2009.

Dabney, Lillian G. "The History of Schools for Negroes in the District of Columbia, 1807–1947." PhD diss., Catholic University, 1949.

Dagbovie, Pero Daglo. "Black Women, Carter G. Woodson, and the Association for the Study of African American Life and History, 1915–1950." *Journal of African American History* 88 (Winter 2003): 21–41.

Dailey, Jane. *Before Jim Crow: The Politics of Race in Postemancipation Virginia.* Chapel Hill: University of North Carolina Press, 2000.

Dailey, Jane, Glenda Elizabeth Gilmore, and Bryant Simon, eds. *Jumpin' Jim Crow: Southern Politics from the Civil War to the Civil Rights Movement.* Princeton, N.J.: Princeton University Press, 2000.

Dailey, Maceo Crenshaw, Jr. "Calvin Coolidge's Afro-American Connection." *Contributions in Black Studies* 8 (1986–87): 77–100.

Davis, Elizabeth Lindsay. *Lifting as They Climb.* Reprint ed. New York: G. K. Hall, 1996.

Davis, John, and Cornelius L. Golightly, "Negro Employment in the Federal Government." *Phylon* 6 (1945): 337–47.

Day, David S. "Herbert Hoover and Racial Politics: The De Priest Incident." *Journal of Negro History* 65, no. 1 (1980): 6–17.

Des Jardins, Julie. *Women and the Historical Enterprise in America: Gender, Race, and the Politics of Memory, 1880–1945.* Chapel Hill: University of North Carolina Press, 2003.

Dill, Bonnie Thornton. "The Means to Put My Children Through: Childrearing Goals and Strategies among Black Female Domestic Servants." In *The Black Woman,* edited by Cheryl Townsend Gilkes, 678–99. Beverly Hills, Calif.: Sage, 1980.

Douglas, Davison M. *Jim Crow Moves North: The Battles over Northern School Integration.* New York: Cambridge University Press, 2005.

Dudziak, Mary L. *Cold War Civil Rights: Race and the Image of American Democracy.* Princeton, N.J.: Princeton University Press, 2000.

Edwards, G. Franklin. *The Negro Professional Class.* Glencoe, Ill.: Free Press, 1959.

Ervin, Keona K. *Gateway to Equality: Black Women and the Struggle for Economic Justice in St. Louis.* Lexington: University of Kentucky Press, 2017.

Fabre, Genevieve. "African-American Commemorative Celebrations in the Nineteenth Century." In *History and Memory in African American Culture,* edited by Genevieve Fabre and Robert O'Meally, 72–91. New York: Oxford University Press, 1994.

Fairclough, Adam. *A Class of Their Own: Black Teachers in the Segregated South.* Cambridge, Mass.: Harvard University Press, 2007.

Fearing, Jeffery John. "African-American Image, History, and Identity in Twentieth-Century Washington, D.C. as Chronicled through the Art and Social Realism Photography of Addison N. Scurlock and the Scurlock Studios 1904–1994." PhD diss., Howard University, 2005.

Feimster, Crystal M. *Southern Horrors: Women and the Politics of Rape and Lynching.* Cambridge, Mass.: Harvard University Press, 2009.

Feldstein, Ruth. *How It Feels to Be Free: Black Women Entertainers and the Civil Rights Movement.* New York: Oxford University Press, 2017.

Felix, Stephanie Yvette. "Committed to their Own: African American Women Leaders in the YWCA: The YWCA of Germantown, Philadelphia, Pennsylvania, 1870–1970." PhD diss., Temple University, 1999.

Felzenberg, Alvin S. "Calvin Coolidge and Race: His Record in Dealing with the Racial Tensions of the 1920s." *New England Journal of History* 55, no. 1 (1998): 83–96.

Ferguson, Karen. *Black Politics in New Deal Atlanta.* Chapel Hill: University of North Carolina Press, 2002.

Ferry, Henry Justin. "Francis James Grimké: Portrait of a Black Puritan." PhD diss., Yale University, 1970.

Fine, Lisa M. *The Souls of the Skyscraper: Female Clerical Workers in Chicago, 1870–1930.* Philadelphia, Pa.: Temple University Press, 1990.

Finnegan, Terence. "Lynching and Political Power in Mississippi and South Carolina." In *Under Sentence of Death: Lynching in the South,* edited by W. Fitzhugh Brundage, 189–218. Chapel Hill: University of North Carolina Press, 1997.

Fitzpatrick, Michael Andrew. "Shaw, Washington's Premier Black Neighborhood: An Examination of the Origins and Development of a Black Business Movement, 1880–1920." MA thesis, University of Virginia, 1989.

Ford, Tanisha C. *Black Women, Style, and the Global Politics of Soul.* Chapel Hill: University of North Carolina Press, 2015.

Fouche, Rayvon. *Black Inventors in the Age of Segregation: Granvile T. Woods, Lewis H. Latimer and Shelby J. Davidson.* Baltimore, Md.: Johns Hopkins University Press, 2003.

Fowler, Andrew. "A Study of the Social Welfare Work of the Shiloh Baptist Church in 1939." BD thesis, Howard University, 1940.

Franklin, John Hope. "'Birth of a Nation': Propaganda as History." *Massachusetts Review* 20, no. 3 (Autumn 1979): 417–34.

Franklin, V. P., and Bettye Collier-Thomas, "For the Race in General and Black Women in Particular: The Civil Rights Activities of African American Women's Organizations, 1915–1950." In *Sisters in the Struggle: African American Women in the Civil Rights-Black Power Movements*, edited by V. P. Franklin and Bettye Collier-Thomas, 21–41. New York: New York University Press, 2001.

Freedman, Estelle B. "The New Woman: Changing Views of Women in the 1920s." *Journal of American History* 62, no. 2 (1974): 372–93.

Fryd, Vivien Green. *Art and Empire: The Politics of Ethnicity in the United States Capitol, 1815–1860.* New Haven, Conn.: Yale University Press, 1992.

Gaines, Kevin. *Uplifting the Race: Black Leadership, Politics, and Culture in the Twentieth Century.* Chapel Hill: University of North Carolina Press, 1996.

Gallagher, Julie. *Black Women and Politics in New York City.* Urbana: University of Illinois Press, 2012.

Gates, Henry Louis. "The Trope of the New Negro and the Image of the Black." *Representations* 24 (Fall 1998): 129–55.

Gatewood, William B. *Aristocrats of Color: The Black Elite, 1880–1920.* Bloomington: Indiana University Press, 1990.

———. "'The Remarkable Misses Rollin': Black Women in Reconstruction South Carolina." *South Carolina Historical Magazine* 92, no. 3 (July 1991): 172–88.

Gellman, Erik S. *Death Blow to Jim Crow: The National Negro Congress and the Rise of Militant Civil Rights.* Chapel Hill: University of North Carolina Press, 2012.

Gerstle, Gary. *Working-Class Americanism: The Politics of Labor in a Textile City, 1914–1960.* New York: Cambridge University Press, 1989.

Gill, Tiffany M. *Beauty Shop Politics: African American Women's Activism in the Beauty Industry.* Chicago: University of Illinois Press, 2010.

Gillette, Howard, Jr. *Between Justice and Beauty: Race, Planning, and the Failure of Urban Policy in Washington, D.C.* Baltimore, Md.: Johns Hopkins University Press, 1995.

Gilmore, Glenda. *Defying Dixie: The Radical Roots of Civil Rights.* New York: W. W. Norton, 2008.

———. "False Friends and Avowed Enemies: Southern African Americans and Party Allegiances in the 1920s." In *Jumpin' Jim Crow: Southern Politics from Civil War to Civil Rights*, edited by Jane Dailey, Glenda Elizabeth Gilmore, and Bryant Simon, 219–38. Princeton, N.J.: Princeton University Press, 2000.

———. *Gender and Jim Crow: Women and the Politics of White Supremacy in North Carolina, 1896–1920.* Chapel Hill: University of North Carolina Press, 1996.

Glenn, Evelyn Nakano. "From Servitude to Service Work: Historical Continuities in the Racial Division of Paid Reproductive Labor." *Signs* 18, no. 1 (1992): 1–43.

Glymph, Thavolia. "'Liberty Dearly Bought': The Making of Civil War Memory in Afro-American Communities in the South." In *Time Longer than Rope: A Century of*

African American Activism, 1850–1950, edited by Charles M. Payne and Adam Green, 111–39. New York: New York University Press, 2003.

————. *Out of the House of Bondage: The Transformation of the Plantation Household*. New York: Cambridge University Press, 2008.

Goggin, Jacqueline. *Carter G. Woodson: A Life in Black History*. Baton Rouge: Louisiana State University Press, 1993.

Goings, Kenneth W. "*The NAACP Comes of Age*": *The Defeat of Judge John J. Parker*. Bloomington: Indiana University Press, 1990.

Gomery, Douglas. "A Movie-Going Capital: Washington, D.C. in the History of Movie Presentation." *Washington History* 9, no. 1 (1997): 5–23.

Gonda, Jeffrey. *Home Front: The Restrictive Covenant Cases and the Making of the Civil Rights Movement*. Chapel Hill: University of North Carolina Press, 2015.

Grant, Donald L. *The Way It Was: The Black Experience in Georgia*. Athens: University of Georgia Press, 2001.

Green, Adam. *Selling the Race: Culture, Community, and Black Chicago, 1940–1955*. Chicago, Ill.: University of Chicago Press, 2007.

Green, Constance McLaughlin. *The Secret City: A History of Race Relations in the Nation's Capital*. Princeton, N.J.: Princeton University Press, 1967.

Greene, Christina. *Our Separate Ways: Women and the Black Freedom Movement in Durham, North Carolina*. Chapel Hill: University of North Carolina Press, 2005.

Gregory, James N. *The Southern Diaspora: How the Great Migrations of Black and White Southerners Transformed America*. Chapel Hill: University of North Carolina Press, 2005.

Gritter, Elizabeth. *River of Hope: Black Politics and the Memphis Freedom Movement, 1865–1954*. Lexington: University Press of Kentucky, 2014.

Gross, Kali N. *Colored Amazons: Crime, Violence, and Black Women in the City of Brotherly Love, 1880–1910*. Durham, N.C.: Duke University Press, 2006.

Hale, Grace Elizabeth. *Making Whiteness: The Culture of Segregation in the South, 1890–1940*. New York: Pantheon Books, 1998.

Haley, Sarah. *No Mercy Here: Gender, Punishment, and the Making of Jim Crow Modernity*. Chapel Hill: University of North Carolina Press, 2016.

Hall, Jacquelyn Dowd. "The Long Civil Rights Movement and the Political Uses of the Past." *Journal of American History* 91, no. 4 (March 2005): 1233–63.

————. *Revolt Against Chivalry: Jessie Daniel Ames and the Women's Campaign Against Lynching*. New York: Columbia University Press, 1993.

Harley, Sharon. "Beyond the Classroom: The Organizational Lives of Black Female Educators in the District of Columbia, 1890–1930." *Journal of Negro Education* 51, no. 3 (1982): 254–65.

————. "The Black Goddess of Liberty: Nannie Helen Burroughs." *Journal of Negro History* 81 (1996): 62–71.

————."Black Women in the District of Columbia, 1880–1920: Their Economic, Social, and Institutional Activities." PhD diss., Howard University, 1981.

————. "Black Women in a Southern City: Washington, D.C., 1890–1920." In *Sex, Race, and the Role of Women in the South*, edited by Joanne V. Hawks and Sheila L. Skemp, 59–74. Jackson: University of Mississippi Press, 1983.

———. "For the Good of Family and Race: Gender, Work, and Domestic Roles in the Black Community, 1880–1930." *Signs* 15, no. 2 (1990): 336–49.

———. "Race Women: Cultural Productions and Radical Labor Politics." In *Women's Labor in the Global Economy*, edited by Sharon Harley, 9–27. New Brunswick: Rutgers University Press, 2007.

———. "When Your Work Is Not Who You Are: The Development of a Working-Class Consciousness among Afro-American Women." In *Gender, Class, Race, and Reform in the Progressive Era*, edited by Noralee Frankel and Nancy S. Dye, 42–55. Lexington: University Press of Kentucky, 1991.

Harper, Glenn T. "'Cotton Tom' Heflin and the Election of 1930: The Price of Party Disloyalty." *Historian* 30, no. 3 (May 1968): 389–411.

Harris, Frederic C. "Rock in a Weary Land: Religious Institutions and African-American Political Activism." In *Something Within: African American Religion and Political Activism*, 86–120. New York: Oxford University Press, 1999.

Harris, LaShawn D. *Sex Workers, Psychics, and Numbers Runners: Black Women in New York City's Underground Economy*. Urbana: University of Illinois Press, 2016.

Hayes, Lawrence H. W. "The Negro Federal Government Worker: A Study of His Classification Status in the District of Columbia, 1883–1938." MA thesis, Howard University, 1941.

Headley, Robert K. *Motion Picture Exhibition in Washington, D.C.: An Illustrated History of Parlors, Palaces, and Multiplexes in the Metropolitan Area, 1894–1997*. Jefferson, N.C.: McFarland and Company, 1999.

Hedstrom, Margaret L. "Beyond Feminisation: Clerical Workers in the United States from the 1920s through the 1960s." In *The White-Blouse Revolution: Female Office Workers since 1870*, edited by Gregory Anderson, 145–69. Manchester: Manchester University Press, 1989.

Hendricks, Wanda. *Gender, Race, and Politics: Black Clubwomen in Illinois*. Bloomington: Indiana University Press, 1998.

Hicks, Cheryl D. *Talk with You like a Woman: African American Women, Justice, and Reform in New York, 1890–1935*. Chapel Hill: University of North Carolina Press, 2010.

Hicks, John D. *Republican Ascendancy: 1921–1933*. New York: Harper and Row, 1960.'

Higginbotham, Evelyn Brooks. *From Strength to Strength: The History of Shiloh Baptist Church, 1863–1938*. Washington, D.C.: Shiloh Baptist Church, 1989.

———. "In Politics to Stay: Black Women Leaders and Party Politics in the 1920s." In *Unequal Sisters: A Multicultural Reader in U.S. Women's History*, edited by Vicki L. Ruiz and Ellen Carol Dubois, 292–306. New York: Routledge, 2000.

———. "Religion, Politics, and Gender: The Leadership of Nannie Helen Burroughs." *Journal of Religious Thought* 44, no. 2 (1988): 7–22.

———. *Righteous Discontent: The Women's Movement in the Black Baptist Church, 1880–1920*. Cambridge, Mass.: Harvard University Press, 1993.

Hill, Hiley H. "Negro Store-Front Churches in Washington, D.C." MA thesis, Howard University, 1947.

Hine, Darlene Clark, "Black Lawyers and the Twentieth-Century Struggle for Constitutional Change." In *African Americans and the Living Constitution*, edited by John

Hope Franklin and Genna Rae McNeil, 33–55. Washington, D.C.: Smithsonian
Institution Press, 1995.

———. "Housewives League of Detroit." In *Visible Women: New Essays on American Activism*, edited by Nancy Hewitt and Suzanne Lebsock, 223–42. Urbana: University of Illinois Press, 1993.

———. ed. *The State of Afro-American History: Past, Present, and Future*. Baton Rouge: Louisiana State University Press, 1989.

Hixson, William B., Jr. "Moorfield Storey and the Struggle for Equality." *Journal of American History* 55, no. 3 (December 1986): 533–54.

Hollis, Daniel W. "Cole L. Blease and the Senatorial Campaign of 1924." *Proceedings of the South Carolina Historical Association* (1978): 53–68.

Holloway, Jonathan Scott. *Confronting the Veil: Abram Harris Jr., E. Franklin Frazier, and Ralph Bunche, 1919–1941*. Chapel Hill: University of North Carolina Press, 2002.

Holt, Roberta B. "The Associated Charities of Washington, D.C., 1892–1935: A History of Activity and Decision of the Board of Managers." PhD diss., Catholic University of America, 1986.

Holt, Thomas C. *Black Over White: Negro Political Leadership in South Carolina during Reconstruction*. Urbana: University of Illinois Press, 1977.

Homel, Michael W. *Down from Equality: Black Chicagoans and the Public Schools, 1920–1941*. Urbana: University of Illinois Press, 1984.

Hovenkamp, H. "Social Science and Segregation before *Brown*." *Duke Law Journal* (June/September 1985): 624–72.

Hoytt, Eleanor Hinton. "International Council of Women of the Darker Races: Historical Notes." *Sage: A Scholarly Journal on Black Women* 3 (Fall 1986): 54–55.

Hull, Gloria T. *Color, Sex, and Poetry: Three Women Writers of the Harlem Renaissance*. Bloomington: Indiana University Press, 1987.

Hundley, Mary Gibson. *The Dunbar Story, 1870–1955*. New York: Vantage Press, 1965.

Hunter, Tera W. *To 'Joy My Freedom: Southern Black Women's Lives and Labors after the Civil War*. Cambridge, Mass.: Harvard University Press, 1997.

———. "'The Women Are Asking for BREAD, Why Give Them STONE?' Women, Work, and Protests in Atlanta and Norfolk during World War I." In *Labor in the Modern South*, edited by Glenn T. Eskew, 62–82. Athens: University of Georgia Press, 2001.

Hutchinson, Louise Daniel. *The Anacostia Story, 1608–1930*. Washington, D.C.: Smithsonian Institution Press, 1977.

Jackson, Kenneth T. *The Ku Klux Klan in the City, 1915–1930*. New York: Oxford University Press, 1967.

Jacobson, Matthew Frye. *Whiteness of a Different Color: European Immigrants and the Alchemy of Race*. Cambridge, Mass.: Harvard University Press, 1998.

Jensen, Joan M. "All Pink Sisters: The War Department and the Feminist Movement of the 1920s." In *Decades of Discontent: The Women's Movement, 1920–1940*, edited by Louis Scharf and Joan M. Jensen, 199–222. Boston, Mass.: Northeastern University Press, 1987.

Johnson, Joan Marie. "'Ye Gave Them A Stone': African American Women's Clubs, the Frederick Douglass Home, and the Black Mammy Monument." *Journal of Women's History* 17, no. 1 (2005): 62–86.

Johnson, Ronald M. "Black and White Apart: The Community Center in the District of Columbia, 1915–1930." *Records of the Columbia Historical Society of Washington, D.C.* 52 (1989): 13–28.

———. "Those Who Stayed: Washington Black Writers in the 1920s." *Records of the Columbia Historical Society of Washington, D.C.* 50 (1980): 485–99.

Jones, Beverly Washington. "Quest for Equality: The Life of Mary Eliza Church Terrell, 1863–1954." PhD diss., University of North Carolina, Chapel Hill, 1980.

Jones, Martha S. *All Bound up Together: The Woman Question in African American Public Culture.* Chapel Hill: University of North Carolina Press, 2007.

Kane, Richard D. "The Federal Segregation of the Blacks during the Presidential Administrations of Warren G. Harding and Calvin Coolidge." *Pan African Journal* 7, no. 2 (1974): 153–71.

Kantrowitz, Stephen. *Ben Tillman and the Reconstruction of White Supremacy.* Chapel Hill: University of North Carolina Press, 2000.

———. "'Intended for the Better Government of Man': The Political History of African American Freemasonry in the Era of Emancipation." *Journal of American History* 96, no. 4 (March 2010): 1001–26.

Kaplan, Temma. "Female Consciousness and Collective Action: The Case of Barcelona, 1910–1918." *Signs* 7, no. 3 (Spring 1982): 545–66.

Katznelson, Ira. *Fear Itself: The New Deal and the Origins of Our Time.* New York: Liveright, 2014.

Kaufman, Herbert. "The Growth of the Federal Personnel System." In *The Federal Government Service,* edited by Wallace S. Sayre, 234–67. Englewood Cliffs, N.J.: Prentice-Hall, 1965.

Kelley, Blair L. M. *Right to Ride: Streetcar Boycotts and African American Citizenship in the Era of Plessy v. Ferguson.* Chapel Hill: University of North Carolina Press, 2010.

Kelley, Robin D. G. "Congested Terrain: Resistance on Public Transportation." in *Race Rebels: Culture, Politics, and the Black Working Class,* 55–75. New York: Free Press, 1994.

———. *Hammer and Hoe: Alabama Communists during the Great Depression.* Chapel Hill: University of North Carolina Press, 1990.

———. "'We Are Not What We Seem': Rethinking Black Working-Class Opposition in the Jim Crow South." *Journal of American History* 80, no. 1 (1993): 75–112.

Kessler-Harris, Alice. *In Pursuit of Equity: Women, Men, and the Quest for Economic Citizenship in 20th Century America.* New York: Oxford University Press, 2001.

Keyssar, Alexander. *The Right To Vote: The Contested History of Democracy in the United States.* New York: Basic Books, 2000.

Kiesel, Diane. *She Can Bring Us Home: Dr. Dorothy Boulding Ferebee, Civil Rights Pioneer.* Lincoln: University of Nebraska Press, 2015.

King, Desmond S. "The Racial Bureaucracy: African Americans and the Federal Government in the Era of Segregated Race Relations." *Governance: An International Journal of Policy and Administration* 12, no. 4 (1999): 345–77.

———. *Separate and Unequal: Black Americans and the US Federal Government.* New York: Oxford University Press, 1995.

———. "A Strong or Weak State? Race and the US Federal Government in the 1920s." *Ethnic and Racial Studies* 21, no. 1 (1998): 21–47.

Klarman, Michael J. *From Jim Crow to Civil Rights: The Supreme Court and the Struggle for Racial Equality*. New York: Oxford University Press, 2004.

Knupfer, Anne Meis. "'If You Can't Push, Pull, If You Can't Pull, Please Get out of the Way': The Phyllis Wheatley Club and Home in Chicago, 1896–1920." *Journal of Negro History* 82, no. 2 (Spring 1997): 221–31.

Kolker, Carole Abrams. "Migrants and Memories: Family, Work, and Community among Blacks, Eastern European Jews, and Native-Born Whites in an Early Twentieth Century Washington, D.C. Neighborhood." PhD diss., George Washington University, 1997.

Kornbluh, Felicia. *The Battle for Welfare Rights: Politics and Poverty in Modern America*. Philadelphia: University of Pennsylvania Press, 2007.

Korstad, Robert. *Civil Rights Unionism: Tobacco Workers and the Struggle for Democracy in the Mid-Twentieth Century South*. Chapel Hill: University of North Carolina Press, 2003.

Korstad, Robert, and Nelson Lichtenstein. "Opportunities Lost and Found: Labor, Radicals, and the Early Civil Rights Movement." *Journal of American History* 73, no. 3 (December 1988): 786–811.

Kousha, Mahanaz. "Race, Class, and Intimacy in Southern Households: Relationships between Black Domestic Workers and White Employers." In *Neither Separate nor Equal: Women, Race, and Class in the South*, edited by Barbara Ellen Smith, 77–90. Philadelphia, Pa.: Temple University Press, 1989.

Lasch-Jones, Adrienne. "Struggle among Saints: African American Women and the YWCA, 1870–1920." In *Men and Women Adrift: The YMCA and the YWCA in the City*, edited by Nina Mjagkij and Margaret Spratt, 160–87. New York: New York University Press, 1997.

Lawson, Steven. *Running for Freedom: Civil Rights and Black Politics in America since 1941*. New York: John Wiley and Sons, 2015.

Lebsock, Suzanne. "Woman Suffrage and White Supremacy: A Virginia Case Study." In *Visible Women: New Essays on American Activism*, edited by Nancy A. Hewitt and Suzanne Lebsock, 62–100. Urbana: University of Illinois Press, 1993.

Lee, Chana Kai. *For Freedom's Sake: The Life of Fannie Lou Hamer*. Urbana: University of Illinois Press, 2000.

Lee, William I. *One-Hundredth Anniversary of the 19th Street Baptist Church*. Washington, D.C.: Murray Brothers, 1939.

Lemons, J. Stanley. *The Woman Citizen: Social Feminism in the 1920s*. Charlottesville: University Press of Virginia, 1990.

Lerner, Adam J. "The Capital City and Mount Rushmore: The Place of Public Monuments in American Political Culture in the Progressive Era and the 1920s." PhD diss., Johns Hopkins University, 2001.

Levenstein, Lisa. *A Movement without Marches: African American Women and the Politics of Poverty in Postwar Philadelphia*. Chapel Hill: University of North Carolina Press, 2009.

Levine, Lawrence. "The Concept of the New Negro and the Realities of Black Culture." In *The Unpredictable Past: Explorations in American Cultural History*, 86–106. New York: Oxford University Press, 1993.

Lewis, David Levering. *District of Columbia: A Bicentennial History*. New York: Norton, 1977.

———. *When Harlem Was in Vogue*. New York: Oxford University Press, 1981.

Lewis, Earl. *In Their Own Interests: Race and Power in Twentieth-Century Norfolk.* Berkeley: University of California Press, 1991.

Lewis-Mhoon, Abena. "Adorning Adversaries, Affecting Avenues: African American Women's Impact on Adornment and Fashion Design in Washington, D.C., 1880–1950." PhD diss., Howard University, 2005.

Lincoln, Charles Eric, and Lawrence H. Mamiya, *The Black Church in the African American Experience,* 13th ed. Durham, N.C.: Duke University Press, 1990.

Lindsey, Treva B. *Colored No More: Reinventing Black Womanhood in Washington, D.C.* Urbana: University of Illinois Press, 2017.

Lisio, Donald J. *Hoover, Blacks, and Lily-Whites: A Study of Southern Strategies.* Chapel Hill: University of North Carolina Press, 1985.

Litwicki, Ellen M. *America's Public Holidays, 1865–1920.* Washington, D.C.: Smithsonian Institution Press, 2000.

Lofton, William H. "The Development of Public Education for Negroes in Washington, D.C.: A Case Study of Separate but Equal Accommodations." PhD diss., American University, 1945.

Logan, Rayford W. *Howard University: The First Hundred Years, 1867–1967.* New York: New York University Press, 1969.

Long, Herman H., and Charles S. Johnson. *People vs. Property: Race Restrictive Covenants in Housing.* Nashville, Tenn.: Fisk University Press, 1947.

Lorini, Alessandra. *Rituals of Race: American Public Culture and the Search for Racial Democracy.* Charlottesville: University Press of Virginia, 1999.

Mack, Kenneth W. *Representing the Race: The Creation of the Civil Rights Lawyer.* Cambridge, Mass.: Harvard University Press, 2012.

MacLean, Nancy. *Behind the Mask of Chivalry: The Making of the Second Ku Klux Klan.* New York: Oxford University Press, 1994.

Masur, Kate. *An Example for All the Land: Emancipation and the Struggle over Equality in Washington, D.C.* Chapel Hill: University of North Carolina Press, 2010.

———. "Patronage and Protest in Kate Brown's Washington." *Journal of American History* (March 2013): 1047–71

Materson, Lisa G. *For the Freedom of Her Race: Black Women and Electoral Politics in Illinois, 1877–1932.* Chapel Hill: University of North Carolina Press, 2009.

McCray, Jack. *Charleston Jazz.* Charleston, S.C.: Arcadia Publishing, 2007.

McDuffie, Erik. *Sojourning for Freedom: Black Women, American Communism, and the Making of Black Left Feminism.* Durham, N.C.: Duke University Press, 2011.

McEyla, Micki. *Clinging to Mammy: The Faithful Slave in Twentieth-Century America.* Cambridge, Mass.: Harvard University Press, 2007.

McGirr, Lisa. *The War on Alcohol: Prohibition and the Rise of the American State.* New York: W. W. & Norton, 2015.

McGovern, James R. *Anatomy of a Lynching: The Killing of Claude Neal.* Baton Rouge: Louisiana State University Press, 1989.

McGuire, Danielle. *At the Dark End of the Street: Black Women, Rape, and Resistance—A New History of the Civil Rights Movement from Rosa Parks to the Rise of Black Power.* New York: Vintage Books, 2010.

McHenry, Elizabeth. *Forgotten Readers: Recovering the Lost History of African American Literary Societies*. Durham, N.C.: Duke University Press, 2002.

McLaurein, Melton A. *Celia, A Slave: A True Story*. Athens: University of Georgia Press, 1991.

McNeil, Genna Rae. *Groundwork: Charles Hamilton Houston and the Struggle for Civil Rights*. Philadelphia: University of Pennsylvania Press, 1983.

McQuirter, Marya Annette. "Claiming the City: African Americans, Urbanization, and Leisure in Washington, D.C., 1902–1957." PhD diss., University of Michigan, 2000.

———. "'Our Cause is Marching On': Parent Activism, Browne Junior High School, and the Multiple Meanings of Equality in Post-War Washington." *Washington History* 16, no. 2 (Fall/Winter 2004–2005): 66–82.

Mead, Rebecca. *How the Vote Was Won: Woman Suffrage in the Western United States, 1868–1914*. New York: New York University Press, 2004.

Meier, August, and Elliott Rudwick. "The Rise of Segregation in Federal Bureaucracy." *Phylon* 28, no. 2 (1967): 178–84.

Mellis, Delia Cunningham. "'The Monsters We Defy': Washington, D.C. in the Red Summer of 1919." Ph.D. diss., City University of New York, 2008.

Mergan, Bernard. "Children's Playgrounds in the District of Columbia, 1902–1942." *Records of the Historical Society of Washington, D.C.* 50 (1980): 383–97.

Meyer, Stephen Grant. *As Long as They Don't Move Next Door: Segregation and Racial Conflict in American Neighborhoods*. Lanham, Md.: Rowman & Littlefield, 2000.

Miller, Frederic M., and Howard Gillette, Jr. *Washington Seen: A Photographic History, 1875–1965*. Baltimore, Md.: Johns Hopkins University Press, 1995.

Miller, George Mason. "'A This Worldly Mission': The Life and Career of Alexander Walters." PhD diss., State University of New York at Stonybrook, 1984.

Miller, M. Sammy. "An Early Venture in Black Capitalism: The Capital Savings Bank in the District of Columbia, 1888–1902." *Records of the Columbia Historical Society of Washington, D.C.* 50 (1980): 359–66.

———. "Robert Heberton Terrell, 1857–1925: Black Lawyer and Community Leader." PhD diss., Catholic University, 1977.

Miller, Nathan. *New World Coming: The 1920s and the Making of Modern America*. New York: Scribner, 2003.

Mintz, Steven. "A Historical Ethnography of Black Washington, D.C." *Records of the Columbia Historical Society of Washington, D.C.* 52 (1989): 235–53.

Mitchell, Michele. *Righteous Propagation: African Americans and the Politics of Racial Destiny after Reconstruction*. Chapel Hill: University of North Carolina Press, 2004.

Moldow, Gloria. *Women Doctors in Gilded-Age Washington: Race, Gender, and Professionalization*. Urbana: University of Illinois Press, 1987.

Moore, Jacqueline M. *Leading the Race: The Transformation of the Black Elite in the Nation's Capital, 1880–1920*. Charlottesville: University Press of Virginia, 1999.

Moore, Sidney Harrison. "Family and Social Networks in an Urban Black Storefront Church." PhD diss., American University, 1975.

Moresi, Michele Gates. "Exhibiting Race, Creating Nation: Representations of Black History and Black Culture at the Smithsonian Institution, 1895–1976." PhD diss., George Washington University, 2003.

Morgan, Francesca. *Women and Patriotism in Jim Crow America*. Chapel Hill: University of North Carolina Press, 2005.

Morris, Aldon. *Origins of the Civil Rights Movement: Black Communities Organizing for Change*. New York: Free Press, 1986.

———. "Political Consciousness and Collective Action." In *Frontiers in Social Movement Theory*, edited by Aldon D. Morris and Carol McClurg Mueller, 351–74. New Haven, Conn.: Yale University Press, 1992.

Morris, Jeffrey B. "The Second Most Important Court: The United States Court of Appeals for the District of Columbia Circuit." PhD diss., Columbia University, 1972.

Moss, Alfred E., Jr. *The American Negro Academy: Voice of the Talented Tenth*. Baton Rouge: Louisiana State University Press, 1981.

Moten, Crystal. "'More than A Job': Black Women's Economic Citizenship in the Twentieth Century Urban North," PhD diss., University of Wisconsin, Madison, 2013.

Mungarro, Angelica. "How did Black Women in the NAACP Promote the Dyer Anti-Lynching Bill, 1918–1923?" 2002, in Kathryn Kish Sklar and Thomas Dublin, eds., *Women and Social Movements in the United States, 1600–2000*. Accessed through the Library of Congress, http://asp6new.alexanderstreet.com/was2/was2.index.map .aspx.

Murdock, Rose M. "The Persistence of Black Women at the Williams Avenue YWCA." *Journal of Women's History* 15, no. 3 (Autumn 2003): 190–96.

Murphy, Mary-Elizabeth B. "African American Women's Politics, Organizing, and Activism in Washington, D.C., 1920–1930." Ph.D. diss., University of Maryland, College Park, 2012.

———. "The Servant Campaigns: African American Women and the Politics of Economic Citizenship in Washington, D.C., in the 1930s." *Journal of Urban History*, 44, no. 2 (March 2018): 187–202.

Naison, Mark. *Communists in Harlem during the Depression*. New York: Grove Press, 1983.

Neverdon-Morton, Cynthia. *Afro-American Women of the South and the Advancement of the Race, 1895–1925*. Knoxville: University of Tennessee Press, 1989.

O'Dell, Samuel. "Blacks, the Democratic Party, and the Presidential Election of 1928: A Mild Rejoinder." *Phylon* 48, no. 1 (1987): 1–11.

Orleck, Annelise. *Common Sense and a Little Fire: Women and Working Class Politics in the United States*. Chapel Hill: University of North Carolina Press, 1995.

———. *Storming Caesars Palace: How Black Mothers Fought their Own War on Welfare*. Boston, Mass.: Beacon Press, 2006.

———. "'We Are that Mythical Thing Called the Public': Militant Housewives during the Great Depression." *Feminist Studies* 19, no. 1 (Spring 1993): 127–72.

Ortiz, Paul. *Emancipation Betrayed: The Hidden History of Black Organizing and White Violence in Florida from Reconstruction to the Bloody Election of 1920*. Berkeley: University of California Press, 2005.

Pacifico, Michelle. "Don't Buy Where You Can't Work: The New Negro Alliance of Washington, D.C." *Washington History* 6, no. 1 (1994): 66–88.

Palmer, Phyllis. *Domesticity and Dirt: Housewives and Domestic Servants in the United States, 1920–1945*. Philadelphia, Pa.: Temple University Press, 1989.

Patler, Nicholas. *Jim Crow and the Wilson Administration: Protesting Federal Segregation in the Twentieth Century*. Boulder: University of Colorado Press, 2004.

Pavis, Jesse A. "The Development of Segregation in the District of Columbia." MA thesis, Howard University, 1949.

Perkins, Kathy A. and Judith L. Stephens, eds. *Strange Fruit: Plays on Lynching by American Women*. Bloomington: Indiana University Press, 1998.

Perkins, Linda M. "The Impact of the 'Cult of True Womanhood' on the Education of Black Women." *Journal of Social Issues* 39, no. 3 (1983): 17–28.

———. "Lucy Diggs Slowe: Champion of the Self-Determination of African-American Women in Higher Education." *Journal of Negro History* 81, no. 1 (Winter–Autumn 1996): 89–104.

Phillips, Kimberly. *AlabamaNorth: African-American Migrants, Community, and Working-Class Activism in Cleveland, 1915–1945*. Urbana: University of Illinois Press, 1999.

———. *War! What Is It Good For: Black Freedom Struggles and the U.S. Military from World War II to Iraq*. Chapel Hill: University of North Carolina Press, 2012.

Pieroth, Doris Hinson. *Seattle's Women Teachers of the Interwar Years*. Seattle: University of Washington Press, 2004.

Pinkett, Harold T. *National Church of Zion Methodism: A History of John Wesley A.M.E. Zion Church, Washington, D.C.* Baltimore, Md.: Gateway Press, Inc., 1989.

Plotkin, Wendy. "Deeds of Mistrust: Race, Housing, and Restrictive Covenants in Chicago, 1900–1953." PhD diss., University of Illinois at Chicago, 1999.

Plummer, Brenda Gayle. *Rising Wind: African Americans and U.S. Foreign Affairs, 1935–1960*. Chapel Hill: University of North Carolina Press, 1996.

Poole, Mary. *The Segregated Origins of Social Security: African Americans and the Welfare State*. Chapel Hill: University of North Carolina, 2006.

Powell, Richard J. *Black Art and Culture in the Twentieth Century*. New York: Thames and Hudson, 1997.

Prather, H. Leon, Sr. "We Have Taken a City: A Centennial Essay." In *Democracy Betrayed: The Wilmington Race Riot of 1898 and Its Legacy*, edited by David S. Cecelski and Timothy B. Tyson, 15–42. Chapel Hill: University of North Carolina Press, 1998.

Quigley, Joan. *Just Another Southern Town: Mary Church Terrell and the Struggle for Racial Justice in the Nation's Capital*. New York: Oxford University Press, 2016.

Quinn, Kelly. "Making Modern Homes: A History of Langston Terrace Dwellings, a New Deal Housing Program in Washington, D.C." PhD diss., University of Maryland, College Park, 2007.

Radcliffe, Florence J. *A Simple Matter of Justice: The Phyllis Wheatley YWCA Story*. Pompano Beach: Exposition Press of Florida, 1985.

Ramsey, Sonya. *Reading, Writing, and Segregation: A Century of Black Women Teachers in Nashville*. Urbana: University of Illinois Press, 2008.

Randall, Terree N. "Democracy's Passion Play: The Lincoln Memorial, Politics and History as Myth." PhD diss., City University of New York, 2002.

Ransby, Barbara. *Ella Baker and the Black Freedom Movement: A Radical Democratic Vision*. Chapel Hill: University of North Carolina Press, 2004.

Reich, Steven A. "Soldiers of Democracy: Black Texans and the Fight for Citizenship, 1917–1921." *Journal of American History* 82, no. 4 (March 1996): 1478–504.

Reynolds, Gary A., and Beryl J. Wright, *Against the Odds: African-American Artists and the Harmon Foundation*. Newark, N.J.: Newark Museum, 1989.

Rice, Roger L. "Residential Segregation by Law, 1910–1917." *Journal of Southern History* 34, no. 2 (May 1968): 179–99.

Rief, Michelle. "Thinking Globally, Acting Locally: The International Agenda of African American Clubwomen, 1880–1940." *Journal of African American History* 89 (Summer 2004): 203–22.

Robertson, Nancy. *Christian Sisterhood, Race Relations, and the YWCA, 1906–1946*. Urbana: University of Illinois Press, 2007.

Robinson, Dormetria La Sharne. "Nannie Helen Burroughs: The Trailblazer." *American Baptist Quarterly* 23, no. 2 (2004): 155–78.

Rollinson, Mary. *Grassroots Garveyism: The Universal Negro Improvement Association in the Rural South, 1920–1927*. Chapel Hill: University of North Carolina Press, 2007.

Rosen, Hannah. *Terror in the Heart of Freedom: Citizenship, Sexual Violence, and the Meaning of Race in the Postemancipation South*. Chapel Hill: University of North Carolina Press, 2009.

Rosen, Mark D. "Was *Shelley v. Kraemer* Incorrectly Decided? Some New Answers." *California Law Review* 95 (2007): 451–512.

Rosenberg, Rosalind. *Jane Crow: The Life of Pauli Murray*. New York: Oxford University Press, 2017.

Rubin, Lawrence. "Washington and the Negro Renaissance." *Crisis* 78, no. 3 (1971): 79–82.

Rudwick, Elliott M. "Oscar De Priest and the Jim Crow Restaurant in the U.S. House of Representatives." *Journal of Negro Education* 35, no. 1 (1966): 77–82.

Ruffins, Fath Davis. "Culture Wars Won and Lost, Part II: The National African-American Museum Project." *Radical History Review* 70 (1998): 78–101.

———. "'Lifting as We Climb': Black Women and the Preservation of African American History and Culture." *Gender and History* 6 (November 1994): 376–96.

———. "Revisiting the Old Plantation: Reparations, Reconciliation, and Museumizing American Slavery." In *Museum Frictions: Public Cultures/Global Transformations*, edited by Ivan Karp, Corrine A. Cratz, Lynn Szwaga, and Tomas Ybarra-Frausto, 394–434. Durham, N.C.: Duke University Press, 2006.

Safranek, S. J. "Race and the Law, or How the Courts and the Law Have Been Warped by Racial Injustice." *Wayne Law Review* 48, no. 3 (Fall 2002): 1025–60.

Sandage, Scott. "A Marble House Divided: The Lincoln Memorial, the Civil Rights Movement, and the Politics of Memory." *Journal of American History*, 80, no 1 (June 1993): 135–67.

Sanders, Crystal. *A Chance for Change: Head Start and Mississippi's Black Freedom Struggle*. Chapel Hill: University of North Carolina Press, 2016.

Sartain, Lee. *Borders of Equality: The NAACP and the Baltimore Civil Rights Struggle, 1914–1970*. Jackson: University of Mississippi Press, 2013.

Savage, Barbara Dianne. *Your Spirits Walk beside Us: The Politics of Black Religion*. Cambridge, Mass.: Harvard University Press, 2008.

Savage, Kirk. *Standing Soldiers, Kneeling Slaves: Race, War, and Monument in Nineteenth-Century America*. Princeton, N.J.: Princeton University Press, 1997.

Schechter, Patricia A. *Ida B. Wells-Barnett and American Reform, 1880–1930*. Chapel Hill: University of North Carolina Press, 2001.

Schneider, Marc R. *Boston Confronts Jim Crow, 1880–1920*. Boston, Mass.: Northeastern University Press, 1997.

———. *"We Return Fighting": The Civil Rights Movement in the Jazz Age*. Boston, Mass.: Northeastern University Press, 2002.

Schuyler, Lorraine Gates. *The Weight of their Votes: Southern Women and Political Leverage in the 1920s*. Chapel Hill: University of North Carolina Press, 2006.

Scott, James C. *Domination and the Art of Resistance: The Hidden Transcripts*. New Haven, Conn.: Yale University Press, 1990.

Seraile, William. *Fire in His Heart: Bishop Benjamin Tucker Tanner and the A.M.E. Church*. Knoxville: University of Tennessee Press, 1998.

Sernett, Milton C. *Bound for the Promised Land: African American Religion and the Great Migration*. Durham, N.C.: Duke University Press, 1997.

Sharpless, Rebecca. *Cooking in Other Women's Kitchens: Domestic Workers in the South, 1865–1960*. Chapel Hill: University of North Carolina Press, 2010.

Shaw, Stephanie. "Black Club Women and the Creation of the National Association of Colored Women." *Journal of Women's History* 3, no. 2 (Fall 1991): 10–25.

———. *What a Woman Ought to Be and Do: Black Professional Women Workers in the Jim Crow Era*. Chicago, Ill.: University of Chicago Press, 1996.

Sherman, Richard B. "The Harding Administration and the Negro: An Opportunity Lost." *Journal of Negro History* 49, no. 3 (1964): 151–68.

———. *The Republican Party and Black America: From McKinley to Hoover, 1896–1933*. Charlottesville: University of Virginia Press, 1973.

Simon, Bryant. *A Fabric of Defeat: The Politics of South Carolina Millhands, 1910–1948*. Chapel Hill: University of North Carolina Press, 1998.

Singh, Nikhil Pal. *Black Is a Country: Race and the Unfinished Struggle for Democracy*. Cambridge, Mass.: Harvard University Press, 2004.

Skarloff, Lauren Rebecca. *Black Culture and the New Deal: The Quest for Civil Rights in the Roosevelt Era*. Chapel Hill: University of North Carolina Press, 2009.

Skocpol, Theda, Ariane Liazos, and Marshall Ganz. *What A Mighty Power We Can Be: African American Fraternal Groups and the Struggle for Racial Equality*. Princeton, N.J.: Princeton University Press, 2006.

Skocpol, Theda, and Jennifer Lynn Oser, "Organization despite Adversity: The Origins and Development of African American Fraternal Associations." *Social Science History* 28, no. 3 (Fall 2004): 367–437.

Simmons, LaKisha. *Crescent City Girls: The Lives of Young Black Women in Segregated New Orleans*. Chapel Hill: University of North Carolina Press, 2015.

Smith, Eric Ledell. "Washington's African-American Diva." *Washington History* 11, no. 1 (1999): 25–43.

Smith, Hedrick. *Duke Ellington's Washington*. Chevy Chase, MD: Hedrick Smith Productions, 2000.

Smith, Jennifer Lund. "The Ties that Bind: Educated African-American Women in Post-Emancipation Atlanta." In *Georgia in Black and White: Explorations in the Race*

Relations of a Southern State, 1865–1950, edited by John C. Inscoe, 97–98. Athens: University of Georgia Press, 1994.

Smith, Kathryn S. "Remembering U Street." *Washington History* 9, no. 2 (1997–98): 29–53.

———, ed. *Washington at Home: An Illustrated History of Neighborhoods in the Nation's Capital.* Washington, D.C.: Windsor Press, 1988.

Smith, Susan L. *Sick and Tired of Being Sick and Tired: Black Women's Health Activism in America, 1890–1950.* Philadelphia: University of Pennsylvania Press, 1995.

Sommerville, Dora Bessie. "A Group Study of a Group of Negro Children Living in an Alley Culture." MA thesis, Catholic University of America, 1941.

Sowell, Thomas. "Black Excellence: The Case of Dunbar High School." *Public Interest* 35 (1974): 3–21.

Splawn, P. Jane, ed. *Carrie Williams Clifford and Carrie Law Morgan Figgs.* New York: G. K. Hall, 1997.

Stewart, Jacqueline Najuma. *Migrating to the Movies: Cinema and Black Urban Modernity.* Berkeley: University of California Press, 2005.

Stewart, Jeffrey C., and Fath Davis Ruffins. "A Faithful Witness: Afro-American Public History in Historical Perspective, 1828–1984." In *Presenting the Past: Essays on History and the Public*, edited by Susan Porter Benson, Stephen Brier, and Roy Rosenzweig, 307–36. Philadelphia, Pa.: Temple University Press, 1986.

Sullivan, Patricia. *Days of Hope: Race and Democracy in the New Deal Era.* Chapel Hill: University of North Carolina Press, 1996.

———. *Lift Every Voice: The NAACP and the Making of the Civil Rights Movement.* New York: New Press, 2009.

Sweet, Leonard. "The Fourth of July and Black Americans in the Nineteenth Century: Northern Leadership Opinion within the Context of the Black Experience." *Journal of Negro History* 61, no. 3 (1976): 256–75.

Taylor, Elizabeth Dowling. *The Original Black Elite: Daniel Murray and the Story of a Forgotten Era.* New York: Harper Collins, 2017.

Taylor, Traki Lynn. "God's School on the Hill: Nannie Helen Burroughs and the National Training School for Women and Girls, 1909–1961." PhD diss., University of Illinois, Urbana-Champaign, 1998.

Terborg-Penn, Rosalyn. *African American Women and the Struggle for the Vote, 1885–1920.* Bloomington: Indiana University Press, 1998.

———. "African-American Women's Networks in the Anti-Lynching Crusade." In *Gender, Class, Race, and Reform in the Progressive Era*, edited by Noralee Frankel and Nancy S. Dye, 148–61. Lexington: University Press of Kentucky, 1991.

———. "Discontented Black Feminists: Prelude and Postscript to the Passage of the Nineteenth Amendment." In *"We Specialize in the Wholly Impossible": A Reader in Black Women's History*, edited by Darlene Clark Hine, Wilma King, and Linda Reed, 487–504. Brooklyn, N.Y.: Carlson Publishing, 1995.

Theoharris, Jean. *The Rebellious Life of Mrs. Rosa Parks.* Boston, Mass.: Beacon Press, 2013.

Thomas, Christopher A. *The Lincoln Memorial and American Life.* Princeton, N.J.: Princeton University Press, 2002.

Thomas, Deobrah Gisele. "Workers and Organizers: African-American Women in the Work Force and Club Movement, 1890–1930." PhD diss., Brown University, 1998.

Thomas, Richard W. *Life for Us Is What We Make It: Building Black Community in Detroit, 1915–1945.* Bloomington: Indiana University Press, 1992.

Thornton, J. Mills. *Dividing Lines: Municipal Politics and the Struggle for Civil Rights in Montgomery, Birmingham, and Selma.* Tuscaloosa: University of Alabama Press, 2002.

Thurber, Bert Henry. "The Negro at the Nation's Capital, 1913–1921." PhD diss., Yale University, 1973.

Thurber, Cheryl. "The Development of the Mammy Image and Mythology." In *Southern Women: Histories and Identities,* edited by Virginia Bernhard, Betty Brandon, Elizabeth Fox-Genovese, and Theda Purdue, 87–108. Columbia: University of Missouri Press, 1992.

Trotter, Joe William, ed. *The Great Migration in Historical Perspective: New Dimensions of Race, Class, and Gender.* Bloomington: Indiana University Press, 1991.

Tucker, Mark. *Duke Ellington: The Early Years.* Urbana: University of Illinois Press, 1991.

Tushnet, Mark V. "Progressive Era Race Relations Cases in their 'Traditional' Context." *Vanderbilt Law Review* 51, no. 4 (May 1998): 993–1003.

Tuuri, Rebecca. "'This Was the Most Meaningful Thing that I've Ever Done': The Personal Civil Rights Approach of Wednesdays in Mississippi." *Journal of Women's History* 28, no. 4 (Winter 2016): 89–112.

Tyson, Timothy B. *Radio Free Dixie: Robert F. Williams and the Roots of Black Power.* Chapel Hill: University of North Carolina Press, 1999.

Van Orsdel, Ralph A. "History of the Telephone System in the District of Columbia." *Records of the Columbia Historical Society of Washington, D.C.* 48 and 49 (1946–47): 171–80.

Van Riper, Paul. *History of the United States Civil Service.* Evanston, Ill.: Row, Peterson, 1958.

Von Eschen, Penny. *Race against Empire: Black Americans and Anti-Colonialism, 1937–1957.* Ithaca, N.Y.: Cornell University Press, 1997.

Vose, Clement E. *Caucasians Only: The Supreme Court, the NAACP, and the Restrictive Covenant Cases.* Berkeley: University of California Press, 1959.

Waldrep, Christopher. *African Americans Confront Lynching: Strategies of Resistance from the Civil War to the Civil Rights Era.* Lanham, Md.: Rowman & Littlefield, 2009.

Walker, Lewis Newton, Jr. "The Struggles and Attempts to Establish Branch Autonomy and Hegemony: A History of the District of Columbia Branch Association for the Advancement of Colored People, 1912–1942." PhD diss., University of Delaware, 1979.

Walls, William J. *The African Methodist Episcopal Zion Church: Reality of the Black Church* Charlotte: A.M.E. Zion Publishing House, 1974.

Wamsley, Janet. "The K.K.K. in Arlington in the 1920s." *Arlington Historical Magazine* 10 (1993): 55–60.

Ward, Jason Morgan. "Causes Lost and Found: Remembering and Refighting Reconstruction in the Roosevelt Era." In *Remembering Reconstruction: Struggles over the Meaning of America's Most Turbulent Era,* edited by Carole Emberton and Bruce E. Baker, 35–58. Baton Rouge: Louisiana State University Press, 2017.

Ware, Leland B. "Invisible Walls: An Examination of the Legal Strategy of the Restrictive Covenant Cases." *Washington University Law Quarterly* 67 (Fall 1989): 737–72.

Weiner, Lynn Y. *From Working Girl to Working Mother: Creating a Female Labor Force in the United States, 1820–1980.* Chapel Hill: University of North Carolina Press, 1985.

Weisenfield, Judith. *African American Women and Christian Activism: New York's Black YWCA, 1905–1945.* Cambridge, Mass.: Harvard University Press, 1997.

Weiss, Nancy J. *Farewell to the Party of Lincoln: Black Politics in the Age of FDR.* Princeton, N.J.: Princeton University Press, 1983.

———. "The Negro and New Freedom: Fighting Wilsonian Segregation." *Political Science Quarterly* 84, no. 1 (1969): 61–79.

White, Deborah Gray. *Aren't I A Woman: Female Slaves in the Plantation South.* New York: W. W. Norton, 1985.

———. *Too Heavy a Load: Black Women in Defense of Themselves.* New York: W. W. Norton, 1999.

Williams, Chad. *Torchbearers of Democracy: African American Soldiers in the World War I Era.* Chapel Hill: University of North Carolina Press, 2013.

Williams, Kidada E. *They Left Great Marks on Me: African American Testimonies of Racial Violence from Emancipation to World War I.* New York: New York University Press, 2012.

Williams, Melvins Roscoe. "Blacks in Washington, D.C., 1860–1870." PhD diss., Johns Hopkins University, 1976.

Williams, Rhonda Y. *The Politics of Public Housing: Black Women's Struggles against Urban Inequality.* New York: Oxford University Press, 2004.

Williams, Zachery R. "In Search of the Talented Tenth: Howard University Intellectuals and the Dilemmas of Race in Academia, 1926–1970." PhD diss., Bowling Green State University, 2003.

Williams-Forson, Psyche A. *Building Houses out of Chicken Legs: Black Women, Food, and Power.* Chapel Hill: University of North Carolina Press, 2006.

Wilson, Francille Rusan. *The Segregated Scholars: Black Social Scientists and the Creation of Black Labor Studies, 1890–1950.* Charlottesville: University Press of Virginia, 2006.

Wilson, Mabel O. *Negro Building: Black Americans in the World of Fairs and Museums.* Berkeley: University of California Press, 2012.

Wiltse, Jeff. *Contested Waters: A Social History of Swimming Pools in America.* Chapel Hill: University of North Carolina Press, 2007.

Winand, Angela Michelle. "Weighed upon a Scale: African-American Women, Class, and Consumer Culture in New Orleans and Washington, D.C., 1880–1950." PhD diss., University of Michigan, 2003.

Wolcott, Victoria. "'Bible, Bath, and Broom': Nannie Helen Burrough's National Training School and African-American Racial Uplift." *Journal of Women's History* 9, no. 1 (1999): 88–110.

———. *Race, Riots and Rollercoasters: The Struggle over Segregated Recreation in America.* Philadelphia: University of Pennsylvania Press, 2012.

———. *Remaking Respectability: African American Women in Interwar Detroit.* Chapel Hill: University of North Carolina Press, 2000.

Wolgemuth, Kathleen L. "Woodrow Wilson and Federal Segregation." *Journal of Negro History* 44, no. 2 (1959): 158–73.

―――. "Woodrow Wilson's Appointment Policy and the Negro." *Journal of Southern History* 24 (1958): 457–71.

Wolters, Raymond. *The New Negro on Campus: Black College Rebellions of the 1920s.* Princeton, N.J.: Princeton University Press, 1975.

Woodson, Carter G. "The Negro Washerwoman: A Vanishing Figure." *Journal of Negro History* 15, no. 3 (1930): 269.

Woodward. C. Vann. *The Strange Career of Jim Crow.* New York: Oxford University Press, 1955.

Wright, R. R., Jr. *The Bishops of the African Methodist Episcopal Church.* Nashville, Tenn.: A.M. E. Sunday School Union, 1963.

Yedell, J. Carlton. "The Role of the Negro Question in the Struggle for Home Rule for the District of Columbia." MA thesis, Howard University, 1940.

Yellin, Eric. *Racism in the Nation's Service: Government Workers and the Color Line in Woodrow Wilson's America.* Chapel Hill: University of North Carolina Press, 2013.

Young, Damon Palma. "Negro-White Contacts in Washington, D.C." MA thesis, Howard University, 1926.

Young, Patricia Alzatia. "Female Pioneers in Afro-American Drama: Angelina Weld Grimké, Georgia Douglas Johnson, Alice Dunbar-Nelson, and Mary Powell Burrill." PhD diss., Bowling Green State University, 1986.

Zangrando, Robert L. *The NAACP Crusade against Lynching, 1909–1950.* Philadelphia, Pa.: Temple University Press, 1980.

Index